Entrepreneurship and Small and Medium-Sized Enterprises (SMEs) in Africa

Emelia Amoako Asiedu
Richard Kofi Asravor
Robert Ebo Hinson
George Oppong Ampong
Editors

Entrepreneurship and Small and Medium-Sized Enterprises (SMEs) in Africa

The Realities of the Post COVID-19 Era

palgrave
macmillan

Editors
Emelia Amoako Asiedu
Department of Marketing
Ghana Communication Technology
University
Accra, Ghana

Robert Ebo Hinson
University of Ghana Business School
Accra, Ghana

Richard Kofi Asravor
Ghana Communication Technology
University
Accra, Ghana

George Oppong Ampong
Ghana Communication Technology
University
Accra, Ghana

ISBN 978-3-032-14173-6 ISBN 978-3-032-14174-3 (eBook)
https://doi.org/10.1007/978-3-032-14174-3

This Palgrave Macmillan imprint is published by the registered company Springer Nature Switzerland AG.
The registered company address is: Gewerbestrasse 11, 6330 Cham, Switzerland

Overview of Chapters

Chapter 2 by Joseph Asare, Stephen Owusu Afriyie, and Emmanuel Atta Kumah looks at "Entrepreneurship and Innovation in Ghana: Post-COVID-19 Realities." They examined the significant effect the pandemic has had on the economy of Ghana, particularly on SMEs. They highlight the crucial role of entrepreneurs in creating SMEs and driving economic growth, and how their well-being plays a critical role in firm performance. They focus on the role of technology in driving entrepreneurship, SMEs, and entrepreneurs, with the use of the Internet increasing access to information and tools. They conclude that the establishment of SMEs in Africa requires a willingness to undertake financial and personal risks while seeking potential returns for flourishing.

In Chap. 3, George Oppong Ampong, Ethel Yiranbon, Esther Asiedu, and Ebenezer Malcalm underline the "Creating and Sustaining Competitive Advantage in Small and Medium-Sized Enterprises (SMEs)." They maintain that Small and medium-sized enterprises (SMEs) operate in a highly competitive business environment where the ability to create and sustain a competitive advantage is crucial for survival and growth. By exploring the various strategies that SMEs can use to create and sustain competitive advantage, they examine the different sources of competitive advantage, including cost leadership, differentiation, and focus strategies, and discuss how SMEs can leverage their resources and capabilities to achieve sustainable competitive advantage.

Chapter 4, by Richard Kofi Asravor, Isaac Ankrah, Christopher Lamptey, Derrick Donkor, Lilian Arthur, and Vera Acheampong, focused on "Technology and Digitization in Small and Medium-Sized Enterprises in Ghana: Impact on Financial Performance." They established that technology and digitization have become crucial for Small and Medium-sized Enterprises (SMEs) in recent years, emphasizing the role of SMEs, which are a vital component of the economy, that have been adapting to digital transformation to improve their competitiveness, efficiency, and profitability.

Chapter 5 had Prince Yaw Amu, Vida Asante Boateng, and Deli Dotse Gli considering "Sustainability Marketing, Social Responsibility, Ethics, and SME Performance: The Moderating Role of Government Regulations." They examine sustainability marketing, corporate social responsibility (CSR), and ethical behavior as potential determinants of small and medium-sized firm (SME) success, while moderating for government regulation. Using the Stakeholder Theory and quantitative analysis, they assess survey data from 110 SMEs using partial least squares structural equation modeling (PLS-SEM). They found that ethical behavior, CSR, and sustainability marketing had substantial and beneficial impacts on business performance. Yet, contrary to expectations, the influence of governmental rules statistically suggests that SMEs' choice to follow responsible practices is motivated by internal or market forces rather than by regulatory frameworks.

Chapter 6 focuses on "Leveraging Digital Technologies for Enhanced Complaint Management in Delivery Service SMEs: Insights from Ghanaian Consumer Behaviour," where Jackson Nuarko Appiagyei, Emelia Amoako Asiedu, Theresa Obuobisa-Darko, Robert Ebo Hinson, and George Asamoah maintain that digital transformation reshapes consumer expectations, small and medium-sized enterprises (SMEs) in Africa's delivery service sector. They explain that digital complaint management strategies affect long-term consumer brand loyalty. Employing a qualitative approach, they found that effective complaint management in delivery service SMEs follows a structured digital process: complaint identification through social media, chatbots, or mobile apps leads to automated or personalized engagement, informing resolution strategies. Also, digital integration enhances response efficiency and customer satisfaction. Aligning findings with Attribution Theory, they provide a nuanced perspective on how SMEs can leverage technology to turn complaints into opportunities for service improvement and long-term customer retention.

In Chap. 7, Charles Asare, William Asamoah Owusu, Derrick Nukunu Akude, Emelia Amoako Asiedu, and Kwame Ntim Sekyere explore "SMEs in the Fourth Industrial Revolution: A Marketing Shift." They emphasize the importance of Small and Medium-sized Enterprises (SMEs) as key contributors to economic development. They explain that the conventional marketing mix (4Ps), a traditional framework, has facilitated marketing development in theory and practice. They use literature related to customer relationship management and its relevance in the fourth industrial revolution in the realm of SMEs with reference to the 4Cs of marketing.

Chapter 8 looks at "The Role and Relevance of Marketing in Small and Medium-Sized Enterprises (SMEs) in Africa." Here, Esther Asiedu, Ebenezer Malcalm, Ethel Yiranbon, George Oppong Ampong, Gertrude Amoakohene, and George Kofi Amoako assert that marketing has a significant influence on many aspects of life, and the global economy is currently going through a significant shift. Marketing is essential to most industries and all facets of the economy since businesses and organizations are constantly undergoing significant changes. Marketing is believed to be essential to the overall survival and growth of economies for both developed and developing countries, as well as transitional countries. They offer a conceptual framework for assessing the function and significance of marketing in SMEs by considering the novel marketing constructs employed by SMEs, specifically transformation, assimilation, prediction, and exceptionality (TAPE).

In Chap. 9, Emelia Amoako Asiedu, Priscilla Otuo, Theresa Obuobisa-Darko, and Ivy Adjei Nketiah focus on "Strategic Marketing Planning in Small and Medium-Sized Enterprises (SMEs)." They stress that strategic marketing planning is critical for the success of small and medium-sized enterprises (SMEs) in that it helps them identify and capitalize on opportunities in the market. They explored the importance of strategic marketing planning in SMEs and provide practical insights on how to develop an effective marketing strategy. They emphasize the need for SMEs to prioritize strategic marketing planning as a means of driving growth, building customer loyalty, and achieving a competitive advantage in their respective markets.

In Chap. 10, Antoinette Yaa Benewaa Gabrah, George Kofi Amoako, and Emelia Amoako Asiedu look at "The Role of Digital Advertising and AI-Based Public Relations in Brand Promotions: Conceptual Framework." They emphasize that Digital advertising, coming in the form of social media advertisements, website advertising, email marketing, and SMS marketing, has overshadowed traditional advertisement. They show that AI-based public relations go to the extent of providing automated tasks, improved user engagement, and personalized and customized content to customers, which increases customer satisfaction.

Chapter 11 focuses on "Financial Management Among SMEs in Africa: The Ghanaian Case," where Richard Asravor and Peter Lawer examine financial management practices among SMEs in Ghana, focusing on challenges, gender disparities, and impacts on sustainability. Applying Resource-Based View and Pecking Order Theory to contextualize financial management in emerging economies, they found that inventory/cost control ($\beta = 1.737, p < 0.001$) and financial advisory engagement ($\beta = 0.836$, $p < 0.001$) are key drivers of sustainability, while financial illiteracy negatively affects performance ($\beta = -0.485$, $p = 0.049$). They emphasize integrated solutions combining foundational practices (e.g., budgeting) with strategic interventions (e.g., cost control).

In Chap. 12, George Kofi Amoako looks at "The Role of Entrepreneurial Orientation and Social Media Marketing on SMEs Performance." He asserts that social media can be perceived as an innovative approach for marketers as well as businesses to increase their sales through creating a lasting relationship with new customers, including maintaining existing ones. Social media platforms such as Twitter, Facebook, Instagram, TikTok, and WhatsApp are used to attract and turn potential consumers into purchasing customers through targeted advertising.

In Chap. 13, Yaa Deheer looks at "Building a Strong Online Presence for Small and Medium Enterprises: An Emerging Market Perspective." She explores how industries are leveraging social media platforms such as Twitter, Facebook, LinkedIn, YouTube, and Instagram to build their competitiveness in the market. She maintains that these platforms have also become important promotional tools and have opened new horizons for online marketing activities. SMEs are now motivated by the importance of social media platforms and how they help them to compete effectively in the domestic and foreign markets.

Chapter 14 looks at "Chatbots and AI-Based Marketing as a Digital Marketing Communication Strategy for SMEs in Africa: Conceptual Framework." Antoinette Yaa Benewaa Gabrah, George Oppong Ampong, and Emelia Amoako Asiedu focused on the adoption of innovative solutions like chatbots and AI-based marketing technologies. They postulate that chatbots and AI-based marketing technologies enable SMEs to streamline their operations, connect more effectively with their customers, and deliver highly personalized services in cost-effective ways.

In Chap. 15, George Kwabena Asamoah looks at the "Dynamics of Small and Medium Enterprises' Borrower Characteristics and Credit Risk in Ghana." He explores the characteristics of SME borrowers and the macroeconomic variables that contribute to credit risk. Using a quantitative approach, he analyzed the relationship between SME borrower characteristics, macroeconomic variables, and credit risk and found that the majority of the loans taken by SMEs were diverted due to agency issues. He emphasized that SMEs should take steps to clarify the conditions that come with loans to reduce the number of unsuccessful applications.

Contents

Notes on Contributors

Vera Acheampong is a lecturer at Ghana Communication Technology University (GCTU), specifically in the Economics department. She's been teaching there since September 2014 and is pursuing a PhD in Development Economics at the University of Ghana. Her research interests include Environmental economics, international trade, gender, and poverty issues.

Ivy Adjei-Nketiah is a lecturer at Wisconsin International University College (WIUC) in Ghana. She holds an MPhil in Industrial Psychology and an MBA in Marketing. Her research areas are in International Marketing, Services Marketing, Marketing Management and entrepreneurship.

Stephen Owusu Afriyie is a Lecturer in the Department of Accounting, Banking and Finance at Ghana Communication Technology University, Accra, Ghana. His research interests are in the areas of forensic accounting, corporate finance, financial inclusion, Fintech, corporate governance, microfinance, and entrepreneurship. He is competent in conducting research using varied scientific tools and procedures in order to interpret results and make inferences. He has a number of research outputs published in reputable journals indexed in SCI, SSCI, ESCI, Scopus, PubMed, DOAJ, and so on, while a number of his studies are still under review for approval and subsequent publication.

Derrick Nukunu Akude is a Lecturer in Marketing and has authored many articles. With over a decade of writing features for the local paper, Derrick has a unique perspective that shines through in his newest collection of articles, which explore the importance we place on service quality perception and the marketing mix. Derrick has an PhD in Business Administration (marketing) from the University of Cape Coast, Ghana and was the recipient of the creative writing award. Derrick has spent over a decade researching services marketing.

George Kofi Amoako is the director at the Directorate of Research Innovation and Consultancy and an associate professor of marketing at the Department of Marketing, School of Business, Ghana Communication Technology University and Durban University of Technology South Africa. His current research areas are Sustainability, Corporate Social Responsibility, Marketing, Branding, Strategy, Environmental Issues, Tourism, and Hospitality. Professor Amoako has conducted several studies to help raise policy options in sustainability and marketing to attain the targets of the United Nations SDGs. Prof. Amoako is in the top 1% of Marketing professors in Africa according to A.D. Scientific 2025. He has published in many high-ranked journals.

Emelia Amoako Asiedu is an Associate Professor in the Business School at the Ghana Communication Technology University. She holds a PhD in Public Administration and Policy Management. Her research area is in public sector performance management, leadership and employee engagement, public policy management, occupational health and safety management, gender issues, tourism and sustainability, and entrepreneurship.

Gertrude Amoakohene is a Senior Lecturer with over 13 years experience in teaching and research and her interest areas include Accounting, Corporate Finance, Financial Institutions, International Finance, Investment, and Development/Sustainable Finance. She possesses analytical abilities oriented towards research-based problems solving and has a flair for academic research, which is the hall mark for scholarly and enterprise activity. She is a results-oriented, hands-on professional who is dutiful to policies and procedures and pays attention to detail. She possesses a strong ability to make well-thought-out decisions.

Prince Yao Amu is a PhD candidate at the University of Ghana Business School, University of Ghana, Legon, and an adjunct lecturer at Ghana Community Technology University. His research interests are sports marketing, management research, FINTECH, consumer behaviour, digital entrepreneurship, and sustainable marketing. He can be contacted through amuprinceyao@gmail.com or pyamu@st.ug.edu.gh

Emmanuel Attah Kumah Amponsah holds a PhD in Financial Accountancy from SHUATS, India, an MBA in Finance and Operations, from SRM University, India, and a BBA in Accounting and Finance from All Nations University, Ghana. He is currently a Senior Lecturer and a head of Accounting, Banking, and Finance Department at Ghana Communication Technology University, Ghana. He is a highly qualified business executive with over twenty (20) years of working experience in senior management positions. He has been actively involved in teaching, research, and consultancy in a distinguished career spanning over 20 years.

Peter Lawer Angmor is a senior lecturer at the Department of Accounting, Banking and Finance, Ghana Communication Technology University and Faculty Exams Coordinator for the Business School. He is a Chartered Accountant with the Institute of Chartered Accountants-Ghana and a member of Chartered Institute of Management Consultants, Canada. He has a strong track record in consultancy, training, assessment, coaching, monitoring, and evaluation and research. His educational background includes a Post Graduate Certificate in Higher Education from Coventry University, an MBA in Accounting and Finance and a BSc in Accounting from the University of Professional Studies, Ghana. He is a PhD student in Forensic Accounting and Audit.

Isaac Ankrah is a senior lecturer at Ghana Communication Technology University (GCTU). He holds a PhD in Technology Economics and Management and a Master's in Economics (Financial Engineering) from Xiamen University. His work spans Applied Economics with a focus on technology, digital economies, and energy economics. He is skilled in econometric modelling and data analytics, using tools such as Python, EViews, Stata, and OxMetrics. At GCTU, he teaches across undergraduate and postgraduate programmes and has supervised numerous Master's theses in economics, technology, and energy-related fields.

Ethel Yiranbon Annor-Tenkorang is a Senior Lecturer and Management policy analyst with 9 years' research and teaching experience in Higher education. She has authored and co-authored 31 peer-reviewed publications and supervised over 60 postgraduate and undergraduate thesis and projects. Her research interest includes Management, Human resource Development, Leadership and Healthcare Technology.

Jackson Nuarko Appiagyei is a dynamic business researcher, innovation consultant, and project strategist specializing in entrepreneurship, marketing, human capital, and M&E. He is currently pursuing a PhD at the University of the Witwatersrand and holds an MPhil in Marketing and Entrepreneurship from the University of Ghana. As Manager of the UGBS Innovation and Incubation Hub, he has led transformative initiatives such as BRIInG, UG-CCReS, NKABOM, etc., securing funding from leading institutions like Mastercard Foundation, British Council, FCDO, etc. A published scholar and conference presenter, Jackson excels at translating academic research into impactful innovation and ecosystem development across Africa's entrepreneurial landscape.

George Kwabena Asamoah is the Dean of Graduate Studies and Research and a Senior Lecturer at the University of Media, Arts, and Communication. With over 15 years of B2B marketing experience, he has held leadership roles in banking, telecoms, insurance, and manufacturing. He holds a PhD and MPhil in Marketing, an MBA, and a B.A. in Political Science and Economics from the University of Ghana, as well as a Diploma in Public Relations and Advertising. A member of the

American Marketing Association, he co-founded ESG Partners and specializes in marketing strategy, communications, and capacity building in environmental, social, and governance (ESG).

Charles Asare is a lecturer of marketing at the Ghana Communication Technology University (GCTU) and a chartered marketer (CIM-UK). He holds an MBA from the University of Sunderland, UK, and is a PhD candidate at UPSA-Ghana. Charles is also a management consultant who provides training for private and public institutions in Ghana and the West African sub-region. His research interests are multichannel and omnichannel integration, consumer behaviour, and contemporary issues in marketing.

Joseph Asare is a Senior Lecturer in Finance at the Business School Faculty of Ghana Communication Technology University in Ghana. He holds a PhD in Business Administration (Finance and Management option), a master's in economics and management, and a BSc Degree in Accounting. His research interest includes Business and Project finance, investment risk analysis and control, Fintech, digital finance, financial innovation, and digital financial inclusion. He has over 15 years of research experience, and several publications in finance.

Esther Asiedu is a Senior Lecturer at the Department of Management Studies, Ghana Communication Technology University (GCTU), with many years of experience in teaching and research. Her research covers leadership, organizational behaviour, supply chain, entrepreneurship, AI in management, and gender issues, with publications in top journals. Dr. Asiedu is a turnaround leader known for her impactful research and exceptional teaching. She mentors youth, supports business planning, and advocates gender equity.

Richard Kofi Asravor is a senior lecturer and Head of the Economics Department at the Ghana Communication Technology University. He has a PhD in Applied Agricultural Economics and Policy. His research areas include the impact of HIV/AIDS on economic growth, farm-level climate adaptation strategies, technology and managerial performance of farm operators.

Vida Asante Boateng is a Lecturer at The Business School of Wisconsin International University College, Ghana. She holds a B.A. (Hons) degree in Industrial and Organizational Psychology (IOP) from the University of Ghana, Legon and further pursued an MPhil in IOP at the University of Oslo, Norway. She was the Head of the Management Department for Human Resource and Marketing at the Business school. Her areas of research interest include but not limited to leadership, diversity and health and safety issues engulfing our organizations. She has over a decade of industry experience in social and marketing research with Research International, Ghana, an affiliate of the WPP Kantar Group (Global), as a Research Manager with extensive insights in both quantitative and qualitative research work.

Felicia de Heer is a Senior Lecturer at the School of Research and Graduate Studies, Central University. She teaches Marketing Management, Integrated Marketing Communication, International Marketing, and Consumer Behaviour. She is also an External Assessor for a University and a Research Institution in Ghana. Her research interests are: Brands Management, Services Marketing Strategy, and Marketing Innovation.

Derrick Ofori Donkor is Lecturer in Economics and Entrepreneurship at Ghana Communication Technology University (GCTU) and a PhD candidate in Economics at the University of Cape Coast, Ghana. He holds advanced degrees in Petroleum Economics and Management from Gubkin Russian State University of Oil and Gas, Moscow, and in Economics of Technology and Development from the University of Cape Coast, alongside professional certification in higher education from Coventry University, UK. With over nine years of academic and consultancy experience across West Africa, his research and professional interests focus on energy economics, innovation, entrepreneurship, and sustainable development. He has written in reputable journals on energy transition and eco-innovation and serves as Chair for Teaching, Learning, and Student Experience at GCTU, while also leading consultancy and capacity-building initiatives within the sub-region.

Antoinette Yaa Benewaa Gabrah holds a PhD in marketing and lecturer at Academic City University, Haatso-Ghana. She teaches contemporary issues in marketing, entrepreneurship, and digital marketing tactics and trends. Her research interests, conferences, and publications are in areas of e-business, digital marketing strategy, international business, entrepreneurial marketing, services marketing, artificial intelligence and emerging technologies, customer satisfaction, customer loyalty, SMEs, entrepreneurial and family ventures management, family businesses in Africa, and digital marketing strategies.

Deli Dotse Gli, PhD is a research associate in the Department of Marketing and Entrepreneurship at the University of Ghana Business School and also an adjunct lecturer in the Department of Marketing at the Ghana Communication Technology University. His research focuses on social marketing, consumer-brand relationships, sustainability, digital and social media, branding, and entrepreneurship. His works have been published in *African Journal of Economics and Management Studies*, *Journal of Digital Business*, *International Journal of Entrepreneurship and Innovation*, and *Journal of Hospitality and Tourism Horizons*. He can be reached via delidg61@gmail.com.

Robert Ebo Hinson is a leading African Marketing Pracademic with nearly 30 years' experience in marketing strategy, communications, customer experience, and education. He holds a DPhil in Marketing from the University of Ghana and a PhD in Business Economics from Aalborg University, Denmark. A Chartered Marketer, he has led brand campaigns for top global firms and delivered hundreds of industry presentations across Africa. He is a Distinguished Visiting Professor at the University of Johannesburg and serves on key academic boards. His research spans marketing, CSR, and sustainability, and he is widely recognized by the AD Scientific Index as Africa's top marketing scholar.

Ebenezer Malcalm is an Associate Professor, Acting Pro Vice-Chancellor, and Dean of the School of Graduate Studies and Research at Ghana Communication Technology University (GCTU). He previously served as Director of the Centre for Online Learning and Teaching (COLT) at

GCTU and was the Pro Vice-Chancellor of Laweh Open University College, Ghana's first Open University. He holds a PhD in Instructional Design and Technology from Ohio University, USA. Prof. Malcalm has published and reviewed articles in leading journals such as Sage, Emerald, Springer, and Taylor & Francis. His research focuses on AI and ICT integration in education and organizations, as well as management, gender, and sustainable development.

Theresa Obuobisa-Darko heads the Department of Management studies at the Ghana Communication Technology University. She holds a PhD in Public Administration and Public Policy from the University of Ghana. Theresa's research interest is in the field of Human Resource Management, Leadership, Organizational Development, and Public Policy.

George Oppong Ampong is an Associate Professor of Management at Ghana Communication Technology University, Accra, Ghana, with experience in both academic and third sector leadership and management. His research interest includes Business and Sustainability strategies, entrepreneurship, SME development, and organizational leadership.

Priscilla Ntriwaa Otuo is a lecturer in the Department of Marketing and Entrepreneurship at the University of Ghana Business School. She holds a PhD in marketing from the University of Hull, UK. Priscilla's research areas include portfolio entrepreneurship, venture start-up, and growth in developing economies. She can be contacted through pnotuo@ug.edu.edu.gh

William Asamoah Owusu is a lecturer in the Department of Marketing at Ghana Communication Technology University and a PhD Candidate. His research interests include SME development, scaling, and internationalization of firms through constrained-based innovations in emerging markets. He holds an MBA (Marketing) from the University of Leicester and a BSc in Agriculture with a specialization in International Agribusiness Management from Van Hall Larenstein, University of Applied Sciences in The Netherlands.

Kwame Ntim Sekyere is a seasoned lecturer and business consultant with over 24 years of experience. He specializes in marketing and entrepreneurship at the Ghana Communication Technology University, where he also serves as a faculty member. Kwame has extensive consulting experience with SMEs. He holds an MPhil in Business Administration and a BSc in Marketing, complemented by several certifications. His research focuses on strategy, international business, and innovation, and he has published in these areas.

List of Figures

List of Tables

1

Entrepreneurship and Small and Medium-Sized Enterprises (SMEs) in Africa: The Realities of Post-COVID-19 Era

Emelia Amoako Asiedu, Richard Kofi Asravor, Robert Ebo Hinson, and George Oppong Ampong

The advancement of entrepreneurship in Africa has not received much attention among scholars, typically because the majority of SMEs operate in the informal sector. Despite this, the literature on SMEs shows that they frequently and easily fail, are subject to government seizures, and encounter limited access to cash and raw materials (Amankwah-Amoah et al., 2018). This comprehensive volume, entitled "Entrepreneurship

E. Amoako Asiedu (✉)
Department of Marketing, Ghana Communication Technology University, Accra, Ghana
e-mail: easiedu@gctu.edu.gh

R. K. Asravor • G. Oppong Ampong
Ghana Communication Technology University, Accra, Ghana
e-mail: rasravor@gctu.edu.gh; gampong@gctu.edu.gh

R. E. Hinson
University of Ghana Business School, Accra, Ghana

E. Amoako Asiedu et al. (eds.), *Entrepreneurship and Small and Medium-Sized Enterprises (SMEs) in Africa*, https://doi.org/10.1007/978-3-032-14174-3_1

and Small and Medium-Sized Enterprises (SMEs) in Africa: The Realities of Post-COVID-19 Era," offers an in-depth exploration of the evolving entrepreneurial landscape across the African continent. The book is structured to provide a balanced viewpoint, with historical context, current challenges, success stories, and policy implications. Its educational features make it a valuable resource for academic institutions, business schools, and training programs seeking to educate future entrepreneurs and business leaders. Ultimately, this book project aims to satisfy the need for up-to-date, contextually rich information that can inform policy decisions, inspire entrepreneurial endeavors, and contribute to the sustainable growth of SMEs in Africa, fostering economic development and resilience in the face of global challenges like COVID-19.

SME development in Africa is key toward the continent's economic progress, yet the SME sector has been impacted by the COVID-19 epidemic, which has brought attention to the need for strategic solutions. The book project is distinctive as it has a dual focus on both historical settings and the contemporary challenges posed by the novel COVID-19 pandemic on SMEs. By examining the realities of the post-COVID-19 era, it provides a unique perspective that combines the resilience and adaptability of African entrepreneurs with the unprecedented disruptions caused by the global health crisis. This book will be beneficial to researchers, policymakers, entrepreneurs, and educators by providing a comprehensive understanding of the African SME ecosystem as well as valuable insights for navigating the post-pandemic landscape among SMEs in Africa.

Several arguments have indicated that to change Africa's economic prospects, however, entrepreneurship must be at the center of efforts (Boly et al., 2018; Salami et al., 2010; Page, 2012). Drawing on the above discussions, this new book on "Entrepreneurship and Small and Medium-Sized Enterprises (SMEs) in Africa: The Realities of Post-COVID-19 Era." Extant literature on sustainable marketing, corporate social responsibility, and business ethics is mostly oriented toward giant organizations (Amu et al., 2024), sometimes neglecting the problems and possibilities faced by small- and medium-sized firms (SMEs). Lin (2024) and Wu and Amoasi (2024) elucidate how sustainability marketing bolsters brand reputation and competitive advantage, whereas Garel and Petit-Romec (2021) and Lin (2024) demonstrate that CSR fosters stakeholder trust and long-term profitability. Waheed and Zhang (2022) assert that ethical frameworks are essential for the success of a sustainable firm. These studies, however, primarily presuppose the availability of financial resources, a specialized department, and economies of scale—circumstances largely inapplicable to SMEs. Dixit and Priya (2023) have highlighted that resource limitations and informal techniques significantly influence the involvement of SMEs in sustainability and CSR. Conversely, the empirical landscape remains deficient, particularly in developing markets and some sectors, in comprehensive understanding how SMEs incorporate such methods into their operations and the subsequent impact on performance.

The effects of government regulations, though counterintuitive, provide significant theoretical and practical reflections for SMEs in developing economic contexts. COVID-19 had spread worldwide, affecting almost every country and region. The economic and sociological consequences of the epidemic have not been adequately acknowledged or grasped. COVID-19's outbreak caused economic hardship on a scale not seen since World War II (Gössling et al., 2020) and has had a substantial impact on global economic development even after the WHO declared the Pandemic was over (Amoako et al., 2024). While the COVID-19 controversy is beneficial to the environment in the short term, it has had a devastating effect on economies and people worldwide (Kugbey et al., 2021).

The advent of the COVID-19 pandemic has further amplified these challenges, exposing vulnerabilities within the SME sector while simultaneously revealing opportunities for resilience and adaptation. The pandemic's disruptive effects—such as disrupted supply chains, reduced demand, and operational restrictions—have necessitated innovative responses and strategic shifts among African entrepreneurs (Engidaw, 2022; Hussain et al., 2021). As such, understanding how SMEs have navigated this crisis and how entrepreneurial practices have evolved in response is critical for identifying pathways toward sustainable recovery and growth.

This volume brings together multidisciplinary insights from academics, policymakers, and practitioners to examine the multiple facets of entrepreneurship in Africa, both before and during the COVID-19 era.

It explores themes including digital transformation and the role of technology in enhancing SME competitiveness (Toukola et al., 2023), strategies for creating and sustaining competitive advantages (Ampong et al., 2024), and the influence of regulatory and institutional frameworks (World Economic Forum, 2023). Additionally, the book emphasizes the importance of social responsibility, ethical business practices, and government interventions, highlighting their significance for fostering sustainable SME development (Amankwah-Amoah et al., 2018; Page, 2012).

Theoretically, this implies that SMEs' engagements in sustainable and ethical undertakings are less a choice dictated by regulatory compliance but more by their intrinsic motivations, governor-manager values, market demands, or stakeholder expectations—as proposed by Stakeholder Theory. SMEs are widely recognized as pivotal drivers of economic growth, innovation, and employment, especially in developing regions where they constitute a significant share of the formal and informal economies (Fjose et al., 2010). In Africa, however, the development and sustainability of SMEs are often hindered by a range of structural and contextual challenges, including limited access to finance, inadequate infrastructure, regulatory complexities, and skill gaps (Hatega, 2007; EU, 2022).

This volume brings together multidisciplinary insights from academics, policymakers, and practitioners to examine the multiple facets of entrepreneurship in Africa, both before and during the COVID-19 era. It explores themes including digital transformation and the role of technology in enhancing SME competitiveness.

References

Amankwah-Amoah, J., Boso, N., & Antwi-Agyei, I. (2018). The effects of business failure experience on successive entrepreneurial engagements: An evolutionary phase model. *Group & Organization Management, 43*(4), 648–682.

Amoako, G. K., Sedalo, G., Asiedu, E. A., Ampong, O. A., & G. (2024). Conceptual framework–sustainability actions, global crises and justice in the future of tourism and hospitality. *Journal of Tropical Futures, 1*(2), 203–217.

Ampong, G. O. A., Plange-Rhule, R., Boakye, A. N., & Afram, K. O. A. O. (2024). Stakeholder management best practices in entrepreneurship. In *Stakeholder management and Entrepreneurship in Africa* (pp. 185–194). Routledge.

Amu, P. Y., Odoom, R., & Mohammed, I. (2024). The Moderating Role of Corporate Social Responsibility on the Relationship between Brand Image and Brand Loyalty: A. *Corporate Social Responsibility-A Global Perspective: A Global Perspective*, 29.

Boly, L., Diallo, D., & Takei, T. (2018). Entrepreneurship in Africa: Opportunities and challenges. *World Journal of Entrepreneurship, Management and Sustainable Development, 14*(2), 150–165.

Dixit, S. K., & Priya, S. S. (2023). Barriers to corporate social responsibility: An Indian SME perspective. *International Journal of Emerging Markets, 18*(9), 2438–2454.

Engidaw, A. E. (2022). Small businesses and their challenges during COVID-19 pandemic in developing countries: In the case of Ethiopia. *Journal of Innovation & Entrepreneurship, 11*, 1. https://doi.org/10.1186/s13731-021-00191-3

EU SME Envoy Network (2022), SMEs and Rising Energy Prices: First findings and Recommendations.

Fjose, S., Grunfeld, L. A., & Green, C. (2010). SMEs and growth in Sub-Sahara Africa: Identifying SME role and obstacles to SME growth. *MENON Publication, 14*, 1–28.

Garel, A., & Petit-Romec, A. (2021). Investor rewards to environmental responsibility: Evidence from the COVID-19 crisis. *Journal of Corporate Finance, 68*, 101948.

Gössling, S., Scott, D., & Hall, C. M. (2020). Pandemics, tourism and global change: a rapid assessment of COVID-19. *Journal of sustainable tourism, 29*(1), 1–20.

Hatega, L. (2007). *SME development in Uganda*. Private Sector Foundation.

Hussain, A., Shahzad, A., Hassan, R., & Doski, S. A. (2021). COVID-19 impact on B2B e-commerce: A multi-group analysis of sports and surgical SME's. *Pakistan Journal of Commerce and Social Sciences (PJCSS), 15*(1), 166–195.

Kugbey, N., Amoah, A., Dotse, S. Q., Amoako-Asiedu, E., Delalorm, C., & Nyarko-Sampson, E. (2021). " The angel within the devil"|: COVID-19 silver linings. *Pan African Medical Journal, 40*(1), p. 251.

Lin, F. (2024). Entrepreneurial performance and marketing analytics: the role of new product innovation. *Journal of Small Business and Enterprise Development, 31*(2), 418–440.

Page, J. (2012). Africa's future: The case for entrepreneurship. *Development Policy Review, 30*(S2), s95–s106.

Salami, A., Kamara, B., & Brixiova, Z. (2010). Doing business in Africa: Policies and business environment. *African Development Review, 22*(2), 201–219.

Toukola, S., Ståhle, M., & Mahlamäki, T. (2023). Renaissance of project marketing: Avenues for the utilisation of digital tools. *Project Leadership and Society, 4*, 100091.

Waheed, A., & Zhang, Q. (2022). Effect of CSR and ethical practices on sustainable competitive performance: A case of emerging markets from stakeholder theory perspective. *Journal of Business Ethics, 175*(4), 837–855.

World Economic Forum. (2023). Why Africa's SMEs need more than money to ensure their growth. https://www.weforum.org/agenda/2023/07/why-priming-africa-s-smes-for-growth-is-about-more-than-money/

Wu, X., & Amoasi, R. (2024). The role of CSR in sustaining corporate brands in the global market: The perspective of telecommunication companies in Ghana. *Corporate Social Responsibility and Environmental Management, 31*(1), 433–447.

2

Entrepreneurship and Innovation in Ghana: Post-COVID-19 Realities

Joseph Asare, Stephen Owusu Afriyie, and Emmanuel Attah Kumah Amponsah

2.1 Introduction

Small and medium businesses (SMEs) account for over 95% of registered businesses and support the African region with about 50% of the total GDP. However, in spite of the huge contributions of SMEs, the sector continues to face significant obstructions that impede their growth and success, which extend beyond the usual barriers to accessing finance. The characteristics of SMEs in developing economies appear to be the same. About 40% of SMEs in developing countries are also faced with difficulty accessing finance. This is a signal that the financial sector in general does not clearly recognize the importance of serving SMEs' financial needs. In addition, the financial sector perceives SMEs as too risky due to the lack of available collateral and poor or no cash flow data on the part of SMEs. On the other hand, Africa's financial market is mired by information irregularity, which has left many small enterprises have poor financial

J. Asare (✉) • S. O. Afriyie • E. A. K. Amponsah
Ghana Communication Technology University, Accra, Ghana
e-mail: jasare@gctu.edu.gh; safriyie@gctu.edu.gh; ekumah@gctu.edu.gh

E. Amoako Asiedu et al. (eds.), *Entrepreneurship and Small and Medium-Sized Enterprises (SMEs) in Africa*, https://doi.org/10.1007/978-3-032-14174-3_2

knowledge. However, the contribution of small and medium-sized enterprises (SMEs) to economic growth cannot be overemphasized. It is for this reason that SMEs are considered as the engine for economic growth and recovery. Recognizing this, African economies have taken steps to encouraging the growth of small and medium enterprises, also known as SMEs. SMEs account for over 95% of all firms in the Sub-Saharan Africa region (Hatega, 2007). Also, SMEs are noted to play a significant role in boosting GDP, providing employment for most of the population, and reducing poverty (Chu et al., 2010). Further, SMEs are recognized for using simple approach in addressing most of Africans' needs by offering inexpensive goods and services in sufficient terms and prices. In addition, SMEs serve as a source of income and employment (Kauffmann, 2006). In both developing and developed economies, small and medium enterprises (SMEs) are considered as the engine that drives both economies and the way to attaining industrialization. In most developing countries, SMEs account for 99% of all businesses, thereby indicating their importance (Fjose et al., 2010). Therefore, addressing SMEs' needs and enhancing their ability to reach full potential is essential to creating a wealthy Africa.

2.1.1 A Global View of Small and Medium-Sized Enterprises

The world all over, small to medium-sized enterprises make up a substantial portion of the total number of global businesses, creating employment, providing goods and services, and supporting economic growth (World Bank, 2019). Small and Medium Enterprises (SMEs) are recognized for playing a major role in most of the world economies, particularly in developing economies, and account for the majority of businesses worldwide, representing about 90% of businesses. SMEs are important in job creation, contributing to more than 50% of employment worldwide and global economic development. Formal SMEs contribute up to 40% of national income (GDP) in emerging economies (Amoah et al., 2022a, b). Empirical evidence has shown that an estimated 600 million jobs will be needed by 2030 to absorb the growing global workforce

(Weerakkody, 2021). It is for this reason that SME development has become a high priority for many governments around the world. In most emerging markets, majority of the formal jobs are created by the SMEs, constituting about 7 out of every 10 jobs. However, access to finance has been identified as a key challenge to SME growth worldwide (Adjabeng & Osei, 2022). In addition, SMEs are behind compared to large companies in terms of productivity. On average, SMEs' labor productivity, or value added per worker, is thought to be half that of larger firms. Therefore, increasing productivity growth has always been the surest way to attain long term growth and survival, and SMEs must consider it as a crucial role. The contribution of SMEs is potentially more important amid the beginnings of the new era of global trade patterns. It is important to note that such changes may translate into a meaningful long-term realignment; however, this could be through a competitive network of SMEs supporting and complementing large companies' efforts (Jeongmin et al., 2024).

2.1.2 Defining SMEs

The world over, small and medium-sized enterprises are defined in a different way. The different definitions of SMEs worldwide reveal that it is difficult to agree on a common definition of SMEs. A study in 75 countries identified more than 75 definitions used in the different (Auciello, 1975). This establishes that there is no commonly accepted definition of SMEs. However, depending on the economy, industry, assets, business size, and products, the definition continues to vary. In most cases, the economy in which SMEs operate through specific legislature and/or authorized institution/body provides the specifics on the definition of SMEs. Almost every emerging economy and most developed countries tend to define SMEs to suit their economic and/or development needs. However, the fundamental criteria used to define SMEs tend to be similar among economies. In most cases, the quantitative measures of the criteria tend to vary from one economy to another, and this relates to balance sheet size, sales turnover, paid-up capital, and number of employees. On the other hand, the quantitative are useful for all purposes of economic analysis (Lexandrina, 2016). However, in recent times, common specific mostly used is the size of the SMEs. The sizing or categorization of a firm as an SME depends on the country, and this can be based on several characteristics. Also, a combination of common traits such as the annual sales, the number of assets owned by the company, number of employees, market capitalization, or other combination of these features (CFI, 2015). The European Union (EU) considers small and medium-sized enterprises (SMEs) as representing 99% of all businesses in the EU. The EU further indicated that the definition of an SME is important to help in accessing finance and the EU support programs targeted specifically at the SMEs (European Union (EU), 2022). In the EU's recommendation 2003/361, small and medium-sized enterprises (SMEs) are defined as shown in Table 2.1 below.

Despite this comprehensive definition, the EU Commission still sees the need to constantly monitor the implementation of the SME definition and review it in irregular intervals.

The United States defines SMEs differently from one industry to another and defines an SME, among other characteristics, as those with no more than 500 workers. On the other hand, Agbeblewu and Boohene (2015) define an SME as country-specific but generally based on three key words: small, single, and local.

Small: These are SMEs/SMBs that are small in nature, based on the number of employees, capital, and assets or overall turnover.

Single: These are SMEs that have a single owner, single service, or single product.

Local: Essentially, these SMEs are locally based in nature and have a localized market. Most of the time, they may be operating from their residence.

Table 2.1 Definition of SMEs based on EU's definition

Company category	Staff headcount	Turnover	Balance sheet total
Medium-sized	<250	≤ € 50 m	≤ € 43 m
Small	<50	≤ € 10 m	≤ € 10 m
Micro	<10	≤ € 2 m	≤ € 2 m

Source: EU Recommendation 2003/361

It is important to remember that while there are similarities, each country, as well as the industries and sectors within them, may adopt different definitions for an SME. In most economies, like Canada, SMEs are considered as businesses that employ less than 500 people, whereas businesses that employ 500 or more are considered large firms. According to Statistics Canada, SMEs have no more than 499 employees and less than $50 million in gross revenue. However, the most agreed definition from numerous research recently defines SMEs as businesses that employ less than 250 employees, noting that very small businesses may have less than 50 employees. Meanwhile, micro-enterprises usually have 5 and 10 employees (Beck & Cull, 2014). However, a common observation is that below 50% of businesses in low- and lower-middle-income economies have less than 100 employees (Katua, 2014).

In Africa, most definitions of SMEs agree that SMEs are the major source of income and employment for about 80% of the majority world population (Kamunge et al., 2014). Micro businesses in Africa constitute about 30% of employment, and small businesses account for 20%, while medium businesses provide about 10% of employment. Also, SMEs in Africa account for over 90% of businesses, contributing about 50% of Gross National Product (GDP) (Fjose et al., 2010). Table 2.2 below shows the characteristics and contribution of five selected SMEs across Africa.

The above information in Table 2.2 clearly shows that SMEs across Africa are defined in many different contexts.

SMEs in Ghana

Small and medium-sized enterprises (SMEs) are the backbone of the Ghanaian economy—they represent about 92% of businesses, largely within the private sector, and contribute about 70% of Ghana's gross domestic product (GDP) in 2018 in terms of corporate taxes, export duties, and import taxes (Doagbodzi, 2024). SMEs constitute the vast majority of businesses in Ghana providing services and goods to large organizations, hence contributing to expanding output, providing value-added activities and widening Ghana's export base (Appiah-Nimo, 2018).

Table 2.2 Characteristics and contribution of SMEs in selected African countries

Country	SMEs vs other business	Firm size (no. of employee)	Average assets $	Contribution to employment	Contribution to GDP	References
Ghana	92%	7–50	≤100,000	80%	60%	GCB (2023). Ghana SME Sector Report 2
Nigeria	95%	10–199	≤305,571	84%	48%	Tobi et al. (2024). Investing in Africa: Small and Medium Enterprises in Nigeria
South Africa	91%	<500	≤35billion	60%	34%	The Banking Association South Africa (2024). Small and Medium Enterprise
Namibia	92%	1–200	≤568,417	20%	12%	Benjamin W. (2023). The Vital Role of SMEs in Namibia's Development
Botswana	95%	<25	< 112521	>30%	16%	Okurut et al. (2015). Determinants of SMEs growth in Botswana
Senegal	99%	<200	<150000	42%	33%	Louis S. (2019). Particularity of informal Senegalese SMEs and Challenges of Their Formalization

Source: this study

According to him, statistics from the National Board for Small Scale Industries (NBSSI) indicate that SMEs constitute about 90% of the private sector's contribution and offer employment in the manufacturing sector as well. These denote that SMEs, therefore, have catalytic impacts on growth. In the Sub-Saharan African country, the majority of businesses operate in the form of a small and medium-sized enterprise. SMEs play a significant role in the economic development of many nations. Ghana's policy priorities are economic diversification, social inclusion, and macro-economic stability. With employment still heavily concentrated in agriculture and the informal sector, and exports concentrated in gold, cocoa, and oil, the government is looking to diversify its economy (Abban et al., 2023). One way of doing this would be to invest its oil and gas resources to support value-added, diversified agricultural exports and ensure that manufacturing is a larger part of GDP and more competitive internationally. SMEs in Ghana would be a critical beneficiary of these policies. They are an integral part of the Ghanaian economy, and they tend to employ vulnerable groups, including women, youth and low-skilled workers. As SMEs often operate in labor intensive, low value-added sectors, wages tend to be low. Actions to boost SME competitiveness through capacity building or national policies (such as the national export strategy or the yam sector strategy) can help increase productivity, raising wages and standards of living. This notwithstanding, SMEs in Ghana face various constraints (including limited access to credit facilities and international markets). Ghana's working population relies on SMEs for income. SMEs are important actors in the transition of and quality of economic growth and sustainable transformation. SMEs quintessentially play an active role in fostering income equality and ensuring that benefits from technological change and globalization are more broadly shared for the benefit of all to the remotest villages. Afrane (2024) asserts that small and medium enterprises (SMEs) are essential to the Ghanaian economy, as they significantly contribute to job creation, poverty reduction, and overall economic growth. Despite these contributions, Ghanaian SMEs encounter substantial obstacles, including inadequate support structures, skills deficits, and restricted access to financing. This makes the governments at both national and local levels recognize the SME sector as a priority area for additional support and development. It is instructive to further note that SMEs form the base from which many successful national brands have emerged over the years. Many of the successful companies we see today started as SMEs before they became large companies or multinational corporations. In this study, the authors take a deep dive into the role of innovation in small and medium-sized enterprises (SMEs) and explore the different ways in which it can drive success, as well as some of the challenges that SMEs face when trying to stay ahead of the curve.

2.1.3 The Old Realities and New Realities of SMEs

The spread of business and cultural activities across the globe has increased due to globalization, a term which most scholars refer to as the efforts to create a global free market for goods and services. However, some scholars also believe the current situation surrounding business is of a fundamentally different order from what has gone before (IMF, 2002). The reality is that virtually all firms, small and large, are facing globalization. And for the SMEs to survive in the twenty-first century, they must confront this global environment with full force (Elikem et al., 2014). The reality is that Globalization, or internationalization, is not a new phenomenon that SMEs have to deal with. The period through the end of the nineteenth century has been characterized by unprecedented economic growth and global integration. However, globalization saw intermittent in the first half of the twentieth century by a wave of protectionism followed by aggressive nationalism, which led to depression and the world war. Unfortunately, international economic and political integration was reversed, with severe consequences which affected most SMEs (Vandenberg, 2009).

SMEs have demonstrated the capacity to promote economic growth. With this, it has been commonly accepted that the drivers of economic growth and long-term sustainability for emerging markets are dependent on the effective development and potentials for small and medium enterprise (SME) sector (World Bank, 2019). The African population has been estimated at more than 1.3 billion people, with a projected growing rate of over 2% annually in most countries. This growing population would require that services, jobs, and economic growth be provided by locally based SMEs. Unfortunately, enterprises on the continent face an array of challenges that far outstretch those of their counterparts in developed countries across the globe (Trevor, 2019).

The major challenge that faces SMEs is access to finance. Financial access is the single biggest obstacle to both start-ups and established SMEs in Africa for growth and expansion. It is estimated that the African formal SME sector has an annual financing gap exceeding $136 billion. However, SMEs account for over 90% of all businesses in Africa. These numbers show that the investment potential of the African continent can be unlocked through financing the SME sector. This reality is since the African population is predicted to double in over 25 years, creating unprecedented market potential for the SME sector (AFI, 2020). About 40% of SMEs in most developing economies are known to grapple with access to finance. This discovery also indicates that the financial sector in general may be struggling to understand and serve SMEs. To address this, the issue of information irregularity in financial markets has to be tackled because it has left many SMEs to become knowledge poor. In addition, the lack of available collateral or cash flow data means that the financial service providers often view SMEs as too risky (WEF, 2023). On the other hand, most small business owners often possess more information about the potential of their businesses, but most at times it tends to be difficult for them to articulate and give detailed information about the business as needed by credit officers (Winborg & Landstrom, 2000).

Currently, SMEs' operational capabilities have been extremely affected by the post-COVID-19 pandemic innovation, forcing many firms to use technology and innovation rather than the old traditional methods of operating business. Most empirical research has shown that there is a higher adoption of the use of technology once SMEs realize the benefits and impact on performance (Shah Alam et al., 2011). Most SMEs before the COVID-19 did not use the most recent technology (Chatterjee et al., 2022). However, an assessment on the impact of technological relative advantage, technology readiness, organizational cost of adoption, top management support, environmental government support, and competitive pressure factors on B2B e-commerce for manufacturing SMEs has shown that technology adoption among SMEs during and after the

COVID-19 pandemic has been high (Hussain et al., 2021). Before the COVID-19 pandemic, Amat and Ishak (2019) had argued that the success of SMEs is determined by their ability to innovate, network, access to capital, and use of technology. Among the common technologies used by SMEs are e-commerce, websites, digital payment, enterprise resource planning, mobile phone, social media, cloud computing, blockchain, and AI tools (Olsen & Saetre, 2007; Mishrif & Khan, 2023).

2.2 Entrepreneurial Ecosystems

Entrepreneurship has been considered a vital organ that drives the economic growth of many countries. Fostering entrepreneurial ecosystems comes as a strategy to nurture a country's economy by promoting entrepreneurial processes and activities that ultimately support the growth of small businesses. Donaldson (2021) referred to entrepreneurial ecosystem as a set of interconnected entrepreneurial support elements such as leadership, culture, capital, markets, human skills, and support. These elements, in turn, create a platform for smooth entrepreneurship development that promotes economic growth and social welfare. Extant studies on entrepreneurial ecosystems focus on distinguishing relevant ecofactors that create vibrant and sustainable entrepreneurial ecosystems. However, less has been done to study the causal relationships between ecofactors and productive entrepreneurship as an eco-output (J. M. P. Kansheba, 2020). Productive entrepreneurship is any productive entrepreneurial activities that contribute directly or indirectly to economic growth and finally increases total welfare through the production of additional output. In response to that inquiry gap, a measurement framework is developed for testing the causal effects among eco-factors, output, and outcome of entrepreneurial ecosystems. These eco-factors are accumulative forms of capital, such as financial, institutional, knowledge, and social capitals, within an ecosystem that enhance productive entrepreneurship (an eco-output). Kansheba (2020) stressed that the effect of entrepreneurial ecosystems on productive entrepreneurship is mediated by innovations. Conducive entrepreneurial ecosystems supply necessary resources that promote innovations among entrepreneurs and bring about innovative and productive startups. Based on evidence drawn from J. M. Kansheba and Wald (2022), the findings reveal that the influence of ecofactors of entrepreneurial ecosystems on productive entrepreneurship is completely mediated by innovation in terms of product and process innovations.

2.2.1 Innovative Entrepreneurship

Innovation involves the generation of new ideas, whether it be new products, processes, upgrades to existing services, or business models (Edwards-Schachter, 2018). It is the act of introducing something new or creating change that adds value to existing products or services. Innovation plays a crucial role in promoting growth, enabling organizations to adapt to evolving market trends, and ultimately driving profitability. While innovation can involve the creation of entirely new concepts, it also includes improvements and enhancements to existing products, services, or ideas. It disrupts the status quo and encourages a departure from the traditional approach. As asserted by Farhan (2024), innovation requires fresh thinking, creativity, and the ability to identify opportunities for change and improvement. It should be noted that innovation is distinct from invention, as it does not necessarily entail the creation of something entirely new. Instead, it focuses on introducing novel ideas or enhancing existing ones to meet the needs of customers, industry demands, and societal changes. Innovation is a vital means for organizations to remain relevant, competitive, and responsive in their respective industries, and it does not inherently involve risk. Kumar and Srivastava (2020) believe innovative entrepreneurship is crucial for identifying emerging trends and market demands, allowing businesses to create new and appealing goods or services for their target audience. To stay relevant in a competitive landscape, businesses must continue to innovate by developing innovative products, services, and evolving their brand. Innovation plays a central role in entrepreneurship as it involves the replacement or improvement of existing offerings, enabling entrepreneurs to meet market trends and satisfy customer demands with innovative strategies.

2.3 Methodology

A survey instrument was specifically designed and pilot-tested for the purpose of this study, utilizing a random sampling method to choose a sample of 100 SMEs from enterprises in Accra, Ghana. The investigators collected data regarding the Ghanaian SMEs, utilizing the International Standard Industrial Classification (ISIC), as specified by the Ghana Statistical Service. The study was also guided by Act 1043 of Ghana Enterprises Agency to ascertain the various types and categories of enterprises. Over 70% of the participants held positions as managing directors and CEOs. The remaining respondents were employed as supporting staff. The SMEs that participated in the study varied in size from two to seven employees, with a mean of three people. All the responses were received and collated using an Excel spreadsheet. Empty cells were removed from the dataset, representing 0.2% of the total responses. The researchers then conducted phone interviews with 25 nonrespondents in order to check for response bias. Analysis of the data turned out with no significant response bias in the selected sample.

2.4 Findings and Discussions

The study revealed that COVID-19 epidemic has taken top stage among all global health issues worldwide. Like life always finds means to survive, so does mankind change to fit into a novel setting. As a result, entrepreneurs must adopt business innovation to overcome these pandemic adversities and post-COVID-19 realities. Evidence from the study revealed that there was a possibility that the inadvertent damage to entrepreneurship in Africa caused by COVID-19 could be long-lasting. As a result, the emergence of COVID-19 has threatened the survival of businesses, especially SMEs, thereby aggravating the unemployment rate over the African continent and posing serious obstacles for the growth of entrepreneurship. However, entrepreneurs could leverage the strengths of creative (innovative) activities to foster a survival perspective, build financial resilience, and modify business models to fit the reality of post-COVID-19 era. This will highlight both short- and long-term aspects of entrepreneurship growth on the African continent.

1. *COVID-19 Impact on SMEs in Developing Economies*

Table 2.3 shows COVID-19 impacts on SMEs in developing economies

Table 2.3 clearly shows that the impact of COVID-19 on SMEs ranges from a decrease in demand and sales, reduction in liquidity and cash flow, and difficulty in getting input, supply, and refinancing. Also, studies by authors including Djankov and Panizza (2020) and Takyi et al. align with the findings of this study.

2. *COVID-19 Impact on Specific Sectors of Ghanaian Businesses*

Table 2.4 shows COVID-19 impacts on specific sectors of Ghanaian businesses.

Table 2.3 COVID-19 impacts on SMEs in developing economies

Country	Decrease in demand/sales %	Reduction in liquidity/cash flow %	Difficulty in input/ supply/refinancing %
Ghana	60.6	75.6	25.4
South Africa	75	54	26
Liberia	67.3	78.4	62.4
Zimbabwe	78	95	68
Mozambique	42	58	44
Sudan	54	81	50
Namibia	68.8	63.8	52.3
Central African Republic	68	24.6	48.6
Tunisia	82.1	88.8	56
Libya	41	36	23
Egypt	55	32	42
Kenya	83	72	63
Zambia	50	50	71
Angola	52.4	64.2	72
Nigeria	72.1	56.2	68

Source: This study, 2024. Compiled from national statistics sources of the economies studied

Table 2.4 COVID-19 impacts on specific sectors of Ghanaian businesses

	Operating status during lockdown		Operating status at time of study		Indicators				
Business sectors	Fully open	Closed	Fully open	Closed	Facing decrease in sales	Average decrease in sales	Facing difficulties in finding inputs	Reporting cash flow problems	Facing decreased access to finance
Household firms	48.2	24.3	78.4	14.6	95.7	66.2	51.2	68.1	29.3
Young SMEs**	49.5	24.2	79	10.5	89.9	67.1	48.4	72.1	24.7
Sector									
Manufacturing	36.9	39.8	79.3	11.6	92.7	65.3	47.6	78.2	17.2
Agric and Other Industries	39.4	24	73.7	9.5	77.2	43.8	52.2	73.9	29.6
Trade	41.4	30.8	84.1	9.3	93.7	56.6	53.7	82.7	26.2
Accommodation / Food	32.7	39.3	66.6	22.2	91.9	65.3	49.7	71.4	27.1
Other Services									
Size									
Micro (1–5)	35.4	37	71.6	18.5	92.2	60.9	51.1	75.2	24.7
Small (6–30)	41.9	33.5	82.6	9.1	89.7	60.8	52.3	77.8	26.6
Medium (31–100)	35.1	12.7	66.4	3.5	89.9	62.1	53.7	69.6	34.6
Large (100+)	46.6	20	93.3	2.6	45.1	16	42.7	47	21.9
Age of Firms									
Young (0–4)	42.3	37.9	64.9	17.2	86.5	52	58	73.5	27.1
Maturing (5–14)	34.8	36.6	73.1	17.1	91.2	60.9	51.9	75	23.9
Established (15+)	38.5	33.8	77	14.5	92.8	62.1	49.2	76.9	27
Other groups									
Informal firms	38.1	35.5	76.1	15.4	90	59.2	51.5	78.3	23.9
Exporters	41.8	36.7	62.2	0	96.1	68.5	46.5	95.9	11.9

Source: This study, 2024. Compiled from national statistical sources of the economy studied

The study results revealed that nearly half of SME businesses in Ghana were closed during the peak of the COVID-19 pandemic. However, some SMEs were fully open for business at the time this study was conducted. In addition, the impact of the COVID-19 pandemic on Ghanaian SMEs are like those observed in Table 2.1. In similar way, studies by scholars including Engidaw (2022) and ITC (2020) align with the findings of this study.

3. *Economic Indicators of COVID-19 Impact on SMEs in Developing Economies*

Table 2.5 shows the economic indicators that caused severe impacts of the COVID-19 pandemic on SMEs.

The results from Table 2.5 show that the three main economic factors that caused adverse impacts on SMEs during the COVID-19 pandemic are GDP, inflation, and interest rates. This study noted that during the pandemic, most of the economies had low or negative GDP growth. Also, prices of common household goods almost doubled, and financial institutions were unwilling to lend to SMEs or did so at a very high rate. Similarly, Peprah et al. (2024) and Jawad and Naz (2023) have affirmed how these factors in this study's findings were impacted by the COVID-19 pandemic.

2.4.1 Innovation in Small and Medium-Sized Enterprises (SMEs)

Small and medium-sized enterprises (SMEs) and entrepreneurs are fundamental to innovation, economic growth and job creation, and play a critical role in social cohesion. Innovation is about finding new and better ways to create value for customers. Innovation in SMEs refers to the process of coming up with new and creative ideas, turning them into products or services, and bringing them to market (Radicic & Alkaraan, 2024). It is the ability to identify a gap in the market and create something that fills that gap, or to find a better way of doing something that has already been done. It is what sets entrepreneurs apart from others and

Table 2.5 Economic indicators of COVID-19 impacts on SMEs in developing economies

	2020			2021			2022		
Country	GDP	Inflation	Interest rate	GDP	Inflation	Interest rate	GDP	Inflation	Interest rate
Ghana	6.5	7.14	14.83	5.9	9.89	15.5	5.1	9.28	14.5
South Africa	0.2	4.13	6.5	-6.3	3.27	6.25	5	4.48	4.4
Liberia	-2.3	26.97	20.36	-2.9	16.95	19.7	7.1	5.87	20
Zimbabwe	-8.1	255.29	38.47	-1.3	557.21	179.8	3.069	92.57	60
Mozambique	2.62	2.78	13.5	-1.23	3.14	14.2	2.46	6.18	13.25
Sudan	-2.18	63.29	14.22	-3.63	163.26	16.09	0.9	359.09	17.3
Namibia	-0.6	3.72	6.5	-8	2.21	6.25	2.6	4.04	5.25
Central African Republic	3	2.69	3.1	0	2.3	3.1	3.3	3.65	3.5
Tunisia	1	6.72	7.75	-8.6	5.64	6.75	0.3	5.73	6.25
Libya	2.5	0.21	3	-31.3	2.82	3	8.9	21.11	3
Egypt	2.97	13.88	12.25	0.97	5.7	9.25	-1	4.5	8.25
Kenya	5.4	5.2	12.44	5.2	5.17	12	5.9	6	7
Zambia	1.4	9.15	14.3	-3	15.73	12.3	1	22.8	14.3
Angola	0.6	17.08	15.5	-5.3	22.28	14.45	-0.66	24.39	20
Nigeria	2.2	12.09	13.5	-1.81.5	13.2	9	0.51	16	11.5

Source: This study, 2024. Compiled from national statistical sources of the economies studied

drives their success. It is also what keeps companies relevant and competitive in a fast-paced and ever-changing world. In short, innovation is the key to staying ahead in entrepreneurship, and it can take many different forms, from creating a new product to improving an existing one to finding a new way to reach customers and bring in sales. Taylor (2017) argued that innovation should be viewed as an economic or social phenomenon rather than a technological term. Innovation is not about making new inventions, but rather about recognizing how to take advantage of opportunities and changes: "Systematic innovation therefore consists in the purposeful and organized search for changes, and in the systematic analysis of the opportunities such changes might offer for economic or social innovation." According to Chirumalla (2021), innovative businesses are able to identify opportunities and create new products or services that fill gaps in the market, and they are able to continuously adapt to new technologies and market trends. They often leverage team extension to bring in specialized skills and scale their operations efficiently without the long-term commitments of traditional hiring. Innovation is often thought of as the lifeblood of entrepreneurship (Ayandibu & Ayandibu, 2024). Without it, companies would quickly become stale and irrelevant in an ever-changing world. The ability to come up with fresh, new ideas and turn them into successful ventures is what sets entrepreneurs apart from the rest. However, the role of innovation in entrepreneurship is not always straightforward. Some entrepreneurs are natural innovators, constantly coming up with new ideas and executing them with precision. Others struggle to keep up with the pace of change, always playing catch-up to their competitors. Biney (2024) corroborates that innovation is often the key to success in entrepreneurship. Entrepreneurs who are able to consistently come up with new and creative ideas are better equipped to remain competitive in a rapidly changing world. They are able to identify opportunities and create new products or services that fill gaps in the market, and they are able to continuously adapt to new technologies and market trends. Innovative businesses often leverage team extension to bring in specialized skills and scale their operations efficiently without the long-term commitments of traditional hiring. Entrepreneurship can drive innovation by creating a culture of risk-taking and experimentation (Donbesuur et al., 2023). Entrepreneurs who are willing to take risks and try new things are often at the forefront of innovation, and they can create new markets and spur economic growth.

2.4.2 The Importance of Innovation in SME Success

Innovation is essential for business success because it allows companies to stand out from their competitors and offer something new and valuable to their customers (YuSheng & Ibrahim, 2020). It helps companies stay relevant in an ever-changing world, where customers are always on the lookout for the next big thing. Companies that embrace innovation are better equipped to adapt to new technologies and market trends, which can give them a significant advantage over those that do not. Innovation can also lead to increased efficiency, reduced costs, and improved customer satisfaction, all of which are critical components of business success. Mensah and Gordon (2020) explicate that when companies invest in innovation, they are investing in their future, positioning themselves for long-term growth and success. Another important aspect of innovation is that it drives economic growth. Companies that innovate create new products, new markets, and new jobs. This, in turn, generates wealth and stimulates economic activity, making innovation a critical driver of prosperity. Innovation is not just a nice-to-have in the world of entrepreneurship; it is a must-have (Adusei et al., 2023). Companies that don't embrace innovation are likely to fall behind and struggle to remain competitive in today's fast-paced business environment. For instance, businesses that integrate cutting-edge technologies like a VPN app to enhance security and privacy for their customers are more likely to stay ahead in the market and build a loyal customer base.

2.4.3 The Role of Technology in Enhancing SMEs and Innovation

Technology plays a critical role in SME activities and innovation. Technology provides entrepreneurs with new tools, platforms, and opportunities to create and bring new products and services to market.

Here are some of the ways technology affects entrepreneurship and innovation:

1. Access to capital: Technology has made it easier for entrepreneurs to access capital through online platforms such as crowdfunding, which can help them get their companies off the ground.
2. Automation: Technology can automate many routine tasks, freeing up time for entrepreneurs to focus on more strategic initiatives.
3. Ease of communication: Technology has made communication faster, easier, and more efficient, which can help entrepreneurs build relationships and networks that can support their companies.
4. Disruptive innovation: Technology has created many new markets and disrupted traditional industries, providing entrepreneurs with opportunities to create new products and services that fill gaps in the market.
5. Access to information: Technology has made it easier than ever for entrepreneurs to access information and research, which can inform their decision-making and help them identify new opportunities.

From the above, technology is an essential tool for entrepreneurs and innovators. By leveraging technology, entrepreneurs can bring new ideas to market, improve efficiency and productivity, and drive economic growth. As technology continues to evolve, it will likely create even more opportunities for entrepreneurs and innovators, and the role of technology in entrepreneurship and innovation will only become more important. With the rapid evolution of technology, especially in fields like application development, entrepreneurs and innovators are poised to seize numerous opportunities for growth and advancement (Amankwah-Amoah et al., 2023).

2.4.4 The Impact of SME Innovation on Job Creation and Economic Growth

Innovation has a significant impact on job creation and economic growth. When entrepreneurs bring new products and services to market, they create new industries, jobs, and opportunities for growth. Innovation can drive job creation and economic growth in many ways. Entrepreneurs who innovate and create new products and services can create new jobs (Asravor & Sackey, 2023) in a range of industries, from manufacturing and distribution to marketing and sales. As these companies grow, they can also create jobs in related industries, such as supply chain management and logistics. Entrepreneurs who innovate and bring new products and services to market can drive economic growth by creating new industries and markets. This can lead to increased investment, higher levels of consumer spending, and improved economic performance (Amoako-Asiedu et al., 2024). As expounded by Amoako and Boateng (2022), innovation can lead to increased productivity by improving existing processes and creating new ones. This can result in greater efficiency, lower costs, and improved competitiveness, which can drive economic growth. Innovation can lead to improved standards of living by creating new products and services that make life easier, more convenient, and more enjoyable (Quaye & Mensah, 2019). This can result in increased consumer spending, which can drive economic growth. It can be deduced that innovation is a key driver of job creation and economic growth. By fostering innovation, entrepreneurs can create new industries, markets, and opportunities for growth, and drive improvements in productivity, competitiveness, and quality of life. These factors can help drive economic growth and create a more prosperous future for everyone (Arthur-Sam, 2024).

2.4.5 Types of Innovation in Small and Medium-Sized Enterprises (SMEs)

Innovation in entrepreneurship can take many different forms, and understanding these different types can help entrepreneurs identify opportunities and focus their efforts in the right areas. Some of the most common types of innovation in entrepreneurship include:

1. Product innovation: This refers to the development of new or improved products, or the introduction of new product features (Adomako et al., 2024). This type of innovation can be anything from a new product in an existing market to the creation of an entirely new mar-

ket. Adopting agile project management can greatly facilitate product innovation by allowing for flexibility, quick iterations, and continuous feedback loops.

2. Process innovation: This refers to the development of new or improved processes that increase efficiency, reduce costs, or provide a better customer experience. This can be anything from streamlining a production process to improving the delivery of goods and services (G. K. Amoako, 2022).
3. Marketing innovation: This refers to new and creative ways of reaching customers and promoting products or services. It can include new forms of advertising, new pricing strategies, or new channels for reaching customers, such as using email software like ActiveCampaign or ClickFunnels to send targeted emails effortlessly, or leveraging mobile app marketing trends to engage users effectively in the app marketplace (Toukola et al., 2023).
4. Business model innovation: This refers to the development of new business models, or the modification of existing models, to create new sources of revenue or to increase efficiency. This can include the use of new technologies, new distribution channels, or new customer engagement strategies (Mignon & Bankel, 2023).
5. Social innovation: This refers to the creation of new solutions to social and environmental problems. Social innovation often involves collaboration and the integration of multiple disciplines and industries, and it can be both for-profit and nonprofit (Vanderpuye, 2024).

These are some of the examples of innovation that exist in entrepreneurship. Understanding these different types can help entrepreneurs focus their efforts and resources, and identify opportunities for growth and success.

2.4.6 The Role of Government in Fostering Innovation for SMEs in the Post-COVID-19 Era

The role of government in fostering innovation is critical, as it can help create an environment that supports and encourages innovation.

Governments can invest in research and development to support the creation of new technologies, products, and services. Government funding can help companies overcome the high costs and long development times associated with R&D (Adjabeng & Osei, 2022). This would help support scientific research, the development of new technologies, and the testing of innovative products and services. The support can help entrepreneurs bring new ideas to market and create new industries. Governments can provide tax incentives for companies or entrepreneurs who start new companies (Thompson Agyapong et al., 2018). The tax incentives generally include exemption from customs import duties on plant and machinery; reduced corporate income tax (CIT); and more favorable investment and capital allowances on plant and machinery. This can help entrepreneurs access the resources they need to innovate and grow their companies. Governments can encourage collaboration between universities, research institutes, and companies, to help foster innovation and create new opportunities (Oduro, 2020). The collaboration between universities and the industry is increasingly perceived as a vehicle to enhance innovation through knowledge exchange. This can involve funding research partnerships or creating innovation hubs that bring together different groups to work on common challenges. Amoah et al. (2022a, b) assert that governments can promote education and skills development to help ensure that the workforce is equipped with the skills needed to drive innovation and compete in the global marketplace. By investing in tech skills training, governments and business organizations can ensure their workforce is prepared to meet the demands of the digital economy needed by SMEs. Also, governments can help protect intellectual property rights of entrepreneurs to encourage innovation (Agyapong et al., 2024). Through government assistance, a number of different national policies can increase the incentives to innovate, including guaranteeing intellectual property rights. They include providing patents, trademarks, and copyrights that give entrepreneurs and companies exclusive rights to their ideas and products. By creating a supportive environment and providing the resources and incentives needed for innovation, governments can help entrepreneurs bring new ideas to market and spur economic growth.

2.4.7 The Future of Innovation in Small and Medium Size Businesses After COVID

After COVID-19, the future of innovation in entrepreneurship is bright and full of potential. With advances in technology, changes in consumer behavior, and new opportunities for growth, entrepreneurs are poised to continue to drive innovation and create new industries and markets. Some of the trends and factors are shaping the future of innovation in entrepreneurship. According to Odei et al. (2023), the rapid pace of technological change is creating new opportunities for entrepreneurs to innovate and bring new products and services to market. From AI and the Internet of Things to virtual and augmented reality, technology is changing the way people live and work, and providing new opportunities for entrepreneurs. Also, the COVID situation has brought changes in consumer behavior and shaping the future of innovation in entrepreneurship (Thukral, 2021). Consumer behavior and purchasing patterns dramatically changed as a result of the COVID-19 crisis. For instance, there has been an increased attention to healthier eating habits and organic and qualitative foods has been observed during and after the pandemic. With the rise of e-commerce and the growth of the gig economy, consumers are looking for new and innovative products and services that meet their changing needs and preferences. However, globalization has drastically altered the business landscape, breaking down geographical boundaries and opening up new opportunities for entrepreneurs. The growth of the global economy is granting entrepreneurs with new prospects to innovate and reach new markets (Agyapong, 2020). With increased access to capital, talent, and markets, entrepreneurs are poised to continue to drive innovation and create new industries and opportunities for growth. The key to business sustainability, particularly in times of economic crisis, is innovation. Quartey (2023) believes the growing focus on sustainability is also shaping the future of innovation in entrepreneurship. Indeed, the quest for sustainability has already started to transform the competitive landscape, which forces SMEs to change the way they think about products, technologies, processes, and business models. As consumers become more environmentally conscious, entrepreneurs are looking for new and innovative ways to create products and services that are sustainable and environmentally friendly. In view of the aforementioned realities, the future of innovation in entrepreneurship is full of potential. With advances in technology, changes in consumer behavior, and new opportunities for growth, entrepreneurs are poised to continue to drive innovation and create new industries and markets that will shape the future of mankind.

2.5 Conclusion

Small and medium-sized enterprises (SMEs) and entrepreneurs are fundamental to innovation, economic growth, and job creation, and play a critical role in social cohesion. It is for this reason that SMEs are considered as the engine for economic growth and recovery. Recognizing this, African economies have taken steps to encouraging the growth of small and medium enterprises, also known as SMEs. The SMEs sector presently has seen much innovation. That is, the SMEs sector is consistently finding new and better ways to create value for customers. Innovation in SMEs includes the process of coming up with new and creative ideas, turning them into products or services, and bringing them to market. It also indicates the ability to identify a gap in the market and create something that fills that gap, or to find a better way of doing something that has already been done. Therefore, innovation is what sets entrepreneurs apart from others and drives their success. It is also what keeps companies relevant and competitive in a fast-paced and ever-changing world. In short, innovation is the key to staying ahead in entrepreneurship, and it can take many different forms, from creating a new product to improving an existing one to finding a new way to reach customers and bring in sales. Africa's financial market is mired by information irregularity which has left many small enterprises have poor financial knowledge. However, the contribution of small and medium size enterprises (SMEs) to economic growth cannot be overemphasized. This study contributes to the body of knowledge on the role of technology in driving entrepreneurship and SMEs. Therefore, this study adds to the literature on small businesses by helping entrepreneurs better understand how to explore innovations in their businesses. SMEs' performance is likely to improve as they increasingly recognize that technology and strategy are closely aligned throughout the innovation process. The findings suggest that the need for increased Internet access to information and tools could help entrepreneurs implement innovative ideas. However, reducing the administrative and bureaucratic load on SMEs seeking government support will help to enable many of them to maximize use of the available resources. Finally, considering the lack of financial resources within most SMEs, future studies on the role of business angels, venture capitalists, and state assistance funds in fostering entrepreneurship and innovation in Ghana are much needed.

References

Abban, R., Omta, J. B., & Aheto, V. S. (2023). Non-traditional agricultural export performance in Ghana. Exporting SMEs' characteristics, export mode, and institutions. *Journal of Economics & Management Research. SRC/JESMR-233, 187*(4), 2–11. https://doi.org/10.47363/JESMR/2023

Adjabeng, F., & Osei, F. (2022). The development of small medium enterprises and their impact on the Ghanaian economy. *Open Journal of Business and Management, 10*(6), 2939–2958. https://doi.org/10.4236/ojbm.2022.106145

Adomako, S., Gyensare, M. A., Amankwah-Amoah, J., Akhtar, P., & Hussain, N. (2024). Tackling grand societal challenges: Understanding when and how reverse engineering fosters frugal product innovation in an emerging market. *Journal of Product Innovation Management, 41*(2), 211–235.

Adusei, E., Demah, E., & Mensah, H. K. (2023). Does going intellectually green matter? Accentuating the role of eco-innovation speed and quality in a competitive post-Covid 19 emerging market. *International Journal of Innovation Science.*

Afrane, Y. O. (2024). *Evaluation of the economic impact of start-ups and small and medium enterprises on Ghana's development: A comprehensive analysis.*

Agbeblewu, S., & Boohene, R. (2015). The interaction between entrepreneurial orientation, firm resources and the performance of tourist accommodation establishments in the Central Region of Ghana. *International Journal of Development Research and Quantitative Analysis, 3*(1), 13–29.

Agyapong, D. (2020). *Review of entrepreneurship, micro, small and medium enterprise financing schemes in Ghana Enterprising Africa* (pp. 142–158). Routledge.
Agyapong, D., Arthur, K. N. A., & Nketsiah, I. (2024). A review of intellectual property laws in Ghana in the context of small enterprises' innovations and inventions. *Entrepreneurship and Enterprise Development in Africa*, 95–105.
Alliance for Financial Inclusion (AFI). (2020). *Scoping and assessment report – MSMEs access to finance ecosystem in Africa*. AFI. https://www.afi-global.org/wp-content/uploads/2020/12/AFI_AfPI_SMEFWG_survey-report_AW2_digital.pdf
Amankwah-Amoah, J., Nyuur, R. B., Hinson, R., Kosiba, J. P., Al-Tabbaa, O., & Cunningham, J. A. (2023). Entrepreneurial strategic posture and new technology ventures in an emerging economy. *International Journal of Entrepreneurial Behavior & Research, 29*(2), 385–407.
Amat, M., & Ishak, S. (2019). Faktor PSiKKIT: Pendorong inovasi pembungkusan dalam kalangan Industri Kecil dan Sederhana berasaskan perusahaan makanan. *Malaysian Journal of Society and Space*. https://doi.org/10.17576/geo-2019-1503-07
Amoah, R., Amponsah, D. A., & Mdletshe, B. (2022a). Assessing the quality of local government training on small medium enterprises (SMEs) in the implementation of local economic development initiatives (LED) in Ghana. *International Journal of Current Science Research and Review, 5*(09).
Amoah, J., Belas, J., Dziwornu, R., & Khan, K. A. (2022b). Enhancing SMEs contribution to economic development: A perspective from an emerging economy. *Journal of International Studies, 15*(2), 63–76. https://doi.org/10.14254/2071-8330.2022/15-2/5
Amoako, G. K. (2022). Customer satisfaction: Role of customer service, innovation, and price in the laundry industry in Ghana. *Journal of African Business, 23*(1), 146–164.
Amoako, S., & Boateng, E. (2022). Considering factors that leads to sustainability of small and medium enterprises in Ghana using PESTEL and theories of entrepreneurship as a measuring tool. *Technium Social Sciences Journal, 31*, 594.
Amoako-Asiedu, E., Otuo, P. N., Obuobisa-Darko, T., & Antwi-Agyei, A. (2024). *Stakeholder legitimacy perceptions and firm innovation: A developing country perspective stakeholder management and entrepreneurship in Africa* (pp. 49–60). Routledge.
Appiah-Nimo, C. (2018). The role of transactional leadership style of owner/managers in adopting a market oriented culture: A case of manufacturing SME'S. *Asian Journal of Economics, Business and Accounting, 7*(3), 1–12.

Arthur-Sam, J. (2024). The role of entrepreneurship in the economic development of Ghana: Evidence from the Mfantseman municipality of Ghana. *International Journal of Applied Research in Business and Management, 5*(2).

Asravor, R. K., & Sackey, F. G. (2023). Impact of technology on macro-level employment and the workforce: What are the implications for job creation and job destruction in Ghana? *Social Indicators Research, 168*(1), 207–225.

Auciello, K. E. (1975). *Employment generation through stimulation of small industries, an international compilation of small-scale industry definitions*. Georgia Institute of Technology.

Ayandibu, A. O., & Ayandibu, E. O. (2024). *The role of innovation in sustainable entrepreneurship sustainable development in industry and society 5.0: Governance, management, and financial implications* (pp. 205–221). IGI Global.

Beck, T., & Cull, R. (2014). *Small and medium-sized enterprise finance in Africa*. African Growth Initiative (working paper 16). Brookings.

Biney, I. K. (2024). Unpacking lifelong learning and entrepreneurial prospects among young adults in Ghana. *Community Development*, 1–22.

Chatterjee, S., Chaudhuri, R., Shah, M., & Maheshwari, P. (2022). Big data driven innovation for sustaining SME supply chain operation in post COVID-19 scenario: Moderating role of SME technology leadership. *Computers and Industrial Engineering, 168*, 108058. https://doi.org/10.1016/j.cie.2022.108058

Chirumalla, K. (2021). Building digitally-enabled process innovation in the process industries: A dynamic capabilities approach. *Technovation, 105*, 102256.

Chu, M., Kara, O., & Benzing, C. (2010). An empirical study of Nigerian entrepreneur: Success, motivation, problems and stress. *International Journal of Business Research, 16*.

Corporate Finance Institute (CFI). (2015). *Small and medium-sized enterprises (SMEs)*. https://corporatefinanceinstitute.com/resources/accounting/small-and-medium-sized-enterprises-smes/

Djankov, S., & Panizza, U. (Eds.). (2020). *COVID-19 in developing economies*. CEPR Press. https://cepr.org/publications/books-and-reports/covid-19-developing-economies

Doagbodzi, R. (2024). Ghanaian small and medium-scale enterprises (SMEs') readiness for African continental free trade area (AfCFTA) implementation. *Journal of Business and Enterprise Development (JOBED), 12*(1).

Donaldson, C. (2021). Culture in the entrepreneurial ecosystem: A conceptual framing. *International Entrepreneurship and Management Journal, 17*(1), 289–319.

Donbesuur, F., Owusu-Yirenkyi, D., Ampong, G. O. A., & Hultman, M. (2023). Enhancing export intensity of entrepreneurial firms through bricolage and international opportunity recognition: The differential roles of explorative and exploitative learning. *Journal of Business Research, 156*, 113467.

Edwards-Schachter, M. (2018). The nature and variety of innovation. *International Journal of Innovation Studies, 2*(2), 65–79.

Elikem, O. C., Akaba, S., & Worwui-Brown, K. D. (2014). Globalization and competitiveness: Challenges of small and medium enterprises (SMEs) in Accra, Ghana. *International Journal of Business and Social Science, 5*(4) Special Issue.

Engidaw, A. E. (2022). Small businesses and their challenges during COVID-19 pandemic in developing countries: In the case of Ethiopia. *Journal of Innovation and Entrepreneurship, 11*, 1. https://doi.org/10.1186/s13731-021-00191-3

European Union (EU). (2022). *SME definition*. EU. https://single-market-economy.ec.europa.eu/smes/sme-fundamentals/sme-definition_en

Farhan, B. Y. (2024). Visionary leadership and innovative mindset for sustainable business development: Case studies and practical applications. *Research in Globalization, 8*, 100219.

Fjose, S., Grunfeld, L. A., & Green, C. (2010). SMEs and growth in Sub-Sahara Africa: Identifying SME role and obstacles to SME growth. *MENON-Publication, 14*, 1–28.

Ghana Commercial Bank. (2023). *Sector industry study – Small medium enterprises (SME's) sector in Ghana*. GCB. https://www.gcbbank.com.gh/research-reports/sector-industry-reports/361-sme-sector-in-ghana-2023-v1/file#:~:text=According%20to%20GEA%20definition%20of,exceeding%2010%20million%20Ghana%20Cedis

Hatega, L. (2007). *SME development in Uganda*. Private Sector Foundation.

Hussain, A., Shahzad, A., Hassan, R., & Doski, S. A. (2021). COVID-19 impact on B2B e-commerce: A multi-group analysis of sports and surgical SME's. *Pakistan Journal of Commerce and Social Sciences (PJCSS), 15*(1), 166–195.

IMF Staff. (2002). *Globalization: A framework for IMF involvement*. IMF. https://www.imf.org/external/np/exr/ib/2002/031502.htm

International Trade Centre (ITC). (2020). *SME competitiveness outlook 2020: COVID-19: The great lockdown and its impact on small business*. ITC. Document Number: P32.E/DMD/RSE/20.VI. https://www.intracen.org/file/itcsmeco2020pdf

Jawad, M., & Naz, M. (2023). Impact of Covid-19 pandemic on macroeconomic aspects. *Journal of Open Innovation: Technology, Market, and Complexity, 9*(3), 100126., ISSN 2199-8531,. https://doi.org/10.1016/j.joitmc.2023.100126

Jeongmin, S., Olivia, W., Michael, B., Lola, W., Camillo, L., Jeffrey, C., & Tiago, D. (2024). *Geopolitics and the geometry of global trade*. Mckinsey Global Institute. https://www.mckinsey.com/mgi/our-research/geopolitics-and-the-geometry-of-global-trade

Kamunge, M. S., Njeru, A., & Tirimba, O. I. (2014). Factors affecting the performance of small and maicro enterprises in Limuru town market of Kiambu County, Kenya. *International Journal of Scientific and Research Publications (IJSRP), 4*(12), 1–20.

Kansheba, J. M. P. (2020). Small business and entrepreneurship in Africa: The nexus of entrepreneurial ecosystems and productive entrepreneurship. *Small Enterprise Research, 27*(2), 110–124.

Kansheba, J. M., & Wald, A. E. (2022). Entrepreneurial ecosystems quality and productive entrepreneurship: Entrepreneurial attitude as a mediator in early-stage and high-growth activities. *Journal of Small Business and Enterprise Development, 29*(2), 311–329.

Katua, N. T. (2014). The role of SMEs in employment creation and economic growth in selected countries. *International Journal of Educational Research, 2*(12), 461–472.

Kauffmann, C. (2006). *Financing SMEs in Africa*. OECD Development Centre, Policy Insight nr 7.

Kumar, V., & Srivastava, R. (2020). New perspectives on business model innovations in emerging markets. *Journal of the Academy of Marketing Science, 48*(5), 815–825.

Lexandrina, M. P. (2016). Entrepreneurship in the Gulf Cooperation Council. *Sciencedirect*. https://www.sciencedirect.com/topics/social-sciences/small-and-medium-sized-enterprise

Mensah, A. M., & Gordon, C. (2020). Strategic partnerships between universities and non-academic institutions for sustainability and innovation: Insights from the University of Ghana. In *Sustainability challenges in Sub-Saharan Africa I: Continental perspectives and insights from Western and Central Africa* (pp. 245–278).

Mignon, I., & Bankel, A. (2023). Sustainable business models and innovation strategies to realize them: A review of 87 empirical cases. *Business Strategy and the Environment, 32*(4), 1357–1372.

Mishrif, A., & Khan, A. (2023). Technology adoption as survival strategy for small and medium enterprises during COVID-19. *Journal of Innovation and Entrepreneurship*. https://doi.org/10.1186/s13731-023-00317-9

Odei, S. A., Odei, M. A., & Toseafa, E. (2023). Determinants of technological and non-technological innovations: Evidence from Ghana'Manufacturing and service sectors. *Journal of African Business, 24*(3), 467–490.

Oduro, S. (2020). Exploring the barriers to SMEs' open innovation adoption in Ghana: A mixed research approach. *International Journal of Innovation Science, 12*(1), 21–51.

Olsen, K. A., & Saetre, P. (2007). ERP for SMEs—Is proprietary software an alternative? *Business Process Management Journal, 13*(3), 379–389. https://doi.org/10.1108/14637150710752290

Peprah, W. K., Anowuo, I., Owusu-Yeboah, O., Ameyaw, D. A. K., & Sabas, L. (2024). *International Journal of Economics and Financial Issues, 14*(6), 145–152. https://doi.org/10.32479/ijefi.17167

Quartey, S. H. (2023). *Business sustainability in SMEs: Towards an Afrocentric research agenda—A research agenda for sustainability and business* (pp. 153–166). Edward Elgar Publishing.

Quaye, D., & Mensah, I. (2019). Marketing innovation and sustainable competitive advantage of manufacturing SMEs in Ghana. *Management Decision, 57*(7), 1535–1553.

Radicic, D., & Alkaraan, F. (2024). Relative effectiveness of open innovation strategies in single and complex SME innovators. *Technology Analysis & Strategic Management, 36*(9), 2113–2126.

Shah Alam, S., Ali, M. Y., & Mohd Jani, M. F. (2011). An empirical study of factors affecting electronic commerce adoption among SMEs in Malaysia. *Journal of Business Economics and Management, 12*(2), 375–399.

Taylor, S. P. (2017). What is innovation? A study of the definitions, academic models and applicability of innovation to an example of social housing in England. *Open Journal of Social Sciences, 5*(11), 128–146.

The World Bank. (2019). *Small and medium enterprises (SMEs) finance*. Improving SMEs' access to finance and finding innovative solutions to unlock sources of capital. https://www.worldbank.org/en/topic/smefinance

Thompson Agyapong, G., Mmieh, F., & Mordi, C. (2018). Factors influencing the growth of SMEs: The case of Ghana. *Thunderbird International Business Review, 60*(4), 549–563.

Thukral, E. (2021). COVID-19: Small and medium enterprises challenges and responses with creativity, innovation, and entrepreneurship. *Strategic Change, 30*(2), 153–158.

Toukola, S., Ståhle, M., & Mahlamäki, T. (2023). Renaissance of project marketing: Avenues for the utilisation of digital tools. *Project Leadership and Society, 4*, 100091.

Trevor, H. (2019). *Why the future is African – And why SMEs should lead the way*. Nextbillion. https://nextbillion.net/future-african-smes/

Vandenberg, P. (2009). *Micro, small and medium-sized enterprises and the global economic crisis: Impacts and policy responses*. International Labour Office, Sustainable Enterprise Programme. 1 v. (Responses to the global economic crisis. ISBN: 9789221224075;9789221224082 (web pdf);9789221224075.

Vanderpuye, E. (2024). *An investigation into organisational hybridity in faith-based social enterprises in Ghana: An organisational spirituality perspective*. 88wwz.

Weerakkody, C., (2021) *Impact of global value chain on the performance of SMEs (October 10, 2021)*. At SSRN: https://ssrn.com/abstract=3941253 or https://doi.org/10.2139/ssrn.3941253

Winborg, J., & Landström, H. (2000). Financial bootstrapping in small businesses: examining small business managers' resource acquisition behaviors. *Journal of Business Venturing, 16*(3), 235–254.

World Economic Forum (WEF). (2023). *Why Africa's SMEs need more than money to ensure their growth*. WEF. https://www.weforum.org/agenda/2023/07/why-priming-africa-s-smes-for-growth-is-about-more-than-money/

YuSheng, K., & Ibrahim, M. (2020). Innovation capabilities, innovation types, and firm performance: Evidence from the banking sector of Ghana. *SAGE Open, 10*(2), 2158244020920892.

3

Creating and Sustaining Competitive Advantage in Small and Medium-Sized Enterprises (SMEs)

George Oppong Ampong,
Ethel Yiranbon Annor-Tenkorang, Esther Asiedu,
Ebenezer Malcalm, and George Kofi Amoako

3.1 Understanding Competitive Advantage in SMEs

According to Algan (2019), SMEs are a significant force in local and global economies, creating jobs and contributing substantially to economic growth. Despite challenges such as inadequate infrastructure in developing countries and limited access to capital, SMEs are finding ways

G. Oppong Ampong • E. Y. Annor-Tenkorang • E. Asiedu (✉) • E. Malcalm
Ghana Communication Technology University, Accra, Ghana
e-mail: gampong@gctu.edu.gh; eyiranbon@gctu.edu.gh;
easaiedu011@gctu.edu.gh; emalcalm@gctu.edu.gh

G. K. Amoako
Ghana Communications Technology University, Accra, Ghana

Durban University of Technology, Durban, South Africa
e-mail: gamoako@gctu.edu.gh

E. Amoako Asiedu et al. (eds.), *Entrepreneurship and Small and Medium-Sized Enterprises (SMEs) in Africa*, https://doi.org/10.1007/978-3-032-14174-3_3

to expand. The increased competition and technological advancements brought about by globalization, along with reduced trade barriers and the presence of e-commerce platforms, have enabled SMEs to adopt a more global outlook (Enaifoghe, 2024). The sustainable growth of the economy relies on the expansion of SMEs, which often form the foundation of economies and nurture private ownership, entrepreneurial drive, and most importantly, adaptability to meet market demands (Puspaningrum, 2020; Yusuf et al., 2023). To thrive in the increasingly interconnected world, SMEs must embrace technology, cross-cultural competence, agility, and an understanding of global markets (Darko Popadić et al., 2022).

In a fiercely competitive market, SMEs face unique challenges that larger corporations do not encounter. Limited resources, reduced market presence, and diminished bargaining power necessitate SMEs to devise distinctive and innovative strategies to set themselves apart from competitors (Gamage et al., 2020; Oliwatosin Abdul-Azeez et al., 2024). Creating a competitive advantage, essentially defining what enables a company to outperform its rivals, is a crucial strategy to achieve (Llave, 2023). This competitive advantage may arise from various factors, such as innovative products, exceptional customer service, or more efficient processes. Recognizing and leveraging these strengths is imperative for SMEs to survive and thrive in a market often dominated by larger competitors (Festa et al., 2022; Kuo, 2020; Mohammad & Solikahan, 2023).

3.2 Role of Innovation in Product and Process Improvement

Innovation assumes a pivotal role in driving a competitive advantage for SMEs (Ayaz Muhammad & Chelliah, 2023; Sair et al., 2023). By continuously improving their processes, products, and services, SMEs can differentiate themselves from competitors and meet evolving consumer demands (Das & Das, 2023; Li, 2023). Technological advancements such as automation and digitization offer SMEs opportunities to enhance productivity, reduce costs, and enhance customer satisfaction. Thus, it is essential for SMEs to carefully weigh the benefits of innovation against the associated risks and expenses, as highlighted by Salami O Afolabi et al. (2024).

The importance of innovation for small and medium-sized enterprises cannot be overstated. SMEs that fail to innovate risk becoming obsolete in a rapidly changing market. Through innovation, SMEs can differentiate themselves from competitors by creating unique value propositions. For example, a small company could develop a new product feature that better addresses consumer needs than existing options, establishing a niche market for itself to dominate. Additionally, innovation is not limited to products; process innovations such as implementing new production methods or improving supply chain management can provide businesses with a significant competitive advantage by reducing costs and increasing productivity (Lelo & Israel, 2024; Monnagaaratwe & Mathu, 2022; Utami et al., 2020).

However, innovation also presents its own set of challenges, especially for small and medium-sized enterprises. Major obstacles may include the cost of research and development (R&D), the risk of product failure, and the need for a skilled workforce to implement new technologies (Utami et al., 2020). To mitigate these risks, SMEs must approach innovation strategically and often leverage alliances, government funding, or collaborative networks (Aswan, 2023; Mawyne Jones & Upadhyay, 2022). By doing so, they can enhance their innovation capabilities without overextending their limited resources. Furthermore, rather than being a one-time effort, innovation can be integrated as a vital component of the company's strategy by fostering a culture of continuous improvement within the organization.

3.3 Differentiation and Cost Leadership Strategies for Competitive Advantage in SMEs

SMEs can gain a competitive edge through two key strategies: cost leadership and differentiation. Becoming the lowest-cost producer in the industry enables a company to offer customers lower prices or generate higher profit margins (Bukoye et al., n.d.; Du & Wang, 2023; Suriani et al., 2024). This is referred to as cost leadership. Conversely, differentiation focuses on providing unique products or services that command a higher price. The suitability of each approach for SMEs' resources, capabilities, and market conditions must be carefully evaluated (Acquah-Hagan et al., 2021; Akingbade, 2020; Pangihutan Situmorang, 2023).

For SMEs, cost leadership can be a highly effective strategy, especially in markets with intense price competition. SMEs can reduce their costs and pass these savings on to customers by streamlining production processes (Łęgowik-Świącik, 2023). They can also achieve this by capitalizing on economies of scale or negotiating better terms with suppliers (Suriani et al., 2024). This approach can attract price-sensitive customers and expand market share. However, quality should not be compromised in pursuit of cost leadership (Pangihutan Situmorang, 2023; Rahman & Hadiyati, 2023). If a brand offers the lowest prices but fails to meet customers' expectations in terms of product performance or customer service, they are unlikely to retain their customer base (Kiyabo & Isaga, 2020; Rahman & Hadiyati, 2023). To ensure that their offerings continue to meet the minimum standards of quality and reliability (Taha et al., 2024; Wushishi, 2024).

Emphasizing non-price aspects allows SMEs to carve out a unique position in the market, providing an opportunity for differentiation. This could involve building a strong brand identity, creating products with distinctive features, or delivering exceptional customer service (Hamid et al., 2022; Tumbelaka, 2022). Through differentiation, SMEs can command premium prices, consequently enhancing their profit margins and cultivating greater customer loyalty (Khan et al., 2024). However, the challenge lies in convincing customers that the unique features justify the higher price, often requiring significant investments in marketing, branding, and customer education (Rahman & Hadiyati, 2023; Zulfikar, n.d.).

3.4 Leveraging Social Media and E-Commerce for Competitive Advantage

Social media and e-commerce have become essential for SMEs to enhance customer engagement and expand their audience (Jercan & Nacu, 2024; Prakoso et al., 2023). Leveraging these platforms enables SMEs to increase sales, foster customer loyalty, and raise brand awareness, ultimately sustaining their competitive advantage (Bano & Ameer Ali, n.d.). In the current digital era, social media and e-commerce platforms offer cost-effective means to reach diverse and vast audiences, a task that would have been challenging and expensive through traditional marketing channels. SMEs can directly engage with consumers, gather feedback, and build communities around their brands on platforms such as Facebook, Instagram, and LinkedIn (Marolt et al., 2022; Rochayatun et al., 2023). This kind of interaction strengthens consumer connections and provides valuable insights to guide marketing and product development strategies (Alenazi & Alanazi, 2023; Ananga et al., n.d.; Zaini et al., 2023).

Additionally, e-commerce has leveled the playing field, enabling SMEs to compete globally with larger enterprises. These platforms also offer various analytics and customer management tools to help SMEs better understand their customers, optimize their operations, and customize their marketing efforts (Prastika & Fachira, 2023; Sukaatmadja et al., 2021). For small fashion retailers, platforms like Instagram can be used to showcase the latest collections, engage with followers, and drive traffic to e-commerce sites, all while capturing real-time data on customer preferences and trends.

3.5 Specialization and Niche Markets in SMEs

SMEs can gain a competitive advantage by focusing on niche markets and specialization, allowing them to serve specific customer segments better than larger competitors. By becoming highly experienced in a particular field, SMEs can offer customized solutions tailored to the specific needs of their target market. According to Dhamija et al. (2023), this strategic focus can also lead to increased brand loyalty and stronger customer relationships.

For SMEs, niche markets present a rare opportunity to become leaders in a particular industry. SMEs can establish a strong presence in smaller, more defined markets where they can offer highly specialized products or services, as opposed to larger enterprises that often aim to capture a broad market (Mohammed & Abdo, 2022). By concentrating on a specific market, SMEs can gain a deep understanding of their customers' needs and preferences. This enables them to provide more personalized and efficient solutions (Wira et al., n.d.). For example, an SME specializing in eco-friendly packaging solutions for organic food producers could position itself as the primary supplier in the industry by offering expertise and products that larger, more diversified packaging companies may not be able to match (Naveen Kumar, 2024).

Creating a strong brand identity is essential for SMEs to differentiate themselves from competitors and build a loyal customer base (Navaia et al., 2023). A well-defined brand identity resonates with customers emotionally by conveying the company's values, mission, and personality. Consistent messaging, visual identity, and customer experience are crucial elements that SMEs should invest in to leave a lasting impression on customers (Hamim Sultoni, 2021; Khan et al., 2024).

Moreover, SMEs with a strong brand identity have the potential to command higher prices and attract a loyal customer base by elevating the perceived value of their products and services. Customers who connect with a brand's values and mission are more likely to become brand advocates, leading to organic business growth and positive word-of-mouth. Maintaining consistency in all aspects of the brand, from visual design to communication tone, helps consumers easily recognize and remember the brand, solidifying its identity in their minds over time (Tumbelaka, 2022).

3.6 Customer Relationship Management in SMEs

Effective customer relationship management (CRM) is not just a tool, but a crucial strategy for SMEs to establish and maintain strong connections with their clients. By leveraging CRM technologies, SMEs can enhance their understanding of customers, personalize interactions, and deliver exceptional service. Additionally, CRM systems provide valuable insights that can inform product development, marketing strategies, and sales efforts, leading to increased customer satisfaction and loyalty (Goyal, 2020; Röser, 2024).

In today's competitive market, SMEs must prioritize the development of long-lasting customer relationships. CRM technologies enable businesses to better comprehend each customer's unique needs and preferences by monitoring and analysing their interactions (Röser, 2024). This knowledge empowers SMEs to deliver personalized experiences, which are essential for retaining customers in the long term. For instance, a CRM system can help an SME identify the products regularly ordered by a specific customer, enabling the business to offer personalized discounts or recommendations, thereby enhancing the customer experience and driving sales (Hamid et al., 2022).

In addition to customization, CRM systems are crucial for improving operational efficiency. By automating repetitive tasks such as data entry, appointment scheduling, and follow-up emails, CRM solutions free up significant time for SME staff to focus on more strategic operations. Furthermore, using CRM solutions' data, SMEs can analyse trends, forecast future sales, and create more effective marketing campaigns (Praba, 2023). Adopting a data-driven approach allows SMEs to anticipate customer needs and deliver exceptional and proactive customer service. Moreover, CRM solutions enable SMEs to manage customer feedback efficiently, leading to prompt resolution of any issues and maintaining high levels of customer satisfaction. Over time, a well-executed CRM strategy can result in increased revenue, loyal customers, and sustained business growth (Hamim Sultoni, 2021).

3.7 Strategic Resource Management

Prudent resource allocation and effective financial management are essential for SMEs to acquire and retain a competitive edge. By carefully managing their finances, including cash flow, budgeting, and investment decisions, SMEs can ensure they have the resources necessary to execute their competitive strategies. Efficient resource allocation enables SMEs to maximize returns on investment and focus on areas that provide the most strategic value (Velykykh, 2023).

In addition to overseeing daily finances, SMEs need to focus on building financial resilience. This involves establishing a financial safety net to protect the company from unforeseen challenges such as market fluctuations, economic downturns, or unexpected expenses (Gubán et al., 2023). By maintaining a healthy cash reserve and cutting unnecessary expenses, businesses can ensure they have the flexibility to adapt to changing market conditions and continue investing in growth opportunities. Furthermore, consistent financial reporting and analysis are crucial aspects of sound financial management as they enable SMEs to track their progress toward financial goals and make well-informed decisions. By emphasizing financial discipline and strategic resource allocation, SMEs can establish a solid foundation for long-term success and sustainable growth (Navaia et al., 2024; Velykykh, 2023).

3.8 Adapting to Market and Consumer Trends

SMEs must be adaptable and nimble in order to respond to evolving consumer preferences and market changes. By staying updated on market trends and consumer preferences, SMEs can adjust their strategies to meet changing needs and maintain their competitive advantage. A company's ability to thrive in a constantly evolving business environment largely depends on its operational flexibility and willingness to innovate (Amoako et al., 2024).

For SMEs to succeed, they must be able to adapt to changing consumer preferences and market shifts. Today's fast-paced corporate environment can see rapid changes due to shifts in consumer behaviour, technological advancements, or global events (Surajwancy & Kulkarni, 2024). Businesses that are slow to adapt to these changes risk losing ground to more agile competitors. To stay ahead of the competition, SMEs need to foster an innovative and flexible culture within their organizations. This involves empowering staff at all levels to implement changes quickly and proactively identify new opportunities and challenges (Enaifoghe, 2024).

3.9 Resources and Capabilities of SMEs

As the global business landscape becomes increasingly competitive, small and medium-sized enterprises (SMEs) in Africa are seeking ways to leverage their resources and capabilities to achieve a sustainable competitive advantage. Several studies have explored the link between internal environmental capabilities and sustainable competitive advantage in manufacturing SMEs, highlighting the mediating role of eco-innovation (Mady et al., 2023). Additionally, the literature emphasizes the importance of knowledge sharing, innovation culture, and entrepreneurial competences in driving SMEs' sustainable competitive advantage (Arsawan et al., 2022; Mokbel Al Koliby et al., 2024a). These studies provide a foundation for further research on the topic of how SMEs in Africa can strategically utilize their resources and capabilities to gain a competitive edge.

Small and Medium Enterprises (SMEs) play a pivotal role in the global economy, often driving innovation, creating jobs, and contributing to economic growth. However, achieving and sustaining a competitive advantage in today's rapidly changing business environment is particularly challenging for SMEs due to their limited resources and capabilities compared to larger firms. Despite these constraints, SMEs can still attain a sustainable competitive advantage by strategically leveraging their resources and capabilities.

The Resource-Based View (RBV) of the firm provides a theoretical foundation for understanding how SMEs can achieve a sustainable competitive advantage. According to Barney (1991), resources are assets, capabilities, organizational processes, firm attributes, information, and knowledge controlled by a firm that enable it to conceive and implement strategies that improve its efficiency and effectiveness. Resources can be tangible, such as physical assets and financial capital, or intangible, such as brand reputation, intellectual property, and organizational culture.

Capabilities, on the other hand, refer to a firm's ability to deploy these resources effectively to achieve a desired outcome (Teece et al., 1997). For SMEs, the challenge lies in identifying and cultivating the resources and capabilities that are valuable, rare, inimitable, and non-substitutable (VRIN) (Barney, 1991). When resources and capabilities meet these criteria, they can provide the firm with a sustainable competitive advantage.

3.10 Competitive Advantage

Competitive advantage, according to Bambang et al. (2021), is a quality that enables an organization to outperform its rivals. Access to natural resources, such as high-grade ores or an inexpensive power source, highly skilled labour, a strategic location, strong entry barriers, and innovative technology are examples of competitive advantages. When a company is implementing a value-creating strategy that no other existing or potential player is doing simultaneously, it is considered to have a competitive edge. The power a company has over its rivals is known as its competitive edge. Gaining this involves providing them with better and more value. Publicizing goods and services that are better or more affordable attracts customers. These distinctive goods or services are known to their target markets (Heriyanto et al., 2021). This explains why consumers are loyal to a certain brand or choose it over a competing one. Grasping competitive advantage requires a grasp of the value proposition. A competitive advantage in the product or service may result from an effective value proposition, which is one that provides customers with better and higher value. Customers' expectations and options may rise as a result of the value proposition.

On the other hand, according to Barney (1991), a business has a competitive edge when it offers its clients advantages that rival those of its rivals but at a cheaper cost. This is a result of the company producing its goods at a significantly reduced cost in comparison to its rivals. It has a cost edge over competitors due to its lower production costs, which enable it to offer items at a lower price. When a company offers its clients perks that are better than those of its rivals while maintaining the same price, it also gains a competitive edge. With these superior perks, the company has a competitive edge (Einsenhardt & Martin 2000; Teece et al., 1997).

According to Haseeb et al. (2019), a number of variables, including cost structure, branding, the calibre of product offers, the distribution network, intellectual property, and customer service, are linked to competitive advantages. Any of the many tasks that an inventive company completes can provide it a competitive edge. Stated differently, every one of these roles contributes to the creation of this highly sought-after and esteemed edge over competitors in the field.

The ideas of competitive advantage put forward by Michael Porter in 1980 and 1985 form the basis of strategic management and are still very applicable to SMEs looking to effectively compete. Porter suggested that businesses use one of three generic strategies: cost leadership, differentiation, or focus to get a competitive edge.

- **Cost Leadership** entails becoming the lowest-cost producer in an industry. This could entail using technology to lower production costs, finding less expensive materials, or leveraging efficient operations for SMEs. SMEs can occasionally attain cost leadership in local or niche markets where larger competitors are less flexible, notwithstanding the difficulty posed by scale constraints.
- **Differentiation** focuses on offering unique products or services that are valued by customers. SMEs often excel in differentiation by providing personalized customer service, introducing innovative products, or developing strong brand identities that resonate within particular markets.
- **Focus Strategy** entails targeting a specific market segment and tailoring the business's offerings to serve that segment better than competitors who target a broader audience. SMEs frequently adopt focus strategies by specializing in niche markets, allowing them to build deep expertise, strong customer loyalty, and defend against larger competitors.

Porter stressed that in order to avoid getting "stuck in the middle" and losing out on a competitive edge, a company had to decide on a clear strategic position. Given their limited resources in comparison to large enterprises, SMEs must make clear strategic decisions and organize their resources toward either cost leadership, distinctiveness, or focus. SMEs can therefore assess and develop their strategy for gaining and maintaining competitive advantage by using Porter's framework, which offers an organized perspective.

1. A significant theoretical breakthrough in comprehending how businesses create and maintain competitive advantage can be found in Jay Barney's (1991) groundbreaking studies on the Resource-Based View (RBV) of the firm. The RBV turns the emphasis inward to the firm's own internal resources and competences as the main source of sustained competitive advantage, in contrast to classic industry structure models like Porter's Five Forces, which place an emphasis on external market positioning.
2. Not every resource contributes to competitive advantage in the same way, claims Barney. According to him, a resource or capability needs to have four essential qualities, which are commonly abbreviated as VRIN, in order to be a source of long-term competitive advantage:
3. **Valuable:** The resource must enable the firm to implement strategies that improve efficiency or effectiveness.
4. **Rare:** The resource must be scarce relative to demand; if many firms possess it, it cannot be a source of competitive advantage.
5. **Inimitable:** The resource must be difficult for competitors to imitate. This could be due to unique historical conditions, causal ambiguity (where it is unclear how the resource provides an advantage), or social complexity (e.g., culture, reputation, interpersonal relationships).
6. **Non-substitutable:** There must be no strategically equivalent valuable resources that are themselves either not rare or imitable.

The RBV is especially effective for SMEs. SMEs can establish long-term advantages through unique capabilities like strong customer relationships, local market knowledge, flexible operations, entrepreneurial leadership, proprietary technologies, specialized expertise, or a distinctive organizational culture, even though they frequently lack the large-scale resources of larger firms. These resources are hard for rivals to imitate since they are frequently ingrained firmly in the business's identity and operations.

Furthermore, Barney stresses that how businesses strategically organize and use their resources is more important than simply having them. Therefore, in order to sustain their competitive positions over time, SMEs must constantly evaluate their internal assets, develop distinctive characteristics, and prevent imitation.

The study highlights the crucial significance of internal strengths in strategy development and execution by firmly explaining why some SMEs perform better than others despite dealing with comparable external conditions by firmly establishing the topic within Barney's RBV framework.

Penrose's (1959) seminal work, The Theory of the Growth of the Firm, laid critical early foundations for the Resource-Based View (RBV) and modern strategic management thinking. Penrose shifted attention from external market forces to the internal resources and capabilities of firms, arguing that the unique characteristics and productive opportunities within each firm largely determine its growth path and competitive advantage.

Penrose (1959) proposed that a firm is fundamentally a collection of productive resources—including human, financial, and physical assets—and that the way a firm utilizes these resources depends on the experience, knowledge, and innovative capacity of its management team. Importantly, she emphasized that the firm's "bundle of resources" is unique, and that growth occurs when firms find new ways to leverage these internal resources efficiently and creatively. A key insight from Penrose's theory is the concept of "firm-specific experience": as firms gain operational experience, they develop unique skills, routines, and knowledge that can be redeployed into new products, services, or markets. This cumulative learning process creates opportunities for expansion that are not immediately available to competitors. Therefore, competitive advantage and firm growth are often the result of how effectively firms nurture, exploit, and expand their internal capabilities over time.

For SMEs, Penrose's insights are particularly valuable. SMEs typically operate with limited external resources and must rely heavily on the creativity, knowledge, and entrepreneurial spirit within their organizations. The ability of SME leaders to discover and exploit new opportunities based on their firm's existing strengths—such as expertise in a particular technology, close customer relationships, or nimble operational structures—is crucial for achieving sustainable growth and competitive positioning.

Moreover, Penrose (1959) cautioned that while firms have the potential for rapid growth, there are limits to growth imposed by the capacities of managerial resources. This is highly relevant for SMEs, which often face human resource constraints that can hinder their ability to scale rapidly without jeopardizing quality or operational control.

Incorporating Penrose's theoretical framework into the discussion enriches the understanding of how internal factors rather than merely external market conditions shape the strategic possibilities and long-term success of SMEs.

Drucker (1985), often referred to as the "father of modern management", made profound contributions to the understanding of entrepreneurship and innovation, particularly emphasizing their critical role in achieving and sustaining competitive advantage—especially for smaller firms. Across works such as Innovation and Entrepreneurship and other management writings, Drucker argued that innovation is not simply about invention but about systematic and purposeful change that creates new wealth-producing resources or endows existing resources with enhanced potential for creating wealth.

According to Drucker (1985), entrepreneurship is the practice of innovation; it is about systematically searching for opportunities, responding creatively, and exploiting change as an opportunity for a different or improved business. He identified seven sources of innovative opportunity, which include unexpected occurrences, incongruities, process needs, industry and market changes, demographic shifts, changes in perception, and new knowledge. These provide a practical framework for small and medium-sized enterprises (SMEs) to identify avenues for growth and competitive differentiation.

For SMEs, Drucker's insights are particularly powerful. Lacking the resource scale of larger firms, SMEs can leverage innovation as a strategic equalizer, allowing them to introduce new products, services, business models, or processes that larger, more bureaucratic organizations may be slower to adopt. Innovation provides SMEs with a way to differentiate themselves, meet niche customer needs, respond flexibly to market changes, and create entirely new markets where competition is less intense.

Importantly, Drucker stressed that innovation should be disciplined and organized, not left to chance. SMEs that build innovation into their organizational cultures—encouraging creativity, learning, and responsiveness—are better positioned to create and sustain competitive advantage over time. Innovation does not necessarily require major technological breakthroughs; it could be as simple as finding new ways to deliver services, reach customers, or reconfigure value chains.

Additionally, entrepreneurship was seen by Drucker (1985) as a behaviour rather than a psychological attribute. According to this viewpoint, innovation is more important than "entrepreneurial heroes" at the organizational level. As a result, SMEs that wish to stay competitive in ever-changing markets must institutionalize entrepreneurial thinking across all departments.

Including Drucker's ideas in the conversation highlights the fact that, for SMEs functioning in dynamic, competitive markets, strategic innovation and an entrepreneurial mindset are essentials rather than extravagances. For SME executives seeking to develop innovation-driven growth plans, Drucker's framework also offers practical advice that will help them establish competitive positions that can be defended even in the face of limited resources and strengths in developing and implementing strategies.

3.11 Sustainable Competitive Advantage

A durable competitive advantage, according to Vinayan et al. (2012), is the foundation of the majority of successful businesses in existence today. Companies who have recognized this and adopted a plan for maintaining a sustainable competitive edge have long held the top spot in their respective markets. Porter (1985) introduced the concept of competitive advantage and distinguished between two primary sources: distinctiveness and cost advantage. Competitive advantage is the result of a company's strengths and resources combined.

According to Barney (1991), competitors find it more challenging to neutralize a competitive advantage that is more sustainable. Gaining a long-term competitive advantage is essential for company success. It is the driving force behind a company's increased focus, sales, profit margins, and staff and customer retention rates as compared to rivals. When looking to acquire a firm, buyers will place the greatest value on it because it is the primary generator of long-term business value. A company that lacks a lasting competitive advantage runs the risk of becoming just another "me too" company that struggles to produce subpar outcomes. There are three main categories of sustained competitive advantage at the most fundamental level:

Cost advantage: When a company engages in pricing competition.

Value advantage: When a company offers a unique product that is thought to be more valuable than others.

Focus advantage: When a company concentrates on a certain market niche and offers a customised product made just for that market segment (Einsenhardt & Martin 2000; Teece et al., 1997).

One definition of a sustainable competitive advantage is a company's unique skills, resources, or advantages that are hard to replicate or outperform in the marketplace. As a result, they maintain their advantage over other comparable and like-minded businesses in the industry.

3.12 SMEs' Resources and Capabilities for Sustainable Competitive Advantage

Using resources and capabilities for a sustainable competitive advantage has become a hot subject in both academic and real-world contexts for small and medium-sized businesses (SMEs) in Africa in recent years. According to several studies (Ijomah et al., 2024a, b; Arsawan et al., 2022; Eikelenboom & de Jong, 2019), this topic is crucial in determining industry practices and policies. Studies like these highlight how important it is to investigate methods and tactics that give SMEs a competitive advantage in the ever-changing African market. The methods by which SMEs can use their assets and competences to gain a long-term competitive edge are covered in the sections that follow.

3.13 Innovative Digital Marketing

A critical analysis of current literature reveals that there are several common themes and findings in the field. For instance, Ijomah et al. (2024a, b) argue that innovative digital marketing strategies are crucial in driving competitive advantage and sustainable growth in SMEs. They highlight the significance of incorporating emerging technologies and digital platforms to enhance SMEs' marketing efforts.

3.14 Dynamic Capabilities

The ability to achieve new forms of competitive advantage is referred to as dynamic capabilities. The ability of an organization to consciously add to, expand, or change its resource base is known as dynamic capability. In order to achieve congruence with the evolving business environment, it can alternatively be defined as the organizational capacity to acquire new forms of competitive advantage through the renewal of organizational resources and capabilities (Hamel & Prahalad, 1989; Prahalad & Hamel, 1994). The concept of a corporation gaining a sustainable competitive advantage through the acquisition of valuable, rare, unique, and non-substitutable (VRIN) resources is not the only one that is supported by dynamic capacity theory. Organizations may integrate, mobilize, and reconfigure their resources and skills to respond to quickly changing contexts thanks to dynamic capabilities (Teece et al., 1997). Therefore, methods that allow an organization to reorganize its resources and strategy in order to attain superior performance and long-term competitive advantages in quickly changing circumstances are known as dynamic capabilities.

Additionally, the impact of dynamic skills on the sustainability performance of SMEs is examined by Eikelenboom and de Jong (2019). According to their research, SMEs need to be able to innovate, adapt, and learn in order to gain a sustained competitive edge. Prabowo et al. (2021) investigate the impact of dynamic capacities on sustained competitive advantage with a particular focus on small enterprises in Indonesia. They discover that SMEs' competitive advantage is greatly enhanced by dynamic capabilities. The relationship between value creation, competitive strategy, and SMEs' dynamic skills is examined by Rashidirad and Salimian (2020). They contend that generating value and securing a long-term competitive advantage require dynamic capabilities. Santos et al. (2023) examine the resources and capabilities needed for Industry 4.0 adoption with a focus on Portuguese SMEs. They stress the significance of employing proactive strategies and efficient resource management while putting Industry 4.0 technology into practice.

Ferreira and Coelho (2020) explore the relationship between dynamic capabilities, innovation, branding capabilities, and competitive advantage in Portugal. They highlight the mediating effects of innovation and branding capabilities in the relationship between dynamic capabilities and competitive advantage. Bari et al. (2022) propose a roadmap to achieve corporate sustainability through dynamic capabilities. They argue that dynamic capabilities are critical in achieving sustained competitive advantage and positioning SMEs for long-term success. Furthermore, Bari et al. (2022) explore the concept of dynamic capabilities in achieving corporate sustainability and sustained competitive advantage.

3.15 Continuous Innovation

Similarly, Arsawan et al. (2022) emphasize the importance of knowledge sharing and innovation culture in fostering sustainable competitive advantage in SMEs. They highlight the need for a collaborative and innovative environment within SMEs to leverage their resources effectively. Additionally, Nimfa et al. (2021) analyse the impact of innovation and competitive advantage on product quality for sustainable growth among

SMEs. Their study highlights the importance of continuous innovation in driving sustainable growth and competitive advantage. Phonthanukitithaworn et al. (2023) investigate how SMEs can leverage intellectual capital, sustainable initiatives, and open innovation to achieve sustainable development. They argue that these factors contribute to SMEs' ability to adapt and remain competitive in a rapidly changing business environment. Moreover, Mokbel Al Koliby et al., (2024b) explore the link between entrepreneurial competences, innovation, and sustainable performance in manufacturing SMEs. They emphasize that SMEs need to develop entrepreneurial capabilities and foster a culture of innovation to gain a sustainable competitive advantage. Koentjoro and Gunawan (2020) conduct a case study of a family company and examine the role of knowledge management, dynamic capabilities, and innovative performance in creating a sustainable competitive advantage. Their study highlights the importance of managing knowledge and capabilities within family-owned SMEs.

3.16 Entrepreneurial Marketing

Khouroh et al. (2020) explore the role of entrepreneurial marketing in achieving sustainable competitive advantage. These studies provide insights into the importance of knowledge management and marketing strategies for SMEs in gaining a competitive edge. Eco-innovation is another area of focus in the literature. Mady et al. (2023) examine the drivers of multiple eco-innovation and its impact on sustainable competitive advantage among manufacturing SMEs in Egypt. This study highlights the importance of eco-innovation as a means to achieve a sustainable competitive advantage.

Furthermore, Nguyen et al. (2021) investigate the influence of competitive advantage on the financial performance of SMEs in Vietnam. They find a positive relationship between competitive advantage and financial performance, suggesting that SMEs with a competitive edge are more likely to achieve better financial outcomes. Wu et al. (2020) examine the effect of relational embeddedness, absorptive capacity, and learning orientation on SMEs' competitive advantage. They argue that building strong relationships, enhancing absorptive capacity, and fostering a learning orientation contribute to SMEs' ability to achieve and sustain competitive advantage.

3.17 Leveraging Human Capital

Human capital is one of the most important resources for SMEs. Employee experience, expertise, and knowledge can be a major source of competitive advantage. SMEs that cultivate a culture of ongoing learning and growth can effectively utilize human capital. In addition to improving labour abilities, investing in staff training and development also raises productivity and innovation levels (Delery & Roumpi, 2017).

Moreover, SMEs can benefit from the agility and flexibility of their workforce. Unlike larger firms, SMEs often have less hierarchical structures, allowing for faster decision-making and better responsiveness to changes in the market. This agility can be a crucial advantage in dynamic industries where the ability to adapt quickly to new trends and customer demands is essential (Wright et al., 2005). Another way SMEs can leverage human capital is by building strong relationships with employees. High levels of employee engagement and commitment can lead to lower turnover rates and higher levels of customer satisfaction, both of which are important for maintaining a competitive edge (Huselid & Becker, 1995). By creating a positive work environment and offering incentives for high performance, SMEs can ensure that their human capital remains a valuable and sustainable resource.

3.18 Developing Organizational Capabilities

Organizational capabilities refer to a firm's ability to manage resources effectively and coordinate activities to achieve strategic objectives. For SMEs, developing strong organizational capabilities is essential for achieving sustainable competitive advantage. One way to enhance organizational capabilities is through process optimization. By streamlining operations and reducing inefficiencies, SMEs can lower costs and improve the quality of their products or services (Teece et al., 1997). This is particularly important in industries where customer retention is a key driver of profitability. In addition, strong customer relationships can lead to valuable insights into market trends and customer preferences, which can inform product development and marketing strategies (Hunt & Morgan, 2017).

3.19 Strategic Alliances and Networks

Another way SMEs can leverage their resources and capabilities is by forming strategic alliances and networks. By collaborating with other firms, SMEs can gain access to resources and capabilities that they may not possess internally. For example, partnering with a larger firm can provide an SME with access to new markets, distribution channels, or advanced technology (Gulati, 1998). Similarly, collaborating with research institutions or universities can help SMEs tap into cutting-edge research and development, leading to new product innovations. Networks are also a valuable resource for SMEs. By participating in industry networks or business associations, SMEs can gain access to valuable information, share best practices, and collaborate on joint projects. Networks can also provide opportunities for SMEs to build relationships with key stakeholders, such as suppliers, customers, and investors, which can enhance their competitive position (Zaheer & Bell, 2005). Furthermore, strategic alliances and networks can help SMEs overcome resource constraints. By pooling resources with other firms, SMEs can achieve economies of scale and reduce costs. This is particularly important in industries where cost leadership is a key competitive strategy. Additionally, alliances can provide SMEs with greater bargaining power when negotiating with suppliers or customers, further enhancing their competitive advantage (Dyer & Singh, 1998).

3.20 Leveraging Technology

In the digital age, technology is a critical resource that SMEs must leverage to achieve a sustainable competitive advantage. The adoption of digital technologies, such as cloud computing, data analytics, and e-commerce platforms, can significantly enhance the efficiency and effectiveness of SMEs' operations (Brynjolfsson & McAfee, 2014). For instance, cloud computing allows SMEs to access advanced software and infrastructure without the need for significant upfront investment. This enables SMEs to scale their operations quickly and respond to market changes more effectively. Data analytics is another powerful tool that is used to obtain a competitive advantage for SMEs. SMEs may improve decision-making and better adjust their products and services to match customer needs by analysing customer data, market trends, and operational indicators (Chen et al., 2012). This enhances consumer satisfaction and raises the possibility of recurring business and good word-of-mouth recommendations. Furthermore, SMEs may affordably access a worldwide audience thanks to e-commerce platforms. SMEs can boost sales, reach a wider market, and compete more fairly with larger companies by creating an online presence (Chaffey, 2015). Additionally, SMEs can more effectively target particular client segments and increase brand awareness with the use of digital marketing tactics like social media marketing and search engine optimization (SEO).

3.21 Building a Strong Brand

Branding is another critical resource that SMEs can leverage to achieve a sustainable competitive advantage. A strong brand can differentiate an SME's products or services from those of competitors, create customer loyalty, and command premium prices. SMEs can build a strong brand by consistently delivering high-quality products or services, maintaining a clear and consistent brand message, and engaging with customers through various channels. In addition to traditional branding strategies, SMEs can also leverage digital platforms to build their brand. Social media, for example, provides SMEs with a cost-effective way to engage with customers, share their brand story, and build a loyal community of followers. By using social media effectively, SMEs can enhance their brand visibility, attract new customers, and increase customer loyalty.

Furthermore, SMEs can differentiate their brand by focusing on sustainability and corporate social responsibility (CSR). As consumers become more conscious of environmental and social issues, SMEs that demonstrate a commitment to sustainability can enhance their brand image and attract socially conscious customers (Porter & Kramer, 2006). This not only contributes to a sustainable competitive advantage but also aligns with the broader societal shift toward more sustainable business practices.

3.22 Overcoming Resource Constraints

While SMEs may have limited resources compared to larger firms, they can overcome these constraints by adopting a resourceful and innovative mindset. For example, SMEs can leverage their agility and flexibility to experiment with new business models, enter niche markets, or adopt a focused differentiation strategy (Porter, 1985). By targeting specific customer segments and offering tailored products or services, SMEs can carve out a unique position in the market and avoid direct competition with larger firms. Additionally, SMEs can adopt a lean approach to resource management. By minimizing waste, optimizing resource allocation, and continuously improving processes, SMEs can achieve higher levels of efficiency and productivity. This not only reduces costs but also frees up resources that can be reinvested in growth initiatives or innovation. Finally, SMEs can overcome resource constraints by leveraging external funding sources, such as venture capital, crowdfunding, or government grants. By securing external funding, SMEs can finance their growth initiatives, invest in new technologies, and expand their operations without depleting their internal resources.

3.23 SME's Challenges in Creating Sustaining Competitive Advantage

In order to gain a lasting competitive edge, small and medium-sized enterprises (SMEs) in Africa must overcome several obstacles. Recent research supports this topic's worldwide significance. For example, stress the significance of utilizing innovation culture and information exchange to create SMEs' long-term competitive advantage. Mokbel Al Koliby et al. (2024a) also draw attention to the connection that exists between innovation, entrepreneurial skills, and long-term success in manufacturing SMEs. These findings highlight the critical need to investigate how African SMEs may best utilize their assets and skills to gain a sustained competitive edge.

Analysing the empirical data is crucial to defining the issue precisely. According to Rashidirad and Salimian (2020), SMEs' adaptable qualities are essential for creating value. Ferreira and Coelho (2020) also look at how branding, innovation, and dynamic capacities affect SMEs' success in Portugal and their competitive advantage. This empirical data provides a solid foundation for the research by highlighting the significance of comprehending the dynamics of SMEs' capabilities in gaining sustainable competitive advantage.

From a global standpoint, it's critical to contrast the difficulties African SMEs encounter with those encountered in other contexts. The impact of dynamic capability on sustained competitive advantage in Indonesian small enterprises is examined by Prabowo et al. (2021).

Small and medium-sized businesses (SMEs) have had difficulty developing a sustained competitive advantage throughout the years. A rising corpus of research (Koentjoro & Gunawan, 2020; Rashidirad & Salimian, 2020; Mady et al., 2023; Ijomah et al., 2024a, b) recognizes the significance of utilizing resources and competences to tackle these difficulties. According to studies (Koentjoro & Gunawan, 2020), SMEs can achieve a sustained competitive advantage by fostering knowledge exchange, innovation, and dynamic skills.

Research indicates that small and medium-sized enterprises (SMEs) can augment their competitive edge by proactive knowledge dissemination and the cultivation of an innovative culture within the company (Koentjoro & Gunawan, 2020). With the use of this strategy, SMEs can use the pooled knowledge and experience of their workforce, resulting in the creation of novel goods and services (Koentjoro & Gunawan, 2020). Moreover, attaining lasting competitive advantage depends heavily on the development of dynamic capacities, such as the capacity to adjust and react to market developments (Rashidirad & Salimian, 2020; Mady et al., 2023). A theoretical framework that helps explain how SMEs might use their resources and competences to obtain a competitive advantage is the resource-based view (El Nemar et al., 2022; Santos et al., 2023).

El Nemar et al. (2022), Santos et al. (2023) highlight the significance of recognizing and using distinct resources and qualities that are priceless, uncommon, one-of-a-kind, and non-replaceable. SMEs may establish a sustainable competitive edge and set themselves apart from rivals by skilfully utilizing these resources and capabilities (El Nemar et al., 2022; Santos et al., 2023). Empirical studies have examined the practical application of these theories in the context of SMEs. For example, Ijomah et al. (2024a, b) conducted a study on innovative digital marketing strategies for SMEs and identified how they can drive competitive advantage and sustainable growth. They explored various strategies, such as social media marketing and personalized marketing, and their impact on SMEs' performance and competitive advantage (Ijomah et al., 2024a, b).

In addition to exploring the application of theories, these studies also consider the methodological approaches employed. For instance, Rashidirad and Salimian (2020) critically assessed the application of dynamic capabilities and value creation in manufacturing SMEs, and they discussed the strengths, limitations, and implications of the research methods utilized. This analysis contributes to a better understanding of how research methods can influence the findings and implications for the field (Rashidirad & Salimian, 2020).

Identifying gaps in the existing literature is essential for guiding future research. Several studies have highlighted unexplored areas within the context of SMEs' resource and capability leveraging for sustainable competitive advantage (Koentjoro & Gunawan, 2020). These gaps emphasize the need for further investigation into specific areas, such as the mediating role of competitive strategy and eco-innovation in achieving sustainable competitive advantage (Rashidirad & Salimian, 2020; Mady et al., 2023).

Lastly, it is important to evaluate the strengths and weaknesses of theories and their practical implications. The resource-based view and dynamic capabilities theory have been widely discussed in the literature (El Nemar et al., 2022; Santos et al., 2023). Various studies have highlighted their strengths, such as their ability to provide a comprehensive framework for understanding the sources of competitive advantage and the dynamic nature of firms (El Nemar et al., 2022; Santos et al., 2023). However, it is also crucial to acknowledge the limitations and potential biases associated with these theories (El Nemar et al., 2022; Santos et al., 2023).

In conclusion, the literature on how SMEs can leverage their resources and capabilities to achieve sustainable competitive advantage provides valuable insights for both academia and industry. The studies discussed in this review highlight the importance of knowledge sharing, innovation culture, and dynamic capabilities in enhancing SMEs' competitive advantage. Theoretical frameworks, empirical studies, and gaps in the literature contribute to a deeper understanding of the challenges and opportunities facing SMEs. Moving forward, further research is needed to explore unexplored areas and address the limitations of existing theories. This ongoing exploration will undoubtedly contribute to the academic discourse and offer practical implications for SMEs aiming to achieve sustainable competitive advantage.

3.24 Conclusion

Small and medium-sized enterprises (SMEs) play an important role in the economic growth of both domestic and international markets by creating jobs and encouraging innovation. To maintain their development and competitive advantage, SMEs must overcome considerable obstacles such as limited resources, strong competition, and the need to stay up with technological improvements. Embracing innovation, strategic distinctiveness, using digital platforms, and maintaining financial discipline are critical tactics for SMEs seeking to survive in today's business climate.

Furthermore, concentrating on niche markets and sustainability can help them strengthen their market position by providing distinct value propositions that appeal to today's conscientious customers. Finally, SMEs that are nimble, inventive, and strategically oriented are better positioned to overcome challenges and capitalize on opportunities in a constantly changing market.

SMEs can achieve a sustainable competitive advantage by strategically leveraging their resources and capabilities. By focusing on human capital, developing organizational capabilities, forming strategic alliances, adopting technology, building a strong brand, and overcoming resource constraints, SMEs can differentiate themselves from competitors and achieve long-term success. While the challenges are significant, the opportunities for SMEs to leverage their unique strengths are vast. With the right strategies and a resourceful mindset, SMEs can not only survive but thrive in today's competitive business environment.

3.25 Recommendations

1. To remain competitive, SMEs should prioritize innovation in all areas of their business, including goods and services. This might include investing in R&D, implementing new technology, and cultivating a culture of continual improvement.
2. SMEs should make full use of social media and e-commerce platforms to broaden their reach, engage customers, and get vital industry data. A consistent and honest brand message across different media is critical to increasing client loyalty.
3. Specializing in specific markets enables SMEs to give customized solutions that bigger rivals may not offer. This strategic approach might result in enhanced brand loyalty and higher profit margins.
4. Integrating sustainability into business models may help SMEs gain a competitive edge, attract environmentally conscientious customers, and perhaps save operational expenses.
5. Effective financial management, such as careful resource allocation and cash flow monitoring, is critical for SMEs to retain operational stability while investing in growth prospects.

6. SMEs must be adaptable and sensitive to changes in market trends and consumer preferences. Continuous market research and a flexible company plan are critical to long-term success.

3.26 Implications for Research, Practice, and/or Society

This book chapter discusses the important implications of how small and medium-sized enterprises (SMEs) can leverage their unique characteristics, such as agility, niche market focus, and resourcefulness, to build and sustain competitive advantage. By understanding and applying strategic frameworks such as Porter's Generic Strategies, Barney's Resource-Based View (RBV), and Drucker's innovation principles, SMEs can better position themselves in increasingly competitive markets.

However, this book is more explicitly bridging the gap between theory and practice. While the theoretical foundations are robust, there is an opportunity to enhance the practical relevance by illustrating how SMEs can operationalize these theories. For example, actionable strategies could include steps for identifying and nurturing valuable internal resources, building an innovation-oriented culture, or selecting the most appropriate competitive strategy based on firm capabilities and market conditions.

From a societal perspective, empowering SMEs with practical strategic tools contributes to broader economic development, job creation, and innovation ecosystems. For research, this highlights the need for more empirical studies that examine how theoretical models can be adapted and implemented in diverse SME contexts across industries and regions.

References

Abdul-Azeez, O., Ihechere, A. O., & Idemudia, C. (2024). SMEs as catalysts for economic development: Navigating challenges and seizing opportunities in emerging markets. *GSC Advanced Research and Reviews, 19*(3), 325–335. https://doi.org/10.30574/gscarr.2024.19.3.0230

Acquah-Hagan, G., Boateng, D., Appiah-Brempong, E., Twum, P., Atta, J. A., & Agyei-Baffour, P. (2021). Access differentials in primary healthcare among vulnerable populations in a health insurance setting in Kumasi Metropolis, Ghana: A cross-sectional study. *Advances in Public Health, 2021*. https://doi.org/10.1155/2021/9911436

Afolabi, S. O., Owoade, Y. A., Iyere, E. A., & Nwobi, T. (2024). Exploring the potential of digital marketing skills development for SMES competitiveness and responsiveness. *World Journal of Advanced Research and Reviews, 23*(1), 1242–1252. https://doi.org/10.30574/wjarr.2024.23.1.2123

Akingbade, W. A. (2020). Service differentiation strategy and organizational performance of Nigerian small and medium enterprises in Lagos State in. *International Journal of Economic Behavior, 10*(1).

Algan, N. (2019, June). *The importance of SMEs on world economies. In Proceedings of International Conference on Eurasian Economies, Turkish Republic of Northern Cyprus* (Vol. 12, pp. 56–61).

Alenazi, S. A., & Alanazi, T. M. (2023). The mediating role of sustainable dynamic capabilities in the effect of social customer relationship management on sustainable competitive advantage: A study on SMEs in Saudi Arabia. *Sustainability (Switzerland), 15*(3). https://doi.org/10.3390/su15031952

Amoako, G. K., Sedalo, G., Asiedu, E. A., & Oppong Appiagyei Ampong, G. (2024). Conceptual framework–sustainability actions, global crises and justice in the future of tourism and hospitality. *Journal of Tropical Futures, 1*(2), 203–217.

Ananga, M. K., Agbefu, R. K., Doku, P. N., Manu, A., Ogum Alangea, D., & Ganle, J. K. (n.d.). The influence of social capital in the utilisation of sexual reproductive health services among the youth in Ghana. A community-based cross-sectional study. https://doi.org/10.1101/2022.10.07.22280832

Arsawan, I. W. E., Koval, V., Rajiani, I., Asnawi, A., & Rahman, A. (2022). Leveraging knowledge sharing and innovation culture into SMEs sustainable competitive advantage. *International Journal of Production and Performance Management*. Retrieved August 15, 2024, from https://www.emerald.com/insight/content/doi/10.1108/IJPPM-04-2020-0192/full/html

Aswan, A. (2023). Moderation role of strategic agility in the relationship between entrepreneurial orientation and competitive advantage in SMEs. *Jurnal Manajemen Bisnis, 14*(1), 125–142. https://doi.org/10.18196/mb.v14i1.16242

Ayaz Muhammad, S., & Chelliah, S. (2023). Innovation, competitive advantage and export performance: A study of Pakistani manufacturing SMEs.

International Journal of Innovative Computing, 13(1), 69–75. https://doi.org/10.11113/ijic.v13n1.395

Bambang, A., Kusumawati, A., Nimran, U., & Suharyono, S. (2021). The effect of spiritual marketing and entrepreneurship orientation on determining sustainable competitive advantage. *The Journal of Asian Finance, Economics and Business, 8*(2), 231–241.

Bano Fatima, R., & Ameer Ali, S. (n.d.). *Competitive advantage in the transformation of social media and E-commerce.*

Bari, N., Chimhundu, R., & Chan, K. C. (2022). Dynamic capabilities to achieve corporate sustainability: A roadmap to sustained competitive advantage. *Sustainability*. Retrieved August 15, 2024, from https://www.mdpi.com/2071-1050/14/3/1531

Barney, J. (1991). Firm resources and sustained competitive advantage. *Journal of Management, 17*(1), 99–120.

Brynjolfsson, E., & McAfee, A. (2014). *The second machine age: Work, progress, and prosperity in a time of brilliant technologies*. W.W. Norton & Company.

Bukoye, B., Ayoola, J., & Francis Sylvanus, U. (n.d.). *Cost leadership strategy on the performance of manufacturing industry: A mediating role of environment.* https://ssrn.com/abstract=4799794

Chaffey, D. (2015). *Digital business and E-commerce management*. Pearson Education.

Chen, H., Chiang, R. H., & Storey, V. C. (2012). Business intelligence and analytics: From big data to big impact. *MIS Quarterly, 36*(4), 1165–1188.

Das, A. K., & Das, M. C. (2023). Productivity improvement using different lean approaches in small and medium enterprises (SMEs). *Management Science Letters, 13*(1), 51–64. https://doi.org/10.5267/j.msl.2022.9.002

Delery, J. E., & Roumpi, D. (2017). Strategic human resource management, human capital and competitive advantage: is the field going in circles?. *Human Resource Management Journal, 27*(1), 1–21.

Dhamija, H., Piaha, R., Rathi, V., Majumdar, R., & Bhatti, K. (2023). Unraveling Niche marketing dynamics. *International Journal of Scientific Research in Engineering and Management.*

Du, Z., & Wang, X. (2023). The impact of cost leadership strategy on the development of high-quality businesses. In *Business, economics and management EMCG* (Vol. 2023).

Dyer, J. H., & Singh, H. (1998). The relational view: Cooperative strategy and sources of interorganizational competitive advantage. *Academy of Management Review, 23*(4), 660–679.

Eikelenboom, M., & de Jong, G. (2019). The impact of dynamic capabilities on the sustainability performance of SMEs. *Journal of Cleaner Production*. Retrieved August 15, 2024, from https://www.sciencedirect.com/science/article/pii/S0959652619323522

Einsenhardt, K., & Martin, J. A. (2000). Dynamic capabilities: What are they? *Strategic Management Journal, 21*(10/11), 1105–1121.

El Nemar, S., El-Chaarani, H., Dandachi, I., & Hassan, Z. (2022). Resource-based view and sustainable advantage: A framework for SMEs. *Journal of Strategic Marketing*. Retrieved August 15, 2024, from https://www.tandfonline.com/doi/abs/10.1080/0965254X.2022.2160486

Enaifoghe, A. (2024). Enhancing small and medium enterprises (SMEs) in a globalized and innovative economy: Challenges and Opportunities. *International Journal of Business, Economics, and Social Development, 5*(2), 130–138.

Ferreira, J., & Coelho, A. (2020). Dynamic capabilities, innovation and branding capabilities and their impact on competitive advantage and SME's performance in Portugal: The moderating effects of digital transformation. *International Journal of Innovation Science*. Retrieved August 15, 2024, from https://www.emerald.com/insight/content/doi/10.1108/IJIS-10-2018-0108/full/html

Festa, G., Rossi, M., & Vrontis, D. (2022). Guest editorial: Reinterpreting competitive strategies in turbulent scenarios. *Competitiveness Review, 32*(3), 277–281). Emerald Group Holdings Ltd. https://doi.org/10.1108/CR-04-2022-172

Gamage, S. K. N., Ekanayake, E. M. S., Abeyrathne, G. A. K. N. J., Prasanna, R. P. I. R., Jayasundara, J. M. S. B., & Rajapakshe, P. S. K. (2020). A review of global challenges and survival strategies of small and medium enterprises (SMEs). *Economies, 8*(4) MDPI AG. https://doi.org/10.3390/ECONOMIES8040079

Goyal, A. (2020). *A critical analysis of Porter's 5 forces model of competitive advantage* (Vol. 7). www.jetir.org

Gubán, Á., Sándor, Á., Udvaros, J., & Gubán, M. (2023). Necessity of enterprise resource planning systems for small and medium-sized enterprises. *International Journal of Advanced Natural Sciences and Engineering Researches, 7*(4), 235–240. https://doi.org/10.59287/ijanser.706

Gulati, R. (1998). Alliances and networks. *Strategic Management Journal, 19*(4), 293–317.

Hamel, G., & Prahalad, C. K. (1989). *STT ATEGIC| NTENT.* Harvard Business Review

Hamid, A., Alshehhi, A., Abdullah, A., & Mohamed, E. (2022). Key success factors for customer relationship management (CRM) projects within SMEs. *Emirati Journal of Business, Economics, & Social Sciences, 1*, 73–85. https://doi.org/10.54878/EJBESS.176

Hamim Sultoni, M. (2021). Loyalty as affecting mediator of service quality and customer satisfaction towards competitive advantage. *Journal of Management Science (JMAS), 4*(2) https://iocscience.org/ejournal/index.php/JMAS

Heriyanto, M., Febrian, A. F., Sugiarto, M., & Handoko, T. (2021). Competitive advantage in small and medium enterprises (smes): a systematic mapping study. *Management Theory & Studies for Rural Business & Infrastructure Development, 43*(1)

Hunt, S. D., & Morgan, R. M. (2017). The resource-advantage theory of competition: A review. *Review of Marketing Research*, 153–205.

Huselid, M. A., & Becker, B. E. (1995, August). The strategic impact of high-performance work systems. *In Academy of Management Annual Meeting, Vancouver* (Vol. 2, No. 1, pp. 33–42).

Ijomah, T. I., Idemudia, C., Eyo-Udo, N. L., & Anjorin, K. F. (2024a). Innovative digital marketing strategies for SMEs: Driving competitive advantage and sustainable growth. *International Journal of Management & Entrepreneurship Research, 6*(7), 2173–2188. https://doi.org/10.51594/ijmer.v6i7.1265

Ijomah, T. I., Idemudia, C., Eyo-Udo, N. L., & Anjorin, K. F. (2024b). Harnessing marketing analytics for enhanced decision-making and performance in SMEs. *World Journal of Advanced Science and Technology, 6*(1), 001–012. https://doi.org/10.53346/wjast.2024.6.1.0037

Jercan, E., & Nacu, T. (2024). The use of information technology in SMEs: Advantages and main challenges. *Proceedings of the International Conference on Business Excellence, 18*(1), 3465–3475. https://doi.org/10.2478/picbe-2024-0281

Khan, M., Farasat, M., Aslam, R., & Gull, M. (2024). Building brand image and loyalty: The role of customer satisfaction and engagement. *Pakistan Journal of Humanities and Social Sciences, 12*(2). https://doi.org/10.52131/pjhss.2024.v12i2.2152

Khouroh, U., Sudiro, A., & Rahayu, M. (2020). The role of entrepreneurial marketing in the relationship between environmental turbulence and dynamic capability with sustainable competitive advantage: An empirical study. *Management Science and Business Review*. Retrieved August 15, 2024, from https://eprints.unmer.ac.id/id/eprint/3328/

Kiyabo, K., & Isaga, N. (2020). Entrepreneurial orientation, competitive advantage, and SMEs' performance: Application of firm growth and personal wealth measures. *Journal of Innovation and Entrepreneurship, 9*(1). https://doi.org/10.1186/s13731-020-00123-7

Koentjoro, S., & Gunawan, S. (2020). Managing knowledge, dynamic capabilities, innovative performance, and creating sustainable competitive advantage in family companies: A case study of a family business. *Journal of Open Innovation: Technology, Market, and Complexity*. Retrieved August 15, 2024, from https://www.mdpi.com/2199-8531/6/3/90

Kuo, T.-N. (2020). Business model of competitive advantage. *Journal of Advanced Management Science*, 11–16. https://doi.org/10.18178/joams.9.1.11-16

Łęgowik-Świącik, S. (2023). Creating Knowledge of the Competitiveness of Enterprises in the Context of Changes in Management Processes. *In European Conference on Knowledge Management* (Vol. 1, pp. 800–R32). Academic Conferences International Limited.

Lelo, J. M., & Israel, B. (2024). Supply chain innovative practices and customer satisfaction: Insights from manufacturing SMEs. *Management Dynamics in the Knowledge Economy, 12*(1), 54–69. https://doi.org/10.2478/mdke-2024-0004

Li, Q. (2023). Frontiers in business, economics and management research on the importance of enterprise culture in improvement in human resources efficiency of small and medium enterprises, *10*(3).

Llave, A. J. (2023). Competitive advantage, strategic management practices, and business sustainability: Inputs to business competency framework. *International Journal of Research Studies in Management, 11*(9). https://doi.org/10.5861/ijrsm.2023.1119

Mady, K., Battour, M., Aboelmaged, M., Youssef, A. M., & Mohamed, Y. (2023). Linking internal environmental capabilities to sustainable competitive advantage in manufacturing SMEs: The mediating role of eco-innovation. *Journal of Cleaner Production*. Retrieved August 15, 2024, from https://www.sciencedirect.com/science/article/pii/S0959652623020863

Marolt, M., Zimmermann, H. D., & Pucihar, A. (2022). Social media use and business performance in SMEs: The mediating roles of relational social commerce capability and competitive advantage. *Sustainability (Switzerland), 14*(22). https://doi.org/10.3390/su142215029

Mawyne Jones, J., Sr., & Upadhyay, A. (2022). SME sustaining strategies. *International Journal of Scientific Research and Management, 10*(10), 4112–4118. https://doi.org/10.18535/ijsrm/v10i10.em10

Mohammad, A., & Solikahan, E. Z. (2023). Create a competitive advantage for Karawo small and medium enterprises. *International Journal of Social Science and Business, 7*(3), 598–610. https://doi.org/10.23887/ijssb.v7i3.54587

Mohammed, A., & Abdo, E.-S. (2022). The interrelationship between niche marketing and Competitiveness. *Alla Abdo 65 International Design Journal, 12*(3) www.onetechtraveller.com

Mokbel Al Koliby, I. S., Abdullah, H. H., Hashim, H. A., & Akhlaghian, F. (2024a). Linking entrepreneurial competencies, innovation and sustainable performance of manufacturing SMEs. *Asia-Pacific Journal of Business Administration*. Retrieved August 15, 2024, from https://www.emerald.com/insight/content/doi/10.1108/APJBA-09-2021-0480/full/html

Mokbel Al Koliby, I. S., Abdullah, H. H., & Mohd Suki, N. (2024b). Linking entrepreneurial competencies, innovation and sustainable performance of manufacturing SMEs. *Asia-Pacific Journal of Business Administration, 16*(1), 21–40.

Monnagaaratwe, K. F., & Mathu, K. (2022). Supply chain management as a competitive advantage for grocery small and medium-sized enterprises in Mahikeng, South Africa. *Journal of Transport and Supply Chain Management, 16*. https://doi.org/10.4102/jtscm.v16i0.791

Navaia, E., Moreira, A., & Ribau, C. (2023). Differentiation strategy and export performance in emerging countries: Mediating effects of positional advantage among Mozambican firms. *Economies, 11*(2). https://doi.org/10.3390/economies11020044

Navaia, E., Moreira, A., & Ribau, C. (2024). The mediating roles of cost leadership and cost focus strategies on innovation capabilities and export performance. Results from an emerging country. *Cogent Business & Management, 11*(1). https://doi.org/10.1080/23311975.2024.2375410

Naveen Kumar, C. M. (2024). Niche marketing strategy for SMEs. *Shanlax International Journal of Economics, 12*(3), 47–50. https://doi.org/10.34293/economics.v12i3.7282

Nguyen, H., Tran, T. H. M., Nguyen, T. H. Y., & Tran, P. T. M. (2021). The influence of competitive advantage on financial performance: A case study of SMEs in Vietnam. The Journal of Asian Finance, Economics, and Business. Retrieved August 15, 2024, from https://koreascience.kr/article/JAKO202112748674986.page

Nimfa, D. T., Uzir, M. U. H., Maimako, L. N., Eneizan, B., & Ibrahim, Z. (2021). The impact of innovation competitive advantage on product quality for sustainable growth among SMES: An empirical analysis. *International Journal of Economic Sciences*. Retrieved August 15, 2024, from https://www.econstor.eu/handle/10419/261658

Pangihutan Situmorang, T. (2023). Quality-based differentiation mediating entrepreneurial orientation and marketing performance, *8*(2), 958–972.

Phonthanukitithaworn, C., Srisathan, W. A., Ketkaew, C., & Naruetharadhol, P. (2023). Sustainable development towards openness SME innovation: taking advantage of intellectual capital, sustainable initiatives, and open innovation. *Sustainability, 15*(3), 2126

Popadić, D., Živanović, V., & Živanovic, N. (2022). The importance of small and medium enterprise development for efficient global market environment. *Chinese Business Review, 21*(3). https://doi.org/10.17265/1537-1506/2022.03.003

Porter, M. E. (1985). *Competitive advantage: Creating and sustaining superior performance*. Free Press.

Porter, M. E., & Kramer, M. R. (2006). The link between competitive advantage and corporate social responsibility. *Harvard business review, 84*(12), 78–92.

Praba, R. S. (2023). Insights on talent acquisition and management: Strategies and practices in IT sector. *Journal of Production, Operations Management and Economics, 41*, 12–21. https://doi.org/10.55529/jpome.41.12.21

Prabowo, H., Sriwidadi, T., & Ikhsan, R. B. (2021). The influence of dynamic capability on sustainable competitive advantage: An empirical study of small businesses in Indonesia. *The Journal of Asian Finance, Economics, and Business*. Retrieved August 15, 2024, from https://koreascience.kr/article/JAKO202115563381822.pagescarr.2024.19.3.0230

Prahalad, C. K., & Hamel, G. (1994). Strategy as a field of study: Why search for a new paradigm?. *Strategic Management Journal, 15*(S2), 5–16.

Prakoso, F. A., Najmudin, N., Novandari, W., Karnowati, N. B., & Apriandi, D. W. (2023). The effect of online customer experience, product quality, and service quality on SMEs customer loyalty. *Journal of Business and Management Review, 4*(5), 363–373. https://doi.org/10.47153/jbmr45.6952023

Prastika, D., & Fachira, I. (2023). Unlocking the competitive advantage: An internal and external analyses of PTIDM as a small enterprise in Indonesia. *European Journal of Business & Management Research, 8*(3), 96–100. https://doi.org/10.24018/ejbmr.2023.8.3.1950

Puspaningrum, A. (2020). Market orientation, competitive advantage and marketing performance of small medium enterprises (SMEs). *Journal of Economics, Business, & Accountancy Ventura, 23*(1), 19–27. https://doi.org/10.14414/jebav.v23i1.1847

Rahman, W., & Hadiyati, R. (2023, July 26). *The relationship of customer satisfaction, perceived service quality, perceived value, and brand image on SMEs customer loyalty*. https://doi.org/10.4108/eai.29-10-2022.2334030

Rashidirad, M., & Salimian, H. (2020). SMEs' dynamic capabilities and value creation: The mediating role of competitive strategy. *European Business Review*. Retrieved August 15, 2024, from https://www.emerald.com/insight/content/doi/10.1108/EBR-06-2019-0113/full/html

Rochayatun, S., Pratikto, H., Wardoyo, C., & Handayati, P. (2023). Competitive advantage as a mediating variable of corporate social responsibility programs' effect on SME sustainability. *Journal of Social Economics Research, 10*(2), 34–46. https://doi.org/10.18488/35.v10i2.3323

Röser, M. (2024). *Customer relationship management in new business models*. www.intechopen.com

Sair, S. A., Anjum, M. N., Ali, W., & Adnan, M. (2023). Empowering small and medium enterprises performance through dynamic marketing strategies and innovations. *Review of Education, Administration & Law, 6*(2), 321–330. https://doi.org/10.47067/real.v6i2.335

Santos, B., Dieste, M., Orzes, G., & Garendo, P. L. (2023). Resources and capabilities for Industry 4.0 implementation: Evidence from proactive Portuguese SMEs. *Journal of Manufacturing Technology Management*. Retrieved August 15, 2024, from https://www.emerald.com/insight/content/doi/10.1108/JMTM-02-2022-0074/full/html

Sukaatmadja, I. P. G., Yasa, N. N. K., Rahyuda, H., Setini, M., & Dharmanegara, I. B. A. (2021). Competitive advantage to enhance internationalization and marketing performance woodcraft industry: A perspective of resource-based view theory. *Journal of Project Management (Canada), 6*(1), 45–56. https://doi.org/10.5267/j.jpm.2020.9.002

Surajwancy, S., & Kulkarni, V. (2024). A study on impact of globalization on small businesses. *International Journal of Scientific Research in Engineering and Management*. https://doi.org/10.55041/IJSREM33247

Suriani, S., Baharuddin, S. M., Nur, I., Abubakar, H., & Abustan. (2024). Driving cost efficiency through operational excellence and sustainability of SMEs in Barru Regency, South Sulawesi, Indonesia. *International Journal of*

Management and Sustainability, 13(2), 448–464. https://doi.org/10.18488/11.v13i2.3790

Taha, A. F., Atheer, A. G., & Asmar, A. (2024). The role of total quality management and target costing in reducing costs. *International Journal of Business and Management Sciences, 04*(05), 367–381. https://doi.org/10.55640/ijbms-04-05-24

Teece, D. J., Pisano, G., & Shuen, A. (1997). Dynamic capabilities and strategic management. *Strategic management journal, 18*(7), 509–533.

Tumbelaka, S. S. X. (2022). Customer bonding, customer satisfaction, and customer loyalty (study on the customer of "SMEs Martabak Hokky Kawanua" in Tondano). *International Journal of Applied Business and International Management.* https://doi.org/10.32535/ijabim.v7i3.1899

Utami, R. D., Program, D., & Teknologi Yogyakarta, U. (2020). A competitive advantage strategy through the use of technology marketing information, and orientation of learning with performance as an intervening variable. *International Journal of Business, Education, Humanities and Social Sciences, 2*(2).

Velykykh, K. (2023). Efficiency of financial resource management as a component part of the financial potential of an enterprise. *Municipal Economy of Cities, 7*(181), 7–11. https://doi.org/10.33042/2522-1809-2023-7-181-7-11

Wira, T., Suryawijaya, E., & Wardhani, M. F. (n.d.). *Tailoring the future of MSME marketing: A study on leveraging customer data for personalized experiences.*

Wright, M., Filatotchev, I., Hoskisson, R. E., & Peng, M. W. (2005). Strategy research in emerging economies: Challenging the conventional wisdom. *Journal of Management Studies, 42*(1), 1–33.

Wu, G. S., Peng, M. Y. P., Chen, Z., Du, Z., & Anser, M. K. (2020). The effect of relational embeddedness, absorptive capacity, and learning orientation on SMEs' competitive advantage. *Frontiers in Psychology.* Retrieved August 15, 2024, from https://www.frontiersin.org/articles/10.3389/fpsyg.2020.01505/full

Wushishi, M. I. (2024). Indirect effect of customer relations on leadership/top management, employee relations and process management in examining the readiness of SMEs to implement lean initiatives. *International Journal of Management, Finance and Accounting, 5*(1), 85–110. https://doi.org/10.33093/ijomfa.2024.5.1.4

Yusuf, M., Surya, B., Menne, F., Ruslan, M., Suriani, S., & Iskandar, I. (2023). Business agility and competitive advantage of SMEs in Makassar City,

Indonesia. *Sustainability (Switzerland), 15*(1). https://doi.org/10.3390/su15010627

Zaheer, A., & Bell, G. G. (2005). Benefiting from network position: firm capabilities, structural holes, and performance. *Strategic Management Journal, 26*(9), 809–825.

Zaini, A., Poernamawati, D. E., & Rahmi, A. (2023). The role of competitive advantage on marketing performance as mediator variable of social capitalin SMEs. *Journal of Economics, Finance and Management Studies, 06*(10). https://doi.org/10.47191/jefms/v6-i10-36

Zulfikar, I. (n.d.). *Neo Journal of Economy and Social Humanities (NEJESH) Building a Strong Brand: Marketing strategy to increase brand awareness and consumer loyalty*. https://internationalpublisher.id/journal/index.php/Nejesh

4

Technology and Digitization in Small and Medium-Sized Enterprises in Ghana: Impact on Financial Performance

Richard Kofi Asravor, Isaac Ankrah, Derrick Donkor, and Vera Acheampong

4.1 Introduction

In an increasingly competitive and rapidly evolving business environment, technology, and digitization have become important drivers of growth and competitiveness, particularly for Small and Medium-sized Enterprises (SMEs). Although significant potential benefits are associated with technology and digitization, SMEs often face obstacles in adopting digital solutions, such as limited digital literacy, high costs, and inadequate infrastructure (Kallmuenzer et al., 2024; Jedynak et al., 2021). As SMEs face increasing pressure to innovate and adapt to global market demands, their adoption of digital technologies has the potential to

R. K. Asravor (✉) • I. Ankrah • D. Donkor • V. Acheampong
Ghana Communication Technology University, Accra, Ghana
e-mail: rasravor@gctu.edu.gh; iankrah@gctu.edu.gh; dodonkor@gctu.edu.gh; vacheampong@gctu.edu.gh

E. Amoako Asiedu et al. (eds.), *Entrepreneurship and Small and Medium-Sized Enterprises (SMEs) in Africa*, https://doi.org/10.1007/978-3-032-14174-3_4

enhance operational efficiency, productivity, and financial performance (Skare et al., 2023). Digital transformation marks a pivotal shift, ushering in what is commonly referred to as the Fourth Industrial Revolution (Lorenz et al., 2015).

Basic digital tools for SMEs in developing countries include cloud computing, social media platforms, e-commerce websites, email marketing software, accounting and invoicing software, project management tools, and digital payment systems, and data analytics offer SMEs new opportunities to streamline operations, reach broader markets, and make more informed decisions (Attaran & Woods, 2019). However, while digitalization is often seen as a pathway to growth, its impact on financial performance can vary depending on factors such as the industry, the scale of investment, and the ability of businesses to integrate new technologies effectively.

SMEs are crucial to the Ghanaian economy; they constitute 92% of businesses and serve as its backbone, contributing 70% to GDP (Ahmed et al., 2023; Osei, 2023). Despite their contribution, SMEs lag larger firms when it comes to technology and digitalization adoption. As technology and digitization become increasingly integral to business operations worldwide, the potential for digital tools to enhance financial performance for Ghanaian SMEs is promising but largely untapped. Technology and digitization are rapidly transforming personal and professional aspects of life, yet their impact on SMEs in Ghana remains less understood.

While some researchers view technology and digitization as crucial drivers for enhancing business performance (Ribeiro-Navarrete et al., 2021), others perceive it as an expensive investment that could disrupt operations (Etemad, 2020). Moreover, the relationship between technology use and financial outcomes among SME businesses is poorly understood, especially in the context of the Ghanaian setting (Frimpong et al., 2022), where resources are constrained. Without a clear understanding of the benefits, SMEs may hesitate to invest in necessary digital upgrades, thus missing out on opportunities to improve profitability. From the foregoing, the objective of this study is to examine the impact of technology and digitization on the financial performance of SMEs in Ghana. Furthermore, the paper assesses the extent of technology adoption among

SMEs in Ghana and identifies the challenges SMEs face in adopting and using technology.

4.2 Literature Review

4.2.1 Theoretical Framework

The Resource-Based View (RBV) theory emphasizes that a firm's internal resources, such as technology, skills, and capabilities, are crucial to achieving sustained competitive advantage and improved financial performance (Assensoh-Kodua, 2019; El Nemar et al., 2022). For Small and Medium-Sized Enterprises (SMEs) in Ghana, adopting and leveraging digital technologies can serve as a strategic resource that enhances operational efficiency, market competitiveness, and financial outcomes (Asravor & Acheampong, 2024; Quaye et al., 2025).

Technology adoption within SMEs is closely linked to the firm's ability to access and utilize digital tools effectively (Battistoni et al., 2023; Canhoto et al., 2021). Access to technical support and after-sales services is crucial, as it ensures that SMEs can troubleshoot and optimize their technology infrastructure. However, the cost of data remains a significant barrier, as high data expenses can limit SMEs' ability to leverage digital platforms effectively (Justy et al., 2023). Moreover, technology skills and the educational level of the owner influence how well SMEs can integrate technology into their business operations. Owners with higher education levels are more likely to embrace digitalization, which translates into improved performance.

The geographical location of the SME also plays a role, as businesses in urban areas typically have better access to digital infrastructure compared to those in rural areas. Marketing accessibility through digital platforms allows SMEs to reach broader markets, increasing their revenue potential. However, risk aversion among SME owners, often due to the fear of failure, can delay technology adoption, impacting financial growth (Hunter et al., 2021). Additionally, access to credit can help SMEs overcome initial financial constraints related to technology adoption.

4.2.2 Empirical Studies

Kallmuenzer et al. (2024) explore the enablers and barriers of digitalization adoption in SMEs, focusing on its impact on performance. By employing the qualitative approach, Kallmuenzer et al. (2024) found that key enablers include appropriate technologies and a digitally skilled workforce, while barriers include a risk-averse culture and outdated systems. The findings highlight the importance of strategic elements for successful digital transformation in SMEs. Also, using a systematic literature review and thematic analysis, Jedynak et al. (2021) identify the development of digital transformation. Jedynak et al. (2021) highlight that most research focuses on digital business models while neglecting the organization itself as a unit of analysis. Their findings emphasize the challenge of developing a digital theory of the organization and reveal several research gaps, offering directions for future studies.

Skare et al. (2023) explored the impact of digital transformation on SMEs, addressing key business challenges such as customer access, competition, finance, rising input costs, skilled labour shortages, and regulatory issues. Using the Digital Economy and Society Index (DESI) and SME data from a survey on European enterprises' access to finance, the findings show that digital transformation enhances SMEs' flexibility and ability to address these challenges. Digitally transformed SMEs face fewer concerns regarding customer access, competition, and finance but also experience risks like labour shortages and loss of competitiveness. The study provides valuable quantitative insights into how digital transformation influences critical business activities for European SMEs.

Attaran and Woods (2019) explored the implementation of Cloud Computing Technology (CCT) in small businesses, proposing a conceptual model for successful adoption. Attaran and Woods (2019) highlight potential implementation challenges and review the key attributes of successful CCT adoption. Additionally, Attaran and Woods (2019) reported in their study technologies, trends, and different deployment strategies for small businesses, offering a case example of successful CCT implementation. Ribeiro-Navarrete et al. (2021) explore the impact of digitalization on the performance of knowledge-intensive business services

(KIBS). They specifically examine how information systems and factors such as manager age, gender, and company size influence KIBS performance, with performance measured by future financial outcomes. Using fuzzy-set qualitative comparative analysis (fsQCA), the study finds that factors like updating social networks, leveraging social networks for business, high digital tool training, and having older managers can positively impact company performance.

4.3 Materials and Methods

4.3.1 Sample

The fieldwork for this study was conducted across various key business hubs in the Greater Accra region of Ghana. The focus was on Small and Medium-Sized Enterprises (SMEs) that have actively integrated technology and digital tools into their operations. The target population consisted of SMEs that have been in continuous operation for a minimum of two years and employ at least one person, excluding the owner. A list of approximately 1,500 registered SMEs was sourced from the Greater Accra Metropolitan Assembly (AMA). Using the Krejcie and Morgan (1970) formula, a sample of 312 SMEs was selected from the population.

4.3.2 Research Instrument

This study employed a self-administered questionnaire to collect data from the selected SMEs. The questionnaire was designed with eight carefully structured items, ensuring ease of completion for the respondents. Additionally, SME owner-managers were asked to provide details on their sales performance over the past three years, offering insights into their business growth and financial trajectory. The questionnaire covered key areas including the financial performance of SMEs, the extent of technology adoption and digitalization, as well as the challenges and factors influencing the adoption of technology within these enterprises.

$$\begin{aligned}\text{Financial\_Performance}_i = {} & \beta_0 + \beta_1\text{Technology\_Adoption} \\ & + \beta_2\text{Access to Technical Support \&} \\ & \text{After Sales Service} + \beta_3\text{Technology Skills} \\ & + \beta_4\text{Risk Aversion}\left(\text{Fear of Failure}\right) \\ & + \beta_5\text{Cost of data} + \beta_6\text{Educational level} \\ & \text{of the owner} + \beta_7\text{Marketing Accessibility} \\ & + \beta_8\text{Availability of Infrastructure} \\ & + \beta_9\text{Access to Credit} \\ & + \beta_{10}\text{Geographical Location} + \varepsilon_i\end{aligned}$$

4.3.3 Definition of Variable

The dependent variable is financial performance. This is the dependent variable, representing the SME's financial outcomes, such as profitability, revenue growth, or overall financial health. The independent variable is technology adoption. In addition to the independent variable, the following control variables included in the models are access to technical support and after-sales service, technology skills, risk aversion (Fear of Failure), cost of data, educational level of the owner, marketing accessibility, availability of infrastructure, access to credit, and geographical location. Technology adoption is measured by the extent to which SMEs have integrated new technologies into their operations, including digital tools, software, or automation systems. The control variables include access to technical support and after-sales service, which can be assessed by the frequency and quality of technical assistance received; technology skills, measured by the level of proficiency in using technological tools or software; and risk aversion (fear of failure), assessed using a scale that measures the owner's hesitance to take financial or operational risks (Sidki et al., 2024). Other controls are the cost of data, represented by the price of Internet or mobile data services, the educational level of the owner, measured by the highest level of formal education attained, marketing accessibility, determined by the SME's ability to reach and engage potential customers through various channels, availability of infrastructure, gauged by access to necessary facilities such as reliable electricity and

Internet, access to credit, assessed by the ease of obtaining financial support from formal sources, and geographical location, indicated by the region or proximity to urban or rural areas, which could influence technology access and business operations.

The apriori expectations are that technology adoption will positively impact financial performance, as adopting new technologies can enhance efficiency, reduce costs, and enable innovation (Bayraktar et al., 2024). However, the degree of impact may depend on the level of access to technical support and after-sales service and the technology skills of the business owner. Risk aversion is expected to have a negative relationship with financial performance, as a higher fear of failure may discourage investment in technologies that can improve business operations. Similarly, a higher cost of data may limit the ability of SMEs to adopt new technologies, thereby negatively impacting performance (Mukherjee & Sen, 2022). The educational level of the owner is anticipated to positively affect financial performance, as more educated owners are likely to have better business acumen (Orobia et al., 2020). Marketing accessibility is expected to positively influence performance, as better marketing channels can lead to increased sales. Availability of infrastructure and access to credit should also positively affect financial performance, as both factors provide the resources necessary for technological investment and business growth. Finally, geographical location may influence technology adoption and financial performance, with urban areas likely showing better outcomes due to greater access to resources and markets (Reddick et al., 2020).

4.4 Results

4.4.1 Extent of Technology Adoption Among SMEs

Table 4.1 presents the extent of technology adoption among SMEs in Ghana. The findings show the highest adoption of mobile payments and mobile money systems (92.63%) among SMEs. In terms of the Point of Sale (POS) systems, 58.65% of the respondents strongly agree that they

Table 4.1 Extent of technology adoption among SMEs in Ghana (%)

Variables	Strongly agreed	Agreed	Neutral	Disagreed	Strongly disagreed
Mobile Payments and Mobile Money Systems	92.63	3.85	1.60	0.64	1.28
Point of Sale (POS) Systems	58.65	10.90	18.59	11.22	0.64
Accounting and Financial Management Software	27.56	17.95	24.36	28.85	1.28
E-Commerce Platforms	38.78	14.42	14.74	28.85	3.21
Customer Relationship Management (CRM) Systems	32.37	12.18	10.90	23.08	21.47
Cloud Storage and Collaboration Tools	1.60	3.21	18.27	49.04	27.88
Inventory and Supply Chain Management Tools	17.95	13.78	18.27	27.24	22.76
Digital Payment Gateways	41.03	18.59	10.90	19.23	10.26
Agricultural Technologies (for Agri-business SMEs)	23.08	14.10	20.19	20.83	21.79
Websites and Blogging Platforms	50.32	23.08	11.54	11.54	3.53
Mobile Apps for SMEs	52.56	20.83	16.99	6.09	3.53

Source: Author's computation

use the POS systems for their business transactions. The study also found that most SMEs were actively involved in using websites and blogging platforms (50.32%) for their SME businesses. In contrast, cloud storage and collaboration tools have the lowest adoption, with only 1.60% strongly agreeing with the statement, suggesting that SMEs in Ghana are less likely to utilize cloud-based services for data storage and collaboration.

Other technologies, such as accounting and financial management software (27.56% strongly agreeing) and E-Commerce platforms (38.78% strongly agreeing), show moderate adoption, but a large percentage of SMEs remain neutral or disagree on their use. Customer relationship management (CRM) systems and inventory and supply chain management tools also show mixed results, with a notable portion of SMEs disagreeing or remaining neutral about their adoption. Technologies like digital payment gateways and agricultural technologies show relatively better adoption rates compared to cloud tools.

4.4.2 Effect of Technology and Digitization on the Financial Performance of SMEs in Ghana

Table 4.2 presents the findings on the effect of technology adoption and digitalization on the financial performance of SMEs in Ghana. Technology adoption (Pr = 0.038), Marketing Accessibility (Pr = 0.013), Availability of Infrastructure (Pr = 0.035), and Access to Credit (Pr = 0.028) are all statistically significant at the 5% level. Additionally, access to technical support and after-sales service (Pr = 0.005) and technology Skills (Pr = 0.001) are highly significant at the 1% level. On the other hand, several factors are not statistically significant. Risk Aversion (Fear of Failure) (Pr = 0.144), Cost of Data (Pr = 0.948), Educational Level of the Owner (Pr = 0.788), and Geographical Location (Pr = 0.906) have Pr(>|*t*|) values well above 0.05, suggesting that these variables do not have a substantial impact on the financial performance of SMEs.

Table 4.2 Technology adoption on financial performance

	Estimate	Std. error	*t* value	Pr(>|*t*|)	Sign. level
(Intercept)	0.130	0.027	4.773	0.000	***
Technology Adoption	0.024	0.012	2.086	0.038	*
Access to Technical Support and After-Sales Service	0.033	0.012	2.829	0.005	**
Technology Skills	0.284	0.082	3.459	0.001	***
Risk Aversion (Fear of Failure)	0.014	0.009	1.466	0.144	
Cost of data	-0.001	0.015	-0.065	0.948	
Educational level of the owner	-0.004	0.017	-0.269	0.788	
Marketing Accessibility	0.039	0.016	2.507	0.013	*
Availability of Infrastructure	0.007	0.003	2.114	0.035	*
Access to Credit	0.032	0.015	2.209	0.028	*
Geographical Location	-0.002	0.015	-0.118	0.906	

Source: Author's computation

*, **, *** implies significant at 5%, 1%, and less than 1%

4.4.3 Challenges in Adoption of Technology

Table 4.3 highlights the various challenges faced by SMEs in Ghana when adopting technology for their businesses. A significant percentage of respondents strongly agreed (68.95%) and agreed (66.35%) that the

Table 4.3 Challenges of technology adoption among SMEs in Ghana (%)

Variables	Strongly agreed	Agreed	Neutral	Disagreed	Strongly disagreed
Lack of Reliable Internet Access	31.73	36.22	10.90	17.31	3.85
High Initial Costs	30.45	35.90	9.94	16.99	6.73
Ongoing Maintenance and Operational Costs	40.06	18.59	13.78	14.10	13.46
Lack of Digital Skills and Technical Expertise	33.01	27.24	12.82	14.42	12.50
Limited Access to Technical Support	23.40	22.12	21.15	17.95	15.38
Cultural Resistance to Change	14.42	15.71	20.83	24.04	25.00
Low Trust in Digital Payment Systems	24.36	26.92	19.55	18.91	10.26
Lack of Infrastructure	31.41	30.77	16.99	17.31	3.53
Inadequate Funding and Access to Capital	28.21	31.41	24.36	14.42	1.60
Poor Data Security and Privacy Concerns	33.33	27.88	24.04	10.90	3.85
Limited Awareness of Available Technologies	28.21	22.12	17.31	20.83	11.54
Complexity of Technology Integration	30.45	24.04	19.23	16.35	9.94
Limited Government Support or Policy Incentives	36.86	22.12	20.83	10.58	9.62
Geographical Barriers	24.36	31.73	17.31	19.87	6.73
Scalability Issues	28.53	26.60	21.47	17.63	5.77
Lack of Localized Solutions	20.19	26.60	25.00	17.31	10.90
Unpredictable Power Supply	25.00	24.36	20.83	15.71	14.10
Limited Collaboration with Other SMEs or Networks	13.14	24.36	18.91	26.60	16.99

Source: Author's computation

challenges of unreliable Internet and high initial costs, respectively, were the major factors challenging their adoption of technology in their businesses. Additionally, the financial burden of maintaining and operating technology is also a critical concern, as 58.65% of respondents noted issues related to ongoing costs. Furthermore, the lack of digital skills and technical expertise was another considerable barrier, with 60.25% of SMEs agreeing with this challenge. While technical support and trust in digital systems were problematic for a significant percentage of SMEs, cultural resistance (39.46%) and trust issues (51.28%) were agreed upon by the responding SME owners as major barriers to the adoption of technology. Additionally, infrastructure-related issues such as poor power supply and geographical barriers, along with the complexity of technology integration and limited awareness of available technologies, were factors that challenged the adoption of technology by SMEs.

4.5 Discussions

Technology adoption has a positive and statistically significant impact on financial performance. This result aligns with a growing body of literature indicating that firms that embrace technological advancements experience enhanced performance through improved efficiency, productivity, and innovation. For instance, studies by Obiki-Osafiele et al. (2024) suggest that firms adopting advanced technology systems can streamline operations, reduce costs, and thus improve profitability. Additionally, technology adoption can enable businesses to access new markets, facilitate data-driven decision-making, and enhance customer experiences (Iyelolu et al., 2024). Access to technical support and after-sales service is another critical factor positively influencing financial performance. As businesses integrate new technologies, having reliable support systems ensures that potential issues are addressed quickly, reducing downtime and minimizing disruptions. According to Shokouhyar et al. (2020), strong after-sales services contribute to higher customer satisfaction and loyalty, which in turn positively affect financial outcomes.

Technology skills are one of the most significant predictors of financial performance. The positive relationship suggests that businesses with a skilled workforce are better equipped to leverage technological tools effectively, leading to higher performance. This is supported by research from Li (2022), who found that a skilled workforce is essential for the successful implementation and use of technology in firms. Furthermore, investing in employee training and development is associated with higher productivity, better decision-making, and improved profitability (Panagiotakopoulos, 2020). Marketing accessibility has a positive effect on financial performance. In the digital age, businesses with better access to online marketing channels, social media platforms, and digital marketing tools can reach a broader audience, increase sales, and enhance brand awareness. Research by Al Koliby et al. (2024) supports this finding, noting that marketing innovation and accessibility in the digital space are essential for achieving a competitive advantage and driving growth.

The availability of infrastructure, such as reliable Internet connectivity, electricity, and technological equipment, significantly contributes to a firm's ability to adopt and integrate technology effectively. According to Huang et al. (2020), infrastructure plays a crucial role in enabling firms to implement technological solutions that improve business processes and outcomes. The positive impact on financial performance suggests that technology adoption could be hindered without adequate infrastructure, limiting its potential benefits. Access to credit is another significant factor influencing financial performance. Firms that can access credit are more likely to invest in technology, which can, in turn, lead to improvements in financial performance. Literature by Beck et al. (2005) suggests that access to financial resources enables firms to fund technology upgrades, expand operations, and increase market share. Credit availability is crucial for business growth, especially in capital-intensive sectors where technology adoption requires substantial upfront investments.

4.6 Conclusion and Recommendations

In conclusion, technology adoption among SMEs in Ghana varies, with mobile payments and mobile money systems being the most widely used. POS systems, websites, and mobile apps have moderate adoption, while technologies like cloud storage, CRM systems, and accounting software face lower uptake due to cost, lack of skills, and resistance to change. Regression results indicate that factors such as technology skills, access to technical support, marketing, infrastructure, and credit access significantly impact financial outcomes for SMEs. The main challenges include high maintenance costs, unreliable Internet access, and a lack of digital skills and technical expertise. Additionally, high initial costs, limited technical support, cultural resistance, and concerns about data security hinder technology adoption. To increase adoption, it is essential to lower costs, improve access to training, and provide tailored support for technologies like cloud storage and CRM systems. Raising awareness, offering incentives, and improving Internet connectivity will also encourage broader integration. Enhancing technology skills, access to technical support, and marketing resources will improve financial performance. Supporting infrastructure development and expanding credit access will foster business growth. Finally, addressing data security concerns, offering technical support, and implementing government policies will help overcome adoption barriers.

References

Ahmed, I. A., Akyen, B., & Anaman, P. D. (2023). Unlocking the growth potential of SMEs in Ghana: An investigation of financial management practices and challenges. *Journal of Research in Business and Management, 11*(10), 55–65.

Al Koliby, I. S., Mehat, N. A., Al-Swidi, A. K., & Al-Hakimi, M. A. (2024). Unveiling the linkages between entrepreneurial culture, innovation capability, digital marketing capability and sustainable competitive performance of manufacturing SMEs: Evidence from emerging countries. *The Bottom Line, 37*(4), 473–500.

Asravor, R. K., & Acheampong, V. (2024). Factors influencing risk attitudes of entrepreneurs in Ghana: The role of gender. *Journal of Small Business & Entrepreneurship, 36*(1), 29–52.

Assensoh-Kodua, A. (2019). The resource-based view: A tool of key competency for competitive advantage. *Problems and Perspectives in Management, 17*(3), 143.

Attaran, M., & Woods, J. (2019). Cloud computing technology: Improving small business performance using the Internet. *Journal of Small Business & Entrepreneurship, 6*, 495–519.

Battistoni, E., Gitto, S., Murgia, G., & Campisi, D. (2023). Adoption paths of digital transformation in manufacturing SME. *International Journal of Production Economics, 255*(108675).

Bayraktar, E., Tatoglu, E., Aydiner, A. S., & Delen, D. (2024). Business analytics adoption and technological intensity: An efficiency analysis. *Information Systems Frontiers, 26*(4), 1509–1526.

Beck, T., Demirgüç-Kunt, A., & Levine, R. (2005). SMEs, growth, and poverty: Cross-country evidence. *Journal of Economic Growth, 10*(3), 199–229. https://doi.org/10.1007/s10887-005-3533-5

Canhoto, A. I., Quinton, S., Pera, R., Molinillo, S., & Simkin, L. (2021). Digital strategy aligning in SMEs: A dynamic capabilities perspective. *The Journal of Strategic Information Systems, 30*(3), 101682.

El Nemar, S., El-Chaarani, H., Dandachi, I., & Castellano, S. (2022). Resource-based view and sustainable advantage: A framework for SMEs. *Journal of Strategic Marketing*, 1–24.

Etemad, H. (2020). Managing uncertain consequences of a global crisis: SMEs encountering adversities, losses, and new opportunities. *Journal of International Entrepreneurship, 18*, 125–144.

Frimpong, S. E., Agyapong, G., & Agyapong, D. (2022). Financial literacy, access to digital finance and performance of SMEs: Evidence From Central region of Ghana. *Cogent Economics & Finance, 10*(1), 2121356.

Huang, H. Y., Ku, E. C., & Chen, C. D. (2020). Cloud infrastructure enhancing product competitive advantage of tourism SMEs on online consumption values of tourists. *Business Process Management Journal, 28*(4), 1146–1163.

Hunter, E., Jenkins, A., & Mark-Herbert, C. (2021). When fear of failure leads to intentions to act entrepreneurially: Insights from threat appraisals and coping efficacy. *International Small Business Journal, 39*(5), 407–423.

Iyelolu, T. V., Agu, E. E., Idemudia, C., & Ijomah, T. I. (2024). Improving customer engagement and CRM for SMEs with AI driven solutions and future enhancements. *International Journal of Engineering Research and Development, 20*(8).

Jedynak, M., Czakon, W., Kuźniarska, A., & Mania, K. (2021). Digital transformation of organizations: What do we know and where to go next? *Journal of Organizational Change Management, 34*(3), 629–652.

Justy, T., Pellegrin-Boucher, E., Lescop, D., Granata, J., & Gupta, S. (2023). On the edge of Big Data: Drivers and barriers to data analytics adoption in SMEs. *Technovation, 127*, 102850.

Kallmuenzer, A., Mikhaylov, A., Chelaru, M., & Czakon, W. (2024). Adoption and performance outcome of digitalization in small and medium-sized enterprises. *Review of Managerial Science*, 1–28.

Krejcie, R. V., & Morgan, D. W. (1970). Determining sample size for research activities. *Educational and Psychological Measurement, 30*(3), 607–610. https://doi.org/10.1177/001316447003000308

Li, L. (2022). Reskilling and upskilling the future-ready workforce for industry 4.0 and beyond. Information Systems. *Frontiers*, 1–16.

Lorenz, M., Rüßmann, M., Strack, R., Lueth, K. L., & Bolle, M. (2015). Man and machine in industry 4.0: How will technology transform the industrial workforce through 2025. *The Boston Consulting Group*, 2.

Mukherjee, T., & Sen, S. S. (2022). Impact of CEO attributes on corporate reputation, financial performance, and corporate sustainable growth: Evidence from India. *Financial Innovation, 8*(1), 40.

Obiki-Osafiele, A. N., Efunniyi, C. P., Abhulimen, A. O., Osundare, O. S., Agu, E. E., & Adeniran, I. A. (2024). Theoretical models for enhancing operational efficiency through technology in Nigerian businesses. *International Journal of Applied Research, 6*(08), 1969–1989.

Orobia, L. A., Nakibuuka, J., Bananuka, J., & Akisimire, R. (2020). Inventory management, managerial competence and financial performance of small businesses. *Journal of Accounting in Emerging Economies, 10*(3), 379–398.

Osei, B. K. (2023). *The difficulties that small business owners in Ghana, West Africa are facing to stay profitable: A qualitative case study*. Northcentral University.

Panagiotakopoulos, A. (2020). Exploring the link between management training and organizational performance in the small business context. *Journal of Workplace Learning, 32*(4), 245–257.

Quaye, W., Akon-Yamga, G., Akuffobea-Essilfie, M., & Onumah, J. A. (2025). Technology adoption, competitiveness and new market access among SMEs in Ghana: What are the limiting factors? *African Journal of Science, Technology, Innovation and Development*, 1–15.

Reddick, C. G., Enriquez, R., Harris, R., & Sharma, B. (2020). Determinants of broadband access and affordability: An analysis of a community survey on the digital divide. *Cities, 106*(102904).

Ribeiro-Navarrete, S., Botella-Carrubi, D. P.-M., & Orero-Blat, M. (2021). The effect of digitalization on business performance: An applied study of KIBS. *Journal of Business Research, 126*, 319–326.
Shokouhyar, S., Shokoohyar, S., & Safari, S. (2020). Research on the influence of after-sales service quality factors on customer satisfaction. *Journal of Retailing and Consumer Services, 56*, 102139.
Sidki, M., Boerger, L., & Boll, D. (2024). The effect of board members' education and experience on the financial performance of German state-owned enterprises. *Journal of Management and Governance, 28*(2), 445–482.
Skare, M., de Obesso, M. D., & Ribeiro-Navarrete, S. (2023). Digital transformation and European small and medium enterprises (SMEs): A comparative study using digital economy and society index data. *International Journal of Information Management, 102594*, 68.

5

Sustainability Marketing, Social Responsibility, Ethics, and SME Performance: The Moderating Role of Government Regulations

Prince Yao Amu, Vida Asante Boateng, and Deli Dotse Gli

5.1 Introduction

The majority of literature on sustainable marketing, corporate social responsibility, and business ethics is predominantly oriented towards giant corporations (Amu et al., 2024b), sometimes neglecting the problems and possibilities faced by small- and medium-sized firms (SMEs). Lin (2024) and Wu and Amoasi (2024) elucidate how sustainability marketing bolsters brand reputation and competitive advantage, whereas Garel and Petit-Romec (2021) and Lin (2024) demonstrate that CSR fosters stakeholder trust and long-term profitability. Waheed and Zhang (2022) assert that ethical frameworks are essential for the success of a sustainable firm. These studies, however, primarily presuppose the

P. Y. Amu (✉) • D. D. Gli
University of Ghana Business School, Accra, Ghana

V. A. Boateng
Wisconsin International University College, Accra, Ghana
e-mail: vida.boateng@wiuc-ghana.edu.gh

E. Amoako Asiedu et al. (eds.), *Entrepreneurship and Small and Medium-Sized Enterprises (SMEs) in Africa*, https://doi.org/10.1007/978-3-032-14174-3_5

availability of financial resources, specialised departments, and economies of scale, circumstances largely inapplicable to SMEs. Dixit and Priya (2023) highlight that resource limitations and informal techniques significantly influence the involvement of SMEs in sustainability and CSR. Conversely, the empirical landscape remains deficient, particularly in developing markets and certain sectors, regarding a comprehensive understanding of how SMEs incorporate such practices into their operations and the subsequent impact on performance.

A crucial but under-examined aspect is the interrelationship between sustainable marketing, corporate social responsibility, ethical considerations, and SME performance, particularly the role of governmental regulation. Although prior research recognises external pressure as a factor influencing SME behaviour (Coudounaris, 2021; Ernst et al., 2022; Agyabeng-Mensah et al., 2022), few studies examine the specific impact of regulatory frameworks on these interactions. Government policies, including environmental regulations, labour legislation, and ethical business standards, can either promote or obstruct SMEs in their pursuit of sustainable and socially responsible activities. However, it remains uncertain whether such legislation enhances or undermines the impact of sustainability measures on SME performance. Furthermore, the research has mostly overlooked the impact of regulatory measures on compliance, innovation stimulation, or the imposition of arbitrary limits on SME expansion. This disparity is especially pronounced in developing countries, where regulatory frameworks are often still being developed, and enforcement levels may fluctuate significantly.

This study seeks to address this gap by examining the moderating influence of government regulation on the links among sustainable marketing, corporate social responsibility, ethics, and small and medium-sized enterprise performance. This specifically examines the impact of regulatory pressure on the strategic implementation of these practices by SMEs and the consequent effects on competitiveness, customer perception, and financial performance. The study will thereby enhance the literature in three substantial ways. Initially, it provides empirical information about the interaction between external regulation and internal sustainability measures for SMEs, a topic that remains generally overlooked in current research. Secondly, it will elucidate whether government

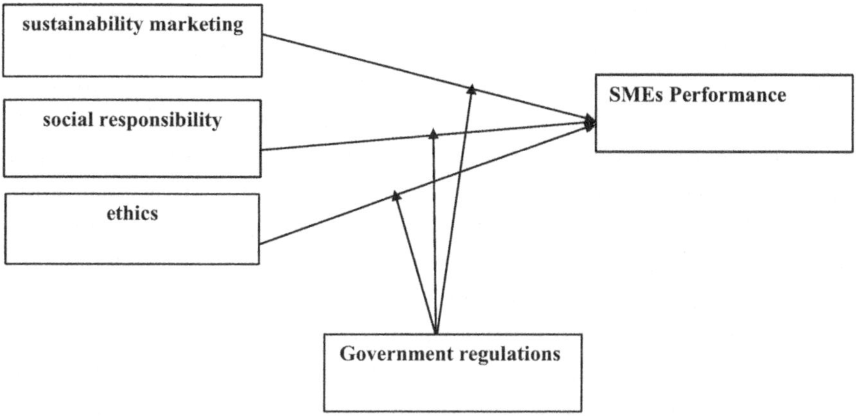

Fig. 5.1 Conceptual framework of the study

policies serve as facilitators or impediments to ethical business activities in contexts of resource constraints. It will eventually provide practical guidance to policymakers and owners of small and medium-sized enterprises on how to adjust regulatory frameworks to coincide with sustainable business growth. This research seeks to provide a sophisticated understanding of SMEs, demonstrating how they may convert regulation into a strategic advantage rather than just a compliance requirement, so improving ethical business practices and fostering long-term success (Fig. 5.1).

5.2 Theoretical Framework

This study is grounded in R. Edward Freeman's Stakeholder Theory from 1984, which posits that firms should generate value not just for shareholders but also for other stakeholders, including customers, employees, suppliers, communities, and the environment—to achieve long-term success. This promotes a shift from a profit-centric perspective of corporations to prioritise ethical responsibility, sustainability, and inclusive decision-making. Over the years, researchers such as Donaldson and Preston (1995) and Post et al. (2002) have broadened its use, illustrating its significance in corporate social responsibility (CSR), sustainable marketing, and ethical business practices.

Stakeholder Theory has been extensively used in evaluating how organisations reconcile opposing stakeholder interests, particularly in the realms of sustainability and ethical research. For instance, Oduro et al. (2024) used it to examine CSR in SMEs, and Agrawal et al. (2025) utilised the theory to comprehend its function in sustainability communication. However, few studies have rigorously applied this theory to examine the confluence of sustainable marketing, social responsibility, and ethics within resource-constrained SMEs. In this context, Stakeholder Theory seeks to analyse how SMEs engage their stakeholders in sustainable and ethical marketing practices. It considers the reasoning of SMEs in prioritising certain stakeholders (e.g., local communities, environmentally sensitive customers) and the consequent effects on competitiveness and legitimacy. The research uses this viewpoint to analyse actual techniques used by SMEs to reconcile stakeholder expectations with sustainable company development, thereby addressing a significant gap in the literature.

5.3 Literature Review

Sustainability marketing, social responsibility, and ethics are increasingly recognised in business literature for their impact on corporate success. While the discourse has been focused on major firms, the significance of SMEs for sustainable and ethical business practices has also emerged. This part elucidates the theoretical and empirical foundations of these notions, their interrelation, and their impact on company performance, culminating in testable predictions.

5.4 Sustainability Marketing and Firm Performance

Sustainability marketing is the strategic integration of environmental and social factors into a company's marketing strategies to effectively meet customer demand for ethical products while maintaining long-term profitability (Park et al., 2022). Proponents of sustainable marketing assert that it would further distinguish companies, bolster client loyalty, and augment market share (Zopounidis & Lemonakis, 2024). Alzghoul et al. (2024) observed that green marketing tactics enhance the financial performance of SMEs by facilitating cost reductions (such as energy efficiency) and enabling premium pricing advantages. Conversely, evidence is present. Proponents such as Chang et al. (2024) argue that sustainable marketing may provide minimal financial benefits in the beginning phases, thereby elevating operating expenses, particularly for resource-constrained SMEs. This may also illustrate the potential moderating influence of variables such as industry type, customer knowledge, and governmental backing on the link between sustainable marketing and company success.

Sustainability marketing necessitates the integration of environmental and social factors into a company's marketing strategy to satisfy customer demand for ethical goods and ensure long-term profitability (Park et al., 2022). Advocates contend that sustainable marketing facilitates brand distinctiveness, fosters consumer loyalty, and augments market share (Zopounidis & Lemonakis, 2024). Empirical research, like Alkandi (2025), indicates that SMEs using green marketing methods tend to achieve enhanced financial performance via cost savings, such as energy efficiency, and the ability to command premium pricing. Nonetheless, this assertion has been contested; for instance, some scholars, such as Teirlinck (2017), caution that sustainability marketing may really increase operational expenses without yielding financial gains, particularly for small and medium-sized enterprises with limited resources. This contradiction supports the notion that the relationship between sustainable marketing and business performance may be influenced by industry type, customer awareness, and regulatory backing (Amoako et al., 2024). Given these debates, we hypothesise:

H1: *Sustainability marketing has a positive and significant effect on firm performance in SMEs.*

5.5 Social Responsibility and Firm Performance

Small and medium-sized firms (SMEs) engage in voluntary CSR initiatives for the purpose of social good, engaging the community, labour, and charity (Amu et al., 2024b). Carroll and Shabana (2010) suggest that CSR improves business image and stakeholder trust while reducing risk, resulting in higher earnings. Gli et al. (2023) support this by demonstrating that CSR-positive SMEs have easier access to finance and are better able to retain clients. However, others believe that such CSR initiatives may detract from core company operations, particularly for SMEs (Stoian & Gilman, 2017; Amu et al., 2024a). Furthermore, the lack of conventional CSR standards in SMEs makes it difficult to quantify performance. Despite these challenges, the prevailing literature suggests a net positive impact, leading to the hypothesis:

H2: *Social responsibility has a positive and significant effect on firm performance in SMEs.*

5.6 Ethics and Firm Performance

Business ethics denote the moral standards governing an organisation's behaviour, including openness, equitable treatment of workers, and the implementation of measures to avert unscrupulous activities (Vasist & Krishnan, 2025). Ethical conduct correlates with enhanced stakeholder trust, less legal risk, and a sustained competitive advantage (Ferrell et al., 2019). Research by Chaanine (2025) indicates that small to medium firms with a robust ethical culture exhibit reduced staff turnover and enhanced customer satisfaction. Conversely, several academics contend that adherence to ethical standards requires substantial administration, especially in highly competitive or very corrupt environments (Vasist & Krishnan, 2025). Consequently, ethical decision-making in SMEs is subjective, since the owner's beliefs often supersede formal rules in determining results (Asawawibul et al., 2025). Despite these complexities, ethical practices are generally associated with sustainable performance, leading to the hypothesis:

H3: *Ethical business practices have a positive and significant effect on firm performance in SMEs.*

5.7 The Moderating Role of Governmental Regulations

The impact of government regulation has been extensively examined in academic literature about its influence on the interplay between sustainable marketing, social responsibility, ethics, and the performance of SMEs. Although stringent regulations are purported to create equitable conditions and foster environmentally sustainable practices, as articulated by certain scholars (Philander & Wimmer, 2025) in relation to the amplification of sustainability marketing's beneficial impacts, others contend that the compliance costs may stifle innovation in SMEs due to excessive regulatory encumbrances (Alzebda, & Matar, 2025; Liao & Xiao, 2025). In accordance with CSR, research indicates that governmental initiatives, such as tax incentives or compulsory reporting, are likely to enhance the correlation between social responsibility and corporate performance by legitimising expenditures on CSR (Philander & Wimmer, 2025; Zhang et al., 2022). In weak regulatory settings, SMEs get more value from short-term survival rather than a long-term commitment to CSR, which often results in diminished effects (Wilson, 2021; Kim et al., 2022). Furthermore, legal enforcement and anti-corruption initiatives are crucial for transforming ethical practices into competitive advantages (Cusumano et al., 2021), whereas, in lenient regulatory environments, ethical SMEs face inequitable competition from unscrupulous competitors (Øyri & Wiig, 2022). Empirical research demonstrates that legislative assistance, such as subsidies for green technology or streamlined compliance requirements, may enhance the success of sustainability projects for SMEs (Leonidou et al., 2013; Torugsa et al., 2013).

Conversely, fragmented or unstable rules may create uncertainties that deter long-term ethical investments (Øyri & Wiig, 2022).

Based on the ensuing argument, *it was hypothesised that governmental regulations positively moderate the relationships between sustainability marketing, social responsibility, and ethics with SME performance.*

5.8 Methodology

The methodology of this study is designed to empirically examine the moderating role of government regulations on the relationships between sustainability marketing, social responsibility, ethics, and firm performance among SMEs. A quantitative research approach is adopted, utilising a cross-sectional survey design to collect data from SME owners and managers. This approach is chosen for its ability to measure relationships between variables and generalise findings across a broader population. The study focuses on SMEs operating across various industries, ensuring diversity in responses while maintaining relevance to the research objectives. The target population consists of registered SMEs within a defined geographical region, selected based on criteria such as business size (typically 10–250 employees) and operational longevity (at least three years in business).

A purposive sampling technique is employed to select 110 SMEs, ensuring representation across different sectors, including manufacturing, retail, and services. This sample size is deemed adequate for statistical analysis while considering practical constraints in data collection. Primary data is gathered through structured questionnaires, with measurement items adapted from established scales in prior studies on sustainability marketing, CSR, ethics, and firm performance. Specifically, items for sustainability marketing are drawn from studies by Belz and Peattie (2012), while CSR measures are adapted from Carroll and Shabana (2010). Ethical business practices are assessed using scales developed by Crane and Matten (2016), and firm performance is evaluated through both financial (e.g., profitability, sales growth) and non-financial (e.g., customer retention, brand reputation) indicators, as suggested by Venkatraman and Ramanujam (1986).

Data analysis is conducted using Statistical Package for the Social Sciences (SPSS) and Partial Least Squares Structural Equation Modelling (PLS-SEM) (Amu et al., 2024a). Descriptive statistics provide an overview of respondent demographics and key variables, while reliability and validity tests (Cronbach's alpha, composite reliability, and discriminant validity) ensure the robustness of the measurement model. PLS-SEM is chosen for its ability to handle complex relationships between latent variables, even with smaller sample sizes, making it suitable for this study. Hypotheses are tested by examining path coefficients and their significance levels, with additional analyses such as mediation or moderation considered if theoretical justification exists. The findings aim to provide actionable insights for SME practitioners and policymakers while contributing to academic discourse on sustainable and ethical business practices.

5.9 Findings

To assess the measurement model, the study first conducted the internal consistent reliability of the model using Cronbach's Alpha, composite reliability, and factor loadings. The findings, as presented in Table 5.1, indicate that the recommended thresholds were met (i.e., Cronbach's Alpha ≥0.70, composite reliability ≥0.70, and factor loadings ≥0.70). The study also calculated the convergent reliability and discriminant validity to assess the construct reliability. To do this, the study used AVE to evaluate convergent validity. As indicated in Table 5.1, the values of the AVEs for each of the related constructs were higher than the recommended threshold of 0.5, establishing convergent validity. Using the

Table 5.1 Loadings, reliability, and validity

	Loadings	C.A	rho_A	C.R	(AVE)
Ethical	0.792–0.832	0.746	0.774	0.85	0.654
GovReg	0.755–0.825	0.86	0.865	0.899	0.642
Perf	0.831–0.825	0.837	0.837	0.902	0.755
Social	0.707–0.886	0.913	0.917	0.933	0.701
Sustainability	0.713–0.854	0.856	0.855	0.897	0.636

Heterotrait-Monotrait (HTMT) ratio, it was identified that discriminant validity was established, as all values were below the threshold of 0.85 (see Table 5.2).

The study then proceeded to assess the structural model by calculating the coefficients of determination (R^2), and the path loadings. Particularly, R^2 values for firm performance (30%) indicated a weak relationship between the model's independent and dependent variables. Among the three hypotheses predicting the main effect, all the direct relationships were supported. Specifically, the paths from Ethics to Performance (β = 0.109, p <.05), Social Responsibility to Performance (β = 0.211, p <.001), and Sustainability Marketing to Performance (β = 0.169, p <.05) were all significant (see Table 5.3). These findings were consistent with extant scholarship (Nguyen et al., 2021; Amu et al., 2024a; Oduro et al., 2025; Rahman et al., 2022). The study proceeded to consider the moderation analysis for all the baseline relationships. The study identified a positive but insignificant relationship for two of the relationships: GovReg*Social → Perf (β = 0.005, p > 0.05) and GovReg*Sustainability → Perf (β = 0.004, p > 0.05). The study also found Govereg*Ethical → Perf (β = -0.025, p > 0.05) to be statistically negative and insignificant.

Table 5.2 Discriminant validity

	Ethical	GovReg	Perf	Social	Sustainability
Ethical					
GovReg	0.459				
Perf	0.352	0.574			
Social	0.362	0.822	0.541		
Sustainability	0.331	0.657	0.494	0.567	

Table 5.3 Model evaluation

	F-square	VIF	*R* square	*Q*-squared
Ethical	0.015	1.172		
GovReg	0.023	2.487		
Perf			0.301	0.215
Social	0.029	2.167		
Sustainability	0.027	1.53		

5.10 Conclusion and Implications of the Study

This research examines the role of government regulations in moderating the relationship between ethical, social, and sustainable practices and firm performance. Considering the potential of SMEs in developing countries such as Ghana, the study provides a model that could influence how these firms can enhance their performance.

This research has some pertinent implications. The direct impacts align with stakeholder theory, suggesting that SMEs' performance may improve in response to stakeholder demands for ethical, social, and sustainable practices, even without regulatory coercion. The lack of significant moderation suggests that the drivers for adopting these practices are primarily intrinsic (e.g., owner-manager values, market demand) rather than extrinsic regulatory pressures. This challenges assumptions about the drivers of social and sustainable activities in resource-constrained SMEs (Table 5.4).

SME owners can gain a competitive advantage by integrating ethical, social, and sustainability factors as core performance drivers, thereby fostering consumer trust and potentially reducing costs. Governments must reevaluate regulations to ensure they provide advantages for SMEs, including tax incentives for green investments and the simplification of regulatory frameworks. The results indicate that current enforcement measures may be absent or insufficient to meet the unique challenges encountered by SMEs, such as elevated compliance costs.

Table 5.4 Path relationships with moderation

Hypothesis	Direct relationships	Beta	STDEV	T Stats	*p*-values	Decision
H1	Sustainability → Perf	0.169	0.060	2.824	0.005	Supported
H2	Social → Perf	0.211	0.065	3.247	0.001	Supported
H3	Ethical → Perf	0.109	0.043	2.513	0.012	Supported
	GovReg*Sustainability → Perf	0.004	0.055	0.077	0.938	
	GovReg*Social → Perf	0.005	0.051	0.095	0.924	
	Govereg*Ethical → Perf	-0.025	0.046	0.550	0.583	

5.11 Limitations and Future Research

Although the current study provides significant theoretical and practical insights, it is not without its limits. The research treated government regulation as a uniform construct. Future study should decompose laws (e.g., into environmental norms and labour standards) into discrete components to identify the most effective policies. Moreover, the cross-sectional survey conducted at a single moment restricted the ability to derive any genuine causal inferences. The impact of regulation may need time to become evident, during which unanticipated repercussions (such as economic shocks) may occur.

References

Agrawal, S., Ray, A., & Rana, N. P. (2025). Effectiveness of sustainability communication on stakeholder engagement: A multi-method qualitative assessment of sustainable development. *Corporate Social Responsibility and Environmental Management, 32*(1), 820–834.

Agyabeng-Mensah, Y., Afum, E., Baah, C., & Essel, D. (2022). Exploring the role of external pressure, environmental sustainability commitment, engagement, alliance and circular supply chain capability in circular economy performance. *International Journal of Physical Distribution and Logistics Management, 52*(5/6), 431–455.

Alkandi, I. (2025). Nexus between green practices, green marketing, and business performance: The mediating role of corporate social responsibility in emerging economy. *Discover Sustainability, 6*(1), 1–28.

Alzebda, S., & Matar, M. A. (2025). Factors affecting citizen intention toward AI acceptance and adoption: The moderating role of government regulations. *Competitiveness Review: An International Business Journal, 35*(2), 434–455.

Alzghoul, A., Aboalganam, K. M., & Al-Kasasbeh, O. (2024). Nexus among green marketing practice, leadership commitment, environmental consciousness, and environmental performance in Jordanian pharmaceutical sector. *Cogent Business & Management, 11*(1), 2292308.

Amoako, G. K., Sedalo, G., Asiedu, E. A., & Oppong Appiagyei Ampong, G. (2024). Conceptual framework–sustainability actions, global crises and justice in the future of tourism and hospitality. *Journal of Tropical Futures, 1*(2), 203–217.

Amu, P. Y., Narteh, B., & Kodua, P. (2024a). The role of perceived value in football club branding: A developing league perspective. *African Journal of Economic and Management Studies, 15*(3), 557–571.
Amu, P. Y., Odoom, R., & Mohammed, I. (2024b). The moderating role of corporate social responsibility on the relationship between brand image and brand loyalty: A. In *Corporate social responsibility – A global perspective: A global perspective* (p. 29).
Asawawibul, S., Na-Nan, K., Pinkajay, K., Jaturat, N., Kittichotsatsawat, Y., & Hu, B. (2025). The influence of cost on customer satisfaction in e-commerce logistics: Mediating roles of service quality, technology usage, transportation time, and production condition. *Journal of Open Innovation: Technology, Market, and Complexity, 11*(1), 100482.
Belz, Frank-Martin, & Ken Peattie. (2012). *Sustainability Marketing: A Global Perspective (2nded)*. UK: John Wiley & Sons, Ltd.
Carroll, A. B., & Shabana, K. M. (2010). The business case for corporate social responsibility: A review of concepts, research and practice. *International Journal of Management Reviews, 12*(1), 85–105.
Chaanine, J. (2025). Strengthening Lebanese health care: Exploring the impact of organizational culture on employee loyalty through trust and job satisfaction. *Leadership in Health Services.*
Chang, H. H. S., Knight, G., & Fong, C. M. (2024). Marketing capabilities, strategy, and performance in international small-and medium-sized enterprises. *Journal of International Marketing, 32*(4), 21–37.
Coudounaris, D. N. (2021). The internationalisation process of UK SMEs: Exporting and non-exporting behaviours based on a four forces behavioural model. *Review of International Business and Strategy, 31*(2), 217–256.
Crane, A., & Matten, D. (2016). Engagement Required. *Re-Imagining Capitalism*, 116.
Cusumano, M. A., Gawer, A., & Yoffie, D. B. (2021). Can self-regulation save digital platforms? *Industrial and Corporate Change, 30*(5), 1259–1285.
Dixit, S. K., & Priya, S. S. (2023). Barriers to corporate social responsibility: An Indian SME perspective. *International Journal of Emerging Markets, 18*(9), 2438–2454.
Donaldson, T., & Preston, L. E. (1995). The stakeholder theory of the corporation: Concepts, evidence, and implications. *Academy of Management Review, 20*(1), 65–91.
Ernst, R. A., Gerken, M., Hack, A., & Hülsbeck, M. (2022). SMES'reluctance to embrace corporate sustainability: The effect of stakeholder pressure on self-

determination and the role of social proximity. *Journal of Cleaner Production, 335*, 130273.

Ferrell, O. C., Harrison, D. E., Ferrell, L., & Hair, J. F. (2019). Business ethics, corporate social responsibility, and brand attitudes: An exploratory study. *Journal of Business Research, 95*, 491–501.

Freeman, R. E. (1984). *Strategic management: A stakeholder approach*. Pitman.

Garel, A., & Petit-Romec, A. (2021). Engaging employees for the long run: Long-term investors and employee-related CSR. *Journal of Business Ethics, 174*(1), 35–63.

Gli, D. D., Tweneboah-Koduah, E. Y., Odoom, R., & Kodua, P. (2023). The effect of corporate reputation on customer loyalty in the Ghanaian banking industry: The role of country-of-origin. *African Journal of Economic and Management Studies, 15*(1), 73–87.

Kim, J., Stern, R. E., Liebman, B. L., & Wu, X. (2022). Closing open government: Grassroots policy conversion of China's open government information regulation and its aftermath. *Comparative Political Studies, 55*(2), 319–347.

Leonidou, C. N., Katsikeas, C. S., & Morgan, N. A. (2013). "Greening" the marketing mix: Do firms do it and does it pay off?. *Journal of the Academy of Marketing Science, 41*(2), 151–170.

Liao, Z., & Xiao, L. (2025). Government environmental regulation, media attention, and corporate green innovation. *International Review of Economics and Finance, 97*, 103751.

Lin, W. L. (2024). The role of corporate social responsibility and corporate social irresponsibility in shaping corporate reputation: An analysis of competitive action and innovation strategies. *Corporate Social Responsibility and Environmental Management, 31*(2), 1451–1468.

Nguyen, N. T. T., Nguyen, N. P., & Hoai, T. T. (2021). Ethical leadership, corporate social responsibility, firm reputation, and firm performance: A serial mediation model. *Heliyon, 7*(4).

Oduro, S., Bruno, L., & Maccario, G. (2024). Corporate social responsibility (CSR) in SMEs: What we know, what we don't know, and what we should know. *Journal of Small Business & Entrepreneurship, 36*(2), 207–238.

Oduro, S., Umar, R. M., De Massis, A., & Haylemariam, L. G. (2025). Corporate social responsibility and family firm performance: A meta-analytic review. *Corporate Social Responsibility and Environmental Management, 32*(2), 1412–1443.

Øyri, S. F., & Wiig, S. (2022). Linking resilience and regulation across system levels in healthcare – A multilevel study. *BMC Health Services Research, 22*(1), 510.

Park, J. Y., Perumal, S. V., Sanyal, S., Ah Nguyen, B., Ray, S., Krishnan, R., et al. (2022). Sustainable marketing strategies as an essential tool of business. *American Journal of Economics and Sociology, 81*(2), 359–379.

Philander, K. S., & Wimmer, B. S. (2025). Playing by the rules: Government regulation and consumer trust in the online Poker Industry. *Computers in Human Behavior Reports*, 100599.

Post, J. E., Preston, L. E., & Sachs, S. (2002). Managing the extended enterprise: The new stakeholder view. *California Management Review, 45*(1), 6–28.

Rahman, H. U., Zahid, M., & Khan, M. (2022). Corporate sustainability practices: A new perspective of linking board with firm performance. *Total Quality Management & Business Excellence, 33*(7–8), 929–946.

Stoian, C., & Gilman, M. (2017). Corporate social responsibility that "pays": A strategic approach to CSR for SMEs. *Journal of Small Business Management, 55*(1), 5–31.

Teirlinck, P. (2017). Configurations of strategic R&D decisions and financial performance in small-sized and medium-sized firms. *Journal of Business Research, 74*, 55–65.

Torugsa, N. A., O'Donohue, W., & Hecker, R. (2013). Proactive CSR: An empirical analysis of the role of its economic, social and environmental dimensions on the association between capabilities and performance. *Journal of Business Ethics, 115*(2), 383–402.

Vasist, P. N., & Krishnan, S. (2025). Navigating the ethical terrain around the challenges of fake news and false narratives: An integrative literature review and a proposed agenda for future research. *Journal of Business Ethics, 196*(2), 473–493.

Venkatraman, N., & Ramanujam, V. (1986). Measurement of business performance in strategy research: A comparison of approaches. *Academy of Management Review, 11*(4), 801–814.

Waheed, A., & Zhang, Q. (2022). Effect of CSR and ethical practices on sustainable competitive performance: A case of emerging markets from stakeholder theory perspective. *Journal of Business Ethics, 175*(4), 837–855.

Wilson, J. Q. (2021). The politics of regulation. In *The political economy: Readings in the politics and economics of American public policy* (pp. 82–103). Routledge.

Wu, X., & Amoasi, R. (2024). The role of CSR in sustaining corporate brands in the global market: The perspective of telecommunication companies in Ghana. *Corporate Social Responsibility and Environmental Management, 31*(1), 433–447.

Zhang, W., Luo, Q., & Liu, S. (2022). Is government regulation a push for corporate environmental performance? Evidence from China. *Economic Analysis and Policy, 74*, 105–121.

Zopounidis, C., & Lemonakis, C. (2024). The company of the future: Integrating sustainability, growth, and profitability in contemporary business models. *Development and Sustainability in Economics and Finance, 1*, 100003.

6

Leveraging Digital Technologies for Enhanced Complaint Management in Delivery Service SMEs: Insights from Ghanaian Consumer Behaviour

Jackson Nuarko Appiagyei, Emelia Amoako Asiedu, Theresa Obuobisa-Darko, Robert Ebo Hinson, and George Kwabena Asamoah

6.1 Introduction

Customer complaints are inevitable in the service industry, as service performance often fails to meet customer expectations (Kim & Baker, 2020). For small and medium-sized enterprises (SMEs), which form the

J. N. Appiagyei (✉) • R. E. Hinson
University of Ghana Business School, Accra, Ghana
e-mail: jnappiagyei@ug.edu.gh; rhinson@ug.edu.gh

E. Amoako Asiedu
Department of Marketing, Ghana Communication Technology University, Accra, Ghana
e-mail: easiedu@gctu.edu.gh

T. Obuobisa-Darko
Ghana Communication Technology University, Accra, Ghana
e-mail: tobuobisa-darko@gctu.edu.gh

E. Amoako Asiedu et al. (eds.), *Entrepreneurship and Small and Medium-Sized Enterprises (SMEs) in Africa*, https://doi.org/10.1007/978-3-032-14174-3_6

backbone of global economies, managing customer complaints effectively is critical to sustaining competitiveness and building customer loyalty. However, SMEs face unique challenges in addressing the diverse behaviours and expectations of different types of complainers: passives, voicers, irates, and activists (Badghish & Shagagi, 2023; Nguyen, 2019). Each group requires tailored strategies, yet SMEs often lack the resources, frameworks, and expertise to handle complaints comprehensively.

The inability to address diverse complaints can have severe consequences. Passive complainers disengage without giving feedback, leaving businesses unaware of their shortcomings (Do et al., 2020). Irates and activists, on the other hand, can amplify dissatisfaction through negative word-of-mouth on public platforms, causing significant reputational damage (Narayanan & Singh, 2024). In the absence of effective strategies, these issues lead to customer attrition, reduced trust, and financial losses, posing an existential threat to SMEs competing against larger firms with more robust customer service systems (Knox & Van Oest, 2014).

Despite the critical role of complaint management in enhancing service excellence, research in this area predominantly focuses on large organizations (Aksoy & Yilmaz 2022; Clavel & Pomey, 2020). Little attention has been paid to how SMEs, with their resource constraints, can implement scalable and effective complaint management strategies. Furthermore, while theories like attribution theory highlight the psychological dimensions of customer complaints, practical insights into applying these frameworks in SME contexts remain limited (Mahato et al., 2024).

It is for this reason that this study aims to investigate how delivery service SMEs in Accra, Ghana, manage diverse customer complaints to enhance service excellence. Specifically, the study seeks to identify effective strategies for managing complaints, categorize types of complainers, and explore the impact of these practices on service quality. The findings aim to provide actionable recommendations for SMEs to tailor their

---

G. K. Asamoah
Ghana Institute of Journalism, Accra, Ghana
e-mail: gasamoah@unicam.edu.gh

complaint management processes and improve customer satisfaction. By bridging theory and practice, this research seeks to contribute to the broader understanding of service recovery while empowering SMEs to thrive in competitive markets through improved customer relationships.

6.2 Literature Review

6.2.1 Service Failure

Service failure occurs when service delivery falls below customer expectations, resulting in dissatisfaction (Zeithaml, 1990; Sahaf & Fazili, 2024). Given the intangible and interpersonal nature of services, occasional failures are inevitable, making effective management crucial for organizational success (Lewis & McCann, 2004; Albrecht et al., 2017). SMEs, characterized by resource constraints, are particularly vulnerable to the impacts of service failure, as their limited operational capacities can magnify customer dissatisfaction and erode loyalty (Nikolić et al., 2019; Caballero-Morales, 2021).

Foundational research categorizes service failures into core and peripheral types. Core failures directly affect the promised service outcome, such as delivery delays, product damage, and billing errors, whereas peripheral failures pertain to supplementary elements like employee behaviour and communication issues (Bitner et al., 1990; Cho & Song, 2012). Contemporary studies reinforce that core failures tend to provoke stronger negative customer reactions and switching behaviours compared to peripheral ones (Sahaf & Fazili, 2024; Nikolić et al., 2019).

Customer perceptions of service failure are also influenced significantly by their attributions regarding cause and responsibility. Attribution theory (Weiner, 1980; Folkes, 1984) argues that customers attribute service failures along dimensions of locus of control, stability, and controllability. Failures perceived as internal, stable, and controllable often result in intense dissatisfaction and negative word-of-mouth (Folkes, 1984; Albrecht et al., 2017). Conversely, customers tend to exhibit greater tolerance for failures viewed as external, unstable, or uncontrollable, perceiving these as isolated events (Weiner, 1980; Chakraborty & Bhat, 2018).

6.2.2 Service Recovery

Service recovery refers to the actions taken by an organization to address service failures and restore customer satisfaction (Miller et al., 2000). Effective service recovery is critical as it not only mitigates the negative effects of service failures but also provides an opportunity to enhance customer trust and loyalty (Pizzutti dos Santos & Basso, 2012). For SMEs, which often operate in highly competitive markets with limited resources, service recovery becomes an indispensable tool for maintaining customer relationships and sustaining business growth (Nikolić et al., 2019).

The concept of the service recovery paradox posits that a customer's satisfaction level can exceed expectations if the recovery effort is exemplary (Krishna et al., 2011). However, Michel and Meuter (2008) argue that this paradox occurs under specific conditions, such as when failures are perceived as minor and recovery efforts are prompt, empathetic, and adequate. The cost and complexity of delivering such recovery, particularly for resource-constrained SMEs, remain significant challenges (Hübner et al., 2018).

Service recovery strategies often focus on fairness dimensions: outcome fairness, procedural fairness, and interactional fairness (Kumar & Kumar, 2016). Customers expect compensations that align with their inconvenience (outcome fairness), clear and efficient recovery processes (procedural fairness), and respectful communication (interactional fairness) (Kumar & Kumar, 2016). Hence, tailoring these strategies to different types of complainers, such as passives, voicers, irates, and activists, is vital for recovery success.

6.2.3 Service Recovery Strategies

Service recovery strategies are vital in addressing customer dissatisfaction and restoring confidence after service failures (DeWitt & Brady, 2003). These strategies involve specific actions aimed at rectifying the failure, minimizing its impact, and fostering loyalty. For SMEs, the design and execution of effective service recovery strategies are critical for maintaining competitive advantage and customer retention (Caballero-Morales, 2021).

Levesque and McDougall (2000) on service recovery strategies highlight two main approaches: fixing the customer and fixing the problem. Fixing the customer focuses on addressing the immediate dissatisfaction through prompt responses, compensation, and empathetic communication. For example, ensuring customers feel heard and valued by providing personalized solutions can significantly enhance satisfaction. Fixing the problem involves identifying and eliminating the root cause of the failure to prevent recurrence. This may include refining processes, training employees, or implementing technological solutions (Levesque & McDougall, 2000).

For instance, some effective recovery strategies include the use of service guarantees, which assure customers of resolution and provide a sense of security. However, in SMEs, such extensive empowerment may not be feasible. Instead, practical methods, such as actively tracking and analysing complaints, prioritizing procedural fairness, and offering symbolic compensations, have proven effective (Kim, 2007).

6.2.4 Service Excellence

Service excellence refers to consistently exceeding customer expectations and delivering memorable experiences that foster trust and loyalty (Gouthier et al., 2012). For small and medium-sized enterprises (SMEs), achieving service excellence is essential for competitive differentiation in a marketplace dominated by larger firms with more resources (Sternad et al., 2019). Service excellence is not only a critical success factor but also a significant driver of customer retention and business growth (Clark & Baker, 2007).

Gouthier et al. (2012) emphasize that service excellence is built on three pillars: service quality, employee empowerment, and customer-centric culture. Service quality frameworks, such as the SERVQUAL model, identify reliability, responsiveness, assurance, empathy, and tangibles as key dimensions influencing customer perceptions (Parasuraman et al., 1988). SMEs, however, often face challenges in consistently delivering these attributes due to resource limitations and operational constraints (Sternad et al., 2019).

According to Den Hartog and Verburg (2002), employee empowerment plays a vital role in fostering service excellence. Empowered employees are better equipped to make decisions, solve problems promptly, and personalize customer interactions, thereby creating positive service experiences (Den Hartog & Verburg, 2002). For example, companies like Zappos prioritize employee autonomy to enhance customer satisfaction. SMEs can adopt similar practices on a smaller scale by investing in training and creating flexible policies (Sternad et al., 2019). A customer-centric culture is the foundation of service excellence. Organizations that prioritize customer needs in their operations tend to deliver higher satisfaction levels. Despite its importance, many SMEs struggle to instill such a culture due to competing priorities or lack of expertise (Nurdiani & Alie, 2023).

6.2.5 Types of Complainers

Understanding the types of complainers is pivotal for businesses aiming to implement effective complaint management strategies. Research categorizes complainers into four primary groups: passives, voicers, irates, and activists (Singh, 1990). Each group exhibits unique behavioural tendencies and expectations, necessitating tailored approaches to service recovery. For SMEs, recognizing these distinctions can significantly enhance their ability to address diverse customer needs and foster satisfaction (Sharma et al., 2010).

Passives are the least likely to complain directly to the provider or spread negative word-of-mouth (WOM) (Oliver, 2014). Their dissatisfaction often remains unvoiced, making it challenging for businesses to identify and address issues. This silent disengagement can lead to reduced loyalty and eventual customer attrition (Singh, 1990). Proactively soliciting feedback through surveys and informal interactions is essential for reaching this group (Gyung Kim et al., 2010).

Voicers, in contrast, actively communicate their complaints to the service provider but refrain from spreading negative WOM (Oliver, 2014).

They are often motivated by a belief in the constructive potential of their complaints and are considered the "best friends" of businesses. SMEs can leverage this behaviour by responding promptly and showing appreciation for their input, turning voicers into loyal advocates (Gyung Kim et al., 2010).

Irates are characterized by their propensity to share dissatisfaction through negative WOM and their lower likelihood of giving providers a second chance (Singh, 1990). Effective handling of irates requires prompt, empathetic recovery actions to rebuild trust and minimize reputational damage (Levesque & McDougall, 1996). While activists are the most vocal, often complaining across multiple channels, including third-party platforms. They demand high responsiveness and accountability from businesses (Oliver, 2014). Ignoring activists can lead to public relations crises, particularly for resource-limited SMEs (Gyung Kim et al., 2010).

6.2.6 Attribution Theory

Attribution theory, developed by Heider (1958) and further refined by Weiner (1980), explains how individuals interpret and assign causes to events, particularly success and failure. This theory is a cornerstone in understanding customer reactions to service failures and the subsequent effectiveness of service recovery strategies. For SMEs, attribution theory offers valuable insights into tailoring complaint management practices based on customers' perceived reasons for service failure (Chakraborty & Bhat, 2018).

According to attribution theory, customers evaluate service failures based on three key dimensions: locus of control, stability, and controllability (Weiner, 1980). The locus of control determines whether the failure is attributed to internal factors (e.g., employee incompetence) or external factors (e.g., unforeseen circumstances). Stability refers to whether the issue is perceived as a recurring problem or a one-time incident, while controllability assesses whether the organization had the ability to prevent the failure (Manusov & Spitzberg, 2008).

Manusov and Spitzberg (2008) also suggest that customers are more forgiving of failures perceived as external, unstable, and uncontrollable. Conversely, failures seen as internal, stable, and controllable often lead to stronger dissatisfaction and reduced trust. SMEs can leverage these insights by shaping recovery strategies to influence customer perceptions positively (Chakraborty & Bhat, 2018). For instance, transparent communication about the cause of a failure, coupled with proactive recovery actions, can mitigate negative attributions.

6.3 Methods

This study employs a qualitative research approach to explore strategies for managing diverse customer complaints to enhance service excellence in delivery service SMEs in the Greater Accra region, Ghana. The qualitative approach is ideal for capturing in-depth insights and understanding the subjective experiences of SME operators regarding complaint management (Creswell, 2013). For the purpose of this study, small and medium enterprises are operationalized based on the number of workers and fixed assets as provided by the National Board for Small Scale Industries (NBSSI). Small enterprises engage 6 to 30 staff; have fixed assets (excluding land and building) not exceeding $100,000 and are formally registered at the Registrar General's department. Medium enterprises have between 30 and 100 workers with fixed assets (excluding land and building) not exceeding $1 million and formally registered at the Registrar General's department (Akpabli, 2019).

The research adopts a case study strategy, focusing on delivery service SMEs operating in the Greater Accra region. The Integrated Business Establishment Survey (IBES) report (GSS, 2016) indicates that the Greater Accra region is home to the largest number of business establishments in Ghana, particularly small and medium enterprises, hence the rationale for selecting Accra as the study area. These businesses represent the study population due to their direct interaction with diverse customer bases and their role in addressing complaints effectively. The purposive sampling technique was employed, with inclusion criteria specifying SMEs that have been in operation for at least 5 years, ensuring the selection of experienced businesses capable of providing rich insights into their complaint management strategies (Malhotra & Birks, 2007).

Primary data were collected through semi-structured interviews guided by a well-constructed interview guide. This instrument ensured consistency in questioning while allowing flexibility to explore respondents' unique perspectives (Malhotra & Birks, 2007). The interviews focused on identifying the types of complaints encountered, strategies for addressing them, and their impact on service excellence. To ensure reliability, the interview guide was pretested with 5 owner-managers of SMEs delivery service firms operating in the Greater Accra region, after which the interview of 15 different owner-managers from the pretest realized data saturation (Creswell, 2013). All interviews were recorded and transcribed verbatim. Validity was also ensured through member checking, allowing participants to review and confirm their responses for accuracy.

Thematic analysis, guided by the Miles and Huberman (1994) approach, was employed for data analysis. This involved coding responses, identifying patterns, and categorizing themes to uncover significant insights. The approach ensured a systematic and rigorous analysis process, enhancing the credibility of the findings.

6.4 Findings

Table 6.1 above presents the profile of respondents for the study. These respondents comprised 15 owner-managers of delivery service SMEs operating in various locations within Accra, Ghana. The sample was diverse, reflecting key demographic and operational characteristics. Eight respondents were male, and seven were female, indicating a near-gender balance. This diversity ensures that the findings incorporate perspectives influenced by both male and female leadership styles.

The firms ranged in age from 5 to 9 years, with the majority being operational for at least 5 years, satisfying the study's inclusion criteria. This criterion ensured that the businesses had sufficient experience to provide valuable insights into managing diverse customer complaints. The firms' longevity also suggests stability and established practices, which enhance the robustness of the findings.

Table 6.1 Profile of respondents

Respondents	Position	Gender	Location	Age of firm	Number of staff
R1	Owner-managers	Male	Madina	6	3
R2	Owner-managers	Male	Haatso	5	5
R3	Owner-managers	Female	Lapaz	8	7
R4	Owner-managers	Male	Tema	5	4
R5	Owner-managers	Female	Pantang	5	8
R6	Owner-managers	Female	East Legon	6	11
R7	Owner-managers	Female	Cantoment	5	5
R8	Owner-managers	Female	Adabraka	7	5
R9	Owner-managers	Female	Osu	6	9
R10	Owner-managers	Male	La	5	3
R11	Owner-managers	Female	Dzowulu	7	8
R12	Owner-managers	Male	Amrahia	8	6
R13	Owner-managers	Male	Pokuasi	9	6
R14	Owner-managers	Male	Weija	6	10
R15	Owner-managers	Male	Dawhenya	5	3

The number of staff employed by these SMEs ranged from 3 to 11, reflecting the resource constraints typical of small businesses. This diversity in staff size contributes to the validity of the findings, as it highlights how complaint management strategies may vary depending on workforce capacity. Furthermore, the geographical spread of respondents—from urban hubs like Madina, Haatso, and East Legon to suburban areas like Dawhenya and Amrahia—ensures representation across different customer demographics and market dynamics within Accra.

The diverse profile of respondents strengthens the robustness of the study by ensuring that findings are not biased towards a specific gender, location, or firm size. The variation in operational contexts and staff sizes adds depth to the data, capturing the complexities of complaint management across SMEs. The inclusion of experienced firms enhances the validity of the findings, as insights are drawn from businesses with proven operational stability. Finally, the study's reliability is supported by the use of purposive sampling, ensuring that all respondents met stringent inclusion criteria, making the data consistent and trustworthy for future applications.

6.4.1 Emerging Themes

In the quest to find answers to the research objective, interviews were conducted with the permission of respondents, who consented to audio recordings and note-taking during the discussions. The recordings and notes were meticulously transcribed to ensure accuracy and to capture the nuanced perspectives of respondents.

The data were systematically sorted and categorized into codes relevant to the research questions. Using the Miles and Huberman qualitative data analysis technique, recurring ideas and statements were identified and grouped into codes. These codes were then organized into overarching themes based on their relevance to the study's objectives. This iterative process ensured that the themes directly addressed the complexities of managing customer complaints and enhancing service excellence in SMEs. After analysing the data, the following themes emerged:

1. Types of Complaints
2. Complaint Handling
3. Tailored Strategies for Different Types of Complainants
4. Challenges in Complaint Management
5. Impact of Complaint Management on Service Excellence
6. Learning and Continuous Improvement

On the types of customer complaints, delivery service SMEs reported various types of customer complaints, with delivery delays being the most common issue. R1 noted, "*Customers often complain about delays, particularly during rush hours and bad weather, making it difficult for us to maintain their trust and loyalty consistently.*" These delays are largely attributed to traffic congestion in Accra and logistical challenges. Miscommunication was another recurring complaint. R10 explained, "*Complaints about wrong delivery times or unclear details to riders are common, and they often frustrate customers who expect better communication from us during their delivery process.*" These issues highlight the need for improved communication strategies between the vendors and the delivery service firms to manage customer expectations. Damage to packages, particularly fragile items, was also a frequent source of dissatisfaction. R8 stated, "*Some complaints focus on goods arriving damaged or in poor condition, especially fragile items, which negatively impacts the trust customers place in our delivery services.*" This indicates a gap in handling and transportation protocols. Lastly, on the types of customer complaints, unclear charges emerged as a significant issue. R13 revealed, "*Several customers express dissatisfaction when they notice they have to pay for the delivery charges after delivery. They often feel misled by vendors that the price of the product they purchased include the delivery charges, which creates tension and demands for better transparency in billing.*" This underscores the importance of clear and upfront pricing structures between the vendors and delivery service firms.

Considering the types of customer complaints presented above, effective complaint handling is critical for managing customer dissatisfaction. Respondents emphasized the importance of prompt responses. R3 shared, "*Whenever complaints arise, we aim to respond within 24 hours to reassure customers that their issues are a priority and to show our commitment to excellent service.*" This approach helps mitigate customer frustration and demonstrates accountability. Apologies and empathy were also central to managing complaints. R9 explained, "*We ensure our riders and staff apologize sincerely, particularly when delays or damaged items are involved, showing empathy to reduce the frustration felt by our valued customers.*" This approach fosters trust and demonstrates customer-centric values. Compensation options, such as refunds and discounts, were frequently employed to resolve issues. R12 noted, "*To address customer dissatisfaction, we often provide refunds, discounts, or free deliveries to resolve issues and ensure they remain satisfied with our services despite the complaints.*" This helps retain customers and rebuild trust. Documentation practices were highlighted as essential for continuous improvement. R5 stated, "*We record every customer complaint in a log to track issues, analyze patterns, and improve training for staff, ensuring we learn and prevent recurring challenges in our operations.*" This systematic approach facilitates long-term improvements.

Tailoring strategies to different types of complainants is key to effective complaint management. After analysing the data, it came to light that passives often require proactive engagement. R7 noted, "*Quiet customers rarely express dissatisfaction openly, so we proactively reach out through calls or surveys to understand their needs and improve our services based on their silent feedback.*" It was also noted that irates demand immediate attention and resolution. R14 shared, "*Angry customers need immediate attention, so we prioritize resolving their complaints by offering refunds or replacements, ensuring they feel valued and reassured about our commitment to service.*" Voicers actively share feedback, making them valuable for improvement. R2 explained, "*Voicers actively share feedback, and we appreciate their constructive criticism by listening, engaging them in discussions, and incorporating their suggestions into our improvement strategies to build trust.*" Likewise, activists require transparency and accountability. R15 stated, "*Activists require transparent communication. We handle their complaints openly, engaging with them publicly when needed, and ensuring accountability to protect our reputation and foster confidence in our services.*"

From the data presented thus far, it was observed that SME delivery services in Accra face significant challenges in managing customer complaints effectively. Limited resources, such as insufficient staff and financial constraints, were a recurring issue. R4 explained, "*As a small business, our limited staff and financial resources make it difficult to handle high complaint volumes during peak seasons or periods of unexpected demand effectively.*" This limitation often leads to delayed resolutions and reduced customer satisfaction. Technology limitations further exacerbate complaint management challenges. R11 noted, "*The lack of advanced tracking systems in our operations results in delays and difficulties for customers, who expect updates and transparency throughout the delivery process.*" This highlights the need for investment in technology to streamline operations and enhance communication. Traffic congestion in Accra was another major challenge impacting timely service delivery. R6 shared, "*Accra's heavy traffic significantly affects our ability to deliver on time and resolve complaints quickly, creating added stress for our staff and dissatisfaction among customers.*" Traffic delays directly contribute to service failures, increasing the volume of complaints. High customer expectations also pose difficulties. R9 stated, "*Customers often expect immediate fixes to their problems, which is hard to achieve with our limited resources. Meeting these high expectations remains a recurring challenge for our team.*" The combination of high expectations and operational constraints makes balancing service quality and complaint resolution particularly demanding for SMEs.

Nevertheless, it is paramount to manage customer complaints effectively, since it has a profound impact on service excellence for delivery service SMEs. Retaining customer loyalty emerged as a key benefit. R1 shared, "*Effectively resolving complaints ensures that customers stay loyal to our brand. They feel reassured and appreciated, even when service issues occur, strengthening their connection to our business.*" Loyal customers contribute to sustained growth and positive brand reputation. Improved customer perceptions were another noted benefit. R8 explained, "*Handling complaints professionally and quickly improves our reputation. Customers see us as reliable and responsive, which enhances their overall perception of our brand.*" This underscores the role of effective complaint management in building trust and credibility. Reducing churn was also significant. R3 noted, "*Proper complaint handling minimizes customer attrition. Even after negative experiences, customers are more likely to stay if we manage their issues effectively and promptly.*" Retaining customers reduces the costs associated with acquiring new ones, ensuring stability. Lastly, on managing complaints, the insights gained from complaints drive operational improvements. R12 stated, "*The insights gained from complaints allow us to refine our delivery systems and operations, ensuring better services for our customers and fewer recurring problems.*" This feedback loop fosters continuous improvement and innovation, reinforcing the importance of customer feedback in achieving service excellence.

From the analysis presented above, it further came to light that continuous learning and improvement are critical for long-term success in managing complaints. Staff training emerged as a foundational strategy. R14 stated, "*We use data from customer complaints to train our staff, helping them develop the skills needed to prevent and handle future issues more effectively, which enhances service delivery.*" Training ensures employees are equipped to handle diverse challenges. Integrating customer feedback into operational strategies was also emphasized. R10 explained, "*Customer feedback is analyzed thoroughly and incorporated into our operational strategies, allowing us to address weaknesses and continuously improve our delivery services.*" This practice enables SMEs to adapt to customer needs effectively. Investments in technology were highlighted as a key area for improvement. R13 shared, "*To address recurring complaints about delays and miscommunication, we have started investing in advanced tracking tools to streamline our operations and meet customer expectations.*" These tools enhance transparency and efficiency. Preventive measures were another important focus. R6 noted, "*Analyzing past complaints helps us identify potential weak points in our operations, allowing us to implement measures that prevent similar issues from happening again in the future.*" This proactive approach reduces the likelihood of repeated complaints and enhances customer satisfaction.

6.5 Discussion and Conceptual Framework

SMEs face unique challenges in complaint handling, stemming from limited resources, high customer expectations, and operational constraints. It is for this reason that this study aimed to investigate how delivery service SMEs in Accra, Ghana, manage diverse customer complaints to enhance service excellence. Specifically, the study sought to identify effective strategies for managing complaints, categorize types of complainants, and explore the impact of these practices on service quality. The findings highlighted six main themes: types of complaints, complaint handling, tailored strategies for different types of complainants, challenges in complaint management, impact of complaint management on service excellence, and learning and continuous improvement. These themes align with the literature on service recovery, customer service excellence, and Attribution Theory, offering valuable insights into SMEs' approaches to handling complaints.

6.5.1 Categorizing Complaint Types and Response

The study identifies delivery delays, miscommunication, damaged packages, and hidden charges as the primary customer complaints. These findings align with Gouthier et al. (2012), who emphasize service reliability as a key determinant of customer satisfaction. Attribution Theory explains that customers often attribute service failures to controllable and stable factors, such as organizational inefficiencies or negligence (Sternad et al., 2019; Weiner, 1980). For example, respondents note that delivery delays result from traffic congestion and operational bottlenecks. While external factors like traffic may reduce perceived controllability, internal issues, such as poor planning, amplify dissatisfaction. This agrees with Manusov and Spitzberg's (2008) assertion that controllable failures elicit stronger negative responses. Addressing these complaints demands improved operational efficiency and transparency, as highlighted by respondents' calls for better communication strategies and clear pricing policies. Critically, the emphasis on hidden charges underscores a gap in customer engagement. Customers feel misled, reflecting a breakdown in procedural fairness, a key dimension of service recovery (Caballero-Morales, 2021). While SMEs recognize the issue, a more proactive approach to transparency and trust-building is essential to preempt such complaints.

In remedying these complaints, prompt responses, apologies and empathy, compensation options, and documentation practices emerge as central to effective complaint handling. These practices align with Levesque and McDougall (2000), who highlight interactional, procedural, and outcome fairness as critical to successful service recovery. The practice of prompt responses aligns with Kim (2007), who suggests that timely resolutions enhance perceptions of interactional fairness and build trust. Attribution Theory supports this by highlighting that swift and empathetic responses can shift customer attributions from organizational negligence to genuine effort (Chakraborty & Bhat, 2018). However, the study reveals gaps in consistency and resource allocation. While some SMEs excel in documenting complaints for long-term improvement, others lack systematic processes, limiting their ability to learn from feedback. This inconsistency raises concerns about scalability and sustainability, especially as SMEs grow (Nikolić et al., 2019). The findings also highlight the psychological impact of apologies and compensation. Respondents note that small gestures, such as refunds or discounts, significantly restore goodwill. This supports the service recovery paradox, where effective handling of minor failures can lead to higher post-recovery satisfaction than if no failure occurred (Krishna et al., 2011). However, reliance on compensation risks becoming costly, especially for resource-constrained SMEs, necessitating a balance between financial feasibility and customer satisfaction.

6.5.2 Strategies for Managing Different Types of Complaints and Its Challenges

The study categorizes complainants into passives, irates, voicers, and activists, mirroring Singh's (1990) typology. Tailored strategies, such as proactive engagement for passives and transparency for activists, align with Oliver (2014), who emphasizes customer segmentation in service recovery. Passives, who rarely voice dissatisfaction, challenge SMEs to adopt proactive feedback mechanisms. Respondents highlight the effectiveness of follow-up surveys, which align with the Attribution Theory principle of reducing ambiguity (Manusov & Spitzberg, 2008). By reaching out, SMEs can address latent dissatisfaction, fostering loyalty among silent customers. Managing irates requires immediate attention and resolution. Respondents prioritize refunds and personalized communication to mitigate anger. This aligns with Weiner's (1980) model, which suggests that customers are more forgiving when they perceive genuine effort to rectify controllable failures. For voicers, respondents emphasize constructive engagement and incorporating feedback into service improvement. This practice aligns with Gyung Kim et al. (2010), who identify voicers as critical to organizational learning. However, the findings reveal limited scalability, as SMEs often rely on ad hoc responses rather than institutionalized feedback systems. Activists, the most vocal and public complainants, require heightened transparency and accountability. Respondents' strategies, such as public engagement and open communication, align with Sharma et al. (2010), who emphasize trust restoration. However, handling activists demands significant resources, posing challenges for smaller SMEs. A structured approach to social media and public relations could mitigate these challenges (Hübner et al., 2018).

While SMEs may attempt to implement these strategies, it is worth noting that it may come with challenges such as limited resources, technology limitations, traffic congestion, and high customer expectations. These findings highlight systemic constraints that impede service recovery efforts (Caballero-Morales, 2021). Limited staff and finances exacerbate delays in complaint resolution. This finding aligns with Nurdiani and Alie (2023), who emphasize resource constraints as a key barrier to SME service excellence. While respondents acknowledge these challenges, few report leveraging collaborative networks or external funding to mitigate resource gaps, indicating a missed opportunity. Furthermore, technology limitations, such as the lack of tracking systems, further hinder SMEs' ability to provide timely updates. This gap contradicts customer expectations for transparency, as outlined in Clark and Baker (2007) on procedural fairness. Respondents' recognition of this issue underscores the need for affordable technological investments. Traffic congestion also represents an external factor beyond SMEs' control. Attribution Theory suggests that external attributions, such as traffic delays, reduce customer dissatisfaction compared to internal attributions (Chakraborty & Bhat, 2018). However, respondents note that customers' expectations for proactive communication remain unmet, reflecting a need for better contingency planning. High customer expectations intensify these challenges. Respondents' frustration with demanding customers highlights a tension between service ideals and operational realities. While Gouthier et al. (2012) acknowledge the difficulty of meeting rising expectations, the findings suggest that SMEs must focus on managing expectations through clear communication and realistic service guarantees.

6.5.3 Impact of Complaint Management on Service Excellence

Complaint management significantly enhances customer loyalty, perceptions, retention, and operational processes. These findings align with Sternad et al.'s (2019) assertion that effective recovery fosters trust and strengthens relationships. Retaining customer loyalty emerges as a primary benefit. Respondents emphasize that resolved complaints reassure customers, reducing churn. This aligns with Clark and Baker (2007) on the relational benefits of service recovery. Attribution Theory supports this, as successful recovery shifts customer attributions from systemic flaws to organizational competence. Reducing churn through complaint management reflects the financial value of customer retention (Manusov & Spitzberg, 2008). Respondents highlight the cost savings of retaining dissatisfied customers compared to acquiring new ones. Pizzutti dos Santos and Basso (2012) support this, emphasizing that loyal customers are more forgiving and less price-sensitive. Improved customer perceptions further validate the importance of complaint management. Respondents note that professional handling enhances brand reputation. This finding aligns with the SERVQUAL model, which highlights responsiveness and assurance as key drivers of perceived quality (Sternad et al., 2019). However, inconsistent practices among SMEs risk undermining these benefits, emphasizing the need for standardization.

Operational improvements, driven by complaint insights, represent a critical outcome. Respondents' focus on using feedback to refine processes aligns with continuous improvement frameworks. However, the findings reveal limited institutionalization of learning mechanisms, suggesting room for more structured approaches to leveraging feedback (Kim, 2007). Nevertheless, it is important for SMEs to prioritize staff training, feedback integration, technology investments, and preventive measures as pillars of continuous improvement (Nurdiani & Alie, 2023). These findings align with Den Hartog and Verburg (2002), who emphasize the iterative nature of service excellence, as staff training emerges as foundational. Respondents emphasize using complaint data to upskill employees, aligning with Caballero-Morales (2021) on employee empowerment. However, the findings reveal disparities in training quality, reflecting resource constraints. Integrating feedback into operational strategies underscores the importance of customer insights. Respondents' practices align with Nikolić et al. (2019), who advocate for feedback loops. However, limited scalability and documentation risk reduce long-term impact. Technology investments also address recurring issues, such as tracking and communication gaps. Respondents' efforts align with Kumar and Kumar (2016) on the role of technology in enhancing procedural fairness. However, high costs remain a barrier for many SMEs, highlighting the need for affordable solutions. Preventive measures, informed by past complaints, reflect proactive management. Respondents' focus on identifying weak points aligns with continuous improvement models. However, the findings reveal limited cross-organizational learning, suggesting opportunities for industry-wide collaboration.

6.5.4 A Conceptual Model for Managing Customer Complaints to Enhance Service Excellence for SMEs

After analysing the data, Fig. 6.1 presents a conceptual model for managing customer complaints to enhance service excellence for SMEs. This model suggests that complaint identification will lead to engagement and response. SMEs begin by identifying complaints through customer feedback or operational monitoring. This stage sets the foundation for engaging customers and addressing their issues, followed by engagement and response leading to resolution. Once a complaint is identified, engagement with the customer follows. Empathy, apologies, and compensation foster trust and pave the way for effective resolutions. However, tailored strategies for complainant type may influence resolution. Tailoring strategies based on customer behaviour (e.g., passives, irates, activists) enhances the effectiveness of engagement. Respondents emphasize that understanding customer psychology, as explained by Attribution Theory, ensures that responses meet specific needs and expectations. Furthermore, continuous learning and feedback integration may enhance or constrain the entire process. Effective integration of feedback improves complaint

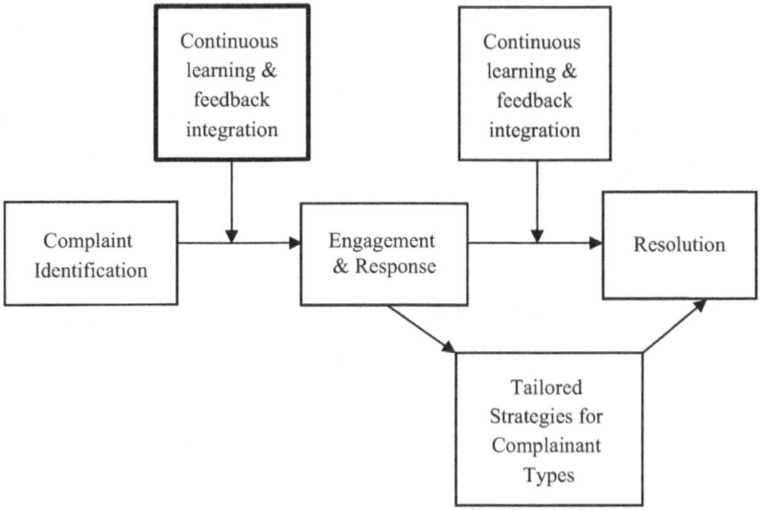

Fig. 6.1 Conceptual model for managing customer complaints. Source: (Author's Construct, 2024)

identification and resolution. The model's propositions are presented below:

P_1: Complaint identification leads to engagement and response.
P_2: Engagement and response lead to resolution.
P_3: Tailored strategies for complainant types may influence how engagement and response lead to resolution.
P_4: Continuous learning and feedback integration may enhance or constrain how complaint identification leads to engagement and response.
P_5: Continuous learning and feedback integration may enhance or constrain how engagement and response lead to resolution.

6.6 Conclusion and Implications

The findings of this study underscore the complexities and opportunities inherent in managing customer complaints within SME delivery services in Accra, Ghana. The research highlights that effective complaint management is a multifaceted process requiring careful attention to complaint identification, tailored engagement strategies, resolution mechanisms, and continuous improvement practices. This structured approach not only addresses immediate customer dissatisfaction but also strengthens the organization's capacity for service excellence and competitiveness.

One significant implication is the need for SMEs to institutionalize processes that ensure consistent and proactive complaint management. By adopting structured complaint identification systems, SMEs can engage dissatisfied customers more effectively, transforming negative experiences into opportunities for trust-building and loyalty. This aligns with Attribution Theory, which emphasizes the importance of shifting customer perceptions from organizational failure to genuine recovery efforts.

The research also highlights the critical role of tailored strategies for different complainant types. By understanding customer behaviours, such as the passivity of silent customers or the vocal tendencies of activists, SMEs can implement targeted interventions that address specific needs. This approach aligns with existing literature emphasizing customer segmentation as a key driver of service recovery success.

Continuous learning and feedback integration emerge as essential components of the complaint management process. SMEs that actively analyse feedback and incorporate insights into operational strategies are better positioned to adapt to evolving customer expectations. This iterative process fosters a culture of innovation and improvement, enhancing both service quality and organizational resilience.

However, the findings also reveal critical challenges, such as resource limitations, technological gaps, and rising customer expectations. Addressing these barriers requires a combination of internal strategies and external support, such as collaborative networks or funding initiatives. Policymakers and industry stakeholders can play a pivotal role in supporting SMEs through capacity-building programs and access to affordable technologies.

The originality of this study lies in its contribution to the Attribution Theory and the broader understanding of complaint management in resource-constrained environments. It offers actionable insights for

SMEs, emphasizing the need for structured, customer-centric strategies that align with theoretical frameworks and practical realities. By addressing the identified gaps and leveraging the proposed process map, SMEs can enhance their service excellence and sustain long-term growth.

6.7 Limitations and Future Research Directions

While this study provides valuable insights, it is not without limitations. First, the research focuses exclusively on delivery service SMEs in Accra, Ghana, which may limit the generalizability of findings to other regions or industries. Future research could expand the geographical scope to include rural areas or other urban centres, providing a more comprehensive understanding of complaint management practices across diverse contexts.

Second, the reliance on qualitative methods, while rich in detail, may introduce subjectivity in data interpretation. Although the study employs rigorous coding and thematic analysis, incorporating quantitative approaches in future research could enhance the robustness of findings. For instance, surveys could be used to quantify the prevalence of specific complaints or the effectiveness of different recovery strategies. Furthermore, future research can also test the propositions of the conceptual model for managing customer complaints to enhance service excellence for SMEs quantitatively.

Third, the study focuses primarily on SME perspectives, potentially overlooking customer viewpoints. Understanding customer expectations and satisfaction levels would provide a more holistic perspective on complaint management. Future studies could adopt a dual-perspective approach, gathering data from both SMEs and their customers to identify potential gaps and align strategies with customer needs. Additionally, the study identifies resource constraints and technological limitations as significant challenges for SMEs. Future research could explore innovative solutions, such as affordable technology platforms or collaborative partnerships, to address these barriers. Investigating the role of government policies and industry associations in supporting SMEs' capacity for complaint management would also be valuable.

Finally, while this study highlights the importance of continuous learning and feedback integration, it does not delve deeply into the mechanisms for institutionalizing these practices. Future research could examine specific tools or frameworks that SMEs can adopt to create sustainable feedback loops and foster a culture of continuous improvement. In conclusion, this study lays the foundation for further exploration of complaint management practices in SMEs. By addressing the identified limitations and pursuing the suggested research directions, future studies can contribute to a deeper and more nuanced understanding of this critical aspect of service excellence.

References

Akpabli, D. A. (2019). *Entrepreneurial capability, institutional factors and SME performance in Ghana*. University of Ghana. http://ugspace.ug.edu.gh/handle/123456789/32660

Aksoy, M., & Yilmaz, Ö. (2022). Consumer complaints and complaint management in the tourism sector. In *Managing risk and decision making in times of economic distress, part A* (Vol. 108, pp. 95–111). Emerald Publishing Limited.

Albrecht, A. K., Walsh, G., & Beatty, S. E. (2017). Perceptions of group versus individual service failures and their effects on customer outcomes: The role of attributions and customer entitlement. *Journal of Service Research, 20*(2), 188–203.

Badghish, S., & Shagagi, A. (2023). Factors influencing consumer complaint intentions: Saudi online shopping. *International Journal of Business and Management, 18*(4), 69.

Bitner, M. J., Booms, B. H., & Tetreault, M. S. (1990). The service encounter: diagnosing favorable and unfavorable incidents. *Journal of marketing, 54*(1), 71–84.

Caballero-Morales, S. O. (2021). Innovation as recovery strategy for SMEs in emerging economies during the COVID-19 pandemic. *Research in International Business and Finance, 57*, 101396.

Chakraborty, U., & Bhat, S. (2018). The effects of credible online reviews on brand equity dimensions and its consequence on consumer behavior. *Journal of Promotion Management, 24*(1), 57–82.

Cho, Y. C., & Song, J. (2012). The effects of customer dissatisfaction on switching behavior in the service sector. *Journal of Business & Economics Research (Online), 10*(10), 579.
Clark, M., & Baker, S. (2007). *Business success through service excellence.* Routledge.
Clavel, N., & Pomey, M. P. (2020). Enhancing patient involvement in quality improvement: How complaint managers see their roles and limitations. *Patient Experience Journal, 7*(3), 112–118.
Creswell, J. W. (2013). *Research design: Qualitative, quantitative, and mixed methods approaches*. Sage Publications.
Den Hartog, D. N., & Verburg, R. M. (2002). Service excellence from the employees' point of view: The role of first line supervisors. *Managing Service Quality: An International Journal, 12*(3), 159–164.
DeWitt, T., & Brady, M. K. (2003). Rethinking service recovery strategies: The effect of rapport on consumer responses to service failure. *Journal of Service Research, 6*(2), 193–207.
Do, D. K. X., Rahman, K., & Robinson, L. J. (2020). Determinants of negative customer engagement behaviours. *Journal of Services Marketing, 34*(2), 117–135.
Folkes, V. S. (1984). Consumer reactions to product failure: An attributional approach. *Journal of consumer research, 10*(4), 398–409.
Ghana Statistical Service, GSS. (2016). *The integrated business establishment survey report.* GSS. Retrieved January 4, 2023, from http://www.statsghana.gov.gh
Gouthier, M., Giese, A., & Bartl, C. (2012). Service excellence models: A critical discussion and comparison. *Managing Service Quality: An International Journal, 22*(5), 447–464.
Gyung Kim, M., Wang, C., & Mattila, A. S. (2010). The relationship between consumer complaining behavior and service recovery: An integrative review. *International Journal of Contemporary Hospitality Management, 22*(7), 975–991.
Heider, F. (1958). *The psychology of interpersonal relations*. New York: Wiley.
Hübner, D., Wagner, S. M., & Kurpjuweit, S. (2018). The service recovery paradox in B2B relationships. *Journal of Business & Industrial Marketing, 33*(3), 291–302.
Kim, G. S. (2007). The service recovery strategies, customer satisfaction, customer loyalty. *Asian Journal on Quality, 8*(1), 76–86.
Kim, K., & Baker, M. A. (2020). The customer isn't always right: The implications of illegitimate complaints. *Cornell Hospitality Quarterly, 61*(2), 113–127.

Knox, G., & Van Oest, R. (2014). Customer complaints and recovery effectiveness: A customer base approach. *Journal of Marketing, 78*(5), 42–57.

Krishna, A., Dangayach, G. S., & Jain, R. (2011). A conceptual framework for the service recovery paradox. *The Marketing Review, 11*(1), 41–56.

Kumar, M., & Kumar, N. (2016). Three dimensions of service recovery: Examining relationship and impact. *Supply Chain Management: An International Journal, 21*(2), 273–286.

Levesque, T. J., & McDougall, G. H. (1996). Customer dissatisfaction: The relationship between types of problems and customer response. *Canadian Journal of Administrative Sciences/Revue Canadienne des Sciences de l'Administration, 13*(3), 264–276.

Levesque, T. J., & McDougall, G. H. (2000). Service problems and recovery strategies: An experiment. *Canadian Journal of Administrative Sciences/Revue Canadienne des Sciences de l'Administration, 17*(1), 20–37.

Lewis, B. R., & McCann, P. (2004). Service failure and recovery: Evidence from the hotel industry. *International Journal of Contemporary Hospitality Management, 16*(1), 6–17.

Mahato, S., Dixit, A. R., Agrawal, R., Antony, J., Garza-Reyes, J. A., & Jamwal, A. (2024). An empirical investigation on the deployment of operational excellence in SMEs. *Benchmarking: An International Journal, 31*(9), 3190–3215.

Malhotra, N., & Birks, D. (2007). *Marketing research: An applied approach: 3rd European edition*. Harlow Prentice Hall Financial Times.

Manusov, V., & Spitzberg, B. (2008). *Attribution theory. Engaging theories in interpersonal communication: Multiple perspectives* (pp. 37–49).

Michel, S., & Meuter, M. L. (2008). The service recovery paradox: True but overrated? *International Journal of Service Industry Management, 19*(4), 441–457.

Miles, M. B., & Huberman, A. M. (1994). Qualitative data analysis: An expanded sourcebook. *Thousand Oaks: Sage Publications*, 338.

Miller, J. L., Craighead, C. W., & Karwan, K. R. (2000). Service recovery: A framework and empirical investigation. *Journal of Operations Management, 18*(4), 387–400.

Narayanan, S., & Singh, G. A. (2024). From stimulus to response: Understanding the causes and outcomes of consumer activism. *Journal of Consumer Behaviour*.

Nguyen, T. A. (2019). *Improving organizational performance by implementing customer complaint management through socio economic approach to management in a case study of SME*. Doctoral dissertation, Université de Strasbourg.

Nikolić, N., Jovanović, I., Nikolić, Đ., Mihajlović, I., & Schulte, P. (2019). Investigation of the factors influencing SME failure as a function of its prevention and fast recovery after failure. *Entrepreneurship Research Journal, 9*(3), 20170030.

Nurdiani, T. W., & Alie, R. M. (2023). Build a service excellence culture of pleasure to customers. *Ejoin: Jurnal Pengabdian Masyarakat, 1*(1), 29–34.

Oliver, R. L. (2014). *Satisfaction: A behavioral perspective on the consumer: A behavioral perspective on the consumer*. Routledge.

Parasuraman, A., Zeithaml, V. A., & Berry, L. L. (1988). Servqual: A multiple-item scale for measuring consumer perc. *Journal of Retailing, 64*(1), 12.

Pizzutti dos Santos, C., & Basso, K. (2012). Do ongoing relationships buffer the effects of service recovery on customers' trust and loyalty? *International Journal of Bank Marketing, 30*(3), 168–192.

Sahaf, T. M., & Fazili, A. I. (2024). Service failure and service recovery: A hybrid review and research agenda. *International Journal of Consumer Studies, 48*(1), e12974.

Sharma, P., Marshall, R., Alan Reday, P., & Na, W. (2010). Complainers versus non-complainers: A multi-national investigation of individual and situational influences on customer complaint behaviour. *Journal of Marketing Management, 26*(1–2), 163–180.

Singh, J. (1990). A typology of consumer dissatisfaction response styles. *Journal of Retailing, 66*(1), 57.

Sternad, D., Krenn, M., & Schmid, S. (2019). Business excellence for SMEs: Motives, obstacles, and size-related adaptations. *Total Quality Management & Business Excellence, 30*(1–2), 151–168.

Weiner, B. (1980). A cognitive (attribution)-emotion-action model of motivated behavior: An analysis of judgments of help-giving. *Journal of Personality and Social Psychology, 39*(2), 186.

Zeithaml, V. A. (1990). Delivering quality service: Balancing customer perceptions and expectations. *Simon and Schuster google schola, 2*, 791–824.

7

SMEs in the Fourth Industrial Revolution: A Marketing Shift

Charles Asare, William Asamoah Owusu, Derrick Nukunu Akude, Emelia Amoako Asiedu, and Kwame Ntim Sekyere

7.1 Introduction

SMEs are vital drivers of economic growth due to their ability to address societal challenges, adapt to market changes, and foster job creation and innovation, especially in emerging economies (Kumar & Gupta, 2020a; Johnson, 2019). To sustain their competitive edge and support economic growth in the evolving consumer landscape, SMEs must revise their marketing strategies in response to the Fourth Industrial Revolution. These marketing strategies adaptation are characterized by advancements in

C. Asare (✉) • W. A. Owusu • D. N. Akude • K. N. Sekyere
Ghana Communication Technology University, Accra, Ghana
e-mail: casare@gctu.edu.gh; wasamoahowusu@gctu.edu.gh; dakude@gctu.edu.gh; ksekyere@gctu.edu.gh

E. Amoako Asiedu
Department of Marketing, Ghana Communication Technology University, Accra, Ghana
e-mail: easiedu@gctu.edu.gh

E. Amoako Asiedu et al. (eds.), *Entrepreneurship and Small and Medium-Sized Enterprises (SMEs) in Africa*, https://doi.org/10.1007/978-3-032-14174-3_7

digital technologies, artificial intelligence, and data analytics. While these innovations offer new ways to engage with customers and improve operations, they also demand continuous adaptation to meet the needs of increasingly tech-savvy consumers (Johnson, 2019).

According to Batat (2024), the marketing mix includes the 4Ps (product, price, place, and promotion) used to create tangible offerings, alongside the 7Ps (product, price, place, promotion, people, processes, and physical evidence) which are utilized for service design. While both the 4Ps and 7Ps play a crucial role in the company's marketing strategy, this chapter focuses on the 4Ps. The traditional 4Ps marketing framework—Product, Price, Place, and Promotion—has long been a cornerstone of marketing strategies, guiding SMEs in product development, pricing, distribution, and promotion (Brown & Lee, 2020). However, this model often emphasizes the business's perspective over the evolving needs and preferences of customers, which can limit an SME's ability to engage effectively with its market. Today's consumers are more informed and empowered, demanding personalized experiences, convenience, and transparency. The conventional 4Ps framework does not fully address these modern consumer expectations. Therefore, necessitating a shift toward a customer-centric approach (Kumar & Gupta, 2020b).

This chapter explores how SMEs can transition from the traditional 4Ps model to the 4Cs framework—Customer, Cost, Convenience, and Communication—proposed by Robert F. Lauterborn in 1990. The 4Cs model centers marketing strategies on customer needs, aligning business efforts with customer preferences to create value. This leads to a shift from a company and "product-centric approach to a more experience-centric way of thinking" (Batat, 2024, p. 101) to foster long-term relationships.

7.2 Understanding SME Customer Relationships

SMEs excel in developing strong customer relationships by providing personalized solutions and maintaining high levels of customer satisfaction (Brown & Wilson, 2021a). This personalized approach gives SMEs a competitive edge, allowing them to respond quickly to customer needs, a challenge that larger companies often face due to their complex structures (Smith, 2020a). Direct engagement with customers fosters a sense of community and loyalty, creating an environment where customers feel valued and understood. This sense of belonging enhances customer retention and advocacy, as satisfied customers are more likely to recommend the business to others (Johnson & Lee, 2019a).

SMEs' ability to build close relationships is rooted in their capacity for individualized engagement. Unlike large organizations with multiple management layers and automated processes, SMEs can interact directly with customers, gather feedback, address complaints, and customize offerings to meet individual preferences (Kumar & Gupta, 2020c). This high level of customer care is appreciated, leading to repeat business and long-term loyalty (Brown & Wilson, 2021a). Beyond transactions, these relationships involve emotional and psychological connections, focusing on creating a positive and memorable customer experience. However, this requires active listening, empathy, and prioritizing the customer's well-being (Johnson & Lee, 2019b).

Again, emotional bonds are formed by consistently delivering exceptional experiences that build trust and satisfaction. SMEs can train employees in customer service skills, particularly empathy and active listening, and use customer relationship management (CRM) tools. This will help to track preferences and predict needs (Smith, 2020a). Essentially, psychological connections develop when customers identify with the company's values and mission. Hence, SMEs can strengthen these connections by aligning their business practices with the values and interests of their customers, such as emphasizing sustainability and ethical sourcing (Johnson & Lee, 2019c).

To establish and maintain these emotional and psychological bonds, SMEs must remain dedicated to a customer-centric approach. This can be achieved by continuously improving the customer experience through feedback, quick complaint resolution, and showing appreciation for loyalty (Smith, 2020a). Small gestures, like personalized thank-you and exclusive offers, can enhance the emotional and psychological connection with the company (Kumar & Gupta, 2020d). Ultimately, SMEs' ability to deliver personalized solutions and maintain customer satisfaction is a significant advantage. This can drive long-term business success by fostering customer loyalty and advocacy (Brown & Wilson, 2021a).

7.3 Identifying Customer Needs and Preferences

SMEs possess a significant advantage in understanding customer needs and preferences due to their ability to establish close, personal relationships with their clientele (Brown & Wilson, 2021a). Their smaller scale allows for direct interactions, ensuring that feedback is quickly addressed rather than lost in bureaucratic layers, which is often the case in larger organizations (Smith, 2020a). SMEs gather first-hand feedback through various methods, including in-person interactions, phone calls, and digital communication channels. This provides direct insights into customer perceptions of their products or services. Informal interactions, such as casual conversations during sales or social media engagement, capture genuine customer sentiments that structured surveys might miss (Johnson & Lee, 2019d; Kumar & Gupta, 2020a).

Community involvement further enhances SMEs' understanding of customer behavior. By being deeply integrated into their communities, SMEs gain valuable insights into their customers' lifestyles, aspirations, and challenges. This involvement ranges from sponsoring local events to participating in business associations, keeping them informed about broader market trends and shifts (Brown & Wilson, 2021b; Smith, 2020a). Leveraging these insights allows SMEs to develop value propositions that resonate with their target audience by understanding not only current customer needs but also anticipating future demands and preferences (Johnson & Lee, 2019a).

SMEs can quickly adapt to feedback and market trends, providing highly tailored and relevant solutions without the need for complex processes that larger organizations require. This agility enables SMEs to deliver products and services that meet immediate customer needs. This enhances satisfaction and provides a competitive advantage (Brown & Wilson, 2021c). By integrating customer feedback into strategic planning, SMEs ensure that product iterations align with customer expectations and that marketing efforts effectively engage their target audience (Kumar & Gupta, 2020b).

The close relationships between SMEs and their customers foster high levels of trust and loyalty. This encourages customers to share honest feedback. This ongoing dialogue improves products and services and strengthens customer relationships. This further turns customers into advocates for the business (Smith, 2020a). Overall, SMEs' ability to deeply understand customer needs is a critical asset that enhances their success. This provides a competitive edge and fosters customer satisfaction and loyalty (Johnson & Lee, 2019a).

7.4 Building Trust and Loyalty

Trust and loyalty are vital for the success of SMEs. Building trust starts with consistently delivering high-quality products and services to ensure customers can rely on the business to meet their needs effectively (Brown & Wilson, 2021a). Reliable service fosters customer confidence, as they trust that the brand will maintain high standards with every interaction. Clear and transparent communication is also crucial for building trust. SMEs should provide straightforward information about their offerings, services, and policies, which makes customers feel informed and valued. This further reduces any uncertainties they might have about the business (Smith, 2020a). Open communication, regular updates, and thorough explanations can help mitigate any negative impacts and bolster trust, especially during challenges (Johnson & Lee, 2019a; Kumar & Gupta, 2020a).

Adhering to ethical standards is another key component in establishing trust. Customers are increasingly concerned with the ethical practices of companies they support, including employee relations, sourcing, and environmental impact (Brown & Wilson, 2021a). SMEs committed to ethical standards can differentiate themselves and attract customers who value corporate responsibility. This enhances their reputation and customer loyalty (Smith, 2020a). To foster customer loyalty, SMEs should focus on creating positive experiences at every touchpoint, from product quality to customer service. Exceptional customer service and exceeding expectations can turn one-time transactions into long-term relationships (Johnson & Lee, 2019a).

Implementing loyalty programs and offering incentives for repeat purchases further cultivates loyalty. Programs such as discounts, personalized rewards, and special offers create a sense of appreciation and encourage customers to continue doing business with the SME (Kumar & Gupta, 2020d). Personalized touches, like birthday messages or exclusive previews, also strengthen the customer-company bond (Smith, 2020a). Active community engagement enhances trust and loyalty. SMEs that support local events, charities, and initiatives demonstrate their commitment to the community, humanizing the business and fostering stronger local customer connections (Brown & Wilson, 2021a).

These efforts help retain customers and turn them into brand ambassadors who promote the business through positive word-of-mouth. Customers who trust and are loyal to a company are more likely to recommend it to others, increasing the business's reach and attracting new customers (Kumar & Gupta, 2020a). By prioritizing trust and loyalty, SMEs can build strong, lasting relationships with their customers, leading to sustainable success in a competitive market (Johnson & Lee, 2019a).

7.5 The Conventional Marketing Mix (4Ps) and SMEs

The conventional marketing mix, known as the 4Ps (Product, Price, Place, Promotion), is a longstanding framework in marketing. It provides a structured approach for businesses to market their products effectively (Kotler & Keller, 2016). This model focuses on four key areas: product, price, place, and promotion (Kotler & Armstrong, 2018; Baker, 2018a; Monroe, 2019; Schiffman & Kanuk, 2019).

The 4Ps framework offers both benefits and drawbacks for SMEs. One advantage is that it provides a straightforward structure for SMEs to develop their marketing strategies, especially for those with limited resources or expertise (Smith, 2020a). By using this model, SMEs can systematically develop their products, set strategic prices, choose suitable distribution channels, and design effective promotional campaigns (Brown & Wilson, 2021a; Johnson & Lee, 2019a).

7.5.1 Product

SMEs often focus on creating products for niche markets, allowing them to cater to specific segments that larger companies may overlook. By identifying unique demands and gaps within these niches, SMEs can develop specialized products that address particular problems or preferences, gaining a competitive advantage and cultivating a loyal customer base (Smith, 2020a; Brown & Wilson, 2021a). However, an overemphasis on product innovation and customization can risk neglecting shifting consumer preferences. The market constantly evolves with emerging trends, technologies, and changing behaviors influencing demand. SMEs that prioritize product development without ongoing customer engagement may miss shifts in consumer expectations. This can potentially lead to decreased satisfaction and sales (Johnson & Lee, 2019a; Kumar & Gupta, 2020a).

To mitigate this risk, SMEs should balance product innovation with continuous market research and customer feedback. Regular data collection through surveys, focus groups, and direct interactions is essential to align product development with market needs (Kotler & Armstrong, 2018). Utilizing data analytics to track and analyze consumer behavior over time provides deeper insights into customer satisfaction and loyalty. This informs more effective product decisions (Baker, 2018a). An agile, iterative approach to product development, including small adjustments tested with limited user groups, can reduce the risk of misalignment with consumer expectations (Schiffman & Kanuk, 2019). Open and honest communication with customers about product changes further aligns development with evolving preferences. This demonstrates a commitment to continual improvement (Smith, 2020a; Kotler & Keller, 2016).

7.5.2 Price

SMEs must consider several factors when developing pricing strategies: cost structures, competitive positioning, and perceived value. Details of the pricing strategies follow.

Cost Structure SMEs need to manage their cost structures, including raw materials, labor, and overhead, to avoid setting prices that jeopardize profitability. A thorough understanding of these costs helps in establishing a price that covers expenses and ensures a profit margin (Smith, 2020a).

Competitive Positioning Pricing should reflect how an SME positions itself in the market. If positioned as a premium brand with superior quality, pricing should mirror this differentiation. Conversely, for those competing on price, it's crucial to ensure prices are competitive while covering costs (Brown & Wilson, 2021a).

Perceived Value The customer's perception of a product's value influences their willingness to pay. Effective communication of a product's unique benefits, such as quality and innovation, is essential. When customers perceive high value, they are more willing to accept higher prices (Johnson & Lee, 2019a). SMEs often use flexible pricing strategies like discounts, promotions, and tiered pricing to attract and retain customers. Effective value communication is critical. SMEs should highlight their products' unique features and benefits through marketing campaigns, social media, and customer testimonials (Kotler & Armstrong, 2018). Ongoing feedback and data collection are necessary for refining pricing strategies. Analyzing sales performance, market research, and customer feedback helps SMEs stay competitive and responsive (Baker, 2018a). Advanced strategies like dynamic and psychological pricing can further boost revenue (Monroe, 2019; Schiffman & Kanuk, 2019).

In summary, balancing competitive pricing with clear value communication is key for SMEs to ensure their products are seen as worthwhile investments, driving business growth and success (Brown & Wilson, 2021a).

7.5.3 Place

The choice of distribution channels is pivotal for SMEs as it significantly impacts their product accessibility, market reach, and sales success.

Efficient distribution strategies ensure timely and convenient product availability. This boosts customer satisfaction and facilitates business growth (Smith, 2021a). SMEs often use local markets, online platforms, and direct sales to connect with their target customers.

Local marketplaces allow SMEs to build strong community ties and a loyal customer base. Participation in local events like farmers' markets and community fairs enables direct customer engagement, prompt feedback, and personal relationships. This fosters trust and long-term success (Brown & Wilson, 2022).

Online platforms are essential for SMEs, offering a cost-effective way to reach a broader audience. E-commerce websites, social media platforms, and online marketplaces such as Amazon and eBay help SMEs expand beyond local areas. These platforms reduce overhead costs compared to physical stores that operate 24/7, resulting in significant business growth (Johnson & Lee, 2020a).

Direct sales, which involve selling products directly to customers without intermediaries, allow SMEs to manage customer experience and retain more earnings. Methods include door-to-door sales, home parties, or online sales through the company's website. This approach is particularly effective for SMEs with specialized or high-value products, enabling personalized service and deeper client relationships.

To adapt to the rise of e-commerce and digital marketplaces, SMEs must rethink traditional distribution strategies. Customers now expect seamless, convenient, and prompt purchasing experiences. SMEs should enhance their online presence with user-friendly e-commerce websites featuring detailed product descriptions, high-resolution images, customer reviews, and secure payment options (Kotler & Armstrong, 2019).

Partnering with established online marketplaces can extend SMEs' reach and provide tools for managing inventory, processing orders, and marketing products. Listing on well-known e-commerce platforms increases visibility and attracts potential buyers (Monroe, 2021a). Social media also plays a crucial role in enhancing distribution strategies. This is achieved via driving traffic to e-commerce sites, generating engaging content, and gathering customer insights (Schiffman & Kanuk, 2020).

Adopting an omnichannel distribution approach, integrating online and offline channels, can further improve convenience and sales. Options like buy online, pick up in-store (BOPIS), and consistent pricing across channels cater to customer preferences (Baker, 2019a). Investing in logistics and supply chain management is vital for meeting customer expectations for timely delivery, potentially through third-party logistics or advanced technology solutions (Smith, 2021a).

Overall, selecting the right distribution channels is essential for SMEs to ensure product accessibility and business success. Embracing online platforms, omnichannel strategies, and investing in logistics can drive market penetration and continuous growth (Brown & Wilson, 2022).

7.5.4 Promotion

SMEs often blend conventional and digital marketing techniques to maximize their reach while managing financial constraints. Instead of simply seeking goods, SMEs now pursue experiences that unfold in hybrid, phygital environments (Batat, 2024). The blending of physical and digital elements, along with technological advancements and environmental shifts, has prompted companies to rethink their marketing strategies, moving away from a product-centered focus toward a more experience-driven approach. Due to limited resources, SMEs employ inventive, cost-effective advertising strategies to capture their target audience's attention (Smith, 2021a).

Traditional marketing remains significant for SMEs, with word-of-mouth being particularly influential. Positive customer recommendations can greatly affect potential buyers. To encourage such recommendations, SMEs must deliver exceptional products and services. Local advertising methods—such as community newspaper ads, event sponsorships, and flyer distribution—can also enhance visibility and foster community trust, promoting customer loyalty and repeat business (Brown & Wilson, 2022).

Digital marketing has opened new avenues for SMEs to engage with customers and build brand recognition. Social media platforms like Facebook, Instagram, Twitter, and LinkedIn offer cost-effective ways to reach a larger audience. By creating engaging content, running targeted advertisements, and interacting with followers, SMEs can boost their visibility and connect personally with potential customers (Johnson & Lee, 2020b).

Electronic mail marketing is another economical digital strategy, allowing SMEs to send personalized communications and promotions directly to their audience. Tailored email campaigns, supported by performance data, can effectively target specific segments. Content marketing, including blogs, videos, and infographics, helps SMEs establish expertise, drive website traffic, and improve search engine rankings. Distributing content through digital platforms further extends its reach (Kotler & Armstrong, 2019).

Search engine optimization (SEO) is crucial for enhancing online visibility. By optimizing websites and content with relevant keywords, SMEs can improve search rankings and attract quality traffic (Monroe, 2021a). Paid advertising platforms like Google and social media, enable targeted engagement and real-time performance monitoring. Pay-per-click (PPC) advertising is particularly effective for lead generation (Schiffman & Kanuk, 2020).

Collaborations and influencer partnerships can also amplify promotional efforts, helping SMEs expand their reach and leverage the influence of others (Baker, 2019b). By combining traditional and digital marketing strategies, SMEs can enhance brand presence, engage their audience, and drive business growth (Brown & Wilson, 2022).

7.6 Limitations of the 4Ps Framework

The 4Ps framework has notable limitations, particularly in addressing customer-focused aspects of marketing. While it offers a structured approach to strategy development, it tends to prioritize the business's perspective over evolving customer needs and preferences. This potentially hinders deep engagement and long-term relationship building (Smith, 2021a; Brown & Wilson, 2022).

The 4Ps focus on controllable elements like product attributes, pricing strategies, distribution channels, and promotional tactics, but this narrow view often overlooks the complexity of customer behavior influenced by cultural trends, technological advancements, competition, and social factors (Johnson & Lee, 2020a). Additionally, the framework's traditional unidirectional communication approach does not account for the interactive and participative nature of modern marketing, where customer engagement and peer influence play significant roles (Kotler & Armstrong, 2019).

Furthermore, the 4Ps often neglect the importance of emotional connections and trust, which are critical for customer loyalty. It emphasizes transactional aspects over intangible elements like brand reputation and customer service (Monroe, 2021a). SMEs focusing solely on the 4Ps may miss opportunities to differentiate based on these key factors, impacting their competitiveness (Schiffman & Kanuk, 2020).

The framework also falls short in addressing contemporary concerns such as sustainability and social responsibility. As consumers increasingly demand ethical practices, SMEs that overlook these factors risk losing socially conscious customers (Baker, 2019a). To overcome these limitations, SMEs should adopt a customer-centric approach, integrating customer feedback and adapting strategies to meet changing demands for more effective and enduring growth (Smith, 2021a).

7.7 Evolving Nature of Consumers in the Fourth Industrial Revolution

In the Fourth Industrial Revolution, consumers are more informed, connected, and empowered, with easy access to product comparisons, reviews, and shared experiences via social media. They now seek not just competitive pricing but meaningful interactions, blended with physical and digital elements (Batat, 2024), aligned with their values and lifestyles. Trust in transparency, authenticity, and ethical practices is crucial. The traditional 4Ps framework falls short in addressing these modern consumer expectations. To meet today's demands, businesses must adopt a customer-centric approach, focusing on personalized experiences, fostering long-term relationships, and delivering exceptional service and innovative solutions for sustainable growth (Smith, 2021a; Brown & Wilson, 2022; Kotler & Armstrong, 2019).

7.8 Customer Relationship Management (CRM) in the Fourth Industrial Revolution

The Fourth Industrial Revolution, driven by advances in AI, machine learning, IoT, blockchain, and big data, significantly impacts corporate processes and customer interactions (Smith, 2021a). For SMEs, the rapid pace of technological change poses challenges in integrating new tools with existing systems, particularly due to limited resources and concerns over cybersecurity and data privacy (Brown & Wilson, 2022). However, digital transformation also offers SMEs exceptional opportunities for enhancing customer relationship management (CRM). By leveraging advanced analytics and AI, SMEs can gain deeper insights into customer needs, personalize interactions, and use digital channels for real-time engagement and seamless omnichannel experiences. Embracing these technologies can strengthen customer connections, boost loyalty, and drive growth, provided that risks associated with innovation are managed effectively (Kotler & Armstrong, 2019).

7.9 Relevance of CRM

CRM systems are crucial for SMEs to manage relationships with existing and potential clients by systematically collecting, retaining, and analyzing consumer data. This data provides insights into customer behavior, preferences, and needs, enabling SMEs to personalize marketing strategies and communications. This enhances customer satisfaction, loyalty, and engagement (Smith, 2021a; Brown & Wilson, 2022). CRM solutions also streamline customer service operations through automated workflows and integrated communication tools. This then improves overall customer experiences (Kotler & Armstrong, 2019).

In the context of the Fourth Industrial Revolution, CRM systems leverage advanced technologies like AI and machine learning to offer predictive insights and automate routine tasks, allowing SMEs to focus on strategic objectives (Smith, 2021a). They identify trends and patterns, facilitate interdepartmental collaboration, and support omnichannel strategies. This is by ensuring a consistent experience across all customer interaction points, whether through social media, email, phone, or in-person (Brown & Wilson, 2022; Kotler & Armstrong, 2019).

Additionally, CRM systems enhance sales growth by optimizing lead management and monitoring sales activities. This helps SMEs refine their strategies and maximize revenue through automated follow-ups and targeted marketing campaigns (Smith, 2021a). Overall, CRM systems provide SMEs with a technological foundation to build strong client relationships, remain competitive, and adapt to the evolving digital market (Brown & Wilson, 2022).

7.10 The 4Cs of Marketing

The shift from the 4Ps to the 4Cs marks a transition to a customer-centric marketing strategy by Bob Lauterborn in the 90s. The 4Cs framework emphasizes understanding and addressing customer needs and preferences rather than focusing solely on product attributes and commercial aspects (Smith, 2021a).

The first "C," Customer, prioritizes grasping and meeting customer expectations, enhancing satisfaction and loyalty (Brown & Wilson, 2022). The second "C," Cost, includes not only the financial price but also the total cost of ownership from the customer's perspective, such as time and effort (Kotler & Armstrong, 2019). Convenience replaces the "Place" aspect of the 4Ps, focusing on streamlining the purchasing process across various channels to improve the customer experience (Smith, 2021a). The final "C," Communication, involves moving from one-way promotion to engaging in meaningful, reciprocal conversations with customers, building trust and lasting relationships (Brown & Wilson, 2022). Adopting the 4Cs approach highlights a commitment to enhancing customer experiences, fostering loyalty, and supporting sustainable growth in a market where consumers are increasingly knowledgeable and interconnected (Kotler & Armstrong, 2019).

7.10.1 Customer

The "Customer" element of the 4Cs framework focuses on understanding and meeting client needs and preferences. SMEs must prioritize customer satisfaction and loyalty by providing excellent value and personalized experiences (Smith, 2021a). A generic approach is insufficient in today's competitive market; instead, SMEs need to deeply understand consumer preferences and behaviors through comprehensive market research and data analysis (Brown & Wilson, 2022). SMEs should gather data from surveys, social media, and purchase records to identify patterns and tailor their offerings to different customer segments (Kotler & Armstrong, 2019). Customization enhances satisfaction and loyalty, with tools like CRM systems enabling targeted marketing campaigns based on customer behavior. Consistent interaction and feedback collection, through online reviews and direct engagement, are vital for maintaining strong relationships (Brown & Wilson, 2022). Recognizing and rewarding loyal customers with loyalty programs or exclusive offers can further strengthen relationships and encourage repeat business. A customer-centric approach across all business operations, including superior products and services, anticipates and exceeds client expectations, leading to improved loyalty and attracting new customers through positive referrals (Kotler & Armstrong, 2019).

7.10.2 Cost

The "Cost" element of the 4Cs framework examines the total expenditure from the customer's perspective, including financial, time, effort, and convenience costs (Smith, 2021a). Unlike the traditional focus solely on price, this broader view of cost considers all factors affecting the customer's overall experience and perceived value. For SMEs, managing both monetary and non-monetary costs is crucial. They should maintain competitive and sustainable pricing while balancing affordability with profitability. This involves effective cost management, operational efficiency, and pricing strategies such as discounts and loyalty programs.

Transparency in pricing is essential to build trust and avoid customer concerns about hidden charges (Brown & Wilson, 2022).

Time is a significant aspect of cost. SMEs should streamline operations to reduce waiting times and enhance efficiency, such as implementing online booking systems, expedited shipping, and prompt customer support. Reducing the time customers spend on transactions improves their overall experience (Kotler & Armstrong, 2019).

Effort is another key consideration. Customers prefer interactions that require minimal effort. SMEs can improve user experience by creating user-friendly websites, providing clear product information, and ensuring accessible customer service. Simplified processes like one-click purchasing and diverse payment options enhance convenience (Smith, 2021a).

Convenience, integrating time and effort, is vital for customer satisfaction. SMEs should ensure their products and services are easily accessible, whether through optimal retail locations, flexible delivery options, or unified online platforms. Providing multiple purchasing and return options increases perceived value and convenience (Brown & Wilson, 2022). To justify the total cost, SMEs must deliver exceptional value by offering high-quality products, superior performance, and excellent customer support. Creating a compelling value proposition and delivering memorable customer experiences can make the overall cost seem more reasonable and attractive, fostering loyalty and satisfaction (Kotler & Armstrong, 2019).

In summary, the "Cost" component requires SMEs to adopt a comprehensive approach to pricing and value assessment, considering all aspects of the customer's expenditure and aiming to build strong, loyal relationships (Brown & Wilson, 2022).

7.10.3 Convenience

The "Convenience" element of the 4Cs framework emphasizes creating a seamless and efficient customer experience. For SMEs, this involves optimizing every aspect of the customer journey to eliminate obstacles and enhance ease of access (Smith, 2021a). Key to convenience is the effective management of distribution channels, ensuring products and services are available when and where customers need them. This can involve a mix of physical stores, online platforms, and partnerships with third-party distributors to create a comprehensive network (Brown & Wilson, 2022). Efficient inventory management is critical, with SMEs using advanced systems to predict demand and adjust stock levels accordingly. This prevents stockouts and overstock situations, ensuring customers consistently find the products they want (Kotler & Armstrong, 2019).

Superior customer support is also essential, providing timely and knowledgeable assistance across various channels like phone, email, live chat, and social media. Quick resolution of inquiries and issues builds trust and strengthens customer relationships (Smith, 2021a).

In this phygital age (Batat, 2024), SMEs should leverage technology to enhance accessibility. User-friendly websites and mobile apps with clear product descriptions and streamlined checkout processes improve the online shopping experience. Offering diverse payment methods and post-purchase support, such as tracking information and easy returns, adds to the convenience (Brown & Wilson, 2022). Products should be designed for ease of use, with straightforward assembly and maintenance. Clear instructions and user-friendly interfaces improve the customer experience beyond the point of purchase (Smith, 2021a).

Ultimately, adopting a customer-centric approach involves actively seeking feedback and monitoring behavior to identify and address areas for improvement. Innovations such as subscription services can further enhance convenience and customer satisfaction (Brown & Wilson, 2022).

7.10.4 Communication

Effective communication in the 4Cs framework involves active, two-way interactions between SMEs and their customers, moving beyond traditional one-way promotional methods (Smith, 2021a). It emphasizes dynamic and participatory engagement, utilizing multiple channels to foster meaningful exchanges. This includes conventional methods like face-to-face meetings and phone calls, as well as digital platforms such as social media, email, websites, and mobile apps. Different channels cater to various customer segments, enabling personalized communication tailored to their preferences (Brown & Wilson, 2022).

Successful communication integrates promotional efforts with active listening and feedback collection. SMEs can use surveys, polls, and direct feedback systems to gather insights on customer needs and preferences. This data helps refine products, services, and marketing strategies to better align with customer expectations (Kotler & Armstrong, 2019).

Engagement is key, with SMEs developing content marketing strategies that offer valuable and relevant content. This can include blog posts, videos, infographics, and social media updates that encourage interaction, such as comments, shares, and discussions. Such content fosters a sense of community and strengthens the connection between the business and its customers (Smith, 2021a).

Transparency is crucial for building trust. SMEs should clearly communicate product details, pricing, and policies, and address any issues openly. Acknowledging and explaining mistakes and outlining corrective actions enhances credibility and customer relations (Brown & Wilson, 2022).

Customization also plays a role, with SMEs using customer data to tailor messages and interactions. Personalization—such as addressing customers by name in emails or suggesting products based on past behavior—creates a sense of value and connection (Kotler & Armstrong, 2019). Regular communication, such as newsletters and updates, helps maintain customer engagement, fostering loyalty and ensuring the business remains top-of-mind (Smith, 2021a).

7.11 Implications

In theory and practice, the 4Ps have not been universally applicable to all markets and situations. This study is on how SMEs can modify their marketing mix to properly take advantage of their market. The study's findings offer valuable insights for marketing managers in the SME sector to consider when developing a marketing mix to effectively reach their target audiences. Managers can implement a range of strategies to improve their engagement with the SME market. These strategies may include:

- Building close relationships for individualized engagement that results in a high level of customer satisfaction;
- Understanding customer needs and preferences without the need for complex processes required by larger competitors, thus providing direct insights in delivering products and services that meet immediate customer needs for a competitive advantage;
- Fostering trust and loyalty through personalized rewards and special offers that encourage customers to be retained and turned into brand ambassadors in the SME business;
- Embracing the 4Cs approach to demonstrate a dedication to improving customer experiences and promoting sustainable growth in a market where consumers are more informed and interconnected than ever.

Rather than focusing solely on managing processes defined by the 4Ps, SME managers should concentrate on the factors that drive customer value. They should build market-oriented, flexible, and innovative businesses that can continuously adapt to rapidly changing market conditions.

7.12 Conclusion

The success and growth of SMEs hinge on their ability to deeply understand and actively engage with their customers. The transition from the traditional 4Ps to the 4Cs marks a significant shift toward a customer-centric approach, focusing on delivering value and exceptional experiences rather than just promoting products (Smith, 2021a). This approach involves prioritizing customer needs, preferences, and feedback, and adapting marketing strategies accordingly (Brown & Wilson, 2022).

CRM systems are essential in this transition, offering valuable data and insights into customer behaviors and preferences. These systems enable SMEs to personalize their marketing efforts and provide a consistent customer experience across various touchpoints (Kotler & Armstrong, 2019).

Effective communication, a key component of the 4Cs, involves reciprocal interactions that build trust and foster long-term relationships. By engaging in meaningful dialogues and addressing customer feedback transparently, SMEs can enhance their credibility and customer satisfaction.

In today's phygital age, driven by the Fourth Industrial Revolution, where consumers are more knowledgeable and connected, SMEs must adapt their marketing strategies to stay relevant. Embracing a customer-centric approach and leveraging CRM solutions can strengthen client relationships and drive growth in a rapidly changing market (Smith, 2021a; Brown & Wilson, 2022). To remain competitive, SMEs need to focus on customer experience and adopt flexible, data-driven strategies as market demands evolve (Kotler & Armstrong, 2019).

References

Baker, M. J. (2018a). *Marketing strategy and management.* Palgrave Macmillan.

Baker, M. J. (2018b). *Marketing theory: A student text.* Sage.

Baker, J. (2019a). *Omnichannel retailing: Integration and strategy.* Cambridge University Press.

Baker, K. (2019b). The power of influencer marketing in small business promotion. *Marketing Strategies Journal, 14*(2), 45–60.

Batat, W. (2024). Why is the traditional marketing mix dead? Towards the "experiential marketing mix" (7E), a strategic framework for business experience design in the phygital age. *Journal of Strategic Marketing, 32*(2), 101–113.

Brown, D., & Lee, J. (2020). Adapting marketing strategies in the digital age. *Journal of Marketing, 54*(3), 72–89. https://doi.org/10.1080/0267257X.2020.1840743

Brown, J., & Wilson, A. (2021a). Customer engagement and SMEs: The role of personalization in business success. *Journal of Small Business Management, 59*(3), 345–367.

Brown, T., & Wilson, A. (2021b). Understanding customer relations in SMEs. *Journal of Small Business Management, 59*(2), 120–135.

Brown, T., & Wilson, M. (2021c). The evolution of the marketing mix: The 4Ps to the 7Ps and beyond. *Journal of Marketing Theory and Practice, 29*(3), 345–362. https://doi.org/10.1080/10696679.2021.1906234

Brown, J., & Wilson, C. (2022). *Effective marketing strategies for SMEs.* Cambridge Business Publishers.

Johnson, M. (2019). The impact of SMEs on economic development in emerging markets. *International Journal of Business Research, 98*(4), 56–70. https://doi.org/10.1016/j.jbusres.2019.07.013
Johnson, M., & Lee, A. (2019a). *Consumer behavior and market trends*. Palgrave Macmillan.
Johnson, M., & Lee, S. (2019b). Customer-centric strategies for SMEs: A comprehensive guide. *International Journal of Business and Management, 14*(3), 65–79.
Johnson, M., & Lee, S. (2019c). Strategies for enhancing customer loyalty in small and medium enterprises. *International Journal of Business and Management, 14*(2), 92–106.
Johnson, P., & Lee, M. (2019d). Marketing strategies for SMEs: Integrating the 4Ps with modern practices. *Journal of Business Research, 98*, 300–310. https://doi.org/10.1016/j.jbusres.2019.01.048
Johnson, M., & Lee, A. (2020a). Leveraging social media for SME growth. *Digital Marketing Review, 18*(3), 112–130.
Johnson, R., & Lee, S. (2020b). *Digital marketing and customer engagement: A comprehensive guide*. Routledge.
Kotler, P., & Armstrong, G. (2018). *Principles of marketing* (17th ed.). Pearson.
Kotler, P., & Armstrong, G. (2019). *Principles of marketing* (17th ed.). Pearson Education.
Kotler, P., & Keller, K. L. (2016). *Marketing management* (15th ed.). Pearson.
Kumar, P., & Gupta, S. (2020a). The role of direct engagement in SME customer satisfaction. *Small Business Economics, 55*(2), 234–252.
Kumar, R., & Gupta, P. (2020b). Leveraging customer feedback in SMEs for competitive advantage. *Business Horizons, 63*(5), 547–555.
Kumar, V., & Gupta, S. (2020c). Adapting the marketing mix for the digital age: Challenges and opportunities for SMEs. *Marketing Intelligence & Planning, 38*(5), 563–575. https://doi.org/10.1108/MIP-02-2020-0140
Kumar, V., & Gupta, S. (2020d). *Data-driven marketing strategies*. Wiley.
Monroe, K. B. (2019). *Pricing: Making profitable decisions*. McGraw-Hill.
Monroe, K. (2021a). Leveraging online marketplaces for SME growth: Opportunities and challenges. *Journal of Business Research, 54*(5), 67–79.
Monroe, K. B. (2021b). *Pricing: Making profitable decisions*. McGraw-Hill Education.
Schiffman, L. G., & Kanuk, L. L. (2019). *Consumer behavior* (11th ed.). Pearson.
Schiffman, L. G., & Kanuk, L. L. (2020). *Consumer behavior* (12th ed.). Pearson Education.

Smith, A. (2020a). Applying the 4Ps in small and medium-sized enterprises: Benefits and challenges. *International Journal of Small Business and Enterprise Development, 27*(4), 499–512. https://doi.org/10.1108/IJSE-08-2019-0302
Smith, J. (2020b). The role of customer feedback in SME growth and development. *Journal of Consumer Marketing, 37*(4), 290–302.
Smith, A. (2021a). Technological advancements and the role of CRM in the Fourth Industrial Revolution. *International Journal of Digital Transformation, 12*(3), 98–110.
Smith, J. (2021b). *Customer-centric marketing: Embracing convenience and innovation*. Harvard Business Review Press.

8

The Role and Relevance of Marketing in Small and Medium-Sized Enterprises (SMEs) in Africa

Esther Asiedu, Ebenezer Malcalm, Ethel Yiranbon Annor-Tenkorang, George Oppong Ampong, Gertrude Amoakohene, and George Kofi Amoako

8.1 The Small and Medium Enterprises (SMEs) in Africa

SME growth is becoming more of an engine for the economy (Zhou & Gumbo, 2021). The attitude has shifted in favour of small and medium-sized businesses because of their adaptability and capacity to support economic expansion, job development, wealth creation, income generation, and the fight against poverty (Manzoor et al., 2021). The achievement of

E. Asiedu • E. Malcalm • E. Y. Annor-Tenkorang • G. Oppong Ampong • G. Amoakohene (✉)
Ghana Communication Technology University, Accra, Ghana
e-mail: easaiedu011@gctu.edu.gh; emalcalm@gctu.edu.gh; eyiranbon@gctu.edu.gh; gampong@gctu.edu.gh; gamoakohene@gctu.edu.gh

E. Amoako Asiedu et al. (eds.), *Entrepreneurship and Small and Medium-Sized Enterprises (SMEs) in Africa*, https://doi.org/10.1007/978-3-032-14174-3_8

the Sustainable Development Goals (SDGs), inclusive and sustainable economic growth, decent job creation, sustainable industrialisation, innovation, and inequality reduction are all made possible in large part by SMEs.

Globalisation and heightened economic competition have made small and medium-sized enterprises (SMEs) a hot topic (Chinomona & Chinomona, 2013; Masroor & Asim, 2019). SMEs are essential to Africa's inclusive socioeconomic growth and development. This is because small and medium-sized enterprises (SMEs) are creating wealth, revenue, and job opportunities—all of which help to end poverty. Interestingly, there is not a commonly agreed definition for the phrase "small and medium-sized enterprise" (SME). Legal definitions of SMEs vary throughout countries. This is because the size of the domestic economy affects a firm's "small" and "medium" dimensions.

The OECD (2005), cited by Ndubisi et al. (2021), defines SMEs as independent, non-subsidiary businesses that are distinguished by their growing workforce and financial assets. Depending on the size of the home economy, different countries have different definitions for SMEs' financial assets. Although there is not a single, widely recognised definition of an SME, scholars have historically defined SMEs based on variables such as total gross asset value, annual turnover, number of employees, and balance sheet.

Businesses with up to 249 employees are classified as SMEs by the Organisation for Economic Co-operation and Development. One to nine people are employed by micro enterprises, ten to forty-nine by small businesses, and fifty to two hundred forty-nine by medium firms. This definition and consideration can enable the best comparability, keeping in mind that different nations utilise different conventions for data collection.

SMEs have a critical role in the advancement of socioeconomic conditions in Africa, where they account for almost 80% of all jobs. For

G. K. Amoako
Ghana Communications Technology University, Accra, Ghana

Durban University of Technology, Durban, South Africa
e-mail: gamoako@gctu.edu.gh

example, the OECD (2017) estimates that there are 44 million SMEs in Sub-Saharan Africa. Additionally, SMEs would have easier access to export markets across the continent and in neighbouring countries thanks to the African Continental Free Trade Area (AfCFTA). In addition, the Sustainable Development Goals and Agenda 2063 of the African Union acknowledge that the potential for the effective development of the SME business model is a requirement for Africa's drivers of economic growth and long-term sustainability for emerging markets.

The fact that small and medium-sized enterprises (SMEs) are found in every sector of the African economy demonstrates the significant influence SMEs have on the socioeconomic growth of the continent. In essence, SMEs are giving a large portion of the African people work and helping to create jobs. For example, up to 90% of workers in African countries like Kenya, Ethiopia, and Uganda are employed by SMEs. This is because small and medium-sized enterprises (SMEs) play a major role in fostering invention, creativity, and the creation of novel ideas and technologies. Small and medium-sized businesses (SMEs) essentially aid in the pre-, during-, and post-commercialisation of innovation and technology (Amoako-Asiedu et al., 2024). This provides a platform for the creation and testing of novel products before they are scaled up and introduced into a larger market through macroeconomic channels.

Furthermore, SMEs are recognised and acknowledged for their role in spotting and developing new markets as well as providing the framework for startup businesses. As a result, millions of Africans now have a source of income. As a result, by stimulating demand for products, services, investments, innovation, technology, and commerce, SMEs are facilitating the production of wealth.

SMEs usually deal with a range of issues, including difficulty obtaining funding, poor infrastructure, and a lack of market expertise. Yet, SMEs still have significant and constrictive barriers that prevent their long-term survival and contribution to the development of Africa, of which marketing is crucial, despite their positive impact on the continent's development (Adomako et al., 2024). As a result, five out of every seven SMEs in African countries fail during the first year of operation, which is an alarming death rate. In Uganda, for example, 30% of recently founded companies fail in their first year of operation. On the other side, South Africa has a 50% to 95% failure rate for new firms, depending on the industry.

By determining client needs, developing value propositions, and setting oneself apart in crowded markets, marketing's strategic role can assist SMEs in overcoming these obstacles. With a focus on the theoretical foundations and real-world applications for managers and policymakers, this chapter examines the function and applicability of marketing in SMEs throughout Africa.

8.2 Africa Country-Specific Insights

Small and medium-sized businesses, or SMEs, are the backbone of many economies, especially those in Africa, where they are essential for generating employment opportunities, lowering poverty rates, and advancing economic growth. The substantial contribution that SMEs make to GDP and employment on the continent highlights their significance. SMEs' success and effect, however, differ greatly among nations due to a variety of factors. These include the business climate, availability of funding, governmental regulations, and the significance of marketing tactics.

Small and medium-sized enterprises (SMEs) play a crucial role in the economic development, social stability, and economic diversity of African nations. The International Finance Corporation (IFC) estimates that small and medium-sized enterprises (SMEs) account for around 90% of firms and over 50% of employment globally. Whilst in Africa, SMEs account for about 80% of all jobs. Although their GDP contribution differs for each nation, it is nevertheless a major factor in encouraging inclusive economic growth.

Contemporary perspectives on SMEs in Africa, with a focus on selected key countries Nigeria, South Africa, Kenya, and Ghana, explore the contribution of SMEs to GDP, employment, and the pivotal role of marketing in their success.

8.3 Nigeria

The largest economy in Africa, Nigeria, mostly depends on its SME sector to fuel job creation and economic expansion. In Nigeria, SMEs make up about 96% of all enterprises, 84% of all jobs, and contribute roughly

48% of the country's GDP. The Nigerian government has worked to strengthen the capabilities of SMEs via a number of programs, including the Micro, Small, and Medium Enterprises Development Fund (MSMEDF) and the National Enterprise Development Programme (NEDEP). The development potential of Nigerian SMEs is still constrained. Nevertheless, issues include unpredictability in the regulatory environment, poor infrastructure, and limited access to capital.

8.4 South Africa

The SME sector is well-established in South Africa and is vital to the nation's economy. Nearly 60% of the workforce is employed by SMEs, which generate roughly 34% of South Africa's GDP. The government has put policies in place to assist SMEs, including market access, skill development, and financing availability, through organisations like the Department of Small Business Development and the Small Enterprise Development Agency (SEDA). Nonetheless, the industry faces difficulties due to problems, including market saturation, fierce rivalry, and the requirement for more effective marketing techniques.

8.5 Kenya

In Kenya, SMEs are the lifeblood of the economy, contributing to approximately 33.8% of GDP and providing about 86% of all employment opportunities. The Kenyan government has made significant strides in creating an enabling environment for SMEs through the Kenya Vision 2030 framework. This emphasises the development of SMEs as a means to achieve industrialisation. Despite these efforts, SMEs in Kenya face challenges, including limited access to capital, market competition, and the need for enhanced marketing strategies to penetrate regional and international markets.

8.6 Ghana

With over 90% of enterprises and a GDP contribution of over 70%, Ghana's SME sector is a vital engine of employment and economic growth. The National Board for Small Scale Industries (NBSSI) and the creation of specific funds to improve financing accessibility are only two of the policies that the Ghanaian government has put in place to assist SMEs. SMEs in Ghana still have to deal with issues like poor infrastructure, restricted market access, and the requirement for better marketing to boost competitiveness.

8.7 The Role and Relevance of Marketing in SMEs

Marketing is an essential component of the growth and sustainability of SMEs. Effective marketing strategies help SMEs to reach new customers, enter new markets, and differentiate themselves from competitors. In the African context, marketing is often constrained by limited budgets, lack of expertise, and insufficient knowledge of digital marketing tools. Marketing is essential for the growth and sustainability of SMEs, as it helps these businesses to identify customer needs, promote their products and services, and build strong relationships with their target markets. In Africa, where SMEs often operate in highly competitive environments with limited resources, marketing can be the differentiating factor that determines success or failure.

8.8 Digital Marketing and Social Media

The rise of digital marketing and social media platforms presents a significant opportunity for African SMEs to reach broader audiences. Social media platforms such as Facebook, Instagram, and Twitter offer cost-effective ways for SMEs to engage with customers, promote their products, and build brand loyalty. For instance, in Nigeria, SMEs have increasingly adopted social media marketing to reach tech-savvy consumers, leading to enhanced brand visibility and sales growth.

Digital marketing also enables SMEs to measure the effectiveness of their campaigns through analytics, allowing for more informed decision-making and strategy refinement. Digital marketing has emerged as a powerful tool for SMEs to enhance their business performance (Nuseir & Aljumah, 2020). The study by Nuseir and Aljumah (2020) emphasises the moderating effect of environmental factors on the relationship between digital marketing and business performance among SMEs in the UAE. This research highlights the importance of understanding the external contextual factors that can either facilitate or hinder the effectiveness of digital marketing efforts. Additionally, social media has gained significant attention as a marketing tool for SMEs. Salam and Hoque (2019) examine the role of social media and the effect of relationship marketing on SME performance in Bangladesh. The study findings suggest that the effective utilisation of social media platforms, combined with relationship marketing strategies, can lead to improved performance for SMEs.

The research by Mathews et al. (2019) underscores the critical role of Internet marketing capabilities in enhancing firm performance, particularly in Japanese SMEs, by influencing risk perceptions and management. Similarly, Davcik et al. (2021) demonstrate the importance of both technological and marketing capabilities in boosting SME performance through effective international R&D activities. Subagja and Ausat (2022) highlight the significant impact of social media utilisation and innovativeness on SME performance. This emphasises the potential of social media to drive innovation and growth. Gameti et al. (2021) further reinforce the importance of entrepreneurial marketing dimensions in fostering SME innovation and sustainable growth through social media. Collectively, these studies illuminate the essential role of marketing in risk management, innovation, and performance improvement within SMEs.

Salam and Hoque (2019) investigated how relationship marketing and social media affected the performance of SMEs in Bangladesh. This highlights the moderating effect of leadership support. Their study emphasises how crucial it is to use social media marketing and cultivate solid connections in order to improve SME success. Osano (2019) looked at

Kenyan SMEs' worldwide market strategies, emphasising the need for strong plans for a successful international expansion. This study highlights how important marketing is in helping SMEs expand internationally. The emergence of digital technology has changed the marketing environment and given SMEs new ways to connect and interact with consumers. Social media, email marketing, and search engine optimisation are examples of digital marketing technologies that help small and medium-sized businesses (SMEs) market and change their goods and services more affordably. E-commerce platforms also help SMEs reach a wider audience by connecting them with regional and international marketplaces in addition to local ones. Digital marketing can be a game-changer for SMEs trying to build their business in Africa, where Internet access is growing quickly (Chaffey & Ellis-Chadwick, 2019).

8.9 Market Research and Customer Insights

Understanding the market and customer preferences is crucial for the success of SMEs. Market research helps SMEs to identify customer needs, preferences, and trends, enabling them to tailor their products and services accordingly. In South Africa, SMEs that invest in market research tend to outperform those that do not, as they are better equipped to respond to market changes and customer demands (Ligthelm, 2010).

Market research is fundamental to understanding predictions of market trends, customer behaviour, and competitive dynamics. African SMEs that invest in market research are better equipped to identify opportunities and mitigate risks. For example, in South Africa, SMEs in the food and beverage sector have utilised market research to understand consumer preferences for organic and healthy foods, leading to the development of niche products that cater to this growing demand (Ligthelm, 2010). Market research involves the systematic collection and analysis of data about consumers, competitors, and market trends. For SMEs, market research is essential for understanding customer needs, identifying new market opportunities, and making informed business decisions. In Africa, where market conditions can be volatile and unpredictable, competitive intelligence is particularly important for SMEs to stay ahead of rivals and adapt to changing market dynamics.

8.10 Entrepreneurial Marketing

Another important dimension of marketing in SMEs is entrepreneurial marketing. Sadiku-Dushi et al. (2019) explore the relationship between entrepreneurial marketing dimensions and SMEs performance. The findings of this study reveal that SMEs that adopt entrepreneurial marketing practices tend to outperform their competitors. This research emphasises the need for SMEs to embrace creative marketing approaches that align with their entrepreneurial nature.

Susanto et al. (2023) examine the role of entrepreneurial orientation and marketing capabilities in influencing the performance of SMEs. They also investigate the moderating effect of social media usage on this relationship. The study findings suggest that a strong entrepreneurial orientation, combined with effective marketing capabilities and strategic use of social media, can significantly enhance SMEs performance.

Presutti and Odorici (2019) identified a positive link between entrepreneurial and market orientations, along with entrepreneurial experience and networks, in driving SME performance growth. This emphasises the need to align marketing strategies with these orientations. Falahat et al. (2020) highlighted the role of product innovation, market intelligence, pricing, and marketing communication capabilities in SMEs' international expansion. This underscores the importance of effective marketing strategies in global growth. Quaye and Mensah (2019) demonstrated that marketing innovation fosters a sustainable competitive advantage in Ghanaian manufacturing SMEs, while Bodlaj and Čater (2022) found that proactive and responsive market orientations, mediated by marketing capabilities, enhance SME export performance.

8.11 Branding and Positioning

Effective branding and positioning can significantly enhance the competitiveness of SMEs. In Kenya, SMEs that have invested in building strong brands have been able to differentiate themselves in a crowded market, leading to increased customer loyalty and market share (Mwangi & Wanjau, 2013).

8.12 Customer Engagement and Relationship Building

One of the core functions of marketing is to engage with customers and build lasting relationships. For African SMEs, understanding customer needs and preferences is critical to tailoring products and services that resonate with their target market. In Ghana, for instance, SMEs in the fashion industry have successfully leveraged social media platforms like Instagram to engage with customers, showcase their designs, and receive feedback. This direct interaction helps build customer loyalty and increases repeat business (Odoom et al., 2017).

8.13 Branding and Positioning

Effective branding and positioning enable SMEs to differentiate themselves in crowded markets. In Kenya, SMEs in the technology sector have successfully built strong brands that are recognised both locally and internationally. Companies like M-KOPA, a Kenyan SME that provides affordable solar energy solutions, have used branding to position themselves as leaders in the renewable energy sector, attracting significant investment and expanding their market reach (Mwangi & Wanjau, 2013). Branding is a critical aspect of marketing that helps businesses create a distinct identity in the minds of consumers. For African SMEs, building a strong brand can be challenging due to limited resources and competitive pressures from larger companies. However, effective branding strategies can help SMEs establish credibility, attract customers, and command premium prices. For instance, SMEs can leverage local culture, traditions, and heritage in their branding efforts to create a unique value proposition that resonates with African consumers (Keller, 2013).

8.14 Content Marketing

Content marketing involves creating and sharing valuable content to attract and retain customers. African SMEs are increasingly adopting content marketing strategies to educate their target audience, build trust, and establish thought leadership. For example, in South Africa, SMEs in the financial services sector have used content marketing to provide financial literacy resources to their customers, helping to build brand credibility and customer loyalty.

8.15 Market Orientation

Another crucial idea in comprehending the function and importance of marketing in SMEs is market orientation. Puspaningrum (2020) investigates the connection between SMEs' marketing performance, competitive advantage, and market orientation. According to the study's findings, SMEs with a strong focus on the market typically have a competitive edge and generate superior marketing results. For SMEs to maintain their competitiveness and experience sustained growth, innovation is essential. The relationship between marketing innovation and sustainable competitive advantage among Ghanaian manufacturing SMEs is examined by Quaye and Mensah (2019). The results underscore the beneficial influence of marketing innovation on small and medium-sized enterprises' competitive edge, underscoring the significance of ongoing innovation in marketing tactics.

Market orientation refers to the extent to which a business prioritises market intelligence, customer focus, and competitor awareness in its operations. Studies have shown that market-oriented SMEs tend to perform better in terms of profitability, customer satisfaction, and market share (Narver & Slater, 1990). In Africa, where markets are often fragmented and underserved, adopting a market orientation can enable SMEs to identify and capitalise on niche opportunities, leading to improved business performance.

8.16 The Concept of TAPE in Marketing

There has been increasing interest in the innovative marketing constructs used by small and medium-sized enterprises (SMEs) to evaluate the role and importance of marketing. These constructs, specifically transformation, assimilation, prediction, and exceptionality (TAPE), offer a conceptual framework for understanding the unique marketing strategies employed by SMEs (O'dwyer et al., 2009).

8.16.1 Transformation

The idea of marketing transformation centres on SMEs' capacity to change and grow in reaction to shifting market conditions (Sollazzo, 2024). This theory highlights the significance of creative thinking and strategic actions that help SMEs maintain their competitiveness in the quickly changing business environment. The fundamental idea of shift in SME creative marketing initiatives is market dynamics. Product enhancement, for instance, describes SMEs that find, create, and implement ways to improve their products and services so that they become more appealing to consumers. This can be seen in the way SMEs modify the marketing mix, adjust marketing strategies and tactics, omit conventional marketing components, or incorporate business-specific components (Kleindl, 1996). Changing the distribution channel to improve customer satisfaction, cost-effectiveness, or competitive advantage is another example of this "transformation" activity (Johne, 1999; Carson et al., 1998).

Moreover, the success of SMEs often depends on their ability to adapt to changing market dynamics and technological advancements (Hilmersson & Hilmersson, 2021). Therefore, understanding the complexities of marketing constructs in the context of SMEs is crucial for enhancing organisational performance and sustainability. The ability of SMEs to change and adapt in response to shifting market conditions is the core idea behind the marketing concept of transformation (Sollazzo, 2024). SMEs to remain competitive in the quickly changing business environment, this theory highlights the significance of strategic initiatives and creative approaches. The fundamental theme of change in SME creative marketing initiatives is market dynamics. According to Mostafa (2005) and McEvily et al. (2004), SMEs that identify, create, and implement product enhancements. According to Cummins et al. (2000) and Kleindl (1996), SMEs exhibit this through modifications to the marketing mix, adaptation of marketing activities and procedures, omission of traditional marketing aspects, and/or inclusion of business-specific elements. The distribution channel may also be changed as part of this "transformation" process to improve customer satisfaction, cost-effectiveness, or competitive advantage (Johne, 1999; Carson et al., 1998).

8.16.2 Transformation: M-PESA (Kenya)

Company: Safaricom (formerly a big corporation, but many SME businesses were motivated by M-PESA)

Context: Kenyan small companies switched from using cash to digital payments thanks to the mobile money app M-PESA.

Impact on SMEs: A lot of small enterprises, such as supermarkets and cab services, swiftly adjusted and redesigned their business plans to focus on mobile money.

TAPE Link: Through new marketing and transaction tactics, SMEs altered their operations, reflecting transformation.

8.16.3 Assimilation

The notion of assimilation is another key marketing construct discussed in the literature. It highlights the process by which SMEs integrate new knowledge and practices into their existing organisational structures, fostering continuous learning and improvement. By effectively assimilating new information, SMEs can enhance their overall performance and increase their competitiveness in the market. One essential component of innovative marketing that helps SMEs make the most use of their resources is the integration of SME marketing practices and activities into all organisational functions. SME employees in non-marketing roles carry out marketing techniques and activities as an essential component of their job due to the pervasiveness of marketing throughout all organisational functions. The process by which marketing techniques and activities are taken in and integrated into SMEs is demonstrated by this assimilation of innovative marketing practices and activities.

8.16.4 Assimilation: Nallem Clothing (Ghana)

- Business: Nallem Clothing (SME in Fashion)
- Context: Using contemporary marketing strategies (social media marketing, pop-up stores, online sales), this SME effectively integrated traditional African fashion.
- SME Impact: It expanded its clientele both domestically and beyond by fusing heritage (African prints) with contemporary branding.
- TAPE Link: Exhibits assimilation by utilising marketing innovation to modify conventional ideas for modern markets.

8.16.5 Prediction

As a marketing concept, prediction is essential for SMEs to assist them predict future consumer behaviour and industry trends so they may make well-informed business decisions. The importance of data analysis and forecasting methods in influencing SMEs' strategic planning and decision-making processes is emphasised by this theory.

The foundation of SME creative marketing approaches and activities connected to customer and market orientation is the ability to predict and forecast the demands of the market and customers. Customer focus is a crucial part of prediction for SMEs because of its ability to maximise customer information to foresee and subsequently profitably service customer requests (Martins & Terblanche, 2003). The significance of prediction is shown in the SME vision, which expresses a strategic vision for the business that is future-focused (Johne, 1999). SME strategic vision that is market-centred and focused on gathering market intelligence to predict conditions and identify marketing practices and activities for the future can maximise efficiency, effectiveness, and profitability (Johannessen et al., 2001; Kleindl, 1996). In SME creative marketing, this prediction process refers to the process of projecting, projecting, or projecting for the purposes of marketing practices and activities.

8.16.6 Prediction: Flutterwave (Nigeria)

The business is Flutterwave, a unicorn fintech that was once a SME.

- Context: Flutterwave foresaw, before many of its rivals, the increasing demand for simple digital payment infrastructure throughout Africa.
- SME Impact: They were able to dominate several marketplaces early on thanks to their vision.
- TAPE Link: Stands for forecasting future market demands and making proactive adjustments to marketing and service offerings.

8.16.7 Exceptionality

Exceptionality, on the other hand, focuses on SMEs' ability to differentiate themselves from competitors by offering unique value propositions and distinctive features. By providing exceptional products or services, SMEs can create a niche market for themselves and establish a strong brand identity. It is important to critically scrutinise the assumptions underlying these theories and assess their relevance and applicability in different contexts.

Investigations on the three components of the unique proposition highlight the importance of outstanding or unusual components to SMEs' creative marketing strategies and activities. According to

Arias-Aranda et al. (2001; Johne, 1999), the variable "new" in this context refers to SMEs' introduction of new goods, services, or procedures as part of their marketing activities and practices, whereas the variable "unique" focuses on how distinctive each newly introduced element is (Johannessen et al., 2001). Furthermore, the non-traditional facet of small and medium-sized enterprises (SMEs) aims to achieve remarkableness by modifying or rejecting the standard industry practises and approaches for marketing at least a portion of their enterprise, merchandise, or service (Kleindl, 1996). As a result, research shows that SMEs are motivated to create marketing strategies and tactics that are unique in some way. Exceptionality in this sense refers to remarkable abilities and achievements that add to the aspects of small and medium-sized enterprises' businesses that they consider uncommon or special.

Four major constructs—transformation, assimilation, prediction, and exceptionality—emerge from this investigation of hierarchies and interactions amongst innovative marketing variables (TAPE). These concepts are reconceived in a brand-new, cutting-edge marketing framework called TAPE, which classifies the constructs according to their function within SMEs, namely, changing marketing initiatives, integrating marketing procedures throughout the SME, anticipating marketing needs, and creating a standout good or service, as demonstrated in Fig. 8.1 for the performance of SMEs.

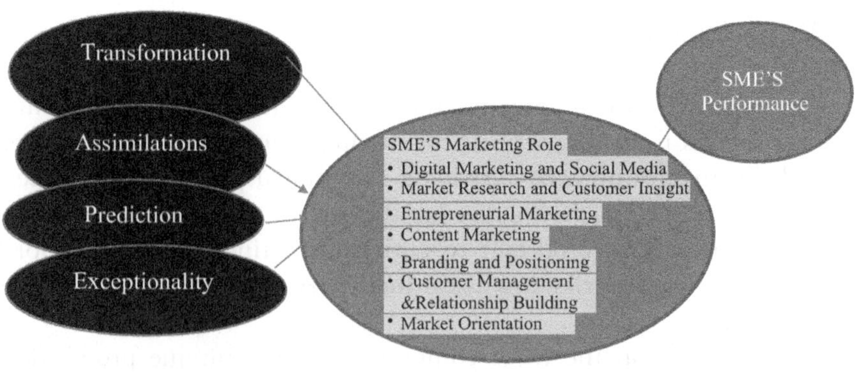

Fig. 8.1 SME's marketing innovative strategies. Source: Authors Own Constructs (2024), Adapted and modified from o'dwyer et al. (2009)

8.16.8 Exceptionality: Kigali Farms (Rwanda)

- Kigali Farms, an agriculture SME, is the company.
- Background: They promoted large-scale mushroom cultivation as a novel and lucrative agricultural enterprise in Rwanda.
- SME Impact: They significantly set themselves apart in marketing and product positioning by providing a product that is not typically widely available in Rwanda.
- TAPE Link: Exemplifies excellence by establishing a distinct market niche with creative advertising techniques and outstanding goods.

Summary table

TAPE element	Real-world SME case	Key insight
Transformation	M-PESA inspired SMEs (Kenya)	Business model shift through mobile money
Assimilation	Nallem Clothing (Ghana)	Traditional meets modern marketing
Prediction	Flutterwave (Nigeria)	Anticipating digital payments growth
Exceptionality	Kigali Farms (Rwanda)	Unique product marketing (mushrooms)

8.17 Contrasting Theories to TAPE

Dynamic Capabilities Theory (DCT)

Teece et al. (1997) developed the Dynamic Capabilities Theory (DCT), which highlights an organisation's capacity to integrate, develop, and reorganise internal and external competences in response to quickly changing circumstances. DCT provides a more comprehensive strategic perspective for how SMEs can dynamically adjust their resources and skills, as opposed to the TAPE framework, which concentrates on particular marketing structures. By highlighting the necessity of ongoing learning and organisational adaptability beyond predetermined marketing models, it thereby challenges TAPE. While DCT stresses an organisation's ability to integrate, develop, and reconfigure internal and external competences to address quickly changing contexts, TAPE assures the importance and relevance of marketing. DCT offers a more comprehensive perspective on how SMEs adjust their resources and competences in dynamic markets, whereas TAPE concentrates on certain marketing constructs. Because it emphasises the value of ongoing learning and adaptation beyond the predetermined constructs of transformation, assimilation, prediction, and exceptionality, this theory contradicts the TAPE framework.

Resource-Based View (RBV)

- Barney (1991) was the main proponent of the Resource-Based View (RBV), which holds that businesses can gain a sustainable competitive edge by utilising special resources and competences that are valuable, rare, inimitable, and non-substitutable (VRIN). RBV concentrates on the underlying strategic assets that underpin these processes, whereas the TAPE framework highlights particular marketing components. Therefore, RBV contests TAPE by claiming that marketing changes or forecasts might not work in the absence of unique internal resources.

According to RBV, businesses can obtain a competitive edge by utilising special resources and competences that are rare, valuable, non-replaceable, and inimitable. RBV concentrates on the strategic assets that support marketing processes, while TAPE stresses marketing processes. RBV challenges the TAPE paradigm by arguing that transformation or prediction tactics may not be as effective in the absence of special resources.

Technology-Organisation-Environment (TOE) Framework

- Tornatzky and Fleischer (1990) created the Technology-Organisation-Environment (TOE) framework, which looks at how organisational, technological, and environmental aspects influence how businesses embrace new technologies. The TOE framework offers a more comprehensive contextual study of internal and external influences on SME operations than the TAPE framework, which concentrates on certain marketing structures. Therefore, by determining the organisational and environmental factors that may facilitate or impede the effective application of TAPE techniques, TOE enhances TAPE.

Technology adoption in businesses is influenced by organisational, technological, and environmental variables, according to TOE.TOE offers a thorough understanding of the internal and external elements influencing SME operations, whereas TAPE focuses on marketing constructs. By providing insights into the contextual elements that either facilitate or impede the use of the TAPE constructs, TOE can be used in conjunction with TAPE.

8.18 Recent Studies Relevant to SME Marketing Frameworks

- A Theoretical Framework for Innovative Marketing in SMEs Carson et al. (2009). The TAPE framework is introduced in the study, but because of its ambiguous applicability in SME situations, it is later suggested to be modified to TAP (excluding Exceptionality). This calls into question the TAPE framework's universality and emphasises the necessity of empirically validating each of its elements.

In their paper "Marketing Capabilities and Competitive Performance in the SMEs Context: A Bi-Theoretical Perspective", Oduro and Mensah-Williams (2023) examine the ways in which different marketing capabilities affect the competitive performance of SMEs in Ghana and was published in the Journal of Small Business Strategy (Vol. 33, Issue 2, 2023). The authors used a quantitative research approach, based on the Resource-Based View (RBV) and Competence-Based View (CBV) theories, and then analysed data from 506 SMEs using Structural Equation Modelling (SEM-PLS). Their results demonstrate the important influence of particular marketing skills—like product development, channel management, and marketing communication—on several aspects of SME success, such as marketing, customer adaptability, and financial results.

Digital Marketing's Effect on SMEs' Performance Sharabati and associates (2024). This study emphasises how important digital marketing tactics like SEO and social media are for improving SME performance. It implies that digital tools, which the TAPE framework might not adequately account for, are essential to contemporary SME marketing.

8.19 Conceptual Framework

The conceptual model was created after the literature review, taking into account the novel marketing structures as well as the role and relevance of the SME.

The mediating variables are digital marketing and social media, market research and customer insight, entrepreneurial marketing, content marketing, branding and positioning, customer management and relationship building, and market orientation. The independent variables are transformation, assimilation, prediction, and exceptionality. The performance of the SME is the dependent variable.

8.20 Challenges Faced by African SMEs in Marketing

The work of seminal authors has been debated, challenged, and expanded upon in the academic community. For instance, studies have examined how these theories apply to various fields and interdisciplinary approaches. By critically assessing key studies, one can understand how these theoretical frameworks have been utilised, adapted, or challenged.

It also shows the complex interactions between various variables within these theories. By identifying and examining both explored and unexplored areas, supported by evidence from academic papers, we can uncover the gaps in current research (Hilmersson & Hilmersson, 2021). Addressing these gaps is crucial in advancing our understanding of marketing constructs used by SMEs and their impact on organisational performance.

Furthermore, it is important to discuss current studies that employ these theories in innovative ways. These studies go beyond traditional interpretations and push the boundaries of these theories, providing fresh insights into their application and potential (Meera & Vinodan, 2024). By evaluating the strengths and weaknesses of these theories, we can substantiate the alignment of our research with them and highlight their theoretical and practical implications.

This theoretical review has explored the marketing constructs used by SMEs for organisational performance, including transformation, assimilation, prediction, and exceptionality. By critically analysing the theories, integrating knowledge from diverse sources, and evaluating their theoretical and practical implications, we can contribute to advancements in academic thought. This study aims to address the gaps in current research and provide original insights into the topic, positioning it as a crucial contribution to the field.

Despite the critical role of marketing in driving the growth of African SMEs, several challenges hinder the effective implementation of marketing strategies.

8.21 Limited Financial Resources

Limited financial resources are one of the biggest issues African SMEs face. Due to their limited operating capital, many SMEs are unable to fund extensive marketing initiatives. This limitation often results in reliance on low-cost marketing methods, which may not be as effective in reaching a broader audience or competing with larger firms.

8.22 Lack of Marketing Expertise

Many SMEs in Africa lack the necessary marketing expertise to develop and execute effective marketing strategies. This skills gap is often due to limited access to formal training and education in marketing. As a result, SMEs may struggle to identify the most effective marketing channels, craft compelling messages, or measure the impact of their marketing efforts.

8.23 Inadequate Access to Technology

While digital marketing presents significant opportunities, many African SMEs face challenges in accessing the necessary technology and infrastructure. This digital divide limits their ability to fully leverage online marketing tools and platforms. In rural areas, where Internet connectivity may be poor, SMEs are particularly disadvantaged in adopting digital marketing strategies.

8.24 Cultural and Linguistic Diversity

Africa's cultural and linguistic diversity presents both opportunities and challenges for SMEs. Marketing messages that resonate in one region may not be effective in another due to differences in language, culture, and consumer behaviour. SMEs must navigate this complexity by tailoring their marketing strategies to local contexts, which can be resource-intensive.

8.25 Implications of Marketing of SMEs

The study on the role and relevance of marketing in Small and Medium-Sized Enterprises (SMEs) in Africa makes significant contributions to various aspects of the field. It aligns with the purpose and objectives of this research by delving into the complexities of marketing in SMEs, particularly in the context of African countries. This study situates itself within the existing body of knowledge by building upon previous research on market orientation, competitive advantage, and marketing performance of SMEs (Puspaningrum, 2020; Sadiku-Dushi et al., 2019).

In terms of theory, this study expands the theoretical framework by exploring unique dimensions such as international R&D activities, technological capabilities, and marketing capabilities on SMEs' performance (Davcik et al., 2021). By combining the ideas of product innovation, market intelligence, and marketing communication capabilities as drivers of SMEs' internationalisation, it presents novel approaches (Falahat et al., 2020). The research also emphasises how crucial market orientation, organisational learning, and organisational culture are to developing an innovative culture in SMEs (Abdul-Halim et al., 2019). These contributions enrich the theoretical underpinnings of marketing in SMEs, providing a more comprehensive understanding of the field.

From a practical perspective, this study has significant implications for industry settings. It emphasises the role of digital marketing in business performance, with a particular focus on the moderating effect of environmental factors (Nuseir & Aljumah, 2020). It also explores innovative digital marketing strategies that drive competitive advantage and sustainable growth in SMEs. Furthermore, the study examines the adoption of social media marketing for sustainable business growth, highlighting the moderating role of leadership support (Chatterjee et al., 2023). These findings offer practical insights for SMEs in Africa and beyond, enabling them to enhance their marketing efforts and improve overall performance.

In terms of policy-making, this study contributes to the development of more effective and equitable policies for SMEs. It emphasises the role of marketing capabilities as a mediator between responsive and proactive market orientation and SMEs' export venture performance (Bodlaj & Čater, 2022). It also underscores the relevance of international marketing strategies in emerging-market exporting firms, providing a conceptual framework for policy development. Additionally, the study highlights the role of business and social networks in the effective internationalisation of SMEs, offering insights for policymakers on fostering supportive networks. These findings can guide policymakers in creating an enabling environment for SMEs to thrive and expand globally.

Lastly, this research has a significant societal impact by addressing the potential application of theories and findings in different geographical and cultural contexts. It recognises the importance of considering cultural factors in understanding risk perceptions and Internet marketing capabilities in Japanese SMEs (Mathews et al., 2019). Additionally, it explores the role of social media and relationship marketing in SME performance in Bangladesh, highlighting the need for tailored strategies in specific cultural contexts (Salam & Hoque, 2019). The study acknowledges the cultural nuances that influence marketing practices and encourages practitioners to adapt their approaches accordingly.

In conclusion, the study on the role and relevance of marketing in SMEs in Africa makes significant contributions to theory, literature, methods, policy, and social impact. It enriches the theoretical framework by incorporating various dimensions and exploring innovative methodologies. It offers practical insights for industry settings, implications for policy-making, and considerations for societal impact. Overall, this research advances the field of marketing in SMEs, both in theory and in practice. Its findings have the potential to enhance marketing strategies, inform policy decisions, and improve the standards of living for SMEs globally.

8.26 Conclusion

Marketing plays a critical role in the growth and sustainability of African SMEs. As these enterprises navigate the challenges of limited resources, inadequate expertise, and diverse cultural landscapes, contemporary marketing strategies such as digital marketing, mobile marketing, and influencer marketing offer new opportunities for success. By leveraging these strategies, African SMEs can enhance their competitiveness, build strong brands, and achieve sustainable growth in both local and international markets. However, addressing the challenges faced by SMEs in implementing effective marketing strategies requires concerted efforts from governments, private sector stakeholders, and development partners to provide the necessary support, training, and infrastructure.

8.27 Recommendation

To ensure the growth and sustainability of African SMEs, it is essential to prioritise the adoption of contemporary marketing strategies, including digital marketing, mobile marketing, and influencer marketing. These strategies present significant opportunities for SMEs to enhance their competitiveness, build strong brands, and achieve sustainable growth both locally and internationally. However, to effectively implement these strategies, it is crucial for governments, private sector stakeholders, and development partners to collaborate in providing the necessary support, training, and infrastructure. By addressing the challenges of limited resources, inadequate expertise, and diverse cultural landscapes, these collective efforts will empower African SMEs to thrive in an increasingly competitive global market.

8.28 Policy Implications for Enhancing SME Marketing and Sustainability

Policymakers must provide an atmosphere that supports SMEs in order to fully utilise the marketing tactics suggested in the TAPE framework. Governments can implement focused initiatives like incentives for SMEs, marketing assistance plans, and discounted access to digital marketing tools. The capacity of SMEs to develop and compete can also be greatly increased by regulatory changes targeted at lowering administrative obstacles, facilitating better access to capital, and safeguarding intellectual property. In addition to enhancing SMEs' marketing capacities, these policy initiatives support the more general objectives of social inclusion and economic growth.

References

Abdul-Halim, H., Ahmad, N. H., Geare, A., & Thurasamy, R. (2019). Innovation culture in SMEs: The importance of organizational culture, organizational learning and market orientation. *Entrepreneurship Research Journal, 9*(3).

Adomako, S., Gyensare, M. A., Amankwah-Amoah, J., Akhtar, P., & Hussain, N. (2024). Tackling grand societal challenges: Understanding when and how reverse engineering fosters frugal product innovation in an emerging market. *Journal of Product Innovation Management, 41*(2), 211–235.

Amoako-Asiedu, E., Otuo, P. N., Obuobisa-Darko, T., & Antwi-Agyei, A. (2024). *Stakeholder legitimacy perceptions and firm innovation: A developing country perspective stakeholder management and entrepreneurship in Africa* (pp. 49–60). Routledge.

Arias-Aranda, D., Minguela-Rata, B., & Rodríguez-Duarte, A. (2001). Innovation and firm size: An empirical study for Spanish engineering consulting companies. *European Journal of Innovation Management, 4*(3), 133–142.

Bodlaj, M., & Čater, B. (2022). Responsive and proactive market orientation in relation to SMEs' export venture performance: The mediating role of marketing capabilities. *Journal of Business Research, 138*, 256–265.

Carson, P. P., Carson, K. D., Eden, W., & Roe, C. W. (1998). Does empowerment translate into action? An examination of service recovery initiatives. *Journal of Quality Management, 3*(1), 133–148.

Chaffey, D., & Ellis-Chadwick, F. (2019). *Digital marketing*. Pearson UK.

Chatterjee, S., Chaudhuri, R., Vrontis, D., & Galati, A. (2023). Influence of managerial practices, productivity, and change management process on organizational innovation capability of small and medium businesses. *European Business Review, 35*(5), 839–859.

Chinomona, R., & Chinomona, E. (2013). The influence of employees' perceptions of organizational politics on turnover intentions in Zimbabwe's SME sector. *South African Journal of Business Management, 44*(2), 57–66.

Davcik, N. S., Cardinali, S., Sharma, P., & Cedrola, E. (2021). Exploring the role of international R&D activities in the impact of technological and marketing capabilities on SMEs' performance. *Journal of Business Research, 128*, 650–660.

Falahat, M., Ramayah, T., Soto-Acosta, P., & Lee, Y. Y. (2020). SMEs internationalization: The role of product innovation, market intelligence, pricing and marketing communication capabilities as drivers of SMEs' international performance. *Technological Forecasting and Social Change, 152*, 119908.

Hilmersson, F. P., & Hilmersson, M. (2021). Networking to accelerate the pace of SME innovations. *Journal of Innovation & Knowledge, 6*(1), 43–49.

Johannessen, J. A., Olsen, B., & Lumpkin, G. T. (2001). Innovation as newness: What is new, how new, and new to whom? *European Journal of Innovation Management, 4*(1), 20–31.

Johne, A. (1999). Successful market innovation. *Innovations Management*, 163–170.

Keller, K. L. (2013). Building strong brands in a modern marketing communications environment. In *The evolution of integrated marketing communications* (pp. 65–81). Routledge.

Kleindl, B. A. (1996). *The impact of mental models on marketing core and technical core new product choice.* Oklahoma State University.

Ligthelm, A. A. (2010). Entrepreneurship and small business sustainability. *Southern African Business Review, 14*(3).

Martins, E. C., & Terblanche, F. (2003). Building organisational culture that stimulates creativity and innovation. *European Journal of Innovation Management, 6*(1), 64–74.

Masroor, N., & Asim, M. (2019). SMEs in the contemporary era of global competition. *Procedia Computer Science, 158*, 632–641.

Manzoor, F., Wei, L., & Asif, M. (2021). Intrinsic rewards and employee's performance with mediating mechanismof employee's motivation. *Frontiers in psychology, 12*, p. 563070.

Mathew, L. S., George, A. D., & Chandramohan, G. (2019). Entrepreneurs to Enterprise (E2E): Facilitating internationalization of SMEs through virtual entrepreneurship. In *Transnational entrepreneurship: Issues of SME internationalization in the Indian context* (pp. 99–116).

Mathews, S. W., Maruyama, M., Sakurai, Y., Perks, K. J., & Sok, P. (2019). Risk perceptions in Japanese SMEs: The role of Internet marketing capabilities in firm performance. *Journal of Strategic Marketing, 27*(7), 599–611.

Meera, S., & Vinodan, A. (2024). Innovative approach and marketing skill: A case study of artisan entrepreneurs of India. *Journal of Entrepreneurship in Emerging Economies, 16*(3), 576–601.

Mwangi, I. W., & Wanjau, K. L. (2013). The role of SACCO in growth of youth entrepreneurship in Kenya: A case of Nairobi County. *Greener Journal of Business and Management Studies, 3*(3), 113–118.

Narver, J. C., & Slater, S. F. (1990). *The effect of a market orientation on business.*

Nuseir, M. T., & Aljumah, A. (2020). The role of digital marketing in business performance with the moderating effect of environment factors among SMEs of UAE. *International Journal of Innovation, Creativity and Change, 11*(3), 310–324.

O'dwyer, M., Gilmore, A., & Carson, D. (2009). Innovative marketing in SMEs. *European Journal of Marketing, 43*(1/2), 46–61.

Odoom, R., Narteh, B., & Boateng, R. (2017). Branding in small-and medium-sized enterprises (SMEs) Current issues and research avenues. *Qualitative Market Research: An International Journal, 20*(1), 68–89.

Osano, H. M. (2019). Global expansion of SMEs: Role of global market strategy for Kenyan SMEs. *Journal of Innovation and Entrepreneurship, 8*(1), 13.

Presutti, M., & Odorici, V. (2019). Linking entrepreneurial and market orientation to the SME's performance growth: The moderating role of entrepreneurial experience and networks. *International Entrepreneurship and Management Journal, 15*, 697–720.

Puspaningrum, A. (2020). Market orientation, competitive advantage and marketing performance of small medium enterprises (SMEs). *Journal of Economics, Business, and Accountancy Ventura, 23*(1), 19–27.

Quaye, D., & Mensah, I. (2019). Marketing innovation and sustainable competitive advantage of manufacturing SMEs in Ghana. *Management Decision, 57*(7), 1535–1553.

Sadiku-Dushi, N., Dana, L. P., & Ramadani, V. (2019). Entrepreneurial marketing dimensions and SMEs performance. *Journal of Business Research, 100*, 86–99.

Salam, S., & Hoque, A. S. M. M. (2019). The role of social media and effect of relationship marketing on SME performance in Bangladesh: Multi-group CFA. *Asian People Journal (APJ), 2*(1), 12–31.

Sollazzo, R. N. (2024). *Financing and innovation in start-ups: A comparative analysis between Italy and the Netherlands.* Doctoral dissertation, Politecnico di Torino.

Zhou, H., & Gumbo, V. (2021). Rural-urban comparison of manufacturing SMMEs performance in KwaZulu Natal province, South Africa. *African Journal of Development Studies, 11*(1), 7.

9

Strategic Marketing Planning in Small and Medium-Sized Enterprises (SMEs)

Emelia Amoako Asiedu, Priscilla Ntriwaa Otuo, Theresa Obuobisa-Darko, and Ivy Adjei Nketiah

9.1 Introduction

In the context of a rapidly evolving and challenging business environment, organisations, particularly small and medium-sized enterprises (SMEs), have acknowledged the necessity of strategic marketing

E. Amoako Asiedu
Department of Marketing, Ghana Communication Technology University, Accra, Ghana
e-mail: easiedu@gctu.edu.gh

P. N. Otuo (✉)
University of Ghana, Accra, Ghana
e-mail: pnotuo@ug.edu.gh

T. Obuobisa-Darko
Ghana Communication Technology University, Accra, Ghana
e-mail: easiedu@gctu.edu.gh; tobuobisa-darko@gctu.edu.gh

I. A. Nketiah
Wisconsin International University College, Accra, Ghana
e-mail: ivy.adjei-nketiah@wiuc-ghana.edu.gh

E. Amoako Asiedu et al. (eds.), *Entrepreneurship and Small and Medium-Sized Enterprises (SMEs) in Africa*, https://doi.org/10.1007/978-3-032-14174-3_9

planning. This approach offers a systematic framework for integrating an organisation's marketing activities with its overarching objectives. The strategic marketing plan is viewed as both a process and a mechanism for growth and sustainability. It integrates the external context and the internal dynamics of the organisation (Bryson et al. 2011), while also incorporating the management's purpose, aspirations, and goals. It delineates specific strategies aimed at marketing activities to facilitate the effective mobilisation of resources and efforts.

The significance of strategic marketing planning is becoming apparent as SMEs endeavour to maintain competitiveness in dynamic markets. In contrast to larger organisations with ample resources, SMEs often function in a resource-constraint environment, rendering a strategic emphasis essential. This approach involves identifying market opportunities and confronting challenges from external competitors and changing customer preferences (Hervani et al., 2005). Strategic marketing planning allows SMEs to proactively adapt to changes, establishing themselves as nimble and customer-centric organisations within their sectors.

A well-crafted marketing strategy aligns an organisation's operational activities with its strategic goals, guaranteeing consistency in decision-making. It facilitates the prioritisation of tasks, allowing firms to focus on high-impact activities that yield competitive advantages. Research indicates that organisations with robust marketing strategies are more adept at managing market volatility and attaining enhanced performance (Porter, 2008). Moreover, strategic marketing planning establishes a framework for ongoing assessment and adjustment, guaranteeing that organisations stay aligned with changing market circumstances.

Small and medium-sized enterprises (SMEs) are a vital element of the global economy, especially in emerging nations like Ghana, where they represent a substantial share of economic activity. These firms foster innovation, provide employment, and alleviate poverty, making them essential for socio-economic development (Agyapong, 2016; Dauda et al., 2010). Nonetheless, SMEs in Ghana encounter several obstacles that impede their development and viability. Critical challenges include restricted access to sophisticated technology, insufficient management proficiency, and obstacles in obtaining financial and human resources (Yi, 2021). These constraints have resulted in a comparatively low survival rate of SMEs in the area (Robson et al., 2009).

Although strategic marketing planning has considerable potential to improve SME performance, research reveals that several SME managers in Ghana lack the requisite skills or resources for successful implementation. Widespread misconceptions, such as the notion that strategic planning is the preserve of large corporations, hinder its implementation (Motwani et al., 2006) Furthermore, the unfamiliarity with advanced planning tactics and processes hinders managers in SMEs from incorporating strategic marketing into their daily operations. Consequently, several SMEs are unable to capitalise on expanding markets for growth and competitiveness.

The competitive environment for SMEs in Ghana is intensifying, particularly in the services sector. The intensified competition emphasises the need for SMEs to use strategic marketing methods to distinguish themselves and address the varied requirements of their target markets. Some organisations have effectively used strategic planning to improve their competitiveness, while others still face challenges due to external influences. The variation in performance across SMEs prompts essential enquiries about the influence of strategic marketing on achieving company success.

Despite the expanding literature on SME performance and strategic planning, little focus has been placed on the interactive influence of market dynamics in determining the effectiveness of marketing strategies in Ghana. This research seeks to examine the impact of strategic marketing planning on the performance of SMEs in a dynamic and competitive market environment. This study aims to provide practical insights for SMEs striving to enhance their marketing strategies and achieve success in a dynamic business environment.

9.2 Literature Review

9.2.1 Strategic Marketing: Defined

Marketing strategy, like all strategy, involves decisions and actions regarding why, where, and how to compete. Schweitzer et al. (2023) state that strategic marketing is a methodical endeavour that helps firms make crucial choices and take actions that determine and direct the identity, activities, and purpose of an organisation, with an emphasis on the future. For an encompassing strategy, Aaker and Moorman (2023) note that the core elements that shape a firm's strategy include why to compete (requires the organisation to consider its purpose—both its larger purpose in society, its employees, and its shareholders—and also points to the all-important role of customer value, which usually goes hand in hand with purpose) and where to compete (involves questions about the selection of the offering market and target market). The authors went on to contend that it is also very crucial to address the idea of competing (which brings concerns of explaining the value the business offers and the selection of the resources, assets, and capabilities essential in delivering the value and the firm's ability to make profits and therefore maintain the strategy) and lastly, organise to compete (this requires looking at the culture of the organisation, the structure of the organisation, the people of the organisation, and the information that will measure strategic performance). Karami and Gorzynski (2022) lament that strategic thinking is not a given capability for every manager and that their expectations may not always be met. Howbeit, the scholars note that managers must establish the guiding principles that steer the firm and must express their vision in a clear, assertive, and positive way. Entrepreneurs who are starting new businesses must engage in business planning, which involves carefully managing the interplay between opportunity, resources, and team dynamics (Wright & Stigliani, 2013).

9.2.2 Strategic Marketing and the Resource-Based View of SMEs

The discourse in the realm of strategic marketing has extensively relied on ideas and concepts derived from strategic management. Strategic management and marketing are both focused on addressing the challenges that arise in the interaction between an organisation and its external surroundings. The customer-centric approach to marketing and key ideas such as segmentation, positioning, and the product life cycle have also had an impact on strategic management thinking (Gellweiler, 2018; Theoharakis et al., 2024). The Resource-Based View (RBV) is founded on the prior contributions of industrial economists and has been a predominant framework in strategy since the 1980s. To exemplify the impact of marketing on strategy, one may reference the research of Agyapong et al. (2021) about marketing capabilities and the studies of Davcik and Sharma (2016) on competitive advantage. It has been specifically used nowadays as a performance assessment tool in international contexts (Tomczak et al., 2017) and for delineating components of positioning strategy (Gellweiler, 2018). Strategic marketing is likely to be more embraced by managers due to its focus on organisational qualities and its appeal as a competitive approach.

9.3 The Need of Structured Planning for SMEs

The primary emphasis in strategy is on identifying the firm's strategic purpose, which encompasses a distinct vision and mission that may provide guidance to the organisation and foster cohesion among key stakeholders, especially workers (Drucker, 2020). The capacity of an owner-manager to recognise a viable trajectory or direction for development is also crucial (Ansoff, 1965). This growth vector is expected to include the identification of novel goods for established markets (e.g. an innovation plan) or the exploration of untapped markets for current products (e.g. a market expansion strategy). According to Herter (1995), it is essential for any firm, regardless of its size, to have a well-designed and thorough strategic plan. This is because the act of creating a plan compels the SMEs to confront the challenging and practical aspects of the business environment, rather than indulging in unrealistic fantasies.

The literature often highlights the need for enhanced and broader planning among SME businesses. For instance, Davidsson (2015) contended that the entrepreneur's first task is to identify a potential opportunity and thereafter develop a comprehensive marketing and financial strategy to exploit the concept. Subsequent to that, it is necessary to acquire authority over the necessary resources and develop a suitable framework. According to Slávik (2019), only around one-third of start-up entrepreneurs develop thorough marketing and financial strategies. However, those that do are more likely to achieve success in their ventures.

Majama and Magang (2017) expanded on the decision-making process in the company, which is hindered by the fact that only the managing director or owner has the authority to make decisions. This is due to a lack of knowledge among other individuals in the firm about the direction and strategy of the organisation. As a result, the firm's human resources have their potential capacity diminished and are not fully used. Contrary to the need for enhanced and broader planning, the actual data presents disagreement. An investigation of strategic planning in SMEs using empirical study shows that traditionally, it has been widely believed that SMEs should use the same management strategies as larger organisations (Hillary, 2017). Research examining the influence of planning on the sales and profit performance of SMEs has found positive associations between the planning function and sales/profits (Otto et al., 2020; Takata, 2016; Inkinen, 2016), as well as no correlation between the utilisation of planning activities by SMEs owner/managers and performance (Majama & Magang, 2017). However, there are other variables that might potentially confuse the interpretation of these results. These aspects include whether the study differentiates between strategic and operational planning, whether it investigates short- or long-term performance, and the amount of planning knowledge seen.

9.3.1 The Process of SME Strategic Management

In SMEs, strategic marketing planning is often a methodical process where owner-managers analyse their industrial environment and define a structure and direction for future actions. Initially, the first step involves crafting a mission statement, analysing the present circumstances that the firm is confronting, and creating predictions for future expansion (Eide et al., 2021). Subsequently, goals and strategies are established. The documentation of these aspects is provided for both internal and external stakeholders, and a monitoring-evaluation process is implemented

(Schonebeck & Pöllinger, 2020). Identifying the optimal alignment between the organisation's objective, available opportunities, and its skills is typically a significant obstacle. As a result, external consultants are often employed to provide assistance in this regard (Volberda et al., 2021). Nevertheless, the owner-manager bears the ultimate accountability for both the formulation and execution of the strategy (Kiron et al., 2016).

9.4 Mission, Vision, and Strategies

Mission and vision are essential components of strategic management. The distinction between vision and mission lies in their temporal aspects. Mission defines the current activities and purpose of the firm, while vision outlines the future state and actions that the company aims to achieve (Henry, 2021). Visions may be seen as reservoirs of energy that drive the attainment of established goals (Henry, 2021). Vision, goal, and strategies are interrelated components of an entrepreneurial viewpoint. They together transform the entrepreneur's desire for a positive change into a management instrument for accomplishing that change (Slamet et al., 2024). Entrepreneurs with ambitious goals who lead growing SMEs possess a focused and powerful vision for the value they can provide (Vanari & Eisenschmidt, 2024). Although entrepreneurs in SMEs often serve as strategic managers, making both strategic and operative choices (Märk & Situm, 2024), the formulation of strategy and strategic planning are grounded in a strategic vision. To facilitate the growth of the organisation, the entrepreneur must develop a precise and unambiguous goal and vision for their company (Slamet et al., 2024).

9.5 Market Analysis

Market analysis is a crucial step that follows the identification of investment opportunities and the initial feasibility study. It is necessary in order to proceed with the detailed economic feasibility study. The market analysis is the first stage of this study and serves as the scientific foundation for justifying the establishment of the business. Thus, engaging in careful preparation prior to initiating spending is not only highly advisable but also the most effective means to ensure the optimum utilisation of economic resources and enhance the likelihood of successful implementation.

SMEs have the option to use either the top-down or bottom-up method for market analysis in strategic planning (Ates et al., 2023). Additional strategies that the SME management might consider include the supply-oriented strategy and the substitute-in-use approach (Halsted, 2019). During the development of the strategic plan, the top-down approach to market analysis necessitates the firm to gather extensive data on market sizes, trends, plant capacities, and other relevant factors. Additionally, the firm must prioritise resource allocation and competitive position. Furthermore, the firm must place importance on evaluating its relative cost standing and the potential to transfer its experience base to new markets beyond its current ones. These criteria need data that adheres to certain formats and categories. Bottom-up techniques for market analysis assume that the market has already been strategically defined. The primary objective is to assess the distinct attributes of brand rivalry and differences among customers within a certain market sector (Yi et al., 2017). However, many of these grassroots techniques do not inherently need such a limited objective. Nevertheless, this limitation is a direct result of the particular method and time in which they have been used. As a result, their ability to address strategic concerns is mostly unknown. This analysis of a certain methodology showcases the possible results that may be achieved.

The situation-in-use analysis is based on identifying important distinctions between functions and technologies, which demonstrate the many ways in which combinations of functions might be provided. However, instead of starting with the provided function, situation-in-use analysis starts by contemplating the perspective of the customer. Consumers place more importance on the advantages that goods provide rather than the actual things. The supply-oriented approach highlights the reliance on public data, which are regularly organised by industry group (Selviaridis & Spring, 2022). The industrial categories are categorised based on supply characteristics, such as the resemblance of production processes, raw materials, physical appearance, technology, or mode of operation. Generally, supply criteria are seldom effective for categorising clients in a meaningful manner.

9.6 SWOT Analysis and Strategic Planning

Stacey (1993) defines SWOT analysis as a process of identifying an organisation's strengths and weaknesses by evaluating its resources and skills. Furthermore, it contains a concise overview of the risks and possibilities that have been found via an analysis of its surroundings. Strategic logic requires the synchronisation of future activities with strengths and opportunities, the reduction of risks, and the resolution of weaknesses. SWOT Analysis is a strategic assessment method used by marketers to examine an organisation's strategic position. The primary objective of SWOT analysis is to offer valuable insights to marketers regarding the core competences of an organisation, based on the evaluation of data obtained through marketing intelligence. This analysis aims to assist marketers in effectively utilising opportunities by leveraging the organisation's strengths, identifying significant threats, and mitigating weaknesses (Palazzo & Micozzi, 2024). It is crucial to note that scholars like Palazzo and Micozzi (2024) and Puyt et al. (2023) stress the importance of examining a company's strengths and shortcomings in comparison to its rivals. They contend that opportunities and risks stem only from the combined actions or lack thereof of the company and its rivals in reaction to shifting environmental conditions. King et al. (2023) assert that SWOT analysis is a crucial and extensively used tool in strategic marketing planning. The SWOT analysis acts as a conduit between marketing information and strategic planning, facilitating the choice of strategies from a range of alternatives (Palazzo & Micozzi, 2024). Abedian and Hejazi (2023) agree that marketing intelligence provides information that is analysed and used in the strategic decision-making process via SWOT analysis. Thus, SWOT analysis acts as a method for bridging the qualitative and quantitative elements of decision-making and improving the process of strategic marketing planning (Puyt et al., 2023).

9.7 Strategic Versus Operational Planning

Simba and Ojong (2017) proposed that within the context of SMEs, the word "strategy" is often used but not comprehensively grasped. It is often used to elevate the significance of a statement or enhance the weight and credibility of a choice. As a result, "strategic selling" is substituted for "effective techniques for the salesperson" and "manpower strategy" is preferred over "personal development plan". DeJeu (2022) said that management jargon has distorted the true meaning of strategy by conflating it with goals or tactics. Thomas and Thomas (2021) categorised planning into two types: strategic planning, which focusses on long-term goals, and operational planning, which deals with short-term objectives. The researchers determined that there was a significant and intricate relationship between planning and performance. Operational planning was mostly prevalent and beneficial for SMEs; however, there were some favourable associations between strategic planning and performance. Due to the limited number of SMEs engaging in strategic planning, it was perceived that there may be a likelihood of SMEs not capitalising on possible benefits.

9.8 Marketing Segmentation

Market segmentation, as described by Ahani et al. (2019), refers to the systematic identification and classification of different client groups based on their individual preferences and varying requirements for products and marketing strategies. Market segmentation involves classifying heterogeneous markets into more homogeneous groups that have comparable needs, characteristics, and responses to marketing initiatives (Kotler & Keller, 2006; Trivedi et al., 2018). According to Armstrong et al. (2014) market segments are defined as clusters of customers who have the same needs and wants. There is no generally applicable approach for market segmentation. Marketers should conduct experiments using several segmentation criteria, either alone or in combination, to determine the most efficient approach for comprehending the market's structure.

In addition, Ahani et al. (2019) said that segmentation may be conducted using the following variables:

a. Geographic segmentation is a method of dividing markets into distinct geographical entities, such as nations, autonomous regions, cities, climates, or residential areas.
b. Demographic segmentation is a method of dividing markets into different categories depending on criteria such as age, gender, family life cycle, income, job, education, religion, race, and country. Consumer groups are often graded based on demographic variables. One factor is that the demands, preferences, and levels of consumer usage are strongly correlated with demographic characteristics. Furthermore, demographic characteristics are more readily quantifiable in comparison to other sorts of data.
c. Behavioural segmentation categorises buyers based on their knowledge, attitudes, use rates, and the advantages they seek when acquiring a product or service.
d. Psychographic segmentation categorises clients into distinct categories based on their lifestyle attributes and personalities (Wijaya, 2006).

According to Wardana et al. (2023), for the market segmentation process to be more successful and valuable for the firm, it should fulfil the following conditions:

a. Market segmentation may be quantified in terms of its size, scope, and the buying power of the segment.
b. Market segmentation is achievable, allowing for targeted targeting.
c. Market segmentation is crucial for profitability if it effectively caters to certain customer groups.
d. Market segmentation may be put into operation, meaning that all initiatives designed to recruit and service a certain market group become successful.
e. Market segmentation is characterised by its distinguishability, allowing for the conceptual separation of groups. These segments might exhibit varying responses to various aspects and programs within the marketing mix.

9.9 Target Market

To develop an exceptional marketing strategy, organisations must first determine their target audience by segmenting the market into customer categories (market segmentation) and choosing which segments to focus on (marketing goals). The target market, also known as market targeting, refers to a certain set of purchasers who have similar demands and preferences, and whom the firm aims to cater to effectively. Target market selection, often known as targeting, is the deliberate choice of one or more market sectors to penetrate (Aljukhadar & Senecal, 2022). The objective of this goal decision is to ensure client happiness by meeting their specific demands and varied desires. According to Khadka and Maharjan (2017), when customers are happy, the demand for a product increases, which in turn leads to a rise in the company's earnings. The outcome of the targeting process is the target market, which refers to a specific and concentrated sector of the market that is the focus of marketing activity.

Aaker and Moorman (2023) propose five target market selection patterns for companies to consider: (1) Single segment concentration, where the company focusses on a single segment due to factors such as limited funds and market opportunities in that segment. (2) Selective specialisation, where the company targets multiple attractive market segments based on its objectives and resources. (3) Market specialisation, where the company focusses on meeting the diverse needs of a specific group of customers. (4) Product specialisation, where the company concentrates on manufacturing specific products to be sold across multiple segments. (5) Full market coverage, where the company strives to serve all customers with all the products they need.

9.10 Positioning

Positioning plays a vital part in a company's strategy inside a certain market and greatly influences its performance in that market (Aaker & Moorman, 2023). The existing literature (Aaker & Moorman, 2023) outlines three distinct perspectives on positioning: the strategic management approach, the marketing management perspective, and the brand management perspective. Strategically, positioning refers to the utilisation of market opportunities and leveraging organisational strengths and resources in order to gain a competitive advantage. The marketing management literature often uses the term "market segmentation, targeting, and positioning (STP)" to describe this process (Kotler & Keller, 2016, p. 267). According to Qazzafi (2020), positioning does not include any activities carried out on a product. "Positioning refers to the deliberate effort to shape the mindset of potential customers" (p. 2). Brand development and brand management are essential elements of the modern resource-based concept of marketing strategy. Positioning is intricately connected to brand identity, brand vision, and value proposition, which are separate components of a brand that have importance for consumers (Abimbola & Kocak, 2007; Aaker, 1996; Ahmad & Salleh, 2019). Aaker (1996) defined brand position as the explicit presentation of a brand's unique attributes and value proposition to the target audience, highlighting its competitive edge over competing brands (p. 176). The concept of positioning may be subject to several interpretations depending on the person. For some people, it represents the resolve to separate into distinct parts. For some individuals, it is a question of visual perception. For some people, it denotes the action of selecting certain attributes of a product to emphasise (Aaker & Shansby, 2009, p. 56). Due to the complex theoretical basis, it is essential to have a deeper understanding of how SME entrepreneurs comprehend it. Positioning is a process that involves two steps: developing a strategy for how a product or brand will be positioned, and then implementing that strategy in the marketing mix. This definition is supported by Armstrong et al. (2009) and Fluhrer and Brahm (2023). Once an organisation has taken a choice and clearly articulated its positioning strategy, the following step is to successfully communicate this desired position to its target audiences, firmly establishing it in their perceptions (Armstrong et al., 2009, p. 220). Research on the expansion of SMEs suggests that SMEs with growth are more inclined to prioritise market orientation and brand development, in contrast to SMEs that are stable or declining (Fluhrer & Brahm, 2023). According to Joensuu-Salo et al. (2022), rapidly expanding SMEs allocate more resources to improve their marketing capabilities. On the other hand, SMEs that expand at a slower pace tend to take a comprehensive strategy by trying to meet the needs of a diverse spectrum of clients (Tan et al., 2014, p. 69).

9.11 The Marketing Mix

According to Kotler et al. (2015), strategy is the process of determining the direction and scope of an organisation in order to achieve long-term goals by effectively managing its resources in the current dynamic business environment. According to Wirtz (2020), strategy is a fundamental notion in strategic management. Therefore, the marketing mix tactics include all the activities taken by a company to ensure that the target market has a favourable impact on the demand for their product. The marketing mix encompasses several techniques, including product, pricing, promotion, venue, physical, process, and human strategies. Product strategy encompasses the range of products and services provided by a firm to the target market with the aim of fulfilling their demands. Goods may be categorised into two groups: tangible goods, which are physical items that can be touched and seen, and intangible products, which are services or experiences that cannot be physically held or seen (Kotler et al., 2015). Price strategy refers to the value assigned to a product or service. Pricing strategy involves a critical assessment of pricing changes inside organisations and how these changes are influenced by the target market (Kotler et al., 2015). The distribution strategy ensures that a company provides clients with high-quality customer service, which directly affects the degree of customer satisfaction (Kotler et al., 2015). The promotion strategy encompasses various components such as personal selling, sales promotion, advertising, public relations, and direct marketing. These elements play a crucial role in strengthening the customer-firm relationship and are essential for boosting the sales of a product or service (Kotler et al., 2015). Physical strategy: Takes into account the visual aspects and physical surroundings that support and ensure high quality. The physical environment and other observable indicators may significantly impact the perception clients have about the quality of the service they get (Kotler et al., 2015). Process strategy refers to a systematic approach that aids in the planning, creation, and execution of service management, which enhances an organisation's capabilities and strategic assets (Kotler et al., 2015). Service marketing emphasises the importance of personnel, especially the interaction between staff and customers, as a key factor in delivering high-quality service and contributing to customer satisfaction (Kotler et al., 2015). In order to provide excellent customer service, employees must first embrace and appreciate their profession, demonstrating a genuine passion for what they do (Wirtz, 2020). However, potential employees may hesitate to work with informal businesses, and customers may be unwilling to purchase from such enterprises. These challenges can hinder growth, competitiveness, and the ability to deliver high-quality products or services (Amoako-Asiedu et al., 2024).

9.12 Business Planning, Growth, and Performance

Majama and Magang (2017) assert that strategic planning is most often studied in terms of its impact on performance. Strategic planning is a powerful tool that enables businesses to gain a competitive advantage by capturing a larger portion of the market. It also helps businesses adapt to a dynamic environment in a profitable manner. Furthermore, strategic planning plays a crucial role in the pursuit of increased revenues and profits. The formal process of planning, rather than only the produced plan, plays a crucial role in determining the success of a business (Halsted, 2019). Efforts to quantify the advantages that SMEs get from using formal strategic planning have been made since at least the mid-1980s. Stacey (1993) discovered a correlation between planning and financial success. However, they observed that informal analytical planning was more advantageous than formal planning. A study by Cheah et al. (2019) examining planning and performance revealed that basic operational planning had a favourable influence on performance. However, the connection between strategic planning and long-term among SME success was weak (Aljukhadar & Senecal, 2022). Kotler and Keller (2016) discovered that SMEs had minimal formal strategic planning. They also showed that performance was not closely linked to formal strategic planning. Additionally, they observed that operational planning had a stronger correlation with increased profitability and sales compared to strategic planning.

According to Kotler et al. (2015), there is a correlation between managers who have a planning orientation and their financial success. The study suggests that managers who are entrepreneurial and opportunistic tend to achieve better financial outcomes when they actively participate in formal planning. Nevertheless, planning yielded more advantages in the long run as opposed to the short run. According to Boyne (2010), the quality of planning is more significant than the amount of time spent on the planning process. However, it was shown that long-term planning does not have a direct impact on a firm's performance among SMEs. Howbeit, Cheah et al. (2019) indicate that it is anticipated that companies who use structured strategic planning in their marketing efforts will achieve superior financial and market success. Based on the available information, we suggest a correlation between the level of strategic marketing planning and the achievement of success among SMEs.

9.13 Conclusion

This study underscores the significance of strategic marketing planning in enhancing the performance of SMEs, particularly in unstable and competitive contexts. Small and medium-sized enterprises (SMEs) serve as the cornerstone of the global economy, contributing to employment, fostering innovation, and combating poverty, particularly in developing nations such as Ghana. However, they cannot achieve their full development potential due to resource shortages, inadequate management, and lack of a clear strategy. Strategic marketing planning enables SMEs to align their marketing initiatives with the overarching organisational goals, facilitating resource optimisation, proactive market adaptation, and enhanced decision-making quality.

Strategic marketing planning is an effective instrument; yet, it is hardly used in SMEs due to misconceptions about its efficacy and the lack of expertise and resources for its execution. This condition hinders SMEs' capacity to fully capitalise on the present market and diminishes their market potential. The findings demonstrate that operational planning influences profitability in the near term, but strategic planning ensures sustainability and a competitive advantage in the long run. The integration of strategic marketing, market segmentation, targeting, positioning, and resource allocation is a crucial dynamic in promoting development in SMEs.

9.14 Implications for Practitioner

Strategic marketing planning is advantageous for small and medium firms (SMEs) since it offers methods for successful competition in diverse marketplaces. This approach ensures that marketing operations align with organisational goals to promote resource efficiency and decision-making. Strategic marketing yields a favourable reaction to evolving market circumstances, enhances consumer happiness, and sustains a competitive advantage over the long term. In management, SME managers in countries like Ghana must confront the perception that strategic planning is only for larger organisations. It is essential to educate SME owners on the significance of such initiatives and to train them in effective planning. Furthermore, legislative initiatives should aim to improve resource availability inside SMEs, notably by increasing financing and market information to promote the utilisation and practice of strategic marketing planning.

9.15 Implications for Research

These findings underscore the need of further examining the correlation between strategic marketing and the success of European SMEs in emerging and dynamic resource-constrained countries. Although contemporary marketing literature emphasises the significance of strategic marketing, its implementation across many sectors and locations remains inadequate. Another area that warrants investigation is the performance measures related to elements such as customer count, market share profitability, and marketing capabilities including segmentation, targeting, and positioning. Also, the connection addressing the marketing strategy of SMEs with external aspects like the advancement of technology by the government or other factors should be investigated too, depending on economic nations like Ghana.

9.16 Future Research Avenues

Organisations, particularly SMEs, must recognise the importance of digital technologies in their strategic marketing efforts. Consequently, an examination of the digital marketing strategies used by SMEs would be beneficial. Cross-industry and geographic sector analyses may identify best practices and creative methods effective across several sectors or locations. Furthermore, longitudinal studies assessing the impact of strategic marketing on the development and sustainability of SMEs over time will have significant industrial and economic importance for practitioners and policymakers. Investigating the reasons that hinder the implementation of strategic marketing, such as insufficient resources and management competences, may provide pragmatic solutions to alleviate these limitations. Additionally, it would be valuable to examine the advantages of joint strategic marketing initiatives among SMEs within the same industry.

References

Aaker, D. A. (1996). Measuring brand equity across products and markets. *California management review, 38*(3).

Aaker, D. A., & Moorman, C. (2023). *Strategic market management.* John Wiley & Sons.

Aaker, D. A., & Shansby, G. (2009). Positioning your product. *Business Horizons.*

Abedian, M., & Hejazi, M. (2023). Optimal strategy selection under fuzzy environment for strategic planning methodology selection: A SWOT approach. *Cybernetics and Systems, 56*, 1–26.

Abimbola, T., & Kocak, A. (2007). Brand, organization identity and reputation: SMEs as expressive organizations: A resources-based perspective. *Qualitative Market Research: An International Journal, 10*(4), 416–430.

Agyapong, G. T. (2016). Factors Influencing the development and growth of small medium-sized enterprises; The case of Ghana (Doctoral dissertation, Brunel University London.).

Agyapong, A., Essuman, D., & Yeboah, A. K. L. (2021). Performance implications of strategic planning and marketing capability in micro and small businesses in an emerging African economy: A contingent resource-based view. *Journal of Small Business & Entrepreneurship, 33*(1), 29–48.

Ahani, A., Nilashi, M., Ibrahim, O., Sanzogni, L., & Weaven, S. (2019). Market segmentation and travel choice prediction in Spa hotels through TripAdvisor's online reviews. *International Journal of Hospitality Management, 80*, 52–77.

Ahmad, A., & Salleh, S. M. (2019). Brand related capabilities and the process of integrated marketing communications (IMC): A Resource Based View (RBV). *Journal of Contemporary Research in Social Sciences, 1*(6), 136–150.

Aljukhadar, M., & Senecal, S. (2022). Targeting the very important buyers VIB: A cluster analysis approach. *Cogent Business & Management, 9*(1), 2088458.

Amoako-Asiedu, E., Otuo, P. N., Obuobisa-Darko, T., & Antwi-Agyei, A. (2024). Stakeholder Legitimacy Perceptions and Firm Innovation: A developing country perspective. In *Stakeholder Management and Entrepreneurship in Africa* (pp. 49–60). Routledge.

Ansoff, H. I. (1965). Corporate strategy: An analytic approach to business policy for growth and expansion. (No Title).

Armstrong, G., Adam, S., Denize, S., & Kotler, P. (2014). *Principles of marketing*. Pearson Australia.

Armstrong, M., Vickers, J., & Zhou, J. (2009). Prominence and consumer search. *The RAND Journal of Economics, 40*(2), 209–233.

Ates, A., McKiernan, P., & Sunner, A. (2023). Reversing the pyramid: Interactive and bottom-up strategy practices in small and medium enterprises. In *Contemporary approaches in equality, diversity and inclusion: Strategic and technological perspectives* (pp. 75–100). Emerald Publishing Limited.

Borden, N. H. (1964). The concept of the marketing mix. *Journal of advertising research, 4*(2), 2–7.

Boyne, G. A. (2010). *Strategic planning. Public service improvement: Theories and evidence* (pp. 60–77). OUP Oxford.

Bryson, J. M., Anderson, S. R., & Alston, F. K. (2011). *Implementing and sustaining your strategic plan: A Workbook for Public and Nonprofit Organizations*. John Wiley & Sons.

Cheah, J., Amran, A., & Yahya, S. (2019). External oriented resources and social enterprises' performance: The dominant mediating role of formal business planning. *Journal of Cleaner Production, 236*, 117693.

Davcik, N. S., & Sharma, P. (2016). Marketing resources, performance, and competitive advantage: A review and future research directions. *Journal of Business Research, 69*(12), 5547–5552.

Dauda, Y. A., Akingbade, W. A., & Akinlabi, H. B. (2010). Strategic management practice and corporate performance of selected small business enterprises in Lagos metropolis. *International journal of Business and Management, 5*(11), 97.

Davidsson, P. (2015). Entrepreneurial opportunities and the entrepreneurship nexus: A re-conceptualization. *Journal of Business Venturing, 30*(5), 674–695.

DeJeu, E. B. (2022). The ethics of delivering bad news: Evaluating impression management strategies in corporate financial reporting. *Journal of Business and Technical Communication, 36*(2), 190–230.

Drucker, P. F. (2020). *The essential drucker*. Routledge.

Eide, A. E., Moen, Ø., Madsen, T. K., & Azari, M. J. (2021). Growth aspirations in SMEs: Managerial determinants and organizational outcomes. *Journal of Small Business and Enterprise Development, 28*(4), 640–665.

Fluhrer, P., & Brahm, T. (2023). Positioning in SMEs: Entrepreneurs' perceptions and strategies. *Journal of Research in Marketing and Entrepreneurship, 25*(3), 431–454.

Gellweiler, C. (2018). Cohesion of RBV and industry view for competitive positioning. *Strategic Management-International Journal of Strategic Management and Decision Support Systems in Strategic Management, 23*(2), 3–12.

Halsted, H. (2019). *How to live in the woods: Expert advice on planning, outfitting, and managing a camping expedition*. Courier Dover Publications.

Henry, A. (2021). *Understanding strategic management*. Oxford University Press.

Herter, G. (1995). Business plan software boosts your chances. *Accounting Technology, 11*, 20–20.

Hervani, A. A., Helms, M. M., & Sarkis, J. (2005). Performance measurement for green supply chain management. *Benchmarking: An international journal, 12*(4), 330–353.

Hillary, R. (Ed.). (2017). *Small and medium-sized enterprises and the environment: Business imperatives*. Routledge.

Inkinen, H. (2016). Review of empirical research on knowledge management practices and firm performance. *Journal of Knowledge Management, 20*(2), 230–257.

Joensuu-Salo, S., Viljamaa, A., & Kangas, E. (2022). Marketing first? The role of marketing capability in SME growth. *Journal of Research in Marketing and Entrepreneurship, 25*(2), 185–202.

Karami, A., & Gorzynski, R. A. (2022). Connection to nature and sustainability in small-and medium-sized environmental organizations: A dynamic strategic thinking approach. *Business Strategy and the Environment, 31*(1), 371–389.

Khadka, K., & Maharjan, S. (2017). Customer satisfaction and customer loyalty. *Centria University of Applied Sciences Pietarsaari, 1*(10), 58–64.

King, T., Freyn, S., & Morrison, J. (2023). SWOT analysis problems and solutions: Practitioners' feedback into the ongoing academic debate. *Journal of Intelligence Studies in Business, 13*(1), 30–42.

Kiron, D., Kane, G. C., Palmer, D., Phillips, A. N., & Buckley, N. (2016). Aligning the organization for its digital future. *MIT Sloan Management Review, 58*(1).

Kotler, P., & Keller, K. L. (2006). *Dirección de marketing*. Pearson educación.

Kotler, P., Burton, S., Deans, K., Brown, L., & Armstrong, G. (2015). *Marketing*. Pearson Higher Education AU.

Kotler, P., & Keller, L. K. (2016). *Marketing management* (15th ed.). Pearson Education.

Majama, N. S., & Magang, T. I. (2017). Strategic planning in small and medium enterprises (SMEs): A case study of Botswana SMEs. *Journal of Management and Strategy, 8*(1), 74–103.

Märk, S., & Situm, M. (2024). Long-term guidance in flux: The evolving significance of mission and vision in strategic management. *Family Business Transformation: Strategic Orientation and Business Modelling, 1*, 1.

Motwani, J., Levenburg, N. M., Schwarz, T. V., & Blankson, C. (2006). Succession planning in SMEs: An empirical analysis. *International Small Business Journal, 24*(5), 471–495.

Otto, A. S., Szymanski, D. M., & Varadarajan, R. (2020). Customer satisfaction and firm performance: Insights from over a quarter century of empirical research. *Journal of the Academy of Marketing Science, 48*(3), 543–564.

Palazzo, M., & Micozzi, A. (2024). The SWOT analysis: An evolving decision-making model. In *Rethinking decision-making strategies and tools: Emerging research and opportunities* (pp. 53–70). Emerald Publishing Limited.

Porter, M. E. (2008). The five competitive forces that shape strategy. *Harvard business review 86*, (1), 78.

Puyt, R. W., Lie, F. B., & Wilderom, C. P. (2023). The origins of SWOT analysis. *Long Range Planning, 56*(3), 102304.

Qazzafi, S. (2020). Factor affecting consumer buying behavior: A conceptual study. *International Journal for Scientific Research & Development, 8*(2), 1205–1208.

Robson, P. J., Haugh, H. M., & Obeng, B. A. (2009). Entrepreneurship and innovation in Ghana: enterprising Africa. *Small business economics, 32*(3), 331–350.

Schonebeck, L., & Pöllinger, T. (2020). Stakeholder management as a tool for the implementation of sustainable supply chains in SMEs in the german food industry(Master's thesis). Malmö University. https://www.diva-portal.org/smash/get/diva2:1481264/FULLTEXT01.pdf

Schweitzer, F., Malek, S. L., & Sarin, S. (2023). Exploring the future of market driving: A dialogue with marketing thought leaders. *Industrial Marketing Management, 113*, 277–294.

Selviaridis, K., & Spring, M. (2022). Fostering SME supplier-enabled innovation in the supply chain: The role of innovation policy. *Journal of Supply Chain Management, 58*(1), 92–123.

Simba, A., & Ojong, N. (2017). Engaged scholarship: Encouraging interactionism in entrepreneurship and small-to-medium enterprise (SME) research. *Journal of Small Business and Enterprise Development, 24*(4), 1009–1027.

Slamet, S., Ridho, A., Marno, M., & Efiyanti, A. Y. (2024). Impact of mission and vision on academic services mediated by governance and human resources in higher education institutions of Indonesia. *Problems and Perspectives in Management, 22*(1), 477–490.

Slávik, Š. (2019). The Business model of start-up—Structure and consequences. *Administrative Sciences, 9*(3), 69.

Stacey, R. (1993). *Strategic Management and Organisational Dynamics*. Pitman

Takata, H. (2016). Effects of industry forces, market orientation, and marketing capabilities on business performance: An empirical analysis of Japanese manufacturers from 2009 to 2011. *Journal of Business Research, 69*(12), 5611–5619.

Tan, S. L. C., Smyrnios, K. X., & Xiong, L. (2014). What drives learning orientation in fast growth SMEs? *International Journal of Entrepreneurial Behavior & Research, 20*(4), 324–350.

Theoharakis, V., Zheng, Y., & Zhang, L. (2024). Dynamic strategic marketing planning: The paradox of concurrently reconfiguring and implementing strategic marketing planning. *Journal of Business Research, 174*, 114525.

Thomas, R. K., & Thomas, R. K. (2021). Strategic planning. *Health services Planning*, 215–245.

Tomczak, T., Reinecke, S., & Kuss, A. (2017). *Strategic marketing: Market-oriented corporate and business unit planning*. Springer.

Trivedi, K., Trivedi, P., & Goswami, V. (2018). Sustainable marketing strategies: Creating business value by meeting consumer expectation. *International Journal of Management, Economics and Social Sciences (IJMESS), 7*(2), 186–205.

Vanari, K., & Eisenschmidt, E. (2024). Missions, visions, and goals for school improvement-A typology of Estonian schools. *Leadership and Policy in Schools, 23*(2), 434–451.

Volberda, H. W., Khanagha, S., Baden-Fuller, C., Mihalache, O. R., & Birkinshaw, J. (2021). Strategizing in a digital world: Overcoming cognitive barriers, reconfiguring routines and introducing new organizational forms. *Long Range Planning, 54*(5), 102110.

Wardana, M. A., Masliardi, A., Afifah, N., Sajili, M., & Kusnara, H. P. (2023). Unlocking purchase preferences: Harnessing psychographic segmentation, promotion and location strategies. *Jurnal Informatika Ekonomi Bisnis*, 713–719.

Wijaya, A. (2006). *The Analysis of Competitive Strategy of PT.* Indo Jaya Motor to Face the Japanese and Non Japanese Motorcycle Brand.

Wirtz, B. W. (2020). *Business model management: Design-process-instruments*. Springer Nature.

Wright, M., & Stigliani, I. (2013). Entrepreneurship and growth. *International Small Business Journal, 31*(1), 3–22.

Yi, S. (2021, July). Research on SMEs Financing Issues. In *2021 International Conference on Economic Development and Business Culture* (ICEDBC 2021) (pp. 57–62). Atlantis Press.

Yi, Y., Gu, M., & Wei, Z. (2017). Bottom-up learning, strategic flexibility and strategic change. *Journal of Organizational Change Management, 30*(2), 161–183.

10

The Role of Digital Advertising and AI-Based Public Relations in Brand Promotions: Conceptual Framework

Antoinette Yaa Benewaa Gabrah, George Kofi Amoako, and Emelia Amoako Asiedu

10.1 Introduction

Digital advertising and AI-based public relations (PR) have become critical tools for brand promotion in the modern marketing landscape (Ziakis & Vlachopoulou, 2023; Makrides et al., 2020). According to Agarwal

A. Y. B. Gabrah (✉)
Academic City University College, Accra, Ghana

Ghana Communication Technology University, Accra, Ghana

Durban University of Technology, Durban, South Africa
e-mail: antoinette.gabrah@acity.edu.gh

G. K. Amoako
Ghana Communications Technology University, Accra, Ghana

Durban University of Technology, Durban, South Africa
e-mail: gamoako@gctu.edu.gh

E. Amoako Asiedu
Department of Marketing, Ghana Communication Technology University, Accra, Ghana
e-mail: easiedu@gctu.edu.gh

E. Amoako Asiedu et al. (eds.), *Entrepreneurship and Small and Medium-Sized Enterprises (SMEs) in Africa*, https://doi.org/10.1007/978-3-032-14174-3_10

and Mittal (2023), with the inception of digital advertising in the marketing space, it has increasingly led to the rise in brand awareness. Digital advertising coming in the form of social media advertisement, website advertising, email marketing, SMS marketing, among others, has overshadowed traditional advertisement (Jeong & Park, 2023), leading to greater and wider audience reach and engagement (Zerfass et al., 2020). The advantage that digital advertising brings includes its ability to reach a wider global audience in real time, at a lower cost, and monitor the analytics related to the advertisement in real time. Literature (Gomez & Roberts, 2022) reveals that there exists a direct correlation between advertising and brand promotion. Branding talks about how well a product is positioned in the minds of consumers (Chen et al., 2021), and how well a product is advertised heavily impacts upon how well a product is positioned in the minds of consumers. Digital advertising provides the platform that augments the promotion of brands through its effectiveness.

Recent breakthroughs in brand promotions have been with regards to the surfacing of artificial intelligence, which has provided a more advanced platform for leveraging technology for business and brands. The PR industry has been affected by the intersection of technology, particularly artificial intelligence (Kumar et al., 2022). AI-based public relations go to the extent of providing automated tasks, improved user engagement, and personalized and customized content to customers, which increases customer satisfaction (Jeong & Park, 2023) and eventually the brand of the product or business organization (Buhmann & White, 2022). In this work, the role of digital advertising and AI-based PR in brand promotions is discussed using a literature-based approach.

This study, therefore, examines the linkage between digital advertising, AI-based public relations, and brand promotion. The work is essentially a non-empirical review of literature, with the development of a conceptual model that can be tested in future studies (Gabrah et al., 2023). Searches were conducted using databases such as Emerald, Wiley, Science direct, and Taylor and Francis for papers which focused on digital advertising, AI-based public relations, and brand promotion. All the articles reviewed are published in English (Gabrah et al., 2023).

This paper, therefore, establishes a relationship between digital advertising, AI-based public relations, and brand promotion using the theory of acceptance and use of technology to achieve this objective and is structured as follows: the next section focuses on the literature review and proposition development; the methodology; and the conceptual framework. In the subsequent section, the implications are discussed, followed by the conclusion.

10.2 Literature Review

10.2.1 Digital Advertising

Digital advertising refers to the promotions of goods and services through the digital space through platforms such as social media, search engines, websites, display ads, and email marketing. This form of advertising has become a cornerstone of modern-day marketing, mainly as a result of its ability to reach out to a larger audience globally with precision (Agarwal & Mittal, 2023). Moreover, the rise of programmatic advertising, which helps automate selling and buying of advert spaces, has, to a large extent, enhanced the efficiency of digital campaigns (Gabrah et al., 2025a, b).

Digital advertising offers several unique advantages that make it indispensable for brand promotion (Kühl et al., 2020). For instance, compared to traditional advertising methods, digital advertising provides a cost-efficient solution for reaching large audiences. Platforms such as Google Ads and Facebook Ads allow brands to allocate budgets effectively and measure performance in real time (Gomez & Roberts, 2022). Unlike traditional advertising, digital platforms enable two-way communication, fostering deeper engagement with consumers. Interactive formats, such as polls and quizzes on Instagram or live streams on YouTube, allow brands to create personalized experiences (Chen et al., 2021). The rise of video ads and augmented reality (AR) ads has revolutionized consumer engagement. AR ads, in particular, allow consumers to visualize products in real-world settings, enhancing decision-making and resulting in higher customer satisfaction (Türksoy, 2022).

Digital Advertising uses strategies such as personalization, retargeting, and omnichannel campaigns. An example of personalization includes ads tailored to individual preferences based on browsing history and behavior in order to increase engagement. The retargeting strategy works by tracking user interactions, which enables advertisers to re-engage potential customers with ads for previously viewed products. Omnichannel Campaigns involve combining multiple platforms, such as Instagram, Facebook, and email marketing, to ensure consistent messaging across channels (Chaffey & Ellis-Chadwick, 2019).

10.2.2 AI-Based Public Relations

The evolution of public relations traces back to ancient practices like Sumerian bulletins and Julius Caesar's newsletters, which evolved from one-way propaganda to mutual benefit exchanges. However, modern PR was pioneered by Ivy Lee and Edward Bernays and used for promotion and persuasion. The development of print media, radio and television accelerated the growth of PR and integrated it into mass media (Bernays, 1951). PR's journey from ancient roots to contemporary practice highlights its dynamic role in shaping communication strategies and maintaining a favorable public image within evolving media landscapes. A study by Jeong and Park (2023) found that AI in public relations enhances efficiency by automating routine tasks, improving stakeholder engagement, and providing deeper insights into public perception and behavior. The downside has been with regard to maintaining transparency and ethical considerations with AI use, which has the propensity to affect public trust. They also revealed that the integration of AI into public relations strategies leads to more strategic decision-making and a stronger ability to effectively manage brand reputation.

Public Relations (PR) is a "*strategic management function that plays a crucial role in establishing and maintaining relationships between an organization and the audiences whose perceptions significantly impact its success or failure*". Rapid advancement has redefined interaction, making face-to-face engagement optional for socializing, shopping, and beyond. Digitalization has opened diverse communication avenues, with AI permeating various sectors like health, education, and marketing (Demirli & Kutuk, 2010). AI is increasingly broadly spreading due to the increase in algorithms. AI technologies display humanoid intellectual abilities and also perform some human abilities in undertaking public relation functions, whether exclusively independently or with the aid of a PR practitioner (Galloway & Swiatek, 2018). AI integration in PR is mushrooming, which is essential for understanding audience expectations. Of a truth, AI has the ability to help improve communication with respect to PR by streamlining processes and empowering PR professional through data-driven insights. AI is widely utilized in the Public Relations Industry, with chatbots prevalent in instant messaging and websites (Forbes, 2020). AI capabilities include text-to-speech, language recognition, translation, emotion detection, and document review. PR now leverages AI tools for tasks like press releases, automated emails, media monitoring, and sentiment analysis, boosting productivity significantly. However, as AI evolves, its usage is poised to surge, raising concerns about its benefits. While new technology offers convenience and advantages, it also sparks numerous problems within the PR community.

Artificial intelligence (AI) is reshaping public relations strategies by automating routine tasks, enabling professionals to allocate more time to strategic and creative activities (Buhmann & White, 2022). This automation not only boosts efficiency but also enhances productivity, allowing PR teams to deliver impactful campaigns with fewer resources. AI-enabled tools such as email automation, content scheduling software, and social media monitoring platforms streamline operations, helping PR professionals focus on critical areas like stakeholder engagement and crisis management (Arief & Saputra, 2019). Furthermore, AI enhances personalized communication through advanced technologies like chatbots and virtual assistants, which analyze user behavior and preferences to deliver tailored responses. Such systems foster meaningful customer interactions, build trust, and strengthen brand loyalty (Kumar et al., 2022).

AI's contribution to crisis management is particularly noteworthy. Its ability to proactively identify potential risks by monitoring public sentiment and analyzing real-time data equips brands to respond swiftly and effectively during crises (Galloway & Swiatek, 2018). Sentiment analysis tools detect shifts in audience attitudes, allowing brands to mitigate potential reputational damage by addressing concerns promptly (Chen et al., 2021). This predictive capability ensures that brands remain in control of their narratives, avoiding negative publicity while maintaining audience trust (Zerfass et al., 2020). Predictive analytics also plays a critical role in campaign planning. By anticipating trends and consumer behavior, AI allows PR professionals to refine their strategies and stay ahead of emerging industry issues. For example, AI provides actionable insights for optimizing content and targeting specific demographics (Jeong & Park, 2023). This forward-looking approach positions brands as thought leaders and enhances their competitive advantage.

Despite its transformative potential, AI should not replace human expertise. While it excels at data-driven tasks, human creativity, critical thinking, and cultural understanding remain essential for crafting authentic messages that resonate with diverse audiences (Austin & Toth, 2011). Ethical considerations, such as transparency and bias mitigation, also necessitate human oversight in AI applications (Bowen, 2007). Professionals must view AI as a complementary tool that augments their abilities to deliver impactful campaigns and adapt to rapidly changing trends (Adams et al., 2012). In today's fast-paced media landscape, the integration of AI into public relations strategies is indispensable. By combining AI's analytical power with human ingenuity, brands can create innovative, audience-centric campaigns that drive engagement and enhance reputation management (Ansip, 2017). This synergy not only improves operational efficiency but also empowers PR professionals to navigate complex communication challenges effectively.

10.2.3 Digital Advertising, AI-Based Public Relations and Brand Promotion

A growing dependence on data, automation, and intelligence characterizes modern marketing strategies (Vlačić et al., 2021). AI-based public relations is a digital marketing communication strategy, with its implementation in mainstream operations intended to achieve faster success (Kumar et al., 2024). However, its implementation among SMEs is still in its infant stages. Marketers can, therefore, capitalize on AI-based public relations as a digital marketing communication strategy to derive value for their customers. Since it provides the capacity to quickly adjust to changing business requirements, producing communications and solution packages that are extremely valuable and profitable for relevant stakeholders. Literature argues for a new marketing mix framework that includes planning, production, personalization, promotion, and more (Marketing Artificial Intelligence Institute, 2024).

Lee and Cho (2020) and Confos and Davis (2016) admit that digital advertising helps to deliver messages through online media outlets, which serve as an integral means of promoting products or services. Previous studies acknowledge that digital advertising serves as a strategic tool for promoting the sustainability of the brand (Ahmed et al., 2019; Makrides et al., 2020; Bruce et al., 2017). For example, Makrides et al. (2020) and Raji et al. (2019) posit that digital advertising is mainly used as a digital marketing communication tool to create brand awareness. This demonstrates that digital advertising, as a key digital marketing communication, has a potential to enhance brand promotion. Thus, this study proposes that:

P1: digital advertising as a digital marketing strategy will have a positive and significant effect on brand promotion of SMEs.

In the current competitive business environment, AI is essential for streamlining processes and guaranteeing quicker success. Artificial intelligence in marketing has a wider use in digital marketing than only including traditional marketing components of the marketing mix. The adoption of AI-enabled marketing techniques, including AI-based public relations, contributes to personalization (Kühl et al., 2020). Furthermore, AI has the ability to overtake human specialists in creative marketplaces. Firms may now use cutting-edge technologies to create powerful brand components to attract customers to a product or service (Cui et al., 2024). Interestingly, on social media, this leads to brand advocacy, love, loyalty, and positive word-of-mouth (Song & Kim, 2022; You et al., 2021). Therefore, this study proposes that:

P2: AI-based public relations as a digital marketing strategy will have a positive and significant effect on brand promotion of SMEs.

10.2.4 Digital Advertising, AI-Based PR and Brand Promotions

Artificial intelligence helps in the engagement of customers. This leads to increased lifetime value and revenue (Bhardwaj et al., 2025). Along different stages of the customer journey, firms can customize content that is highly valuable to a wide range of customers (Dixit, 2022). Previous studies suggest that marketing teams can use artificial intelligence (AI) to help them carry out needs-based studies (Gupta et al., 2021). It is important to note that the creative and innovative marketing strategies are highly tailored and human-centered experiences, due to AI. This will promote improved brand advocacy. Without a question, artificial intelligence (AI) will help marketers combine cutting-edge technology with human creativity to identify, understand, and interact with modern consumers on a personal level. This can be achieved through hyperpersonalized, relevant, and timely advertising (Kumar et al., 2024). The use of digital advertising and AI-based public relations as a digital marketing strategy has a positive impact on the attitude formation of customers, and this, in turn, affects brand positioning and brand promotion positively (Melović et al., 2020). In the same vein, Labanauskaitė et al. (2020) admit that digital advertising and AI-based public relations serve as important e-marketing tools that help to communicate new products to customers and to ensure customer engagement. This study proposes that:

P3: Digital advertising and AI-based public relations as a digital marketing strategy will have a positive and significant effect on brand promotion of SMEs.

10.3 Ethical Considerations and Approach Using Digital Advertising and AI-Based Public Relation

Early public relations practices sparked ethical concerns with a press agentry approach, emphasizing exaggeration and sensationalism over truthfulness, as noted by Grunig and Hunt in 1984, creating ethical dilemmas. Most communication managers may embrace technologically mediated processes without a thorough understanding. Communication professionals acknowledge the need for further education and competency in utilizing AI tools for communication practices, recognizing AI's significant impact on the industry (Zerfass et al., 2020). It is a primary concern that evolving communication and PR technologies be approached with ethical considerations regarding AI usage. Professionals must grasp how algorithms are constructed and employed within their organizations, alongside a nuanced understanding of data ethics and the ramifications of AI implementation (Valin & Gregory, 2020). Moreover, PR professionals must steer moral decision-making regarding AI utilization and emerging technologies, considering their development and organizational application. AI's potential to enhance communication persuasiveness and target audiences based on psychological susceptibilities raises ethical concerns regarding public opinion engineering (Bachmann, 2019). However, like any evolving profession, its historical path reflects a shift toward more self-aware and ethical communication models. By examining this progression, we witness the profession's evolution from merely disseminating information to actively fostering ethical communication practices. Public Relations has been observed as unethical due to its behavior of persuasion, lying, and spin doctoring; the practice itself is akin to manipulation and propaganda. Many criticize the PR industry for lacking ethics and lobbying as threats to truthful journalism (Shannon et al., 2021). Ivy Lee's prominent practice of Public Relations emphasizes telling the truth and providing accurate information. Corporate conscience was highly focused on public relations (Ryan & Martinson, 1983).

The evolution of ethics in public relations opened a broader sense of social responsibility and accountability, and ethically responsible policy for balanced decision-making. Many ethical advisors in the industry have contributed to historical public relations developments with more self-aware and moral communication models. Today, the profession has matured, and the industry depends heavily on the codes of ethics of significant professional associations. Ethical principles hold not only the broader discourse of business ethics but also in the specific realm of public relations ethics (Baskin et al., 2005). Practitioners must be committed to serve the client's interests through upright promotion and

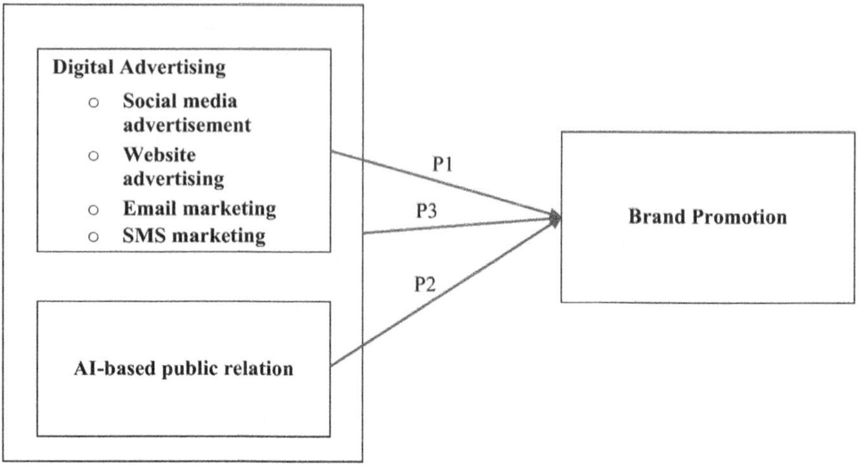

Fig. 10.1 Conceptual framework of the study. (Author's Construct (2024))

Table 10.1 Summary of the review

Themes	Source	Finding
Digital advertising	Ahmed et al. (2019), Amoako et al. (2023), Bruce et al. (2017), Chaffey and Ellis-Chadwick (2019), Lee and Cho (2020), Makrides et al. (2020), Song and Kim (2022)	Digital advertising enhances consumer engagement and brand visibility, particularly through personalization, interactivity, and social media.
AI-based public relations	Agarwal and Mittal (2023), Buhmann and White (2022), Galloway and Swiatek (2018), Kumar et al. (2022), Jeong and Park (2023), Zerfass et al. (2020), Gabrah et al. (2025a, b)	AI technologies are transforming public relations by enabling real-time reputation management, stakeholder analysis, and message personalization.
Ethical considerations	Austin and Toth (2011), Bachmann (2019), Bowen (2004), Shannon et al. (2021), Valin and Gregory (2020), Chen et al. (2021)	The integration of AI in communication raises ethical concerns such as bias, transparency, and the need for revised codes of professional conduct.

Source: Author's Construct (2025)

concealment, meanwhile serve an undefined public interest (Bowen, 2004). The PR professions require making judgment calls and ethical decisions. Public relations practitioners must navigate complex situations, manage crises, and make strategic decisions. Advertisers need to consider ethical implications and societal impacts when creating campaigns (Fig. 10.1). A summary of the review is presented in Table 10.1.

10.4 Methodology

The study used a traditional review of literature using articles published in English from 2017 to 2025. In this study, a desk-based research style was used. Prior research is summarized, compiled, and synthesized as part of secondary research. We used a range of datasets to better comprehend how to make more informed business selections. In addition, we studied periodicals, new publications, books, and digital resources from various sectors. During our search, we eliminated any research that did not meet our expansive criteria. Using this method, we gathered the necessary data: First, we conducted an electronic search of relevant databases (Emerald Online Journals; JSTOR Online Journals; Elsevier Online Journals). Keywords used for searching literature include digital advertising, AI-based public relations, digital marketing strategy, and brand promotion of SMEs. Google scholar was used as the main search engine. These keywords should be covered in the abstract as well as the main document. Articles, as well as reports from other organizations, were also reviewed. In all, 53 papers were sourced, and after screening and scanning, 43 were valid for the review.

10.5 Discussion of Proposed Conceptual Framework

This study conceptualizes that digital advertising and AI-based public relations as a digital marketing communication strategy are employed by firms. Digital advertising can take forms such as social media advertisement, website advertising, email marketing and SMS marketing. The study proposes that digital advertising, if effectively implemented and managed by an organization, could positively and significantly affect brand promotion irrespective of the category of the brand (Gabrah et al., 2025a). Also, AI-based public relations could yield a positive and significant impact on brand promotion. Again, both digital advertising and AI-based public relations, if applied together as a combined digital marketing communication strategy, can also bring in positive brand promotion effects for firms. Key firms that implement digital advertising and AI-based public relations in Africa, particularly Ghana and Nigeria, include Interactive digital, which is a full-service digital agency and has key customers like MTN, Stanbic (The Business & Financial Times Online, 2025). Effect studios also uses digital advertising and AI-based public relations as a strategy and has customers like Meta, Ecobank, and Total Energies (The Business & Financial Times Online, 2025). Also, Red Media Africa implements this strategy and hosts customers like Access Bank and Lipton (Lamphills Blog, 2025).

10.6 Implications

This paper provides evidence that there is a need to explore digital advertising and artificial Intelligence-based public relations as key digital marketing communication strategies, particularly to drive brand promotion among small and medium-sized enterprises from the emerging market perspective (Amoako et al., 2023). This will help to ensure sustainability, leading to the attainment of the SDGs (Gabrah et al., 2023). The implementation and effective management of digital advertising and artificial Intelligence-based public relations by SMEs such as Interactive digital would help firms to improve their overall brand performance (Amoako et al., 2024). Therefore, managers and CEOs of SMEs in emerging market like Effect studios should be deliberate about the implementation of digital advertising and artificial Intelligence-based public relations as a digital marketing communication strategy (Gabrah et al., 2024). Again, they should invest in digital advertising and artificial Intelligence-based public relations to help them derive the positive market outcome. Managers and CEOs of SMEs such as Red Media Africa should further monitor and estimate the digital marketing performance of such strategies (Melović et al., 2020). Marketing professionals should put in measures to implement digital advertising and artificial Intelligence-based public relations as key digital marketing communication strategies to improve the promotion of brands. Regulatory bodies should endeavor to monitor and sanction firms that deviate from the data protection laws to ensure consumers' privacy concerns are addressed. The integration of digital advertising and AI-based public relations in brand promotion offers consumers personalized, interactive, and responsive experiences, enhancing engagement and convenience. However, it also raises concerns about data privacy, potential manipulation, and trust erosion, especially when AI systems lack transparency. As consumers grow accustomed to seamless digital interactions, their expectations rise, which can boost satisfaction but also lead to digital fatigue or reduced brand loyalty if the experience feels intrusive or inconsistent. Overall, while these strategies improve communication effectiveness, they require ethical implementation to maintain consumer trust from regulators.

10.7 Conclusion, Limitations, and Suggestion for Further Studies

As the public relations industry embraces digital advertising, artificial Intelligence, and other emerging technologies, it marks a significant shift in how professionals engage with audiences and manage communication strategies to promote brands. Presently, AI in PR is currently focused on data monitoring, analysis, and content creation, and there is a huge potential for growth and innovation. Despite not reaching High-Level Machine Intelligence (HLMI), individual use of AI tools, particularly Generative AI, is prevalent, enhancing productivity and work quality. Digital advertising and AI-based PR are transformative tools in brand promotion, offering unparalleled opportunities for engagement and competitive advantage. By leveraging these technologies, brands can achieve sustainable growth and long-term success. Managers should invest in integrating digital advertising and AI-based PR to streamline operations and enhance brand visibility. Focusing on tools that provide actionable analytics and foster customer relationships is essential for maintaining relevance in competitive markets. Future research could explore ethical concerns in AI-driven PR and the impact of digital advertising on consumer trust.

Additionally, studies could analyze the effectiveness of these tools in emerging markets such as Ghana. The study is non-empirical; hence, the claims made should be empirically tested. Therefore, the propositions made could be tested in further studies using empirical data. The suggested conceptual framework is put to the test in both developed and developing nations through more research. Further propositions could be made based on a theory. Further studies could explore how the use of digital advertising and AI-based public relations could lead to brand promotion.

References

Adams, J., Tyrrell, R., Adamson, A. J., & White, M. (2012). Socio-economic differences in exposure to television food advertisements in the UK: a cross-sectional study of advertisements broadcast in one television region. *Public Health Nutrition, 15*(3), 487–494.

Agarwal, P., & Mittal, S. (2023). Artificial intelligence in customer engagement: Implications for online reputation management. *Journal of Business Analytics, 15*(1), 45–42.

Ahmed, R. R., Streimikiene, D., Berchtold, G., Vveinhardt, J., Channar, Z. A., & Soomro, R. H. (2019). Effectiveness of online digital media advertising as a strategic tool for building brand sustainability: Evidence from FMCGs and services sectors of Pakistan. *Sustainability, 11*(12), 3436.

Amoako, G. K., Bonsu, G. A., Gabrah, A. Y. B., & Ampong, G. O. A. (2023). Digital marketing and sustainability competitive advantage: A conceptual framework. In *Handbook of research on achieving sustainable development goals with sustainable marketing* (pp. 170–188). IGI Global.

Amoako, G. K., Dartey-Baah, K., Naatu, F., Acquah, I. S. K., & Gabrah, A. Y. B. (2024). Corporate social responsibility and brand performance: Evidence from Ghana. *Journal of International Management, 30*(4), 101161.

Ansip, A. (2017). Making the most of robotics and artificial intelligence in Europe. *European Commission*. ec.europa.eu.

Arief, N. N., & Saputra, M. A. (2019). Kompetensi Baru Public Relations (PR) Pada Era Artificial Intelligence: Case Study Praktisi PR di Indonesia. *Jurnal Sistem Cerdas, 2*(1), 1–12.

Austin, L. L., & Toth, E. L. (2011). Exploring ethics education in global public relations curricula. *Public Relations Review, 37*(5), 506–512.

Bachmann, P. (2019). Public relations in liquid modernity: How big data and automation cause moral blindness. *Public Relations Inquiry, 8*(3), 319–331.

Baskin, O., Aronoff, C., & Lattimore, D. (2005). *Public relations: The profession and the practice*. McGraw-Hill.

Bernays, E. L. (1951). *Public relations*. Norman.

Bhardwaj, S., Sharma, N., Goel, M., Sharma, K., & Verma, V. (2025). Enhancing customer targeting in E-Commerce and digital marketing through AI-Driven personalization strategies. In *Advances in Digital Marketing in the Era of Artificial Intelligence* (pp. 41–60). CRC Press.

Bowen, S. A. (2004). Organizational factors encouraging ethical decision-making: An exploration into the case of an exemplar. *Journal of Business Ethics, 52*(4), 311–324.

Bowen, S. A. (2007). *Ethics and public relations*. Gainesville, FL: Institute for Public Relations.

Bruce, N. I., Murthi, B. P. S., & Rao, R. C. (2017). A dynamic model for digital advertising: The effects of creative format, message content, and targeting on engagement. *Journal of Marketing Research, 54*(2), 202–218.

Buhmann, A., & White, C. L. (2022). Artificial intelligence in public relations: Role and implications. In J. H. Lipschultz, K. Freberg, & R. Luttrell (Eds.), *The Emerald handbook of computer-mediated communication and social media* (pp. 625–638). Emerald Publishing Limited.

Chaffey, D., & Ellis-Chadwick, F. (2019). *Digital marketing: Strategy, implementation, and practice*. Pearson Education.

Chen, L., Zhang, Y., & Sun, W. (2021). Detecting biases in AI-based reputation management tools. *AI Ethics Review, 7*(2), 98–113.

Confos, N., & Davis, T. (2016). Young consumer-brand relationship building potential using digital marketing. *European Journal of Marketing, 50*(11), 1993–2017.

Cui, Y. G., van Esch, P., & Phelan, S. (2024). How to build a competitive advantage for your brand using generative AI. *Business Horizons, 67*(5), 583–594.

Demirli, E., & Kutuk, M. (2010). AI applications in social systems. *Artificial Intelligence Studies, 3*(2), 45–60.

Dixit, S. (2022). Artifical intelligence and crm: A case of telecom industry. In *Adoption and Implementation of AI in Customer Relationship Management* (pp. 92–114). IGI Global.

Forbes, C. (2020). The role of AI in shaping the future of PR. Available at https://www.forbes.com/councils/forbesbusinesscouncil/2023/11/30/four-ways-ai-is-changing-the-public-relations-industry/

Gabrah, A. Y. B., Amoako, G. K., & Ampong, G. O. A. (2023). Africa's response to SDGs: Barriers and challenges. In *Corporate sustainability in Africa: Responsible leadership, opportunities, and challenges* (pp. 47–63). Springer International Publishing.

Gabrah, A. Y. B., Amoako, G. K., & Anwana, E. (2024). Stakeholder Integration and Corporate Entrepreneurship. In *Stakeholder Management and Entrepreneurship in Africa* (pp. 9–22). Routledge.

Gabrah, A. Y. B., Boateng, H., Twum, K. K., & Antwi, E. O. (2025a). AI Integration, PR Strategies, Brand Reputation, and Stakeholder Perceptions: A Conceptual Framework. In *Redefining Public Relations in Emerging Markets: Regional Insights from Africa, South America and Asia* (pp. 143–157). Cham: Springer Nature Switzerland.

Gabrah, A. Y. B., Boateng, H., Twum, K. K., & Antwi, E. O. (2025b). The Significance and Challenges of AI-Driven PR Campaigns in Diverse Cultural Contexts: A Conceptual Framework. In *Strategic Public Relations in Emerging Economies: Public and Private Sector Perspectives* (pp. 195–210). Cham: Springer Nature Switzerland.

Galloway, C., & Swiatek, L. (2018). Public relations and artificial intelligence: It's not (just) about robots. *Public Relations Review, 44*(5), 734–740.

Gomez, R., & Roberts, M. (2022). The impact of AI on global brand reputation management. *International Journal of Marketing Studies, 12*(3), 56–72.

Gupta, S., Justy, T., Kamboj, S., Kumar, A., & Kristoffersen, E. (2021). Big data and firm marketing performance: Findings from knowledge-based view. *Technological Forecasting and Social Change, 171*, 120986.

Jeong, J. Y., & Park, N. (2023). Examining the influence of artificial intelligence on public relations: Insights from the Organization-Situation-Public-Communication (OSPC) model. *Asia-Pacific Journal of Convergent Research Interchange, 9*(7), 485–495.

Kühl, N., Mühlthaler, M., & Goutier, M. (2020). Supporting customer-oriented marketing with artificial intelligence: Automatically quantifying customer needs from social media. *Electronic Markets, 30*(2), 351–367.

Kumar, A., Singh, P., & Yadav, M. (2022). AI-driven chatbots in reputation management: Opportunities and challenges. *Journal of Digital Marketing, 14*(4), 33–47.

Kumar, V., Ashraf, A. R., & Nadeem, W. (2024). AI-powered marketing: What, where, and how? *International Journal of Information Management, 77*, 102783.

Labanauskaitė, D., Fiore, M., & Stašys, R. (2020). Use of E-marketing tools as communication management in the tourism industry. *Tourism Management Perspectives, 34*, 100652.

Lamphills Blog. (2025). *Top communication agencies in Nigeria*. https://blog.lamphills.com/pr/top-communication-agencies-in-nigeria/?utm_

Lee, H., & Cho, C. H. (2020). Digital advertising: Present and future prospects. *International Journal of Advertising, 39*(3), 332–341.

Melović, B., Jocović, M., Dabić, M., Vulić, T. B., & Dudic, B. (2020). The impact of digital transformation and digital marketing on the brand promotion, positioning and electronic business in Montenegro. *Technology in Society, 63*, 101425.

Makrides, A., Vrontis, D., & Christofi, M. (2020). The gold rush of digital marketing: assessing prospects of building brand awareness overseas. *Business Perspectives and Research, 8*(1), 4–20.

Raji, R. A., Rashid, S., & Ishak, S. (2019). The mediating effect of brand image on the relationships between social media advertising content, sales promotion content and behaviuoral intention. *Journal of Research in Interactive Marketing, 13*(3), 302–330.

Ryan, M., & Martinson, D. L. (1983). Ethical public relations: Codes of ethics and what they mean. *Public Relations Quarterly, 28*(4), 25–30.

Shannon, A., Brown, C., & Davis, T. (2021). AI ethics in media and public relations. *Journal of Communication Ethics, 18*(2), 129–140.

Song, S., & Kim, H. Y. (2022). Is social media marketing worth it for luxury brands? The dual impact of brand page satisfaction and brand love on word-of-mouth and attitudinal loyalty intentions. *Journal of Product & Brand Management, 31*(7), 1033–1046.

The BFT Online. (2025). *Best advertising and marketing agencies in Ghana 2025*. https://thebftonline.com/2025/02/07/best-advertising-and-marketing-agencies-inghana-2025/

Türksoy, N. (2022). The future of public relations, advertising, and journalism: How artificial intelligence may transform the communication profession. *Türkiye İletişim Araştırmaları Dergisi, 40*, 394–410.

Valin, J., & Gregory, A. (2020). *Ethics guide to artificial intelligence in PR*. Chartered Institute of Public Relations.

Vlačić, B., Corbo, L., e Silva, S. C., & Dabić, M. (2021). The evolving role of artificial intelligence in marketing: A review and research agenda. *Journal of Business Research, 128*, 187–203.

You, Y., He, Y., Chen, Q., & Hu, M. (2021). The interplay between brand relationship norms and ease of sharing on electronic word-of-mouth and willingness to pay. *Information & Management, 58*(2), 103410.

Zerfass, A., Hagelstein, J., & Tench, R. (2020). Artificial intelligence in communication management. *Journal of Communication Management, 24*(4), 377–389.

Ziakis, C., & Vlachopoulou, M. (2023). Artificial intelligence in digital marketing: Insights from a comprehensive review. *Information, 14*(12), 664.

11

Financial Management Among SMEs in Africa: The Ghanaian Case

Richard Kofi Asravor and Peter Lawer Angmor

11.1 Introduction

Small and Medium Enterprises (SMEs) are the mainstay of Africa's economic development, contributing substantially to employment, Gross Domestic Product (GDP) growth, and poverty reduction (Mugano & Dorasamy, 2023). According to the World Bank (2020), SMEs account for nearly 70% of businesses in Ghana and contribute approximately 50% of the country's GDP. Thus, SMEs play a vital role in employment generation (Abisuga-Oyekunle et al., 2020), innovation (Maksimov et al., 2017), and poverty alleviation (Okpara, 2011). SMEs account for almost 90% of registered businesses in Ghana and are pivotal to its economic stability and landscape. However, despite their importance, earlier studies by Abor and Quartey (2010) posit that many Ghanaian SMEs face substantial challenges and struggle

R. K. Asravor • P. L. Angmor (✉)
Ghana Communication Technology University, Accra, Ghana
e-mail: rasravor@gctu.edu.gh; plawer@gctu.edu.gh

E. Amoako Asiedu et al. (eds.), *Entrepreneurship and Small and Medium-Sized Enterprises (SMEs) in Africa*, https://doi.org/10.1007/978-3-032-14174-3_11

with financial management, which hinder their growth and sustainability, leading to high failure rates. Mensah et al. (2019) and Asravor et al. (2025) opined that further exacerbating the financial instability among SMEs are the high interest rates, limited financial literacy, and the lack of government support. As indicated by some research findings, several initiatives have been implemented by the Government of Ghana and private individuals to curb and alleviate the financing constraints faced by these SMEs (Oduro, 2020). For instance, to overcome the credit constraints, the Government of Ghana established the Development Bank Ghana which seeks to make credit easier to these SMEs (Domeher, 2012).

Inspite of the numerous efforts, the poor financial management practices among Ghanaian SMEs remain a major challenge, as many SMEs owners lack sound and formal training in financial record-keeping, financial planning, budgeting, cash flow management, and access to credit (Mang'ana et al., 2024).

Only 30% of SMEs maintain proper financial records, making it difficult to secure loans or attract investors (Ghana Statistical Service, 2021). The lack of technical skills aggravates SMEs' vulnerability, leading to high failure rates within the first few years of operation (Skouloudis et al., 2023).

Recent studies suggest that approximately 60% of SMEs in Ghana fail within their first 5 years, primarily due to poor financial practices (Agyapong, 2021). Despite the growing body of research on SME financial management in Africa, critical gaps remain that this study addresses, particularly in the Ghanaian context. In Ghana, a plethora of studies have generally focused on credit and the effect of credit constraints on SMEs growth (Akanyonge et al., 2023), very limited studies have focused on issues of financial management and how that affects operations. While previous studies (Abor & Quartey, 2010; World Bank, 2020) have broadly examined SME financing challenges, very few have analyzed how owner financial literacy influences financial management effectiveness. Furthermore, limited studies have evaluated how access to financing influences financial decision-making, and management practices within SMEs remains underexplored. From the aforementioned gaps in the literature, the motivation of this study is to:

- identify the challenges hindering effective financial management among SMEs,
- analyze the impact of financial management on SMEs growth and sustainability,
- assess the effect of SME owner financial literacy on its financial management.

By addressing these objectives, the study will first contribute to understanding the correlation between financial literacy level among SME owners and the adoption of sound financial management practices. This will provide valuable insights for policy formulation and educational programs aimed at enhancing SME performance and sustainability in the long run. Addressing these gaps is essential for developing targeted strategies that enhance the financial management competencies of SMEs in Ghana, thereby fostering their growth and contribution to the national economy. The rest of this paper is structured as follows: Sections 11.2 and 11.3 elucidate the literature review and materials and methods, respectively. The analysis of results is presented in Sect. 11.4, and conclusions are given in Sect. 11.5.

11.2 Literature Review

11.2.1 Theoretical Literature Review

Resource-Based View (RBV) Theory

The Resource-Based View (RBV) is a strategic management theory developed by Barney (1991) that argues a firm's competitive advantage stems from its unique internal resources and capabilities. According to RBV, resources must be valuable, rare, inimitable, and non-substitutable (VRIN) to sustain long-term success. These resources can be tangible (physical assets, financial capital) or intangible (knowledge, brand reputation, managerial skills). RBV suggests that firms should develop, acquire, and leverage superior resources to outperform competitors. For example, a company with proprietary technology, skilled employees, or strong financial management systems can achieve efficiency and innovation that rivals cannot easily replicate. The theory has been widely applied in entrepreneurship, particularly in SMEs, where effective resource utilization, such as financial literacy, cash flow management, and digital tools, can compensate for limited scale.

In this study, the Resource-Based View (RBV) theory is used to highlight how various financial management practices contribute to SME competitiveness, with effective budgeting enabling efficient resource allocation and future investment planning while helping firms withstand economic shocks (Wernerfelt, 1984). Quality record-keeping enhances financial transparency and tax compliance while improving access to external financing, though poor practices in this area remain a significant constraint for Ghanaian SMEs (Abor & Quartey, 2010). Proper cash flow management serves as a critical survival mechanism by maintaining liquidity and avoiding insolvency risks (Brealey et al., 2020). SME owners' financial literacy functions as a key intangible resource that directly influences financial decision-making quality regarding investments and debt (Lusardi & Mitchell, 2014). The adoption of FinTech solutions provides competitive advantages through enhanced operational efficiency and reduced transaction costs (Ozili, 2018), while engagement with financial advisors facilitates the adoption of improved financial reporting and tax planning practices (Bennett & Robson, 2004). Finally, effective inventory and cost control systems contribute directly to profitability through reduced holding costs and prevention of stockouts (Chand & Katou, 2012), collectively demonstrating how these interrelated financial management practices constitute valuable organizational resources under the RBV framework.

Pecking Order Theory (POT)

The Pecking Order Theory (POT), developed by Myers and Majluf (1984), provides a framework for understanding how Ghanaian SMEs prioritize their financing sources in response to information asymmetry and transaction costs. This theory explains the observed financing hierarchy where firms prefer internal funds (retained earnings and personal savings) first, then debt, with external equity as a last resort. In Ghana's SME sector, this manifests through heavy reliance on informal loans and personal savings (Agyapong et al., 2017), as limited financial records and low owner financial literacy create information barriers that restrict access to formal credit. The preference for internal financing stems from its lower costs and reduced disclosure requirements, while debt is favored over equity to avoid ownership dilution, despite challenges posed by high interest rates and collateral demands.

Financial literacy emerges as a critical factor influencing this financing behavior, with more knowledgeable owners demonstrating strategic debt management (Coleman & Cohn, 2000), while financial illiteracy exacerbates information asymmetry (Beck & Demirgüç-Kunt, 2006). The growing adoption of FinTech solutions is gradually transforming this landscape by introducing alternative credit scoring through digital platforms (Demir et al., 2022), potentially reducing traditional information gaps. However, the full impact of these technological innovations remains uneven across different SME segments in Ghana, as adoption rates vary and traditional financing constraints persist. This theoretical perspective helps explain why Ghanaian SMEs typically exhaust internal financing options before considering external sources, while also highlighting how emerging digital solutions may alter these long-standing financing patterns.

11.2.2 Empirical Literature Review

Studies in Africa confirm that SMEs with strong internal financial management systems perform better. Abor and Biekpe (2007) found that Ghanaian SMEs with structured financial controls had higher profitability. Similarly, Fatoki (2014) highlighted that financial literacy among South African SME owners improved access to credit. Research shows that Ghanaian SMEs face severe constraints in accessing bank loans, forcing them to rely on internal funds (Aryeetey, 2005). Stevenson and St-Onge (2005) found that SMEs in Kenya followed POT by first using retained earnings before seeking external financing. The empirical literature on financial management practices among SMEs in Africa, with a particular focus on Ghana, reveals several critical insights. Abdul-Rahaman et al. (2022) examined the impact of digital financial services on SME growth in Ghana through a mixed-methods approach, combining surveys of 300 SMEs with interviews of financial service providers. Their study, utilizing primary data collected from SME owners in Accra and Kumasi in 2021, found that SMEs adopting digital financial services reported 23% higher revenue growth due to faster transactions and improved credit access, while also highlighting regulatory challenges in FinTech adoption that particularly affected rural SMEs.

Adomako et al. (2022) investigated the relationship between record-keeping quality and SME profitability through a quantitative survey of 450 SMEs across Ghana and Kenya. Their research, based on structured questionnaires assessing accounting practices between 2020 and 2021, demonstrated that SMEs maintaining formal record-keeping systems experienced 30% fewer tax disputes and achieved 18% higher profit margins, while poor record-keeping was strongly correlated with cash flow crises. The study recommended government-led training programs to improve financial documentation practices among SME owners.

The importance of cash flow management was underscored by Agyapong et al. (2023), who analyzed its role in SME resilience during economic crises through case studies of 200 Ghanaian SMEs and financial statement analysis. Their examination of secondary data from bank records (2019–2022) revealed that SMEs employing cash flow projections survived COVID-19 lockdowns at 2.5 times the rate of those without such practices, with 60% of failed SMEs lacking adequate liquidity buffers, prompting calls for emergency cash flow training programs.

Budgeting practices were specifically examined by Alhassan and Asare (2021), who assessed their impact on SME profitability through regression analysis of survey data from 180 manufacturing and retail SMEs in Ghana. Their 2020 data showed that SMEs implementing annual budgets achieved 15% higher returns on investment, though the study noted budgeting adoption remained low at just 35% among micro-SMEs, particularly in informal sectors.

Financial literacy's role in SME success was quantified by Anarfo et al. (2023) through a cross-sectional survey of 500 SME owners across Ghana and Nigeria. Their 2022 Likert-scale questionnaire data found financially literate owners were 40% more likely to secure loans, while financial illiteracy correlated strongly with high debt defaults, leading to recommendations for integrating financial education into vocational training programs.

The value of professional financial advice was evaluated by Boachie-Mensah and Acquah (2022) through interviews and financial metrics from 120 advisory clients in Ghana. Analyzing pre- and post-advisory performance data from 2018 to 2021, they found advisory clients achieved 28% revenue growth compared to 12% for non-clients, though high costs were identified as a significant barrier for micro-SMEs.

Inventory management practices were linked to operational efficiency by Danso et al. (2023) through a survey of 250 retail SMEs in Accra. Their analysis of 2021–2022 inventory turnover ratios demonstrated that just-in-time inventory systems reduced waste by 22%, while poor controls resulted in 35% stockout rates, with technology adoption (particularly POS systems) showing significant improvements in inventory accuracy.

Frimpong et al. (2023) explored FinTech's role in financial inclusion through logistic regression of 400 SME responses in Ghana. Their 2022 survey data revealed mobile money users saved an average of 8 banking hours monthly, though 70% of non-adopters cited trust issues, suggesting the need for enhanced cybersecurity education alongside FinTech promotion.

Finally, Owusu et al. (2022) examined optimal debt levels through financial ratio analysis of 300 SME balance sheets from 2017 to 2021. Their findings indicated SMEs maintaining debt below 30% of assets experienced 50% lower bankruptcy rates, while cautioning against predatory lending practices that threaten SME financial sustainability.

11.3 Materials and Methods

11.3.1 Research Approach

To achieve the research objectives, a quantitative research approach was adopted. This approach was used because it helped in the facilitation of the generalization of results to a larger population, increasing the study's applicability to SMEs across Ghana and other African economies with similar and equal financial structures. Furthermore, it helps in identifying measurable and statistically reliable patterns, relationships, and trends in financial management practices among SMEs in Ghana.

11.3.2 Research Design

A cross-sectional survey design was employed to collect data at a single point in time from a sample of SMEs in the Accra Metropolis. This design was selected because it allows for the efficient assessment of financial management practices among SMEs without the need for longitudinal tracking, which can be time-consuming and resource-intensive. The cross-sectional approach provides a snapshot of current financial behaviors, including budgeting, record-keeping, and access to financing, which are critical in evaluating the financial health of SMEs. Greater Accra is a major economic hub in Ghana; hence, by focusing on SMEs in the Greater Accra Region, the study captures significant insights from a diverse range of businesses, including retail, manufacturing, and service-based enterprises.

11.3.3 Target Population

The study's target population consists of SMEs operating within the Accra Metropolis. According to the Ghana Statistical Service (2021), there are 20,412 registered SMEs in Accra, making it an ideal location for assessing financial management trends. The selection of Accra is strategic due to its high concentration of SMEs, which contribute significantly to employment and economic growth. The study focuses on registered SMEs to ensure that sampled businesses have a formal structure, making financial management practices more traceable. The population includes micro, small, and medium-sized enterprises across various sectors, ensuring a comprehensive analysis of financial behaviors.

11.3.4 Sampling Technique

A random sampling method was used to ensure a representative and unbiased selection of SMEs. This technique enhances the reliability of the data by giving each SME in the target population an equal chance of being selected. The researcher utilized Microsoft Excel's Random Number Generation function to systematically assign numbers to registered SMEs, from which a sample was drawn. Random sampling minimizes selection bias and improves the generalizability of findings. Given the large population size (20,412 SMEs), this method ensures efficiency in data collection while maintaining statistical validity. The approach also aligns with the study's quantitative nature, as it allows for precise data analysis and hypothesis testing.

11.3.5 Sample Size

The study adopted a two-stage sampling approach to determine the appropriate sample size for reliable statistical analysis. First, 47 SMEs were selected for a pilot study to test the validity and reliability of the questionnaire. The pilot study helped refine the questionnaire by identifying ambiguous questions and ensuring clarity before full-scale data collection. For the main study, the sample size was determined using Krejcie and Morgan's (1970) sample size formula, which is suitable for finite populations. Given the total population of 20,412 registered SMEs in Accra (Ghana Statistical Service, 2021), a 95% confidence level and 5% margin of error were applied, yielding a minimum required sample size of 377. However, to account for potential non-responses and incomplete data, the sample size was adjusted to 242 SMEs based on resource constraints and feasibility.

11.3.6 Sources of Data

The study primarily relies on primary data collected through closed-ended structured questionnaires. This method was chosen because it allows for standardized responses, making data analysis more efficient.

The questionnaire was designed to capture key financial management variables such as budgeting, cash flow management, and financial literacy levels. Also, the choice of primary data for this study was to ensure that findings are directly relevant to the research objectives.

11.3.7 Procedure for Data Collection

Questionnaires were physically and electronically distributed to SME operators in the Greater Accra region of Ghana. To enhance response rates, the researcher engaged directly with business owners, explaining the study's purpose and ensuring clarity in responses. Data collection was conducted over a 4-week period, allowing sufficient time for participants to provide accurate information.

11.3.8 Analysis of Data

The collected data were processed using SPSS version 27.0, a robust statistical tool for quantitative research. Descriptive statistics (mean, frequency, percentages) were used to summarize financial management practices (Objective 1). For Objectives 2 and 3, a multiple regression model was applied to examine the relationship between financial management variables and SME performance. The model is expressed as:

$$Y_i = \beta_0 + \beta_1 X_1 + \beta_2 X_2 + \ldots + \beta_9 X_9 + \varepsilon_i$$

Where: X_1: Budgeting Practice; X_2: Record Keeping Quality; X_3: Cash Flow Management; X_4: Access to External Finance; X_5: Financial illiteracy Level; X_6: Debt Management Strategy; X_7: Use of Financial Technology (FinTech); X_8: Financial Advisory Engagement; X_9: Inventory and Cost Control Practice.

11.3.9 Apriori Expectation

The study's hypotheses are grounded in contemporary financial management literature, with expectations that structured budgeting (X_1)

enhances financial performance through disciplined resource allocation (Alhassan & Asare, 2021), while quality record-keeping (X_2) improves decision-making accuracy and tax compliance (Adomako et al., 2022). Effective cash flow management (X_3) is anticipated to boost SME sustainability by maintaining liquidity (Agyapong et al., 2023), and access to external finance (X_4) is expected to foster growth through capital infusion (Abdul-Rahaman et al., 2022). Financial illiteracy (X_5) likely negatively impacts performance due to poor financial decisions (Anarfo et al., 2023), whereas prudent debt management (X_6) reduces default risks (Owusu et al., 2022). FinTech adoption (X_7) is projected to enhance efficiency through digital transactions (Frimpong et al., 2023), financial advisory engagement (X_8) improves strategic planning (Boachie-Mensah & Acquah, 2022), and robust inventory control (X_9) optimizes costs and profitability (Danso et al., 2023).

11.4 Results and Discussion

11.4.1 Descriptive Statistics of Respondents

Table 11.1 presents an overview of the demographic, educational, and operational characteristics of SMEs surveyed. The findings show that 80.58% of SME owners are female, and only 19.42% are male. Also, the majority of SME owners (51.65%) fall within the 40–49-year age bracket, while those aged 30–39 years constitute 35.95% of the sample. Younger entrepreneurs, aged 18–29 years, account for only 10.33%, and participation drops sharply beyond 50 years (2.07%). In terms of the highest educational level, 57.44% of SME owners have only basic education, with 31.82% having vocational training. Only 0.83% have attained tertiary education, while 9.92% completed high school.

The majority of the respondents (98.35%) have received no financial training, and the SMEs in the service sector dominate the sample, constituting 49.18% of businesses, followed by trading enterprises (41.32%), and manufacturing firms (9.50%). Furthermore, most SMEs (59.09%) have been in operation for 3–5 years, with 27.27% operating for 6–10

Table 11.1 Descriptive statistics of SMEs

	Variable	Frequency	Percent
Sex:			
	Male	47	19.42
	Female	195	80.58
Age Group:			
	18–29 years	25	10.33
	30–39 years	87	35.95
	40–49 years	125	51.65
	50–59 years	5	2.07
Education			
	Basic Educ.	139	57.44
	High School	24	9.92
	Tertiary	2	0.83
	Vocational	77	31.82
Financial Training			
	No	238	98.35
	Yes	4	1.65
Type of SMEs			
	Manufacturing	23	9.5
	Service	119	49.18
	Trading	100	41.32
Years Operated			
	Less than 1 year	8	3.31
	1–2 years	18	7.44
	3–5 years	143	59.09
	6–10 years	66	27.27
	More than 10 years	7	2.89

Source: Authors Computation

years. SMEs with less than 1 year of operation account for only 3.31%, and businesses surviving beyond 10 years represent just 2.89% of the sample.

11.4.2 Challenges Hindering Effective Financial Management

Table 11.2 highlights the key financial and operational challenges confronting SMEs sampled for this study. The most prominent issue identified is poor record-keeping, reported by 15.29% of respondents. This is closely followed by limited financial literacy (14.88%) and lack of access

Table 11.2 Challenges faced by SMEs

Variable	Frequency	Percent
Economic and Market Volatility	13	5.37
Fraud and Financial Misconduct	2	0.83
High Operating Costs	14	5.79
Inadequate Financial Planning and Budgeting	31	12.81
Lack of Access to Finance	34	14.05
Limited Financial Advisory Services	3	1.24
Limited Financial Literacy	36	14.88
Limited Use of Financial Technology	18	7.44
Over-reliance on Informal Financial Systems	24	9.92
Poor Debt Management	22	9.09
Poor Record Keeping	37	15.29
Regulatory and Compliance Burdens	8	3.31

Source: Author's Computation from field survey

to finance (14.05%), underscoring the persistent financial capability gaps among SME owners. Additionally, inadequate financial planning and budgeting account for 12.81%, while over-reliance on informal financial systems (9.92%) and poor debt management (9.09%) also emerge as notable constraints.

Other challenges include limited use of financial technology (7.44%), high operating costs (5.79%), and economic and market volatility (5.37%). Less frequently cited but still significant are regulatory and compliance burdens (3.31%), limited financial advisory services (1.24%), and fraud and financial misconduct, which, although only mentioned by 0.83%, may have outsized impacts when they occur.

Furthermore, Table 11.3 presents a gender-disaggregated analysis of the challenges faced by SMEs, revealing notable differences in the financial and operational experiences of male and female entrepreneurs. The data indicate that female SME owners disproportionately bear the brunt of nearly all the challenges listed.

The analysis shows that poor record-keeping is significantly more prevalent among female entrepreneurs (12.40%) compared to their male counterparts (2.89%). Similarly, limited financial literacy affects 11.98% of female respondents, relative to 2.89% of males. This trend extends to lack of access to finance (females: 11.16%, males: 2.89%) and inadequate financial planning and budgeting (females: 10.74%, males: 2.07%).

Table 11.3 Gender comparison of challenges faced by SMEs

	Male		Female	
	Frequency	Percent	Frequency	Percent
Economic and Market Volatility	0	0.00	13	5.37
Fraud and Financial Misconduct	1	0.41	1	0.41
High Operating Costs	4	1.65	10	4.13
Inadequate Financial Planning and Budgeting	5	2.07	26	10.74
Lack of Access to Finance	7	2.89	27	11.16
Limited Financial Advisory Services	0	0.00	3	1.24
Limited Financial Literacy	7	2.89	29	11.98
Limited Use of Financial Technology	7	2.89	11	4.55
Over-reliance on Informal Financial Systems	4	1.65	20	8.26
Poor Debt Management	5	2.07	17	7.02
Poor Record Keeping	7	2.89	30	12.40
Regulatory and Compliance Burdens	0	0.00	8	3.31

Source: Author's Computation from field survey

Furthermore, while high operating costs are a concern for both genders, a greater proportion of female respondents (4.13%) cited this issue compared to males (1.65%). The same pattern holds for challenges such as over-reliance on informal financial systems (females: 8.26%, males: 1.65%) and poor debt management (females: 7.02%, males: 2.07%). Also, economic and market volatility and regulatory and compliance burdens were exclusively reported by female SME owners, suggesting that women may be more sensitive to macroeconomic shocks and administrative constraints.

11.4.3 Effect of Financial Management on SMEs Growth and Sustainability

Table 11.4 presents the results of an Ordinary Least Squares (OLS) regression model assessing the influence of various dimensions of financial management on the sustainability of small and medium-sized enterprises (SMEs). The regression model shows an *R*-squared value of 0.2548, indicating that approximately 25.5% of the variation in SMEs' sustainability is explained by the financial management variables included in the

Table 11.4 Effect of financial management on SMEs sustainability

	Estimate	Std. Error	*t* value	Pr(>|t|)	Sign
(Intercept)	2.0154	0.39589	5.091	7.43E-07	***
X_1: Budgeting Practice	-0.05911	0.20789	-0.284	0.7764	
X_2: Record Keeping Quality	0.35646	0.30124	1.183	0.237922	
X_3: Cash Flow Management	0.78774	0.21464	3.67	0.000302	***
X_4: Access to External Finance	1.27833	0.69287	1.845	0.06633	.
X_5: Financial ILLiteracy Level	-0.48534	0.24476	-1.983	0.048572	*
X_6: Debt Management Strategy	0.21884	0.20382	1.074	0.284098	
X_7: Use of Financial Technology (FinTech)	0.41512	0.21727	1.911	0.057307	.
X_8: Financial Advisory Engagement	0.8361	0.20656	4.048	7.07E-05	***
X_9: Inventory and Cost Control Practice	1.73709	0.2407	7.217	7.75E-12	***
R-Square	0.2548		*F*-Statistics	6.526	

.,*, and **** imply significance at 10%, 5%, and less than 1%

model. The F-statistic of 6.526 further confirms that the model is statistically significant overall, implying that the independent variables collectively have a meaningful impact on the dependent variable.

Among the variables examined, inventory and cost control practices exert the most substantial influence on sustainability, with a coefficient of 1.73709 and a *p*-value well below the 0.001 threshold. This highlights the critical role of internal efficiency and resource management in determining long-term business outcomes. Similarly, financial advisory engagement shows a strong positive and statistically significant effect (β = 0.8361, $p < 0.001$), underscoring the importance of expert guidance and informed financial decision-making in enhancing SME resilience.

Cash flow management also demonstrates a statistically significant and positive relationship with sustainability (β = 0.78774, $p < 0.001$). This result is consistent with theoretical expectations in finance literature, where maintaining liquidity and managing short-term assets and liabilities effectively are key to operational continuity and survival, particularly in financially constrained environments.

Two variables, that is, access to external finance and use of financial technology, show marginal statistical significance at the 10% level. The effect of access to external finance ($\beta = 1.27833$, $p \approx 0.066$) indicates that while external funding is not universally accessible or effective for all SMEs, it has the potential to enhance sustainability for firms that can leverage it strategically. Likewise, the adoption of financial technology ($\beta = 0.41512$, $p \approx 0.057$) appears to contribute positively to sustainability outcomes, possibly reflecting the growing relevance of digital tools and innovations in modern business operations.

In contrast, the level of financial illiteracy is negatively associated with sustainability, with a coefficient of -0.48534 and a *p*-value of 0.04857, indicating statistical significance at the 5% level. This finding is crucial, as it confirms that poor understanding of financial concepts can significantly hinder SMEs' ability to make sound financial decisions, manage risk, and respond effectively to market challenges.

Other variables, including budgeting practice, record-keeping quality, and debt management strategy, do not show statistically significant effects on sustainability. While these practices are generally considered foundational to good financial management, their lack of significance in this model may suggest either limited variation among firms or that these practices alone are insufficient to drive sustainability without complementary strategic initiatives.

11.5 Discussion

The demographic profile of surveyed SMEs reveals critical structural characteristics that shape financial management challenges in Ghana's SME sector. The overwhelming female predominance (80.58%) aligns with Ghana Statistical Service (2021) reports on SME ownership patterns, though the stark gender disparity in financial challenges—particularly in record-keeping (females 12.40% vs males 2.89%) and financial literacy (females 11.98% vs males 2.89%)—corroborates Adomako et al.'s (2022) findings that female entrepreneurs often face greater financial management constraints due to limited formal training opportunities. The concentration of owners in the 40–49 age bracket (51.65%) with basic education (57.44%) explains the prevalent financial capability gaps, as Anarfo et al. (2023) established that such demographic groups typically have lower financial literacy levels.

The sectoral distribution (49.18% services, 41.32% trading) and operational longevity (59.09% in business for 3–5 years) mirror Frimpong et al.'s (2023) observation that Ghana's SME sector remains dominated by short-term, service-oriented ventures with high mortality rates. The finding that only 2.89% survive beyond 10 years reinforces Agyapong et al.'s (2023) conclusion about cash flow management being a critical survival factor during economic shocks.

The identified financial challenges present a hierarchy of intervention priorities. Poor record-keeping (15.29%) as the foremost challenge validates Danso et al.'s (2023) emphasis on documentation quality as a prerequisite for financial control. The compounding effect of limited financial literacy (14.88%) and access to finance (14.05%) reflects Abdul-Rahaman et al.'s (2022) findings about how financial exclusion perpetuates informal practices. The gender-differentiated challenges particularly highlight systemic barriers facing women entrepreneurs, with regulatory burdens being exclusively reported by females—a finding that extends Boachie-Mensah and Acquah's (2022) work on gendered financial constraints.

The regression results provide empirical validation for several theoretical propositions. The strong positive effect of inventory/cost control (β = 1.737, $p < 0.001$) confirms Harris's (1913) classical inventory theory in contemporary Ghanaian contexts. Financial advisory's significance (β = 0.836, $p < 0.001$) supports Berry et al.'s (2006) advocacy for professional guidance, while cash flow management's impact (β = 0.788, $p < 0.001$) empirically substantiates Peel and Wilson's (1996) liquidity management principles.

The marginal significance of FinTech adoption (β = 0.415, $p \approx 0.057$) suggests digital finance's evolving role, aligning with Ozili's (2018) technology adoption curve theory. The negative financial illiteracy effect (β = -0.485, $p = 0.049$) quantifies Lusardi and Mitchell's (2014) human capital arguments, while the non-significance of budgeting and record-keeping contradicts Abor and Quartey's (2010) assumptions, possibly indicating these are necessary but insufficient conditions for sustainability in Ghana's volatile market context.

These findings collectively suggest that SME sustainability interventions should prioritize: (1) gender-sensitive financial literacy programs targeting middle-aged female entrepreneurs, (2) inventory management capacity building, (3) subsidized financial advisory services, and (4) targeted FinTech adoption support—while recognizing that foundational practices like budgeting may need complementary strategic support to yield measurable sustainability impacts. The evidence underscores the need for integrated financial management solutions that address both capability deficits and systemic barriers in Ghana's SME ecosystem.

11.6 Summary, Conclusion, and Recommendation

This study examined financial management practices among Ghanaian SMEs, analyzing demographic characteristics, operational challenges, and their impact on business sustainability. Key findings reveal a predominantly female-owned SME sector (80.58%) with significant financial literacy gaps, particularly among middle-aged entrepreneurs with basic education. The most pressing challenges include poor record-keeping (15.29%), limited financial literacy (14.88%), and restricted access to finance (14.05%), with female entrepreneurs disproportionately affected. Regression analysis demonstrated that inventory/cost control ($\beta = 1.737$, $p < 0.001$), financial advisory services ($\beta = 0.836$, $p < 0.001$), and cash flow management ($\beta = 0.788$, $p < 0.001$) were the most significant predictors of SME sustainability, while financial illiteracy had a strong negative effect ($\beta = -0.485$, $p = 0.049$). Interestingly, traditional practices like budgeting and record-keeping showed no statistically significant impact, suggesting they may be necessary but insufficient alone for ensuring sustainability.

The study confirms that Ghana's SME sector faces systemic financial management challenges rooted in both capability deficits and structural barriers. The gender disparities in financial constraints highlight how socioeconomic factors compound operational difficulties for women entrepreneurs. While digital financial solutions show promise ($\beta = 0.415$, $p \approx 0.057$), their marginal significance indicates an ongoing adoption barrier. The findings challenge conventional assumptions about universal best practices, revealing contextual nuances in what drives SME sustainability in emerging economies. Ultimately, the research underscores that financial management effectiveness in Ghana's SME sector depends on integrating strategic operational controls (inventory/cost management), expert guidance, and liquidity management, while addressing foundational literacy gaps.

To address these challenges, the study recommends implementing gender-sensitive financial literacy programs focusing on practical skills like inventory control and cash flow management for female entrepreneurs. Public-private partnerships should be developed to provide affordable financial advisory services, particularly for women-owned SMEs. FinTech adoption should be accelerated through SME-focused training on mobile money and accounting platforms, while addressing cybersecurity concerns. Policy reforms are needed to streamline regulatory processes and develop gender-inclusive financing schemes to reduce barriers identified by female entrepreneurs. Finally, SME support programs should adopt a holistic approach by combining basic financial practices (record-keeping) with advanced strategies (cost control), recognizing their complementary roles in enhancing business sustainability. These evidence-based recommendations aim to create an enabling ecosystem where financial management practices can effectively drive SME growth and sustainability in Ghana and similar contexts. Future research should explore longitudinal effects of these interventions and sector-specific financial management solutions.

References

Abdul-Rahaman, A., & Abdulai, A. (2022). Mobile money adoption, input use, and farm output among smallholder rice farmers in Ghana. *Agribusiness, 38*(1), 236–255.

Abisuga-Oyekunle, O. A., Patra, S. K., & Muchie, M. (2020). SMEs in sustainable development: Their role in poverty reduction and employment generation in sub-Saharan Africa. *African Journal of Science, Technology, Innovation and Development, 12*(4), 405–419.

Abor, J., & Biekpe, N. (2007). Corporate governance, ownership structure and performance of SMEs in Ghana: implications for financing opportunities. Corporate Governance: *The international journal of business in society, 7*(3), 288–300.

Abor, J., & Quartey, P. (2010). Issues in SME development in Ghana and South Africa. *International Research Journal of Finance and Economics, 39*(6), 215–228.

Adomako, S., Danso, A., & Uddin, M. (2022). Financial record-keeping practices and SMEperformance in emerging economies. *Journal of Small Business Management, 60*(3), 567–585. https://doi.org/10.1111/jsbm.12567

Agyapong, D. (2021). Analyzing financial risks in small and medium enterprises: Evidence fromthe food processing firms in selected cities in Ghana. *International Journal ofEntrepreneurial Behavior & Research, 27*(1), 45–77.

Agyapong, D., Agyapong, G. K. Q., & Darfor, K. N. (2017). SME financing in Ghana: The role of internal funds and trade credit. *Journal of Small Business and Enterprise Development, 24*(3), 544–561. https://doi.org/10.1108/JSBED-11-2016-0179

Agyapong, D., Boachie, R. T., & Mensah, L. O. (2023). Cash flow management and SME survival during economic crises. *Journal of Small Business and Enterprise Development, 30*(1), 112–130. https://doi.org/10.1108/JSBED-03-2022-0121

Akanyonge, J., Obeng-Amponsah, W., & Owusu, E. L. (2023). Financial development and SMEs in African countries. In *Finance for Sustainable Development in Africa* (pp. 252–276). Routledge.

Alhassan, F., & Asare, N. (2021). Budgetary control and financial performance of SMEs inGhana. *African Journal of Economic and Management Studies, 12*(4), 501–518. https://doi.org/10.1108/AJEMS-01-2021-0023

Anarfo, E. B., Abor, J. Y., & Osei, V. (2023). Financial literacy and SME performance in sub-Saharan Africa. *Review of Development Finance, 13*(1), 45–60. https://doi.org/10.1016/j.rdf.2023.02.003

Aryeetey, E. (2005). Informal finance for private sector development in Sub-Saharan Africa. *Journal of Microfinance/ESR Review, 7*(1), 3.

Asravor, R. K., Essah, N., & Sackey, F. G. (2025). Effects of COVID-19 and government stimulus packages on the resilience and recovery of micro, small, and medium enterprises in Ghana. *African Identities*, 1–23.

Barney, J. (1991). Firm resources and sustained competitive advantage. *Journal of management, 17*(1), 99–120.

Berry, A. J., Sweeting, R., & Goto, J. (2006). The effect of business advisers on the performance of SMEs. *Journal of Small Business and Enterprise Development, 13*(1), 33–47. https://doi.org/10.1108/14626000610645298

Beck, T., & Demirgüç-Kunt, A. (2006). Small and medium-size enterprises: Access to finance as a growth constraint. *Journal of Banking & Finance, 30*(11), 2931–2943. https://doi.org/10.1016/j.jbankfin.2006.05.009

Bennett, R. J., & Robson, P. J. A. (2004). The role of boards of directors in small and medium-sized firms. *Journal of Small Business and Enterprise Development, 11*(1), 95–113.

Boachie-Mensah, P., & Acquah, I. S. K. (2022). Financial advisory services and SME growth in Ghana. *Journal of Entrepreneurship in Emerging Economies, 14*(2), 210–228. https://doi.org/10.1108/JEEE-08-2021-0312

Brealey, R. A., Cooper, I. A., & Habib, M. A. (2020). Cost of capital and valuation in the public and private sectors: Tax, risk and debt capacity. *Journal of Business finance & accounting, 47*(1–2), 163–187.

Chand, M., & Katou, A. A. (2012). Strategic determinants for the selection of partner alliances in the Indian tour operator industry: A cross-national study. *Journal of World Business, 47*(2), 167–177.

Coleman, S., & Cohn, R. (2000). Small firms' use of financial leverage: Evidence from the 1993 National Survey of small business finances. *Journal of Business Entrepreneurship, 12*(3), 81–98.

Danso, A., Adomako, S., & Damoah, J. O. (2023). Inventory management practices and operational efficiency of SMEs. *International Journal of Productivity and Performance Management, 72*(3), 401–420. https://doi.org/10.1108/IJPPM-04-2022-0189

Demir, A., Pesqué-Cela, V., Altunbas, Y., & Murinde, V. (2022). Fintech, financial inclusion and SME financing. *Journal of Financial Stability, 58*, 100966. https://doi.org/10.1016/j.jfs.2022.100966

Domeher, D. (2012). Land rights and SME credit: Evidence from Ghana. *International Journal of Development Issues, 11*(2), 129–143.

Fatoki, O. (2014). The causes of the failure of new small and medium enterprises in South Africa. *Mediterranean Journal of Social Sciences, 5*(20), 922–927.

Frimpong, S., Asuming, P. O., & Agyapong, D. (2023). FinTech adoption and financial inclusion among Ghanaian SMEs. *Technological Forecasting and Social Change, 186*, 122–135. https://doi.org/10.1016/j.techfore.2022.122135

Ghana Statistical Service. (2021). *National survey on small and medium enterprises in Ghana*. Author.

Krejcie, R. V., & Morgan, D. W. (1970). Determining sample size for research activities. *Educational and Psychological Measurement, 30*(3), 607–610. https://doi.org/10.1177/001316447003000308

Lusardi, A., & Mitchell, O. S. (2014). The economic importance of financial literacy: Theory and evidence. *Journal of Economic Literature, 52*(1), 5–44. https://doi.org/10.1257/jel.52.1.5

Maksimov, V., Wang, S. L., & Luo, Y. (2017). Reducing poverty in the least developed countries: The role of small and medium enterprises. *Journal of World Business, 52*(2), 244–257.

Mang'ana, K. M., Hokororo, S. J., & Ndyetabula, D. W. (2024). An Investigation of the Extent of Implementation of the Financial Management Practices of Agri-SMEs in developing countries: Evidence from Tanzania. *Sustainable Technology and Entrepreneurship, 3*(1), 100049.

Mensah, A. O., Fobih, N., & Adom, Y. A. (2019). Entrepreneurship development and new business start-ups: Challenges and prospects for Ghanaian entrepreneurs. *African Research Review, 13*(3), 27–41.

Mugano, G., & Dorasamy, N. (Eds.). (2023). *SMEs and Economic Development in Africa*. Taylor & Francis Group.

Myers, S. C., & Majluf, N. S. (1984). Corporate financing and investment decisions when firms have information that investors do not have. *Journal of Financial Economics, 13*(2), 187–221. https://doi.org/10.1016/0304-405X(84)90023-0

Oduro, S. (2020). Exploring the barriers to SMEs' open innovation adoption in Ghana: A mixed research approach. *International Journal of Innovation Science, 12*(1), 21–51.

Okpara, J. O. (2011). Factors constraining the growth and survival of SMEs in Nigeria: Implications for poverty alleviation. *Management Research Review, 34*(2), 156–171.

Owusu, G. M. Y., Anokye, F. K., & Bekoe, R. A. (2022). Debt management strategies and financial sustainability of SMEs. *Journal of Small Business and Enterprise Development, 29*(4), 589–607. https://doi.org/10.1108/JSBED-05-2021-0198

Ozili, P. K. (2018). Banking stability determinants in Africa. *International Journal of Managerial Finance, 14*(4), 462–483.

Peel, M. J., & Wilson, N. (1996). Working capital and financial management practices in the small firm sector. *International Small Business Journal, 14*(2), 52–68.

Skouloudis, A., Leal Filho, W., Deligiannakis, G., Vouros, P., Nikolaou, I., & Evangelinos, K. (2023). Coping with floods: Impacts, preparedness and resilience capacity of Greek micro-, small-and medium-sized enterprises in flood-affected areas. *International Journal ofClimate Change Strategies and Management, 15*(1), 81–103.

Stevenson, L., & St-Onge, A. (2005). *Support for growth-oriented women entrepreneurs in Ethiopia, Kenya and Tanzania*. Geneva, Switzerland: International Labour Office.

Wernerfelt, B. (1984). A resource-based view of the firm. *Strategic management journal, 5*(2), 171–180.

World Bank. (2020). *SME finance: Improving SMEs' access to finance and finding innovative solutions*. World Bank. https://www.worldbank.org/en/topic/smefinance

12

The Role Entrepreneurial Orientation and Social Media Marketing on SMES Performance

George Kofi Amoako

12.1 Introduction

Social media has become one of the vital communication channels for businesses (Hanafizadeh et al., 2021). According to Liao et al. (2021), the popularity of social media has enabled consumers to socially interact with and share information in relation to their brands or product. This can lead to more rational buying decisions (Gupta, 2019). Social media platforms such as Twitter, Facebook, Instagram, TikTok, and WhatsApp can be used to attract and turn potential consumers into purchasing customers through targeted advertising. Social media can also be seen as an innovative approach for marketers as well as businesses to increase their sales through creating a lasting relationship with new customers, including maintaining existing ones (Malthouse et al., 2013). To be able to

G. K. Amoako (✉)
Ghana Communications Technology University, Accra, Ghana

Durban University of Technology, Durban, South Africa
e-mail: gamoako@gctu.edu.gh

E. Amoako Asiedu et al. (eds.), *Entrepreneurship and Small and Medium-Sized Enterprises (SMEs) in Africa*, https://doi.org/10.1007/978-3-032-14174-3_12

communicate and connect with prospects and customers, several companies, enterprises as well as marketers are establishing their social media presence. This shows that businesses are constantly striving to publish relevant brand content as well as respond to buyers' comments, queries, and questions on time.

Studies such as Teng et al. (2022) asserted that social media has changed the way businesses or companies interact with their customers as well as created a new stream of electronic commerce usually referred to as social commerce. According to Alayón et al. (2022), social media is a strategic innovative tool used to share information as well as create profitable customer long lasting relationship. Due to social media's effectiveness, small, medium and large companies have adopted social media platform applications to improve their business performance, including achieving a competitive advantage over their rivals (He, 2022). Companies have used social media for market penetration, advertising including networking with prospective clients (George & Schillebeeckx. 2022). Hitchen et al. (2017) propose that social media platforms help business strategic partnerships through collaborative information as well as knowledge sharing. The advancement in Internet technologies, for instance, social media, provides unprecedented opportunities for small and medium enterprises (SMEs), which play a significant role in the economic development of any country (Rana et al., 2019).

Admittedly, social media's popularity among SMEs can be partially explained by its lower costs, minimum technical requirement as well as positive and wide range effect (Chatterjee & Kar, 2020). For example, social media creates value for SMEs in relation to customer service, sales, marketing, and internal operations (Abed, 2020). According to Adelakun et al. (2025), consumers spending more time on the Internet and traditional marketing channels becoming ineffective, SMEs are using social media marketing strategies to connect with their target audience, engaging them to attain sustainable growth. Online marketing offers SMEs the opportunity to reach out to a global audience, target specific demographics with precision, and measure the effectiveness of their marketing efforts in real time (Sharabati et al., 2024). By utilizing Internet marketing channels, for instance, email marketing, search engine optimization, and social media, SMEs can increase their product or brand visibility, develop leads, drive sales, which, in the long term, leads to business growth and success. Creating valuable as well as relevant content to attract, educate, and engage target audiences ultimately drives brand awareness and customer loyalty (Lou & Xie, 2021). In conclusion, innovative online marketing strategies play a significant role in driving competitive advantage as well as sustainable growth for SMEs (Quaye & Mensah, 2019). By utilizing digital marketing tactics, including staying ahead of industry trends, SMEs can effectively reach and involve their target audience, drive business results, and thrive in today's digital economy (Al Koliby et al., 2024).

12.2 Literature Review and Proposition Development

12.2.1 Social Media

Online platforms are recognized as a vital tool for small and medium enterprises (SMEs) to build close connections with buyers (Scuotto et al., 2017; Marolt et al., 2022). Therefore, it can be linked with the secured development of web creation, including designs that are targeted to enhance communication, ideas, sharing of information, interactivity as well as liaison on the Internet. According to Borge et al. (2022), the rise of many social media sites, for instance, Facebook, Instagram, and Twitter, currently known as X, makes it easier for businesses to influence their marketing environment, capabilities, as well as engage their buyers in discussions. Twitter (X) is a well-known online site for customers to communicate among themselves. Due to its flexibility, individuals can express their views or ideas (Fitriyyah et al., 2019; Fraccastoro et al., 2021).

As social media gains much attention due to the options it gives to businesses, companies, especially consumers, it has become a critical tool for contemporary marketing communication (Mazzarol, 2015; Eggers et al., 2017). The increasing information on social media reveals an in-depth understanding of the extent to which this knowledge can influence people's purchasing decision-making toward a firm's product, goods, and/or services (Khairiza & Kusumasari, 2020). Internet contribution to the community domain, as well as its effects on SMEs or firms' involvement, are extraordinary, relative, as well as inclusive (Eggers et al., 2017). The importance of SMEs experiences with consumers utilization of online platforms, for instance, the level of marketing engagement as well as advertising, are some of its fundamental assets (Borge et al., 2022).

Online platforms present new opportunities for buyers or people, including SMEs and companies, to inform, educate, and entertain their shareholders, explain general concerns, give ideas as well as their desires, including executing and controlling actions (Crammond et al., 2018; Li et al., 2018). With different kinds of people actively connecting as well as participating in online platforms such as Facebook, WhatsApp, Instagram, and Twitter (X), it is necessary to deliberate on grouping consumers on Internet based on their online handles (Farzam et al., 2022). According to Lawelai et al. (2022), buyers' perspective and judgment on social media platforms, for instance, Instagram, WhatsApp, Facebook, and so on, can be recognized as online sentiments. These may be brand reviews, impressions about ongoing issues, or individual ideology concerning numerous subject matters. Social media opinions are significant since they can influence how buyers judge things in addition to their attitude (Gunawan & Huarng, 2015). It can also enable SMEs, firms, and businesses to acquire knowledge and understand how people think of them, as well as analyze information that can be used to enhance their brand, goods, and/or services (Palalic et al., 2021).

12.2.2 Social Media Marketing

Social media has been recognized as a cornerstone of online marketing strategies for SMEs, delivering a cost-effective way to connect to a large audience, establish brand awareness as well as create involvement (Udeh et al., 2024). Social media marketing plays an important role in building brand awareness as well as creating a strong digital presence for SMEs (Alkhasoneh et al., 2024). With many users actively involving themselves on the Internet, SMEs have the chance to connect with a global audience and identify potential or prospective buyers (Alkhasoneh et al., 2024; Ali Qalati et al., 2020). Through constantly sharing valuable and engaging content, SMEs can increase their product visibility, foster consumer loyalty, including gaining traffic to their websites (Guha et al., 2018). With several social media platforms that are available, SMEs can select the platform that aligns with their target customers and business objectives. Currently, Facebook offers a wide audience for SMEs to connect with consumers (Oguanobi & Joel, 2024). It is good for sharing different types of content, including posts, videos, and images. Instagram is a visual platform that is specifically designed for businesses that solely rely heavily on visuals, for instance, fashion, food, and travel. It is ideal for sharing visually appealing content and engaging a younger audience.

SMEs must actively engage their followers or customers by replying to their messages, comments and suggestions as this can help build a strong lasting relationship as well as foster loyalty (Cheng & Shiu, 2019; Mahalakshmi et al., 2025). Online platforms offer powerful advertising options that enable SMEs to choose specific demographics, behaviors and interests as well (Mahalakshmi et al., 2025; Lim et al., 2024). Paid advertisements can help SMEs reach a bigger audience and create conversions. Businesses can again collaborate with social media influencers within their sector to help enlarge their audience in order to increase brand reliability (Mahalakshmi et al., 2025). Influencers can promote products or services to their followers, helping companies reach a highly engaged audience (Campbell & Farrell, 2020; Tafesse & Wood, 2021). Therefore, social media marketing is a powerful tool for SMEs to create brand awareness, engage their audience, and drive business growth. By selecting the right platforms, executing effective market strategies, and assessing performance, SMEs can leverage social media to achieve their marketing objectives and stay ahead of the competition (Delbaere et al., 2021).

12.2.3 Entrepreneurial Orientation

Entrepreneurial orientation (EO) is defined as the practices, processes, as well as decision-making that drive companies or businesses to initiate new products, services, markets, ideas, innovations, or business models that are not in existence (Covin et al., 2019). Entrepreneurial orientation can again be identified as a basis for achieving a competitive edge as it shows how SMEs or companies can change their operations for new growth directions (Kiyabo & Isaga, 2020). Entrepreneurial orientation is the process by which SMEs or firm owners take decisions for spreading the mission of the company. Luu and Ngo (2019) asserted that entrepreneurial orientation continues to expand with the passage of time; also, new dimensions have constantly been included successively. Innovativeness, which is the creative capability of companies leading to new product development, followed by proactiveness, which involves anticipating as well as planning to address those anticipations in advance (Kiyabo & Isaga, 2020; Hashem et al., 2024). Later, risk-taking was added as a further dimension, along with competitive aggressiveness, which includes challenging the competitor rather than following them, which involves high risk (Kiyabo & Isaga, 2020; Linton, 2019). Heryadi et al. (2023) propose that entrepreneurial orientation is the most important concept for small and medium enterprises (SMEs). Orientation is defined as the degree to which firms, companies, or businesses focus on meeting the needs, wants, and desires of its consumers (Riswanto et al., 2019). Research articles carried out by Semrau et al. (2019) reveal that the important role of entrepreneurial orientation is to enhance marketing performance. According to Keh et al. (2002), entrepreneurial orientation has a direct positive effect on organizational performance and long-term sustainability. Market-oriented SMEs have superior business competencies due to owners, managers or entrepreneurs' orientation (Belás et al., 2021).

12.2.4 Small and Medium Enterprises (SMEs)

Small and medium enterprises (SMEs) amount to a significant part of the global economy as well as play a vital role in achieving innovation, job creation including economic growth (Gherghina et al., 2020). SMEs usually operate with limited financial resources, infrastructure, and human capital making it difficult to compete with bigger firms or companies. According to Familoni and Onyebuchi (2024), SMEs are normally recognized with the aim of attaining rapid growth and scalability. With the current exciting opportunities for expanding and success, it poses a threat in terms of managing growth effectively, maintaining business culture, including scaling operations without sacrificing brand quality. SMEs many times are at the forefront of innovation, business models, leveraging new technologies and market trends to obstruct traditional businesses (Onesi-Ozigagun et al., 2024). This requires managers or marketers to be active, adaptive, and willing to accept change in order to stay ahead of the dynamic business environment. SMEs must be intelligent as well as flexible in responding to changing market conditions, buyers' preferences, including competitors' threats. Small and medium enterprises (SMEs) are found to act as important suppliers of semifinished and/or, in some cases, finished raw materials to large companies, and as such, they are considered amongst the most vital organizational suppliers (Seifzadeh et al., 2021).

Furthermore, Muñoz-Pascual et al. (2019) asserted that SMEs, which are both diversified and heterogeneous, are also considered as the economic backbone of the country of their operations. Al-Kwifi et al. (2021) again propose that superior marketing practices, recognized for their cost-effectiveness, can enable SMEs to achieve successful sustainable business growth as well as development. These practices require SMEs to include new technologies into already existing and well-established business practices, thus requiring the use of ICT in their daily business activities as an important and promising tool for promoting their brands and enabling further sustainable business growth (Kapoor et al., 2018). In conclusion, SMEs are characterized by a mixture of challenges, opportunities, resource constraints, uncertainties, rapid growth, globalization, technological disruption, and intense competition (Ololade, 2024). By understanding these dynamics and leveraging their strengths, managers or marketers can steer the complexities of the market as well as position their firms for success and long-term sustainable growth (Nyquist et al., 2025).

12.2.5 Social Media Marketing and Entrepreneurial Orientation of Owners: SMEs

Social media marketing (SMM) is a strategy of using social media or digital platforms to advertise any brand, product or services, information, or an idea (Kenton, 2018). SMM serves many purposes. According to Crammond et al. (2018), it can be used effectively to increase awareness of a product, service, information, idea, and/or opinion. It is a powerful tool for branding. SMM helps in developing brand awareness, enhancing brand recognition, including increasing brand recall. Kaur (2019) proposes that social media marketing is possibly one of the easiest ways to achieve traffic to the business website. Entrepreneurial orientation (EO) can be recognized as an overall strategic posture of businesses (Fadda, 2018).

In the context of business or firm growth, EO is expected to help SME entrepreneurs to create current software or applications early enough to enhance their business operations as the marketing environment changes. The EO is seen to be proactive as well as guide entrepreneurs to take the requisite steps toward developing innovative ideas, products, and/or services. With the help of EO, owners of SMEs will be able to enjoy the advantages connected to availing themselves to higher risk of opportunities. SMM adoption by entrepreneurs can affect both economic as well as social value; it can also enhance the socio-economic conditions of a country (Audretsch & Belitski, 2021). According to Vrontis et al. (2022), the utilization of social media marketing can also have a positive effect on the performance of SMEs. Business owners or entrepreneurs can use social media marketing strategies to achieve their company objectives. For instance, marketing, advertising, branding, public relations, customer service, problem-solving, including human resources (Nisar & Whitehead, 2016). SMM as well as entrepreneurial orientational activities can have a significant impact on SMEs' expansion, competitive advantage, including their output performance. Thus, it is asserted that:

P1: Social media marketing (SMM) has a positive impact on entrepreneurial orientation (EO).

12.2.6 Social Media Marketing and SMEs Performance

Social media marketing (SMM) can help SMEs to increase their business performance since it offers an opportunity for them to develop as well as strengthen their product, brand, or service name (Amoako et al., 2023). This includes obtaining a complete platform through which they can eventually gain benefits (Sahaym et al., 2021). Social media marketing sites are a crucial part of the business-related activities, as well as it is more beneficial for SMEs due to its cost-effective nature as a way to compete with limited resources against bigger firms (Veldeman et al., 2017). SMM can also enable SMEs to create more knowledge about their products, brand, and/or services, thus convincing existing and non-existing customers which in turn increase SMEs or company performance (Tajudeen et al., 2018). SMEs can use SMM to create and execute communities, distribute content that increases traffic on their websites to identify new business opportunities, including establishing direct contact with their consumers and prospective buyers as well (Kumar et al., 2016).

SMM again improves SMEs' performance outcomes by building strong relationships with buyers, influencing consumers' decisions to purchase, gaining access to knowledge that is shared, not only between businesses and buyers but also between buyers themselves (Trainor et al., 2014). According to Bocconcelli et al. (2017), SMM provides opportunities for SMEs that want to establish strong connections with purchasers as well as enhance their capabilities, skills, and expertise, which in turn affects their competitive edge, including business performance. Achieving competitive advantage is very significant to SMEs since it plays a vital role in driving higher business performance (Kumar et al., 2016; Devereux et al., 2020). A higher level of competitive edge enables businesses or companies to create superior value for buyers, which in the long run increases sales volume, customer satisfaction, market share, including loyalty (Kumar et al., 2016; Sundararaj & Rejeesh, 2021). Leonardi and Vaast (2017) propose that researchers should focus on how social media marketing helps enterprises as well as expand their examinations related to knowledge co-creation and performance. Therefore, we propose that:

P2: SMM has a significant effect on SMEs' Performance.

12.2.7 Entrepreneurial Orientation of Owners and SMEs Performance

Over the years, the connection that exists between entrepreneurial orientation and SMEs performance has gained much attention (Buli, 2017; Álvarez Jaramillo et al., 2019). Scholars have recognized EO as a strong predictor of SMEs' performance and as such more studies are required (Ciampi et al., 2021; Acosta et al., 2018; Boso et al., 2013). Based on the positive impact of EO on business performance, scholarly articles propose that companies achieve long-term performance and sustainability from building proactiveness, risk-taking, including innovative attitude. Del Rosario and René (2017) identified that EO can enable SMEs to move faster as well as stay ahead of the competition in this changing business environment. While SMEs and their business performance are essential to business Owners, CEO or Managers, research indicates an absence of accurate understanding and information about how entrepreneurial aspects influence SMEs' performance (Mason et al., 2015).

Previous articles have investigated how EO influences business performance in-depth (Sadiku-Dushi et al., 2019). Rostain (2021) recognizes that most articles have identified that EO has a positive impact on SMEs performance. Several scholars have handled EO as if it is a single entity. They show that EO has a similar impact on SMEs performance in different settings, including diverse countries, marketplaces, and types of businesses (Perera et al., 2019). Khedhaouria et al. (2020) also suggested that there is a tilted connection between EO and SMEs or companies' performance. The magnitude of the relationship between EO and business or SMEs performance has been seen to vary depending on the type of performance measurements used. The positive association between EO and performance is resistant to alternative measures of EO, as well as changes in performance measurement (financial versus nonfinancial). According to Kashan et al. (2021), there is evidence of a direct connection between entrepreneurial orientation and SMEs performance. Their meta-analysis (Sadiku-Dushi et al., 2019) academically affirms that there is a positive connection between EO and SMEs performance.

Creative ideas, inventive behavior, including entrepreneurial-oriented knowledge, skill, capabilities are important variables in generating industry-based SME activities (Yadav et al., 2024; Taipale et al., 2019). SMEs can attain the strongest growth results with an entrepreneurial strategic posture that holds temporally salient market information, which is more structurally adaptive (e.g., is younger), and has an intangible resource advantage relative to their industry rivals (Somohano-Rodriguez et al., 2022). SMEs with higher EO can do better in international markets since they have the competencies required to create new strategies that provide an edge in the foreign market and may discover and utilize new technologies that better correspond with the needs, wants, and desires of foreign market consumers, and are also prepared to assume the business risks that come with executing new strategies, including technology, in new markets (Taipale et al., 2019). Based on the following relationship, it is proposed that:

P3: There is a positive effect of entrepreneurial orientation (EO) on SMEs Performance.

12.3 Methodology

The conceptual research model was designed based on the literature review. The study used a traditional review of literature using articles published in English from 2015 to 2024. Keywords used for searching literature include *social media marketing*, *social media*, *entrepreneurial orientation*, *risk-taking*, *proactiveness*, *innovativeness*, *performance*, and *SMEs performance*; these keywords should be covered in the abstract as well as the main document. Articles as well as reports from World bank and other organizations were also reviewed. This data was sourced from google scholar, emerald insight and science direct. Thematic analysis was used in analyzing the data sourced. In all, 92 papers were sourced, and after screening and scanning, 81 were valid for the review (Fig. 12.1).

12.4 Discussions of the Conceptual Framework

The outcome of this literature review and synthesis suggests that social media marketing can enhance the performance of SMEs and entrepreneurial orientation also leads to SMEs performance. Moreover, the proposed conceptual framework also points out that social media marketing can also enhance entrepreneurial orientation. The proposed conceptual framework suggests further that the combination of social media marketing and entrepreneurial orientation can lead to SME performance. The

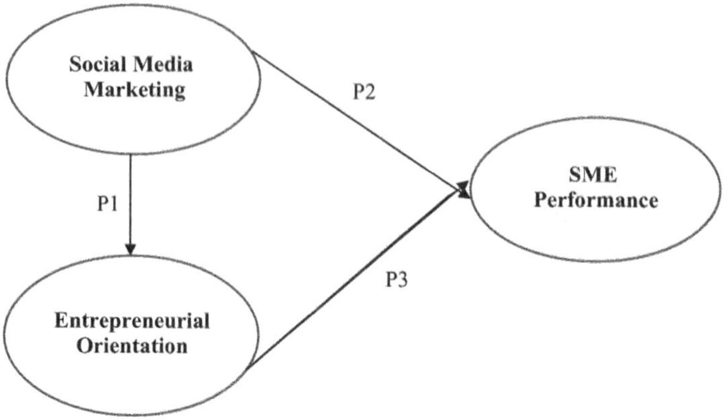

Fig. 12.1 Conceptual framework of the study. Source: Authors construct, 2024)

conceptual framework suggests that managers of SMEs must engage in social media marketing effectively and invest in orienting staff more on the elements of good entrepreneurship to increase their profitability and performance. Moreover, the proposed conceptual framework indicates that rooting social media marketing through good entrepreneurial orientation can boost SME performance. As indicated in Figure 12.1 above, the relationships amongst the variables are indicated.

12.5 Implication to Practice

Recent articles have revealed many implications for practice. The outcome shows positive guidelines to owners and managers of SMEs who have in mind to technologically change their business by utilizing online platforms, for instance, Facebook, WhatsApp, Twitter(X), Instagram, and so on, to increase sales as well as achieve business performance. Thus, SMEs owners and managers of SMEs, such as Free the Youth, who use social media marketing to promote streetwear, must recognize as well as examine their business appropriately in the current changing market environment both internal and external before financing in these Internet tools. As this can enable SMEs like Aftown, a Ghanaian digital music platform agency that uses social media channels to market and distribute music from local artists to take advantage of the opportunities, including reducing uncertainty that comes with online marketing. Therefore, SMEs such as Akosua Afriyie-Kumi, a renowned Ghanaian handbag brand that wants to change their business through online sites, must know the abilities of workers in relation to their technological level.

SMEs, including So Her, a Ghanaian SME that specializes in wigs, accessories, and shoes, who has leveraged WhatsApp as a key platform for operations, must employ technologically intelligent people who can direct as well as educate managers on the strategies to adopt to achieve market growth and long-term performance. This can be done through training, seminars, including conferences. SMEs owners as well as managers can establish whether their business or companies have the skills to identify the opportunities in online sites. They must again evaluate whether their company has the capabilities to update current as well as obtain intellectual property in addition to fixed assets that effectively lead to profitable as well as public interest that enhances business performance (Dzogbenuku et al., 2024). Managers and owners of SMEs, such as Biishville, a nomadic dining and event outfit owned and managed by a Ghanaian who used Instagram to position it as a sought-after chef service in Africa, can organize training for their staff on how to operate these technologies, as well as encouraging them to comply with eco-friendly requirement that SMEs must follow. Thus, it will enable SMEs to develop economics, including social values, which will lead to better performance.

In this proposed conceptual framework, owners and managers of SMEs can enhance their entrepreneurial orientation (EO), must communicate the utilization of interconnected systems (for example, people and equipment) in addition to the duties of individuals as well as devices used together in the company or business. According to Akter et al. (2020), many consumers have a dubious conception about bots as well as some online assistance tools. Current research proves that social media platforms enable SMEs to improve their business performance. From this point of view, SMEs must address the difficulties in both technological and managerial contexts for effective extortion of value from the volume of data. Therefore, owners as well as managers of SMEs must emphasize how technological advancement can significantly combine all the current devices, including online platforms, to gain a better overall performance of SMEs.

12.5.1 Limitations and Future Scope

The research work reveals limitations that allow additional or future perspectives. First, the study findings do not rely on real sample data. That only consists of the issues of determination of the association that linked the constructions, thereby improving the possibility of flaws in the correlation between the independent variable and unexplained variations. Thus, it is recommended that future academic investigations can be based on real sample collected and tested using the proposed model. Second, the proposed model is only conceptual and needs to be tested empirically. Thus, it may not easily back the hypothesis of the research results. Researchers can execute studies based on different geographical locations, taking into consideration the opinions of other owners as well as managers of SMEs working in other regions in any geographical zones.

12.6 Conclusion

SMM helps SMEs to gain exposure, marketing insights, as well as increase traffic (Dwivedi et al., 2021), including providing assets that SMEs can utilize to improve their competitive edge and business performance. According to Ahmad et al. (2018), SMM and EO of owners do not necessarily lead directly to superior marketing or SMEs performance. Thus, the main aim of this article is to better understand the way SMM and EO of owners influence SMEs performance in the long term. Based on resource-based views as well as dynamic capabilities perspective, it is asserted that SMM and EO improve Internet capabilities in a way that positively increases SMEs' competitive advantage and performance as well. Though the research gives valuable insights into social media platform sites, it is not without limitations.

First, as a conceptual paper, the conclusion is only based on assumptions since the proposed model has not been tested. Second, the findings lack generalizability as data were not collected to test the proposed model. Third, this study applied a simple measure of SMM and EO. For broader assessment of SMM and EO on SMEs performance, another research can be done with more advanced criterion. Furthermore, future studies can extend beyond the conceptual research model by scoping moderating effects. For instance, corporate social responsibility, environmental turbulence, and so on. Also, businesses normally undertake a whole range of marketing activities as well as utilize several pieces of information, including communication technologies, with SMM as part of omnichannel marketing. Consequently, future studies can deliberate on a wider context by adding other relational capabilities that arise, not only from SMM, but also from other e-commerce sites as well as m-commerce sites, and new technologies. Lastly, other marketing performance indicators can be employed to give additional knowledge on market performance outcomes.

References

Abed, S. S. (2020). Social commerce adoption using TOE framework: An empirical investigation of Saudi Arabian SMEs. *International Journal of Information Management, 53*, 102118.

Acosta, A. S., Crespo, Á. H., & Agudo, J. C. (2018). Effect of market orientation, network capability and entrepreneurial orientation on international performance of small and medium enterprises (SMEs). *International Business Review, 27*(6), 1128–1140.

Adelakun, C. G., Olaleye, B. R., Khumalo, N., & Omikunle, Y. E. (2025). Impact of total quality management on organizational learning among Nigerian SMEs: The moderating role of strategic thinking. *Acta Universitatis Danubius. OEconomica, 21*(4), 197–214. Retrieved from https://dj.univ-danubius.ro/index.php/AUDOE/article/view/3502.

Ahmad, S. Z., Abu Bakar, A. R., & Ahmad, N. (2018). Social media adoption and its impact on firm performance: The case of the UAE. *International Journal of Entrepreneurial Behavior & Research, 25*, 84–111.

Akter, S., Michael, K., & Uddin, M. R. (2020). Transforming business using digital innovations: The application of AI, blockchain, cloud and data analytics. *Annals of Operations Research, 308*, 7–39.

Al Koliby, I. S., Mehat, N. A. B., Al-Swidi, A. K., & Al-Hakimi, M. A. (2024). Unveiling the linkages between entrepreneurial culture, innovation capability, digital marketing capability and sustainable competitive performance of manufacturing SMEs: Evidence from emerging countries. *The Bottom Line, 37*(4), 473–500.

Alayón, C. L., Säfsten, K., & Johansson, G. (2022). Barriers and enablers for the adoption of sustainable manufacturing by manufacturing SMEs. *Sustainability, 14*(4), 2364.

Ali Qalati, S., Li, W., Ahmed, N., Ali Mirani, M., & Khan, A. (2020). Examining the factors affecting SME performance: The mediating role of social media adoption. *Sustainability, 13*(1), 75.

Alkhasoneh, O. M., Jamaludin, H., Bin Zahar, A. R. I., & Al-Sharafi, M. A. (2024). Drivers of social media use among SMEs and its impact on brand awareness and customer engagement. *Asia-Pacific Journal of Business Administration, 17*(15). https://doi.org/10.1108/APJBA-02-2024-0102

Al-Kwifi, O. S., Ongsakul, V., Abu Farha, A. K., Zafar, A. U., & Karasneh, M. (2021). Impact of product innovativeness on technology switching in global market. *EuroMed Journal of Business, 16*, 25.

Álvarez Jaramillo, J., Zartha Sossa, J. W., & Orozco Mendoza, G. L. (2019). Barriers to sustainability for small and medium enterprises in the framework of sustainable development – Literature review. *Business Strategy and the Environment, 28*(4), 512–524. https://doi.org/10.1002/bse.2261.

Amoako, G. K., Bonsu, G. A., Gabrah, A. Y. B., & Ampong, G. O. A. (2023). Digital marketing and sustainability competitive advantage: A conceptual framework. In *Handbook of research on achieving sustainable development goals with sustainable marketing* (pp. 170–188). IGI Global.

Audretsch, D. B., & Belitski, M. (2021). Towards an entrepreneurial ecosystem typology for regional economic development: The role of creative class and entrepreneurship. *Regional Studies, 55*, 735–756.

Belás, J., Amoah, J., Dvorský, J., & Šuleř, P. (2021). The importance of social media for management of SMEs. *Economics & Sociology, 14*(4), 118–132. https://doi.org/10.14254/2071-789X.2021/14-4/7

Bocconcelli, R., Cioppi, M., & Pagano, A. (2017). Social media as a resource in SMEs' sales process. *Journal of Business & Industrial Marketing, 32*, 693–709.

Borge, R., Boulianne, S., Dennis, J., Vaccari, C., & Valeriani, A. (2022). Political participation in the digital technology era: A symposium on Outside the Bubble: Social media and Political Participation in Western Democracies By Cristian Vaccari and Augusto Valeriani. *Italian Political Science Review, 53*, 1–19.

Boso, N., Story, V. M., & Cadogan, J. W. (2013). Entrepreneurial orientation, market orientation, network ties, and performance: Study of entrepreneurial firms in a developing economy. *Journal of Business Venturing, 28*(6), 708–727.

Buli, B. M. (2017). Entrepreneurial orientation, market orientation and performance of SMEs in the manufacturing industry: Evidence from Ethiopian enterprises. *Management Research Review, 40*(3), 292–309.

Campbell, C., & Farrell, J. R. (2020). More than meets the eye: The functional components underlying influencer marketing. *Business Horizons, 63*(4), 469–479.

Chatterjee, S., & Kar, A. K. (2020). Why do small and medium enterprises use social media marketing and what is the impact: Empirical insights from India. *International Journal of Information Management, 53*, 102103.

Cheng, C. C., & Shiu, E. C. (2019). How to enhance SMEs customer involvement using social media: The role of Social CRM. *International Small Business Journal, 37*(1), 22–42.

Ciampi, F., Demi, S., Magrini, A., Marzi, G., & Papa, A. (2021). Exploring the impact of big data analytics capabilities on business model innovation: The mediating role of entrepreneurial orientation. *Journal of Business Research, 123*, 1–13.

Covin, J. G., Wales, W., & J. (2019). Crafting high-impact entrepreneurial orientation research: Some suggested guidelines. *Entrepreneurship Theory and Practice, 43*(*1*), 3–18.

Crammond, R., Omeihe, K. O., Murray, A., & Ledger, K. (2018). Managing knowledge through social media: Modelling an entrepreneurial approach for Scottish SMEs and beyond. *Baltic Journal of Management, 13*(3), 303–328.

Del Rosario, R.-S. M., & René, D.-P. (2017). Eco-innovation and organizational culture in the hotel industry. *International Journal of Hospitality Management, 65*, 71–80.

Delbaere, M., Michael, B., & Phillips, B. J. (2021). Social media influencers: A route to brand engagement for their followers. *Psychology & Marketing, 38*(1), 101–112.

Devereux, E., Grimmer, L., & Grimmer, M. (2020). Consumer engagement on social media: Evidence from small retailers. *Journal of Consumer Behaviour, 19*(2), 151–159.

Dwivedi, Y. K., Ismagilova, E., Hughes, D. L., Carlson, J., Filieri, R., Jacobson, J., Jain, V., Karjaluoto, H., Kefi, H., & Krishen, A. S. (2021). Setting the future of digital and social media marketing research: Perspectives and research propositions. *International Journal of Information Management, 59*, 102168.

Dzogbenuku, R., Keelson, S., Amoako, G. K., & Gabrah, A. Y. B. (2024). Retail mix and retail image amongst women: The mediating role of employee attitude. *Cogent Business & Management, 11*(1), 2329042.

Eggers, F., Hatak, I., Kraus, S., & Niemand, T. (2017). Technologies that support marketing and market development in SMEs—Evidence from social networks. *Journal of Small Business Management, 55*(2), 270–302.

Fadda, N. (2018). The Effects of Entrepreneurial Orientation Dimensions on Performance in the Tourism Sector. *The New England Journal of Entrepreneurship, 21*, 22–44.

Familoni, B. T., & Onyebuchi, N. C. (2024). Augmented and virtual reality in us education: A review: Analyzing the impact, effectiveness, and future prospects of ar/vr tools in enhancing learning experiences. *International Journal of Applied Research in Social Sciences, 6*(*4*), 642–663.

Farzam, A., Moradi, P., Mohammadi, S., Padar, Z., & Siegel, A. A. (2022). Opinion manipulation on Farsi Twitter. *Scientific Reports, 13*, 1–18.

Fitriyyah, S. N. J., Safriadi, N., & Pratama, E. E. (2019). Analisis Sentimen Calon Presiden Indonesia 2019 dari Media Sosial Twitter Menggunakan Metode Naive Bayes. *Journal Edukasi Dan Penelitian Informatika (JEPIN), 5*(3), 279.

Fraccastoro, S., Gabrielsson, M., & Pullins, E. B. (2021). The integrated use of social media, digital, and traditional communication tools in the B2B sales process of international SMEs. *International Business Review, 30*(4), 101776.

George, G., & Schillebeeckx, S. J. (2022). Digital transfor_mation, sustainability, and purpose in the multinational enterprise. *Journal of World Business, 57*(*3*), 101326.

Gherghina, Ş. C., Botezatu, M. A., Hosszu, A., & Simionescu, L. N. (2020). Small and medium sized enterprises (SMEs): The engine of economic growth through investments and innovation. *Sustainability, 12*(*1*), 347.

Guha, S., Harrigan, P., & Soutar, G. (2018). Linking social media to customer relationship management (CRM): A qualitative study on SMEs. *Journal of Small Business & Entrepreneurship, 30*(3), 193–214.

Gunawan, D. D., & Huarng, K. H. (2015). Viral effects of social network and media on consumers' purchase intention. *Journal of Business Research, 68*(11), 2237–2241.

Gupta, V. (2019). The influencing role of social media in the consumer's hotel decision-making process. *Worldwide Hospitality and Tourism Themes, 11*, 378–391.

Hanafizadeh, P., Shafia, S., & Bohlin, E. (2021). Exploring the consequence of social media usage on firm performance. *Digital Business, 1*, 100013.

Hashem, G., Aboelmaged, M., & Ahmad, I. (2024). Proactiveness, knowledge management capability and innovation ambidexterity: An empirical examination of digital supply chain adoption. *Management Decision, 62*(1), 129–162.

He, H. (2022). A comprehensive review on the role of online media in sustainable business development and decision making. *Soft Computing, 26*, 1–15.

Heryadi, D. Y., Ekowati, D., Chusumastuti, D., Siliwangi, U., Tinggi, S., Ekonomi, I., Megarkencana, N., & Tinggi, S. (2023). Pengaruh Kehadiran Media Sosial, Orientasi Pasar Terhadap Kinerja UMKM di Jawa Barat. *Journal Businessman: Riset Dan Management, 5*(*1*), 94–107.

Hitchen, E. L., Nylund, P. A., Ferràs, X., & Mussons, S. (2017). Social media: Open innovation in SMEs finds new support. *Journal of Business Strategy, 38*(*3*), 21–29.

Kapoor, K. K., Tamilmani, K., Rana, N. P., Patil, P., Dwivedi, Y. K., & Nerur, S. (2018). Advances in social media research: *Past, present and future. Information Systems Frontiers, 20*, 531–558.

Kashan, A. J., Wiewiora, A., & Mohannak, K. (2021). Unpacking organizational culture for innovation in Australian mining industry. *Resource Policy, 73*, 102149.

Kaur, D. (2019). Social media marketing. Digital Kaur. www.digitalkaur.com›social-media-marketing.

Keh, H. T., Foo, M. -D., & Lim, B. C. (2002). Opportunity evaluation under risky conditions: the cognitive processes of entrepreneurs. *Entrep Theory Pract, 27*, 125–148.

Kenton, W. (2018). *Social media marketing (SMM)*. Investopedia. https://www.investopedia.com/terms/s/socialmedia-marketing-smm.asp.

Khairiza, F., & Kusumasari, B. (2020). Analysing political marketing in Indonesia: A palm oil digital campaign case study. *Forestry and Society, 4*(*2*), 294–309.

Khedhaouria, A., Nakara, W. A., Gharbi, S., & Bahri, C. (2020). The relationship between organizational culture and small-firm performance: Entrepreneurial orientation as mediator. *European Management Review, 17*, 515–528.

Kiyabo, K., & Isaga, N. (2020). Entrepreneurial orientation, competitive advantage, and SMEs' performance: Application of firm growth and personal wealth measures. *Journal of Innovation and Entrepreneurship, 9*(1), 12.

Kumar, A., Bezawada, R., Rishika, R., Janakiraman, R., & Kannan, P. K. (2016). From social to sale: The effects of firm-generated content in social media on customer behavior. *Journal of Marketing, 80*(1), 7–25. https://doi.org/10.1509/jm.14.0249

Lawelai, H., Sadat, A., & Suherman, A. (2022). Democracy and Freedom of Opinion in Social Media: Sentiment Analysis on Twitter. *PRAJA: Journal Ilima Pemerintahan, 10*(*1*), 40–48.

Leonardi, P. M., & Vaast, E. (2017). Social media and their affordances for organizing: A review and agenda for research. *Academy of Management Annals, 11(1)*, 150–188.

Li, L., Su, F., Zhang, W., & Mao, J. Y. (2018). Digital transformation by SME entrepreneurs: A capability perspective. *Information Systems Journal, 28*(6), 1129–1157.

Liao, S. H., Widowati, R., & Hsieh, Y. C. (2021). Investigating online social media users' behaviors for social commerce recommendations. *Technology in Society, 66*, 101655.

Lim, X. J., Quach, S., Thaichon, P., Cheah, J. H., & Ting, H. (2024). Fact or fake: information, misinformation and disinformation via social media. *Journal of Strategic Marketing, 32*(5), 659–664.

Linton, G. (2019). Innovativeness, risk-taking, and proactiveness in startups: A case study and conceptual development. *Journal of Global Entrepreneurship Research, 9*(1), 20.

Lou, C., & Xie, Q. (2021). Something social, something entertaining? How digital content marketing augments consumer experience and brand loyalty. *International Journal of Advertising, 40*(3), 376–402.

Luu, N., & Ngo, L. V. (2019). Entrepreneurial orientation and social ties in transitional economies. *Long Range Planning, 52(1)*, 103–116.

Mahalakshmi, L., Anbalagan, E., Tawil, S., & Joshi, K. P. (2025, December). A Hybrid Attention-Driven Recurrent Neural Network Model for Sentiment Classification of Social Media Texts. *In Proceedings of International Conference on Innovation in Computing, Science, Engineering and Technology, 2*,(1).

Malthouse, E. C., Haenlein, M., Skiera, B., Wege, E., & Zhang, M. (2013). Managing customer relationships in the social media era: Introducing the social CRM house. *Journal of Interactive Marketing, 27*(4), 270–280.

Marolt, M., Zimmermann, H. D., & Pucihar, A. (2022). Social media use and business performance in SMEs: The mediating roles of relational social commerce capability and competitive advantage. *Sustainability, 14*(22), 15029.

Mason, M. C., Floreani, J., Miani, S., Beltrame, F., & Cappelletto, R. (2015). Understanding the impact of entrepreneurial orientation on SMEs' performance. The role of the financing structure. *Procedia Econ. Financ., 23*, 1649–1661.

Mazzarol, T. (2015). SMEs engagement with e-commerce, e-business and e-marketing. *Small Enterprise Research, 22*(1), 79–90.

Muñoz-Pascual, L., Curado, C., & Galende, J. (2019). The triple bottom line on sustainable product innovation performance in SMEs: A mixed methods approach. *Sustainability, 11*, 1689.

Nisar, T. M., & Whitehead, C. (2016). Brand interactions and social media: Enhancing user loyalty through social networking sites. *Computers in Human Behavior, 62*, 743–753.

Nyquist, A. -M., Farshid, M., & Brown, T. E. (2025). Employing digital twin technology in the pursuit to avert sustainable marketing myopia. *Journal of Research in Marketing and Entrepreneurship, 27*(2), 277–293. https://doi.org/10.1108/JRME-01-2024-0007

Oguanobi, V. U., & Joel, O. T. (2024, May). Scalable business models for startups in renewable energy: Strategies for using GIS technology to enhance SME scaling. *Engineering Science & Technology Journal, 5*, 1571–1587.

Ololade, B. M. (2024). Internal control systems of SMEs in Nigeria: a proactive or reactive strategy against employees' fraud?. *Journal of Financial Crime, 32*(1), 49–63. https://doi.org/10.1108/JFC-10-2023-0259

Onesi-Ozigagun, O., Ololade, Y. J., Eyo-Udo, N. L., & Ogundipe, D. O. (2024). Revolutionizing education through AI: A comprehensive review of enhancing learning experiences. *International Journal of Applied Research in Social Sciences, 6*(*4*), 589–607.

Palalic, R., Ramadani, V., Mariam Gilani, S., Gërguri-Rashiti, S., & Dana, L. P. (2021). Social media and consumer buying behavior decision: what entrepreneurs should know?. *Management Decision, 59*(6), 1249–1270.

Perera, D. N., Nag, D., & Venkateswarlu, P. (2019). A Study on the Relationship of Entrepreneurial Orientation and Business Performance in the SMEs of Kurunegala District in Sri Lanka. *Theor. Econ. Lett., 9*, 2324–2336.

Quaye, D., & Mensah, I. (2019). Marketing innovation and sustainable competitive advantage of manufacturing SMEs in Ghana. *Management Decision, 57*(7), 1535–1553.

Rana, N. P., Barnard, D. J., Baabdullah, A. M. A., Rees, D., & Roderick, S. (2019). Exploring barriers of m-commerce adoption in SMEs in the UK: Developing a framework using ISM. *International Journal of Information Management, 44*, 141–153.

Riswanto, A., Hurriyati, R., Wibowo, L. A., & Gaffar, V. (2019). Effect of market orientation on business performance in MSMEs as mediating by dynamic marketing capabilities. *Quality - Access to Success, 20*, 78–83.

Rostain, M. (2021). The impact of organizational culture on entrepreneurial orientation: A meta-analysis. *Journal of Business Venturing Insights, 15*, e00234.

Sadiku-Dushi, N., Dana, L.-P., & Ramadani, V. (2019). Entrepreneurial marketing dimensions and SMEs performance. *Journal of Business Research, 100*, 86–99.

Sahaym, A., Datta, A., & Brooks, S. (2021). Crowdfunding success through social media: Going beyond entrepreneurial orientation in the context of small and medium-sized enterprises. *Journal of Business Research, 125*, 483–494.

Scuotto, V., Caputo, F., Villasalero, M., & Del Giudice, M. (2017). A multiple buyer–supplier relationship in the context of SMEs' digital supply chain management. *Production Planning & Control, 28*(16), 1378–1388.

Seifzadeh, M., Salehi, M., Abedini, B., & Ranjbar, M. H. (2021). The relationship between management characteristics and financial statement readability. *EuroMed Journal of Business, 16*, 108–126.

Semrau, T., Ambos, T., & Kraus, S. (2019). Entrepreneurial orientation and SME performance across societal cultures: An international study. *Journal of Business Research, 69*(5), 1928–1932

Sharabati, A. A. A., Ali, A. A. A., Allahham, M. I., Hussein, A. A., Alheet, A. F., & Mohammad, A. S. (2024). The impact of digital marketing on the performance of SMEs: An analytical study in light of modern digital transformations. *Sustainability, 16*(19), 8667.

Somohano-Rodríguez, F. M., Madrid-Guijarro, A., & López-Fernández, J. M. (2022). Does Industry 4.0 really matter for SME innovation? *Journal of Small Business Management, 60*(4), 1001–1028.

Sundararaj, V., & Rejeesh, M. R. (2021). A detailed behavioural analysis on consumer and customer changing behaviour with respect to social networking sites. *Journal of Retailing and Consumer Services, 58*, 102190.

Tafesse, W., & Wood, B. P. (2021). Followers' engagement with Instagram influencers: The role of influencers' content and engagement strategy. *Journal of Retailing and Consumer Services, 58*, 102303.

Taipale-Erävala, K., Henttonen, K., & Lampela, H. (2019). Entrepreneurial competencies in successfully innovative SMEs. *International Journal of Entrepreneurship and Small Business, 38*(3), 251–276.

Tajudeen, F. P., Jaafar, N. I., & Ainin, S. (2018). Understanding the impact of social media usage among organizations. *Information & Management, 55*(*3*), 308–321.

Teng, X., Wu, Z., & Yang, F. (2022). Research on the Relationship between Digital Transformation and Performance of SMEs. *Sustainability, 14*, 6012.

Trainor, K. J., Andzulis, J. M., Rapp, A., & Agnihotri, R. (2014). Social media technology usage and customer relationship performance: A capabilities-based examination of social CRM. *Journal of Business Research, 67*, 1201–1208.

Udeh, E. O., Amajuoyi, P., Adeusi, K. B., & Scott, A. O. (2024). The integration of artificial Intelligence in cybersecurity measures for sustainable finance platforms: An analysis. *Computer Science & IT Research Journal, 5*(6), 1221–1246.

Veldeman, C., Van Praet, E., & Mechant, P. (2017). Social media adoption in business-to-business: IT and industrial companies compared. *International Journal of Business Communication, 54*(3), 283–305. https://doi.org/10.1177/2329488415572785

Vrontis, D., Siachou, E., Sakka, G., Chatterjee, S., Chaudhuri, R., & Ghosh, A. (2022). Societal effects of social media in organizations: Reflective points deriving from a systematic literature review and a bibliometric meta-analysis. *European Management Journal, 40*, 151–162.

Yadav, U. S., Vyas, S., Kanchan, G. I., & yadav, A. K. (2024). Impact of entrepreneurial leadership, social media, digital technology, Entrepreneurial orientation and innovation on business performance in the handicraft sector: Talent management as mediating construct. *Journal of Innovation and Entrepreneurship, 13*(1), 72.

13

Building a Strong Online Presence for Small and Medium Enterprises: An Emerging Market Perspective

Felicia de Heer

13.1 Introduction

Small and medium-scale enterprises (SMEs) are found all over the world (Disse & Sommer, 2020). In Africa, entrepreneurial activity by SMEs is an important driver of economic growth (Amoah et al., 2022; Agyapong et al., 2018; Abbasi et al., 2017) and has significantly impacted employment and poverty levels (ADA, 2016). According to the International Trade Centre (2018), SME activities in Africa help in generating domestic and foreign revenue.

In general, about 50% of the labour force worldwide is employed by SMEs (Ayyagari et al., 2007). In Ghana, it is reported that SMEs form 70% of the informal sector (Rural Enterprise program, 2017), and owners of these SMEs depend on the proceeds from their businesses to support their household expenditures (Frimpong et al., 2022). The

F. de Heer (✉)
Department of Marketing, Central Business School, Central University, Accra, Ghana
e-mail: fdeheer@central.edu.gh

E. Amoako Asiedu et al. (eds.), *Entrepreneurship and Small and Medium-Sized Enterprises (SMEs) in Africa*, https://doi.org/10.1007/978-3-032-14174-3_13

International Trade Center (2018) indicated that ensuring SME growth could lead to the achievement of Sustainable Development Goals (SDGs). Subsequently, Eniola and Entebang (2015) posited that attention should be given to SMEs to realize their full economic impact. Unfortunately, SMEs in Ghana are faced with a number of challenges, including poor funding, technology, high transactions, high default risk, high interest rate, lack of collateral and poor management (International Trade Centre, 2019). Several studies have been undertaken to assist SMEs overcome these challenges and propel growth. These studies include Agyapong and Attram (2019); Gathungu and Sabana (2018); Hussain et al. (2018); Frimpong et al. (2022). For example, Frimpong et al. (2022) examined financial literacy, access to digital finance and SME performance. Agyapong and Attram (2019) examined the financial literacy of owner–managers of SMEs and its impact on performance. Also, in a related study, Hussain et al. (2018) explored the variables that determined SMEs' performance and utilized access to financial products and financial risk attitude as the mediating variables. Amoah et al. (2021) examined the use of social media by SMEs as an advertising tool. Using an intercept and online survey, the study revealed that social media significantly impacted SME financial performance, increased market share and boosted business motivation. All these studies, however, paid less attention to establishing a strong online brand presence for SMEs.

With the advancement in technology and the spread of the Internet, consumers live at two levels, physical and virtual. Marketing online, also sometimes referred to as digital marketing, makes use of websites, online adverts, emails, interactive kiosks and TV (Chaffey & Smith, 2008), enabling customers to engage with diverse brands at competitive prices (Vineran et al., 2013; Wang et al., 2015). It is estimated that by 2026, 40% of all products will be purchased via the Internet (Febrian et al., 2020). SMEs can leverage online brand presence to help identify market needs and offer appropriate market solutions (Tolstoy et al., 2020; Weber, 1999). However, studies in this area are scant.

In addition, the increased use of smartphones in recent times offers consumers the ability to find, locate and purchase goods from any part of the world (Dzisi & Ofosu, 2014). The Internet World Stats (2019) indicates that the five top African countries with high Internet usage are:

Nigeria (119.5m), Egypt (49.2m), Tanzania (43.6m), Kenya (43.3m) and South Africa (32.6m). Ghana is currently ranked 97th in the e-commerce market globally (Go–Globe, 2023) and, as of November 2022, had 8.8 million social media users (Statista, 2022). It must be emphasized that SMEs' competitiveness and survival depend upon their capability to employ robust marketing strategies, including innovation and technology (Fan et al., 2021; European Commission, 2018).

Despite this current technological landscape and subsequent usage by many, SMEs, particularly in emerging markets, do not have a strong online presence (Costa & Castro, 2021). Subsequently, the SME failure rate is very high in Africa (Jamil, 2023), with about 70% being extinguished in the first year of market entry (Chinje, 2015). In the last two decades, despite the clarion call for a paradigm shift, SMEs' response to online activities is still not noticeable (Lin et al., 2019). Efforts in building a strong online presence can be described as abysmal, as researchers anticipate successful pathways to assist policy decisions. From the competitive point of view, SMEs currently face a challenge in the market, as more and more brick-and-mortar sales points for large manufacturers are replaced with an online ecosystem leveraging digital tools and social media platforms such as Twitter, Facebook, LinkedIn, YouTube and Instagram to improve their brand engagement and competitiveness on the market (Amoa-Gyarteng et al., 2024). Building an online presence is therefore critical for SMEs in Sub-Saharan Africa as the competition from businesses in the formal sector is becoming more and more intense (Avenyo et al., 2021; Attrams & Tshehla, 2022). To further strengthen the need for this current research, Damoah and Peprah (2021) reported that although there are some SME research studies in Ghana, the pace of scholarly investigation is slow, and the current study fills that gap in the literature.

Important dimensions for effective SME online marketing indicated in the literature until now include profitability, market value, social and environmental performance and satisfaction (Tarute & Gatautis, 2014; Bouwman et al., 2019; Shettima & Sharma, 2020). Despite the proliferation of research, there is a limited understanding of how dimensions such as: interactiveness of the brand website, brand reputation, past performance of the brand, customer experience, e-WOM and user-friendliness of the website can assist SMEs in building a strong brand presence. This study, therefore, sets out to investigate whether these variables can ignite online SME brand presence.

This paper aims to identify the major factors for building a strong SME online presence in Africa, particularly Ghana. Current trends show that customers of SMEs are turning to online shopping as a result of the spread of the Internet. Also, the legislative solutions proffered in Ghana for retailers have improved the use of online marketing activities. Exploring this topic as a result of these happenings makes it even more justified to boost the earnings of SMEs.

This study contributes to the literature by exploring the factors that build a strong SME online brand presence and contextualizes the investigation to SMEs in Africa, a clear departure from earlier studies which focused on advanced countries (Agyapong et al., 2018). In Africa, there is a gradual shift from an agrarian economy to an industrial and technologically based economy (Dana et al., 2018). Identifying the factors for SMEs to build a strong online brand presence will bolster businesses.

Also, understanding the factors that influence SME online brand presence by academics will set the agenda for future research. The current study will elucidate the variables to be used for research in SME online marketing activities and serve as a guideline for selecting constructs in future studies. Similarly, practitioners will receive practical guidance based on the study to incorporate the factors identified in their online marketing strategies. The author will make available research conclusions, recommendations and limitations which will assist policymakers in this direction.

The structure of this conceptual paper is organized as follows: the literature review, which presents the theoretical background. This is followed by the methodology, the study's findings, discussion of results, implications for theory and practice, limitations of the study and recommendations for further research work.

13.2 Theoretical Framework

Many studies have explained how online businesses become successful using the Technology and Acceptance Model (TAM) (Davis, 1989). Most of these studies used the theory to explain the intention to use and accept information systems (Foshay & Kuziemsky, 2014; Popovic et al., 2009). However, according to Venkatesh et al. (2003), acceptance of an information system may not lead to the usage of technology and may only provide support for the behavioural intent to use. As a result, the current study utilized the model by DeLone and McLean (2003) as a theoretical lens to approach the underlying mechanisms of the study objective. The original (DeLone & McLean, 1992) model, which was used to measure the success of information systems, was based on theoretical and empirical studies in the information technology space by researchers in the 1970s and 1980s. The model was later revised in 2003, and it captured critical areas of quality in the information environment (Al- Kofahi et al., 2020), which, to a large extent, are relevant to the current study: information, system, service quality and user satisfaction. Information quality in online technology refers to the website application content in terms of relevance, accuracy, completeness and reliability. This means the content at the SMEs organization website must be personalized, complete, relevant, easy to understand and secure. This quality dimension ensures customers keep returning to the website of the SME constantly. System quality refers to the characteristics desired by website users: usability, reliability, availability, adaptability and response time. Service quality encompasses trust, empathy, response time and support delivered by the SME. Finally, user satisfaction denotes the level of satisfaction users derive, including interface satisfaction.

The model evidently provides a useful framework for firms in the SME sector in emerging markets to be able to understand, explain and assess information system success, such as user satisfaction, service quality, system quality and use. It has been widely applied in related sectors in online business, and many studies have confirmed different relationships in the model (Ghani et al., 2019; Machani et al., 2021; Akrong et al., 2022). Ghani et al. (2019) applied the (DeLone & McLean, 2003) model to examine the effect of Enterprise Resource Planning (ERP) post-implementation on employee performance in a Malaysian SME. Three quality dimensions of the model were explored: system quality, information quality and service quality. Findings revealed that system quality and service quality had a significant positive effect on SME employees' performance, whilst information quality did not have any significant effect in Malaysia.

Similarly, Machani et al. (2021) employed the DeLeone and McLean model for SMEs in Nairobi and extended the factors. The results showed that all the independent variables were positively related to the independent variable. Finally, Akrong et al. (2022) adopted the model to investigate the factors that influence the ERP system usage, employee satisfaction, information quality, service quality and system quality. The findings revealed that the model significantly measures the ERP system successfully and is a predictor of user satisfaction.

It can be concluded from the above discussion that the (DeLone & McLean, 2003) model is a useful theory that can be used in investigating building online brand presence for SMEs in emerging markets by examining its user friendliness, interactiveness of the brand, past performance of the brand, e-WOM, ease of use, customer experience of website and brand reputation.

13.3 User Friendliness of a Website

Just as a friendly atmosphere is an important attribute for human beings to thrive, it is also beneficial to incorporate friendliness in service delivery, particularly in online service delivery. A strong online presence is important to keep and attract new customers to ensure business sustainability in the current SME competitive environment (Tardan et al., 2017; Dinesh & Sushil, 2019), and this is determined to a large extent by the user-friendliness of the website. User-friendliness refers to the total customer impressions of the website with regard to the ease of use (Saura et al., 2017; Zheng et al., 2015). The user-friendliness of a website is made up of two critical factors: it must be simple and also personalized to suit the interests and preferences of potential customers so as to generate a positive customer experience (Sakas et al., 2022; Butkiewicz et al., 2015). Extant literature posits that physically challenged individuals are able to use Amazon because of its user-friendly plug-ins with e-book assistance (Raza et al., 2020). As part of ensuring a friendly online environment, SMEs must offer a wide range of products and develop strategies that assist customers who visit their websites and choose products that will satisfy their needs. Previous studies have revealed that websites that load very quickly enhance user experience (Sakas et al., 2022; Sikder, 2023; Bansal, 2024). Websites that are not user-friendly may suffer from poor brand image, low sales and profitability (Hokkanen et al., 2016; Jayaram et al., 2015).

Prior studies by Amin (2016) showed a positive relationship between user-friendliness and electronic customer satisfaction. Similarly, Tabash et al. (2019) studies in the banking sector revealed that user-friendliness was a major quality dimension of electronic customer satisfaction.

13.4 Interactiveness of the Brand Website

Interactiveness of a website has been defined from two major perspectives in the literature. First, Kelleher (2009) and Lowry et al. (2015) discussed interactiveness from a communication process perspective. A second perspective of interactiveness focused on communicating using technological devices such as personal computers, laptops and smartphones (Oh & Sundar, 2015; Sicilia et al., 2005). Interactivity ensures that the firm and customers interact, and this is seen as an important feature in online business (Kankam-Kwarteng et al., 2021; Shilbury et al., 2014; Alalwan, 2018).

Akincilar and Dagdeviren (2014) reported that a brand website is an important promotional tool for increased sales and customer retention. Its influence on brand identification or differentiation is unparalleled. A brand's website provides interaction with existing and potential customers to influence purchase decisions (Quan et al., 2020) and obtain value in the market (Smith, 2019). Abdullah et al. (2016) also posited that a brand website ensures proper information flow to customers, which helps build relationships. Innovations such as social media, search engines, voice-over-IP technologies among others are used to enhance interactivity and to personalize customer experiences (Gao & Liu, 2023). SMEs are increasingly using websites to improve their business performance (Suryani et al., 2020). In West Africa, there has been a significant surge in online purchases in recent times. Survey results in 2020 and 2021 indicated an 81% increase in online shopping in Nigeria and a 79%

increase in Ghana (Agyapong, 2022). This shows that the number of online users is growing rapidly, and therefore, the interactiveness of SME websites is critical.

Barreda et al. (2015) studies revealed that customers are attracted to use websites that provide interactivity to potential customers. UI Islam and Rahman (2017) studies also indicate that website interactivity draws customers to the focal company, increases the rate of return and builds brand visibility. Furthermore, website interactiveness facilitates two-way communication, thereby improving customer satisfaction (Ho & Lee, 2015) and customer engagement with the focal brand (UI Islam & Rahman, 2017).

13.5 Past Performance of the Brand

The past performance of an online SME is becoming important. More importantly, customers evaluate online firms with regard to their competences in handling customer complaints, the efficiency of their channels and sales policies (Alzola & Robaina, 2010). Online customers prefer buying from firms that offer a wide array of channels, making the purchase process more flexible and convenient, which will lead to customer satisfaction and retention (Choudhary et al., 2011). The past sales performance reduces uncertainty and, in a study, was found to have a strong relationship with the attitude and behaviour of Chinese online consumers (Javed et al., 2020).

13.6 e -WOM

e-WOM, like the offline WOM, is an interactive communicative process that enables potential, current and previous customers to meet online and share opinions about products and services that they are likely to purchase (Ismagilova et al., 2017; King et al., 2014). Currently e-WOM is seen as an important information communication tool for firms online (Filieri et al., 2018; Floyd et al., 2014; Nam et al., 2018) and invariably affects purchase decisions (Lin et al., 2018). The search for information from customers who have used the product before reduces the search cost and fear of product failure by current customers (Awad & Ragowsky, 2008; Wang et al., 2009). In addition, information obtained from other product users on the Internet is seen as unexaggerated and helps consumers to shape their attitudes towards the focal brand. Several studies have confirmed that 93% of consumers reported that e-WOM communication influenced their purchase intention (Fullerton, 2017; Ruiz-Mafe et al., 2018; Tata et al., 2019). Empirical studies in different industries have indicated that e-WOM influenced consumers' intention to purchase. They include Erkan and Evans (2016) and Plotkina and Munzel (2016) for products and services; Aerts et al. (2017) for laptops; Uribe et al. (2016) for cars; and Chen et al. (2016) for smartphones.

13.7 Ease of Use

Elling et al. (2007) indicated that usability or ease of use is a website quality dimension. According to Davis (1989), ease of use refers to perceptions by a buyer that online purchases will be effortless. Baker-Eveleth and Stone (2015) defined ease of use as "the relative ease with which a novice manoeuvres around an actual website and does something" (p. 82). It refers to the fact that the use of a website is not burdensome. Ease of use encompasses aspects of the website such as user interface, design and functionality that ensures a seamless and user-friendly experience. This means that potential customers are able to navigate, interact and complete transactions on a website (Davis, 1989).

Ease of use is a necessary quality dimension to encourage consumers to use a website efficiently and effectively. The importance of this website feature was reinforced by van Iwaarden et al. (2004), who stated that easy navigation on a website is a critical ingredient for a strong online activity. Thus, intended users of a technology are encouraged to use the innovation if they believe it will be easy to use (Kikawa et al., 2022). Ease of use of a system, therefore, positively influences customer perception and overall satisfaction (Alyabes & Alsalloum, 2018; Pratiwi & Dewi, 2018; Syahdan, 2021). In addition, ease of use leads to customer loyalty (Andre et al., 2021; Suleman et al., 2019).

This is reinforced by the empirical study of Kikawa et al. (2022), which investigated the factors that assist Ugandan SMEs in implementing social media marketing strategies. This study used TAM and Innovation Diffusion Theory (IDT). The findings indicated that perceived ease of use has a significant relationship with SMEs' adoption of social media marketing. Ease of use as a construct has been investigated in other domains, including electronic mail (Szajna, 1996), e-commerce (Bruner & Kumar, 2005) and intention to employ Internet applications (King & He, 2006). Studies by Moridis et al. (2018) and Aremu and Shahzad (2023) indicated a positive relationship between the adoption of e-commerce by SMEs and perceived ease of use. All these studies have shown that ease of use is important for owners of SMEs to build online brand presence.

13.8 Customer Experience on the Website

Customers go through several experiences as they search for information about a product or service online. There is a burgeoning literature on online transactions but limited information on online customer experience (Schmitt, 1999; Edvardsson et al., 2005). Customer experience is explained as the "internal and subjective response that customers have to any direct or indirect contact with a company". Pine and Gilmore (1999, p.2) also defined the term customer experience as "events that engage individuals in a personal way". This means that customers' emotional, physical, intellectual and spiritual attachment to a brand or product emanates from their own experiences. Other researchers have indicated that customer experiences result from feelings or knowledge that occur throughout their interactions with the organization (Mascarenhas et al., 2006).

If a customer is successful in purchasing at an online shop, it will lead to a positive customer experience and vice versa (Barari et al., 2020). To ensure an effective customer experience, firms must understand the importance of the influence of cultural values and perceptions of website design. Cultural artefacts used, like language, symbols, colours and navigation styles of a website, are influenced by cultural beliefs and norms of target consumers. Hagag et al. (2015), therefore, posited that firms must conduct research using cultural models such as Hofstede's cultural dimensions and Hall (1960) in order to positively influence purchase behaviour. Hall (1960) posits that consumers prefer verbal communication in low-context cultures and non-verbal communication in high-context cultures. The studies in the literature proffer several variables that influence customer experience. They include website aesthetics, ease of use, customization, interactivity, engagement, enjoyment and flow (Martin et al., 2015; Trevinal & Stenger, 2014; Rose et al., 2012).

However, there are very few studies on how customer experience influences building online brands in the SME sector. Several studies have reported that customer experience leads to the creation of impressions, which are later stored in the memory of the individual. These studies revealed that positive experiences can lead to satisfaction, trust, revisit and intention and/or repurchase intention (Schmitt, 1999; Edvardsson et al., 2005). These authors also reported that good customer experience is a critical ingredient for gaining a competitive advantage. Subsequently, Lemon and Verhoef (2016) outlined that good customer experience is important for expanding a firm's market share. Based on these findings, the current study proposes that the customer experience of a website has a relationship with building online brand presence for SMEs.

13.9 Brand Reputation

Brand reputation refers to the sum of all stakeholders (including consumers') perceptions with regard to product attributes, which form a personal association with the brand (Nareswari et al., 2021). A brand is a name, term, design, symbol or a combination of them that is used to differentiate a product or service from another (Jain, 2017). A product from a particular SME can be considered a brand because it is distinct from other brands on the market. An individual's brand perceptions are self-expressive and entail how well a brand matches with his/her self-concept and eventually affects their image (Bai et al., 2021). Brand reputation shows the attractiveness of the brand elements that a consumer wants to associate with. Subsequently, Moliner et al. (2018) argued that brands are used to develop individual and public self-concept. Highly reputable brands can be used to enhance one's self-concept and image in society (Le, 2021). A brand with a high reputation indicates higher prestige (Choi & Burnham, 2021) and vice versa. Customers, therefore, seek brands with a high reputation to enhance their self-esteem.

According to Choi and Burham (2021) and Veloutsou and Moutinho (2009), it must be understood that "the development of brand reputation means more than keeping customers satisfied, it is something a company earns over time and refers to how various audiences evaluate the brand" (p. 315). Studies have revealed that firms with a high reputation can earn positive word of mouth, which leads to increased customer acquisition and lower defections (Rogerson, 1983; Su et al., 2016; Walsh et al., 2009). The role of brand reputation in building online brand presence has received very little attention.

Earlier research of significance investigated how brand reputation can influence customer behaviour. Most of these studies reported that a positive reputation boosts customers' associations with brands and ensures positive customer behaviours. For example, Su et al. (2016) investigated how customer commitment, identification and satisfaction mediate the relationship between brand reputation and word of mouth. Findings showed that in the service sector, satisfaction plays an important role in translating reputation into word of mouth. In addition, studies by Bartikowski and Walsh (2011) established that customer commitment and loyalty play an intervening role between reputation and company—helping customer behaviour. To extend these findings, this study proposes that brand reputation has a positive impact on building SME online brand presence.

13.10 Methodology

The research was based on a systematic literature review of studies that focused on building a resilient SME online brand presence from an emerging market perspective. Literature was obtained from ScienceDirect,

Scopus, JSTOR and Google Scholar databases. This ensured that the data and information collected were systematic and included studies relevant to the topic of investigation.

The researcher used keywords such as "online SMEs" and "SMEs in Africa" among others to obtain results from peer-reviewed articles. Fifty publications were obtained initially and screened for eligibility. The criteria for screening included:

- Relevance to SME activities in emerging markets
- Emphasis on online brand presence or marketing
- Peer-reviewed journals
- There was a second screening, which ensured that unrelated and duplicate articles were removed. Out of the 50 studies downloaded from the databases, only 32 were within the inclusion criteria and were finally reviewed. Thus, relevant and appropriate information from high-quality journals was used for the study.

13.11 Discussions

The study investigated the factors for building a strong SME online brand presence. To this end, the analysis focused on seven major variables: user-friendliness of the website, interactiveness of the brand website, past performance, e-WOM, ease of use, customer experience and brand reputation effect in building an online brand presence. It is reported in the literature that large marketing organizations with huge financial resources are more predisposed to incorporating online marketing activities in their businesses as compared to SMEs (Wang & Ahmed, 2009). However, the literature indicates that SMEs will enjoy a competitive advantage by building an online presence (Farida & Setiawan, 2022).

The conceptual findings underscored positive relationships between the variables under investigation and building a strong online brand presence. This means that SMEs effectively leveraging these variables can build a strong online brand presence. For example, in terms of the user-friendliness of websites, previous studies opined that user-friendliness attracted customers, ensured customer retention and boosted operational efficiency of SMEs (Nwachukwu & Okoye, 2019; Yang & Jun, 2019; Edokobi et al., 2024). According to the research, user-friendliness of a website will have a positive relationship in building a strong online SME brand presence. This finding concurs with studies by Raza et al. (2020).

The past performance of a brand has a significant effect on building a strong SME brand website. This study concurs with findings by Javed et al. (2020). Similarly, e-WOM in the current study has positive relations with building an online SME brand presence. In online purchases, previous users of a product share their experiences to boost the confidence of potential users. This result is confirmed by previous studies such as eMarketer (2014) and Eneizan et al. (2020). The studies also revealed a positive relationship between ease of use and building SME online brand presence. Studies by Tang and Chi (2005), Alsaghier et al. (2011) and Eneizan et al. (2020) confirmed the relationship. Similarly, ease of use is a determinant for building an online presence. The findings of Bendary and Al-Sahouly (2018) indicated that SMEs' use of e-commerce is significantly influenced by perceived ease of use.

The research findings clearly show that the customer experience of a website has a strong impact on an SME brand website. This means that if a customer has a positive emotional and cognitive experience with the website, it will lead to increased customer visits. This finding is supported by online customer satisfaction studies (Jaiswal & Singh, 2020; Quach et al., 2020).

Brand reputation can be leveraged by SMEs to build an online presence. In the studies of Anagnostopoulou et al. (2020), it was revealed that positive online reviews resulted in high overall financial performance. This finding concurs with Choi and Burnham (2021), whose studies show that brands with higher reputations are perceived by customers as prestigious.

The implementation of online marketing activities by SMEs in emerging markets using the constructs identified in this study will ensure efficient use of the website, influence customer perception and improve overall customer satisfaction.

13.12 Theoretical Implications

Theory development about the factors that assist in building a strong SME online brand presence is relevant. Building on the model by DeLone and McLean (1992, 2003), the factors identified can ensure a strong online environment. The study therefore contributes to research by using a conceptual validation of the independent variables in the context of online SMEs in emerging markets. These factors are even more important for resource-constrained SMEs that have to compete in both domestic and international markets by adapting to consumer needs, entering into new market segments and offering unique customer experiences on their websites.

13.13 Managerial Implications

Online marketing has become the new normal as customers seek for more flexibility and convenience in the purchase process. They are also bombarded with a wide range of product offerings from different companies at brick-and-mortar sales points, and e-WOM can assist potential customers in making the right choices. SMEs can therefore accelerate their business growth by leveraging a strong online brand presence and selling their wares. Customers will then have access to quality attributes such as user-friendliness, ease of use and brand reputation, among others, which are necessary for purchasing online.

Many SMEs in Africa face critical challenges to be innovative because of a lack of finance (Disse & Sommer, 2020). Availability of finance is an enabler for building an SME online brand presence. Unfortunately, accessing capital by SMEs in Africa through traditional banks is difficult because of their inability to provide collateral security (Hendratmi et al., 2019). Thus, ensuring SMEs have enough funding for their operations is crucial for policymakers. Crowdfunding is seen as an alternative source of funding in the literature for African SMEs, where formal financial intermediaries are bypassed and a pool of funds raised by individuals and investors is used to assist SMEs in generating capital for expansion (Courtney et al.,

2017). Through crowdfunding, SMEs in Africa can manage their demand and supply adequately, ensure cutting innovation such as building an online presence, improve efficiency and broaden their markets

It is also necessary for policymakers to improve and expand the Internet connectivity in Africa for building SME online brand presence. Reliable Internet access is a prerequisite for building an online brand presence, but in Africa, many areas are underserved and struggle with poor Internet connectivity and coverage. Rapid infrastructural development by governments is necessary for building a successful online brand presence.

13.14 Recommendations

Building an online presence by SMEs offers immense growth opportunities. However, to fully exploit these benefits, coordinated efforts from various stakeholders are essential. Policymakers must ensure an enabling environment for a transformation to online business by SMEs. Governments in emerging markets must provide a reliable and affordable infrastructure so that SMEs have continuous access to electricity and Internet connectivity for online activities. Similarly, the cost involved in using Internet services must be reduced considerably to encourage SMEs to provide services online.

Collaboration with industry associations and other stakeholders can strengthen these efforts to rope in several SMEs. Policymakers should work together with all stakeholders to address all possible challenges SMEs may face, such as digital literacy and accounting skills.

13.15 Conclusion

This study provides a synthesis of the literature on building an online brand presence by SMEs. The main objective of the study was to identify the factors that can assist in building a strong online brand presence. The main contribution is therefore the identification of the constructs for building an online brand presence for SMEs. The findings of the study revealed a strong relationship between user-friendliness of the website, interactiveness of the brand website, past performance of the brand, e-WOM, ease of use, customer experience on the website and brand reputation and building SME online brand presence. The study is of utmost importance to SME expansion and growth, given the current trend in the market. The researcher, therefore, hopes that the study will offer the basis for further research and provide a guide to both SME owners and policymakers. The study also noted a few limitations: it was conceptual, and not all related literature was reviewed.

13.16 Limitations and Further Research

The study has a few limitations. First, the current study is conceptual and only reviewed related literature. Other researchers must undertake empirical studies to confirm or refute the findings. It may also be necessary to add other independent variables during further research to have a better understanding of the phenomenon. Finally, although the study reviewed many related articles, the author may not have included all the studies on SME online brand presence.

References

Abbasi, W. A., Wang, Z., & Abbasi, D. A. (2017). Potential sources of financing for small and medium enterprises (SMEs) and role of government in supporting SMEs. *Journal of Small Business and Entrepreneurship Development, 6*(1), 39–47.

Abdullah, D., Jayaraman, K., & Kamal, S. B. (2016). A conceptual model of interactive hotel website: The role of perceived website interactivity and customer perceived value toward website revisit intention. *Procedia Economics and Finance, 37*, 170–175.

ADA. (2016). Small and growing businesses in Africa: Profiles, successes and challenges. https://www.ada-microfinance.org/sites/default/files/2020-12/study-sgbs-en-.pdf

Aerts, G., Smits, T., & Verlegh, P. (2017). How online consumer reviews are influenced by the language and valence of prior reviews: A construal level perspective. *Computers in Human Behavior, 75*, 855–864.

Agyapong, D., & Attram, A. B. (2019). Effect of owner–manager's financial literacy on the performance of SMEs in the Cape Coast Metropolis in Ghana. *Journal of Global Entrepreneurship Research, 9*, 67. https://doi.org/10.1186/s40497-019-0191-1

Agyapong, G. T., Mmieh, F., & Mordi, C. (2018). Factors influencing the growth of SMEs: The case of Ghana. *Thunderbird International Business Review, 60*(4), 549–563. https://doi.org/10.1002/tie.21945

Agyapong, G. K. (2022). *Marketing communications during a pandemic: Perspective from a developing Country. In marketing communications and brand development in emerging markets volume II: Insights for a changing World* (pp. 109–129). Springer International Publishing.

Akincilar, A., & Dagdeviren, M. (2014). A hybrid multi-criteria decision making model to evaluate hotel websites. *International Journal of Hospitality Management, 36*, 263–271.

Akrong, G. B., Yunfei, E., & Owusu, E. (2022). Development and validation of an improved DeLone–McLean IS success model: Application to the evaluation of a tax administration ERP. *International Journal of Accounting Information Systems, 47*, 100579.

Alalwan, A. A. (2018). Investigating the impact of social media advertising features on customer purchase intention. *International Journal of Information Management, 42*, 65–77.

Al-Kofahi, M. K., Hassan, H., & Mohamad, R. (2020). Information systems success model: A review of literature. *International Journal of Innovation, Creativity and Change, 12*(8), 397–417.

Alsaghier, H. M., Ford, M., Nguyen, A., & Hexel, R. (2011). Conceptualising citizen's trust in e-Government: Application of Q Methodology. *Electronic Journal of e-Government, 7*(4), 295–310.

Alyabes, A. F., & Alsalloum, O. (2018). Factors affecting consumers' perception of electronic payment in Saudi Arabia. *European Journal of Business and Management, 10*(27), 36–45.

Alzola, L. M., & Robaina, V. P. (2010). The impact of pre-sale and post-sale factors on online purchasing satisfaction: A survey. *International Journal of Quality & Reliability Management, 27*(2), 121–137. https://doi.org/10.1108/02656711011014267

Amin, M. (2016). Internet banking service quality and its implication on E-customer satisfaction and E-customers loyalty. *International Journal of Bank Marketing, 34*(3), 280–306.

Amoa-Gyarteng, K., Dhliwayo, S., & Adekomaya, V. (2024). Innovative marketing and sales promotion: Catalysts or inhibitors of SME performance in

Ghana. *Cogent Business & Management, 11*(1). https://doi.org/10.1080/23311975.2024.2353851

Amoah, J., Jibril, A. B., & Akram, U. (2021). Social media as a promotional tool towards SME's development: Evidence from the financial industry in a developing economy. *Cogent Business & Management, 8*(1), 1923357.

Amoah, J., Belas, J., Dziwornu, R., & Khan, K. A. (2022). Enhancing SME contribution to economic development: A perspective from an emerging economy. *Journal of International Studies, 15*(2), 63–76.

Anagnostopoulou, S. C., Buhalis, D., Kountouri, I. L., Manousakis, E. G., & Tsekrekos, A. E. (2020). The impact of online reputation on hotel profitability. *International Journal of Contemporary Hospitality Management, 32*(1), 20–39.

Andre, Pebriyanti, H. L., Kartono, R., & Sundjaja, A. M. (2021). The effect of perceived usefulness, perceived ease of use, perceived risk and technology readiness on intention to use e-banking in Jakarta. *Turkish Journal of Computer and Mathematics Education (TURCOMAT), 12*(10), 6829–6836.

Aremu, A. Y., & Shahzad, A. (2023). Factors influencing the usage of e-business to improve SME performance. *International Journal of E-Business Research, 19*(1), 1–16. https://doi.org/10.4018/IJEBR.324065

Attrams, A. S., & Tshehla, M. (2022). Challenges of services sector SMEs in a developing country: A case of Ghana. *Journal of the International Council for Small Business, 3*(3), 228–236.

Avenyo, E. K., Konte, M., & Mohnen, P. (2021). Product innovation and informal market competition in sub-Saharan Africa. *Journal of Evolutionary Economics, 31*(2), 605–637.

Awad, N. F., & Ragowsky, A. (2008). Establishing trust in electronic commerce through online word of mouth: An examination across genders. *Journal of Management Information Systems, 24*(4), 101–121.

Ayyagari, M., Beck, T., & Demirgüç-Kunt, A. (2007). Small and medium enterprises across the globe. *Small Business Economics, 29*, 415–434.

Baker-Eveleth, L., & Stone, R. W. (2015). Usability, expectation, confirmation, and continuance intentions to use electronic textbooks. *Behaviour & Information Technology, 34*(10), 992–1004.

Bansal, G. (2024). Wisdom of the experts, not the wisdom of the crowds: The power of case-based research in the age of AI. *Journal of Information Technology Case and Application Research, 26*(1), 90–90.

Barari, M., Ross, M., & Surachartkumtonkun, J. (2020). Negative and positive customer shopping experience in an online context. *Journal of Retailing and Consumer Services, 53*, 101985.

Barreda, A. A., Bilgihan, A., Nusair, K., & Okumus, F. (2015). Generating brand awareness in online social networks. *Computers in Human Behavior, 50*, 600–609.

Bartikowski, B., & Walsh, G. (2011). Investigating mediators between corporate reputation and customer citizenship behaviors. *Journal of Business Research, 64*(1), 39–44.

Bendary, N., & Al-Sahouly, I. (2018). Exploring the extension of unified theory of acceptance and use of technology, UTAUT2, factors effect on perceived usefulness and ease of use on mobile commerce in Egypt. *Journal of Business & Retail Management Research, 12*(02), 60–71.

Bouwman, H., Nikou, S., & De Reuver, M. (2019). Digitalization, business models, and SMEs: How do business model innovation practices improve performance of digitalizing SMEs? *Telecommunications Policy, 43*(9), 101828.

Bruner, G. C., & Kumar, A. (2005). Explaining consumer acceptance of handheld internet devices. *Journal of Business Research, 58*(5), 553–558.

Butkiewicz, M., Wang, D., Wu, Z., & Madhyastha, H. V. (2015). Klotski: Reprioritising web content to improve user experience on mobile devices. In *Proceedings of the 21st USENIX Symposium on Networked Systems Design and Implementation (NSDI).*

Chaffey, D., & Smith, P. (2008). *E-marketing excellence: Planning and optimising your digital marketing*. Routledge.

Chen, J., Teng, L., Yu, Y., & Yu, X. (2016). The effect of online information sources on purchase intentions between consumers with high and low susceptibility to informational influence. *Journal of Business Research, 69*(2), 467–475.

Chinje, N. (2015). Harnessing digital marketing to access markets: Opportunities for Africa's SMEs. *Africa Growth Agenda, 12*, 14–18.

Choi, L., & Burnham, T. (2021). Brand reputation and customer voluntary sharing behavior: The intervening roles of self-expressive brand perceptions and status seeking. *Journal of Product & Brand Management, 30*(4), 565–578.

Choudhary, A. I., Asif, M., Choudhry, R. M., Siddique, Z., & Mughal, A. M. (2011). Impact of after sale service characteristics on customer satisfaction. *Information Management and Business Review, 3*(6), 360–365.

Costa, J., & Castro, R. (2021). SMEs must go online—e-Commerce as an escape hatch for resilience and survivability. *Journal of Theoretical and Applied Electronic Commerce Research, 16*(7), 3043–3062.

Courtney, C., Dutta, S., & Li, Y. (2017). Resolving information asymmetry: Signaling, endorsement, and crowdfunding success. *Entrepreneurship Theory and Practice, 41*(2), 265–290.

Damoah, O. B., & Peprah, A. A. (2021). Synthesis of small and medium enterprise research in Ghana. *Journal of Global Entrepreneurship Research, 11*(1), 451–468.

Dana, L., Ratten, V., & Honyenuga, B. Q. (2018). Introduction to African entrepreneurship. In *African Entrepreneurship: Challenges and opportunities for doing business* (pp. 1–8). https://doi.org/10.1007/978-3-319-73700

Davis, F. D. (1989). Perceived usefulness, perceived ease of use, and user acceptance of information technology. *MIS Quarterly, 13*(3), 319.

DeLone, W. H., & McLean, E. R. (1992). Information systems success: The quest for the dependent variable. *Information Systems Research, 3*(1), 60–95.

DeLone, W. H., & McLean, E. R. (2003). The DeLone and McLean model of information systems success: A ten-year update. *Journal of Management Information Systems, 19*(4), 9–30.

Dinesh, K. K., & Sushil, N. (2019). Strategic innovation factors in startups: Results of a cross-case analysis of Indian startups. *Journal for Global Business Advancement, 12*(3), 449.

Disse, S., & Sommer, C. (2020). *Digitalisation and its impact on SME finance in Sub-Saharan Africa* (Discussion Paper 4/2020). German Development Institute.

Dzisi, S., & Ofosu, D. (2014). Marketing strategies and the performance of SMEs in Ghana. *European Journal of Business and Management, 6*(5), 102–111.

Edokobi, O., Okoli, C. M., & Ugochukwu, I. (2024). Evaluating the operational impact of e-commerce tools in Nigerian SMEs: A VAR model approach. *African Journal of Business and Economic Research, 19*(2), 101.

Edvardsson, B., Gustafsson, A., & Roos, I. (2005). Service portraits in service research: A critical review. *International Journal of Service Industry Management, 16*(1), 107–121.

Elling, S., Lentz, L., & De Jong, M. (2007). Website evaluation questionnaire: Development of a research-based tool for evaluating informational websites. *Lecture Notes in Computer Science, 4656*, 293–304.

EMarketer. (2014). "Digital Ad spending benchmarks by industry: The Complete eMarketer Series for 2014". www.emarketer.com

Eneizan, B., Alsaad, A., Abdelbaset Alkhawaldeh, H. N., & Rawash, O. E. (2020). E-WOM, trust, usefulness, ease of use, and online shopping via websites: The moderating role of online shopping experience. *Journal of Theoretical and Applied Information Technology, 98*(13), 2554–2565.

Eniola, A. A., & Entebang, H. (2015). SME firm performance—Financial innovation and challenges. *Procedia – Social and Behavioural Sciences, 195*, 334–342.

Erkan, I., & Evans, C. (2016). The influence of eWOM in social media on consumers' purchase intentions: An extended approach to information adoption. *Computers in Human Behavior, 61*, 47–55.

European Commission. (2018). *Erasmus+ annual report 2017: Annexe*. Publications Office of the European Union.

Fan, M., Qalati, S. A., Khan, M. A. S., Shah, S. M. M., Ramzan, M., & Khan, R. S. (2021). Effects of entrepreneurial orientation on social media adoption and SME performance: The moderating role of innovation capabilities. *PLOS ONE, 16*(4), e0247320.

Farida, I., & Setiawan, D. (2022). Business strategies and competitive advantage: The role of performance and innovation. *Journal of Open Innovation: Technology, Market, and Complexity, 8*(3), 163.

Febrian, F., Adnan, A. Z., Wibawa, L. S., Ahmadi, R. S., & Agustina, G. (2020). Diversity of innovation to enhance customer loyalty in Batik Slamethadipriyanto Banyumas. *Dinasti International Journal of Digital Business Management, 1*(6). https://doi.org/10.31933/dijdbm.v1i6.574

Filieri, R., Raguseo, E., & Vitari, C. (2018). When are extreme ratings more helpful? Empirical evidence on the moderating effects of review characteristics and product type. *Computers in Human Behavior, 88*, 134–142.

Floyd, K., Freling, R., Alhoqail, S., Cho, H. Y., & Freling, T. (2014). How online product reviews affect retail sales: A meta-analysis. *Journal of Retailing, 90*(2), 217–232.

Foshay, N., & Kuziemsky, C. (2014). Towards an implementation framework for business intelligence in healthcare. *International Journal of Information Management, 34*(1), 20–27.

Frimpong, S. E., Agyapong, G., & Agyapong, D. (2022). Financial literacy, access to digital finance and performance of SMEs: Evidence from central region of Ghana. *Cogent Economics & Finance, 10*(1), 2121356.

Fullerton, L. (2017). Online reviews impact purchasing decisions for over 93% of consumers, report suggests. http://www.thedrum.com/news/2017/03/27/onlinereviews-impact-purchasing-decisions-over-93–consumers-report suggests

Gao, Y., & Liu, H. (2023). Artificial intelligence-enabled personalisation in interactive marketing: A customer journey perspective. *Journal of Research in Interactive Marketing, 17*(5), 663–680. https://doi.org/10.1108/JRIM-01-2022-0023

Gathungu, J. M., & Sabana, B. M. (2018). Entrepreneur financial literacy, financial access, transaction costs and performance of microenterprises in

Nairobi city County in Kenya. *Global Journal of Management and Business Research, 18*(6), 41–51.

Ghani, E. K., Yasin, S. A., & Ali, M. M. (2019). Examining Enterprise resource planning post implementation and employees' performance in small and medium enterprises using DeLone and McLean's information system success model. *International Journal of Financial Research, 10*(3), 153.

GO-Globe. (2023). Ghana's SME trailblazers: Accelerating ecommerce innovation. https://www.go-globe.com/ghanas-sme-trailblazers-accelerating-ecommerce-innovation

Hagag, W., Clark, L., & Wheeler, C. (2015). A framework for understanding the website preferences of Egyptian online travel consumers. *International Journal of Culture, Tourism and Hospitality Research, 9*(1), 68–82.

Hall, E. T. (1960). The silent language in overseas business. *Harvard Business Review, 38*(3), 87–96.

Hendratmi, A., Sukmaningrum, P. S., Ryandono, M. N., & Ratnasari, T. (2019). The role of Islamic crowdfunding mechanisms in business and business development. *GATR Journal of Business and Economics Review, 4*(1), 10–23.

Ho, C., & Lee, P. (2015). Are blogs still effective to maintain customer relationships? *Journal of Hospitality and Tourism Technology, 6*(1), 5–25.

Hokkanen, L., Xu, Y., & Väänänen, K. (2016). Focusing on user experience and business models in startups: Investigation of two-dimensional value creation. In *Proceedings of the 20th International Academic Mindtrek Conference* (pp. 59–67).

Hussain, N., Rigoni, U., & Orij, R. P. (2018). Corporate governance and sustainability performance: Analysis of triple bottom line performance. *Journal of Business Ethics, 149*(2), 411–432.

International Trade Centre. (2018). Promoting SME competitiveness in Africa: Data for de-risking investment.

International Trade Centre. (2019). *SME Competitiveness Outlook 2019: Big money for small businesses*. ITC.

Internet World Stats. (2019). World Internet Users Statistics and 2019 World Population Stats, Internet World Stats. Available at: https://www.internetworldstats.com/stats.htm, accessed on November 15, 2019.

Ismagilova, E., Dwivedi, Y. K., Slade, E., & Williams, M. D. (2017). *Electronic word of mouth (eWOM) in the marketing context: A state of the art analysis and future directions* (SpringerBriefs in Business). Springer.

Jain, R. (2017). Basic branding concepts: Brand identity, brand image and brand equity. *International Journal of Research in Business and Social Sciences, 6*(3), 1–10.

Jaiswal, S., & Singh, A. (2020). Influence of the determinants of online customer experience on online customer satisfaction. *Paradigm: A Management Research Journal, 24*(1), 41–55.

Jamil, M. I. (2023). A discourse on entrepreneurial discontinuance, failure rates, and failed business models. In *Advances in business strategy and competitive advantage* (pp. 115–135). Business Science Reference; IGI Global Scientific.

Javed, M. K., Wu, M., Qadeer, T., Manzoor, A., Nadeem, A. H., & Shouse, R. C. (2020). Role of online retailers' post-sale services in building relationships and developing repurchases: A comparison-based analysis among male and female customers. *Frontiers in Psychology, 11*, 1–14.

Jayaram, D., Manrai, A. K., & Manrai, L. A. (2015). Effective use of marketing technology in Eastern Europe: Web analytics, social media, customer analytics, digital campaigns and mobile applications. *Journal of Economics, Finance and Administrative Science, 20*(39), 118–132.

Kankam-Kwarteng, C., Amo, F., Osei, F., & Bediako, D. O. (2021). Service innovation and service quality effects on marketing performance of SMEs. *Innovation, 2*, 1–10.

Kelleher, T. (2009). Conversational voice, communicated commitment, and public relations outcomes in interactive online communication. *Journal of Communication, 59*(1), 172–188.

Kikawa, C. R., Kiconco, C., Agaba, M., Ntirampeba, D., Ssematimba, A., & Kalema, B. M. (2022). Social media marketing for small and medium enterprises' performance in Uganda: A structural equation model. *Sustainability, 14*(21), 14391.

King, R. A., Racherla, P., & Bush, V. D. (2014). What we know and don't know about online word-of-Mouth: A review and synthesis of the literature. *Journal of Interactive Marketing, 28*(3), 167–183.

King, W. R., & He, J. (2006). A meta-analysis of the technology acceptance model. *Information & Management, 43*(6), 740–755.

Lemon, K. N., & Verhoef, P. C. (2016). Understanding customer experience throughout the customer journey. *Journal of Marketing, 80*(6), 69–96.

Lin, X., Featherman, M., Brooks, S. L., & Hajli, N. (2018). Exploring gender differences in online consumer purchase decision making: An online product presentation perspective. *Information Systems Frontiers, 21*(5), 1187–1201.

Lin, X., Wang, X., & Hajli, N. (2019). Building e-Commerce satisfaction and boosting sales: The role of social commerce trust and its antecedents. *International Journal of Electronic Commerce, 23*(3), 328–363.

Lowry, P., Gaskin, J., & Moody, G. (2015). Proposing the Multimotive information systems continuance model (MISC) to better explain end-user system evaluations and continuance intentions. *Journal of the Association for Information Systems, 16*(7), 515–579.

Machani, M. Z., Kinoti, P., & Obare, I. (2021). A model focusing on success factors of health information systems in small and medium enterprises: Case study of Nairobi County. *Academic Journal of Social Sciences and Education, 9*(3), 28–35.

Martin, J., Mortimer, G., & Andrews, L. (2015). Re-examining online customer experience to include purchase frequency and perceived risk. *Journal of Retailing and Consumer Services, 25*, 81–95.

Mascarenhas, O. A., Kesavan, R., & Bernacchi, M. (2006). Lasting customer loyalty: A total customer experience approach. *Journal of Consumer Marketing, 23*(7), 397–405.

Melián Alzola, L., & Padrón Robaina, V. (2010). The impact of pre-sale and post-sale factors on online purchasing satisfaction: A survey. *International Journal of Quality & Reliability Management, 27*(2), 121–137.

Moliner, M. A., Monferrer, D., & Estrada, M. (2018). Consequences of customer engagement and customer self-brand connection. *Journal of Services Marketing, 32*(4), 387–399.

Moridis, C. N., Terzis, V., Economides, A. A., Karlovasitou, A., & Karabatakis, V. E. (2018). Using EEG frontal asymmetry to predict IT user's perceptions regarding usefulness, ease of use and playfulness. *Applied Psychophysiology and Biofeedback, 43*(1), 1–11.

Nam, K., Baker, J., Ahmad, N., & Goo, J. (2018). Dissatisfaction, disconfirmation, and distrust: An empirical examination of value Co-destruction through negative electronic word-of-Mouth (eWOM). *Information Systems Frontiers, 22*(1), 113–130.

Nareswari, N., Balqista, A. S., & Negoro, N. P. (2021). The impact of behavioural aspects on investment decision-making. *Jurnal Manajemen dan Keuangan, 10*(1), 15–27. https://doi.org/10.33059/jmk.v10i1.3125

Nwachukwu, C., & Okoye, P. (2019). Website quality and performance of SMEs in Anambra State. *Journal of Business and Management, 21*(7), 45–54.

Oh, J., & Sundar, S. S. (2015). How does interactivity persuade? An experimental test of interactivity on cognitive absorption, elaboration, and attitudes. *Journal of Communication, 65*(2), 213–236.

Pine, J., & Gilmore, J. H. (1999). *The experience economy: Work is theatre and every business a stage*. Harvard Business School Press.

Plotkina, D., & Munzel, A. (2016). Delight the experts, but never dissatisfy your customers! A multi-category study on the effects of online review source

on intention to buy a new product. *Journal of Retailing and Consumer Services, 29*, 1–11.
Popovič, A., Coelho, P. S., & Jaklič, J. (2009). The impact of business intelligence system maturity on information quality. *Information Research, 14*(4).
Pratiwi, D., & Dewi, C. (2018). Factors (benefits, trust, self-efficacy, ease of use, security) affecting consumers' perception of e-money in Indonesia. *Jurnal Sekretaris dan Administrasi Bisnis, 2*(2), 24–37. https://doi.org/10.31104/jsab.v2i2.60
Quach, S., Barari, M., Moudrý, D. V., & Quach, K. (2020). Service integration in omnichannel retailing and its impact on customer experience. *Journal of Retailing and Consumer Services, 65*, 102267.
Quan, N. H., Chi, N. T., Nhung, D. T., Ngan, N. T., & Phong, L. T. (2020). The influence of website brand equity, E-brand experience on E-loyalty: The mediating role of E-satisfaction. *Management Science Letters*, 63–76. https://doi.org/10.5267/j.msl.2019.8.015
Raza, S. A., Umer, A., Qureshi, M. A., & Dahri, A. S. (2020). Internet banking service quality, E-customer satisfaction and loyalty: The modified e-SERVQUAL model. *The TQM Journal, 32*(6), 1443–1466.
Rogerson, W. P. (1983). Reputation and product quality. *The Bell Journal of Economics, 14*(2), 508.
Rose, S., Clark, M., Samouel, P., & Hair, N. (2012). Online customer experience in E-retailing: An empirical model of antecedents and outcomes. *Journal of Retailing, 88*(2), 308–322.
Ruiz-Mafe, C., Chatzipanagiotou, K., & Curras-Perez, R. (2018). The role of emotions and conflicting online reviews on consumers' purchase intentions. *Journal of Business Research, 89*, 336–344.
Sakas, D. P., Reklitis, D. P., Trivellas, P., Vassilakis, C., & Terzi, M. C. (2022). The effects of logistics websites' technical factors on the optimization of digital marketing strategies and corporate brand name. *Processes, 10*(5), 892.
Saura, J. R., Palos-Sánchez, P., & Cerdá Suárez, L. M. (2017). Understanding the digital marketing environment with KPIs and web analytics. *Future Internet, 9*(4), 76.
Schmitt, B. H. (1999). *Experiential marketing*. Free Press.
Shettima, M., & Sharma, N. (2020). Impact of digitalisation on small and medium enterprises in Nigeria. *Adalya Journal, 4*(2), 635–644.
Shilbury, D., Quick, S., Funk, D., Westerbeek, H., & Karg, A. (2014). *Strategic sport marketing*. Routledge.

Sicilia, M., Ruiz, S., & Munuera, J. L. (2005). Effects of interactivity in a web site: The moderating effect of need for cognition. *Journal of Advertising, 34*(3), 31–44.

Sikder, A. S. (2023). Revolutionising web user experience: A pioneering investigation into web performance optimisation's impact on user experience and business success. *International Journal of Imminent Science & Technology, 1*(1), 186–198.

Smith, C. D. (2019). *Entrepreneurial marketing in online home-based businesses: Narratives from immigrant entrepreneurs* (Doctoral dissertation, Walden University). Walden Dissertations and Doctoral Studies, 7428.

Smith, A. D., Shock, J. R., & Beaves, R. G. (2019). Customer relationship management and the impact of E-coupons on B2C retail markets. *International Journal of Business Information Systems, 30*(2), 203.

Statista. (2022). Available online: https://www.statista.com/statistics/1171416/number-of-internet-users-ghana/ (accessed on 30 November 2022)

Steiner, R. L., Bai, X., Bejleri, I., Han, M., & Yan, X. J. (2021). Partnerships between agencies and transportation network companies for transportation-disadvantaged populations: Benefits, problems, and challenges. *Transportation Research Record, 2675*, 1260–1271. https://doi.org/10.1177/03611981211032629

Su, L., Swanson, S. R., Chinchanachokchai, S., Hsu, M. K., & Chen, X. (2016). Reputation and intentions: The role of satisfaction, identification, and commitment. *Journal of Business Research, 69*(9), 3261–3269.

Suleman, D., Ali, H., Nusraningrum, D., & Ali, M. M. (2019). Perceived ease of use, trust and risk toward attitude and intention in shopping for online fashion products in Indonesia. *Business Research, 7*(4), 240–253.

Suryani, T., Fauzi, A. A., & Nurhadi, M. (2020). SOME-Q: A model development and testing for assessing the consumers' perception of social media quality of small medium-sized enterprises (SMEs). *Journal of Relationship Marketing, 20*(1), 62–90.

Syahdan, R. (2021). Factors influencing Gen-Z customer perception online shopping in Indonesia. *International Journal of Communication and Society, 3*(2), 99–111.

Szajna, B. (1996). Empirical evaluation of the revised technology acceptance model. *Management Science, 42*(1), 85–92.

Tabash, M. I., Albugami, M. A., Salim, M., & Akhtar, A. (2019). Service quality dimensions of E-retailing of Islamic banks and its impact on customer satisfaction: An empirical investigation of Kingdom of Saudi Arabia. *The Journal of Asian Finance, Economics and Business, 6*(3), 225–234.

Tang, T. W., & Chi, W. H. (2005). *The role of trust in customer online shopping behaviour: Perspective of technology acceptance model.* Paper presented at the Procedings of NAACSOS Conference 2005 Indiana, USA.

Tardan, P. P., Shihab, M. R., & Yudhoatmojo, S. B. (2017). Digital marketing strategy for mobile commerce collaborative consumption startups. *2017 International Conference on Information Technology Systems and Innovation (ICITSI)*, 309–314.

Tarutė, A., & Gatautis, R. (2014). ICT impact on SMEs' performance. *Procedia – Social and Behavioural Sciences, 110*, 1218–1225. https://doi.org/10.1016/j.sbspro.2013.12.968

Tata, S. V., Prashar, S., & Gupta, S. (2019). An examination of the role of review valence and review source in varying consumption contexts on purchase decision. *Journal of Retailing and Consumer Services, 52*, 101734.

Tolstoy, D., Nordman, E. R., Hånell, S. M., & Özbek, N. (2020). The development of international e-commerce in retail SMEs: An effectuation perspective. *Journal of World Business, 56*(3), 101165.

Trevinal, A. M., & Stenger, T. (2014). Toward a conceptualisation of the online shopping experience. *Journal of Retailing and Consumer Services, 21*(3), 314–326.

Ul Islam, J., & Rahman, Z. (2017). The impact of online brand community characteristics on customer engagement: An application of the Stimulus–Organism–Response paradigm. *Telematics and Informatics, 34*, 96–109.

Uribe, R., Buzeta, C., & Velásquez, M. (2016). Sidedness, commercial intent and expertise in blog advertising. *Journal of Business Research, 69*(10), 4403–4410.

van Iwaarden, J., van der Wiele, T., Ball, L., & Millen, R. (2004). Perceptions about the quality of websites: A survey amongst students at Northeastern University and Erasmus University. *Information & Management, 41*, 947–959.

Veloutsou, C., & Moutinho, L. (2009). Brand relationships through brand reputation and brand tribalism. *Journal of Business Research, 62*(3), 314–322.

Venkatesh, Morris, Davis, & Davis. (2003). User acceptance of information technology: Toward a unified view. *MIS Quarterly, 27*(3), 425.

Vineran, S., Iuliana, C., Luigi, D., & Mihai, T. (2013). The effects of social media marketing on online consumer behaviour. *International Journal of Business and Management, 8*(14), 66–79.

Walsh, G., Mitchell, V., Jackson, P. R., & Beatty, S. E. (2009). Examining the antecedents and consequences of corporate reputation: A customer perspective. *British Journal of Management, 20*(2), 187–203.

Wang, M. C., Wang, E. S., Cheng, J. M., & Chen, A. F. (2009). Information quality, online community and trust: A study of antecedents to shoppers' website loyalty. *International Journal of Electronic Marketing and Retailing, 2*(3), 203.

Wang, Y., & Ahmed, P. K. (2009). The moderating effect of the business strategic orientation on ecommerce adoption: Evidence from UK family run SMEs. *The Journal of Strategic Information Systems, 18*(1), 16–30.

Weber, T. E. (1999). How a purple box helps one company entice its customers Online. *Wall Street Journal, 81.*

Yang, S., & Jun, M. (2019). Website quality and SME performance: A user experience perspective. *Information & Management, 56*(6), 103198.

Zheng, X., Cheung, C. M., Lee, M. K., & Liang, L. (2015). Building brand loyalty through user engagement in online brand communities in social networking sites. *Information Technology & People, 28*(1), 90–106.

14

Chatbots and AI-Based Marketing as a Digital Marketing Communication Strategy for SMEs in Africa: Conceptual Framework

Antoinette Yaa Benewaa Gabrah, George Oppong Ampong, and Emelia Amoako Asiedu

14.1 Introduction

Africa's business environment presents significant hurdles for small and medium enterprises (SMEs), including limited financial and technological resources, underdeveloped infrastructure, and intense competition from both local and global players (Naradda Gamage et al., 2020; Khan,

A. Y. B. Gabrah (✉)
Academic City University College, Accra, Ghana

Ghana Communication Technology University, Accra, Ghana

Durban University of Technology, Durban, South Africa
e-mail: antoinette.gabrah@acity.edu.gh

G. Oppong Ampong
Ghana Communication Technology University, Accra, Ghana
e-mail: gampong@gctu.edu.gh

E. Amoako Asiedu et al. (eds.), *Entrepreneurship and Small and Medium-Sized Enterprises (SMEs) in Africa*, https://doi.org/10.1007/978-3-032-14174-3_14

2023). These challenges often hinder the ability of SMEs to scale operations, retain customers, and achieve long-term sustainability (Shahadat et al., 2023; Carrasco-Carvajal et al., 2023; Hernita et al., 2021). To address these issues, the adoption of innovative solutions like chatbots and AI-based marketing is increasingly seen as a necessity rather than a luxury. These technologies enable SMEs to streamline operations, connect more effectively with their customers, and deliver highly personalised services in cost-effective ways (Chaffey & Ellis-Chadwick, 2019; Zuhroh & Rini, 2024).

Chatbots, powered by artificial intelligence, have become vital tools for enhancing customer interaction (Krishnan et al., 2022; Cheng & Jiang, 2022). Unlike traditional customer service approaches that require substantial human resources, chatbots offer 24/7 support, ensuring customers receive immediate responses to their inquiries (Wang et al., 2022; Vashishth et al., 2024). This capability not only improves service efficiency but also builds trust and strengthens customer relationships (Majumder & Mondal, 2021). According to Chaffey and Ellis-Chadwick (2019) and Behera et al. (2024), chatbots go beyond basic communication by personalising the customer experience. For example, they can recommend products based on past purchases or guide customers through their buying journey (Shumanov & Johnson, 2021; Gabrah, 2024). This makes chatbots indispensable for SMEs aiming to build brand loyalty in competitive markets (Behera et al., 2024). Furthermore, by automating repetitive tasks, chatbots free up valuable human resources, allowing businesses to focus on innovation and strategic planning (Haugeland et al., 2022).

AI-based marketing takes customer engagement to a new level by leveraging data-driven insights (Magableh et al., 2024). Tools like predictive analytics and recommendation engines allow businesses to understand their customers deeply, forecast market trends, and deliver highly targeted marketing campaigns (Haleem et al., 2022). These tools are

E. Amoako Asiedu
Department of Marketing, Ghana Communication Technology University, Accra, Ghana
e-mail: easiedu@gctu.edu.gh

particularly valuable for SMEs with limited marketing budgets, as they ensure that every dollar spent achieves maximum impact (Magableh et al., 2024). Saura and Palos-Sanchez (2020) highlight how AI minimises operational inefficiencies, enabling resource-constrained businesses to compete with larger, more established players. For instance, an SME can use AI algorithms to determine the best time to run ads on social media or tailor its messaging for different customer segments, ensuring relevance and engagement.

In Africa, the widespread use of social media platforms such as WhatsApp, Facebook, and Instagram provides SMEs with unprecedented opportunities to connect with a vast audience (Amoako et al., 2023). These platforms serve as effective channels for deploying chatbots and executing AI-driven marketing campaigns. However, the full potential of these technologies remains untapped due to significant challenges. Many SMEs struggle with inadequate Internet infrastructure, high data costs, and a lack of technical expertise to deploy and manage AI tools effectively (Schwaeke et al., 2025; Kumar et al., 2024). Kaur and Kumar (2020) argue that bridging these gaps requires concerted efforts from both the government and the private sector. Governments can improve digital infrastructure and lower data costs, while private-sector initiatives can focus on upskilling SME owners and employees in technology adoption (Rawindaran et al., 2023). The integration of chatbots and AI-based marketing into SMEs' operations has transformative potential. These technologies enable businesses to overcome operational bottlenecks, enhance customer engagement, and scale their reach efficiently (Gabrah, 2024; Liu et al., 2022). However, their successful implementation depends on addressing existing barriers. Collaboration between policymakers, industry stakeholders, and SMEs is essential to foster an enabling environment that supports digital innovation and drives economic growth across the continent (Gabrah et al., 2023, 2024).

This study, therefore, helps marketers to utilise chatbot and AI-based marketing as key digital marketing tactics among SMEs, particularly in emerging markets such as Ghana. This study highlights the dynamic relationships that exist between chatbot and AI-based marketing and digital marketing communication as a strategy. This objective is achieved by a review of the literature from 2015 to 2025. This paper is a non-empirical review of the literature. This study concentrates on the market outcome of chatbot and AI-based marketing as well as the challenges faced in implementing chatbot and AI-based marketing as a digital marketing communication strategy. The following sections focus on the literature review, discussion of the conceptual framework, the implications: managerial and societal implications, the conclusions, limitations, and suggestions for further research.

14.2 Literature Review and Theoretical Framework

14.2.1 Chatbots in Digital Marketing

In an increasingly digital world, customer engagement has shifted to online platforms, where businesses must respond promptly to consumer needs (Rasool et al., 2020; Perez-Vega et al., 2021). Chatbots, artificial intelligence-powered tools, have emerged as a game-changer in digital marketing (Kshetri et al., 2024; Sun et al., 2024). These automated systems simulate human conversations through text or voice, enabling businesses to provide instant, round-the-clock responses (Gołąb-Andrzejak, 2023). Unlike traditional methods, chatbots handle multiple customer inquiries simultaneously, significantly reducing wait times and ensuring consistent communication (Adam et al., 2021). According to Chaffey and Ellis-Chadwick (2019), chatbots are particularly effective in personalising customer interactions, which is essential for building trust and fostering loyalty. For instance, a chatbot integrated into an e-commerce platform can guide customers by offering personalised product recommendations based on browsing history or past purchases (Shafi et al., 2020). In competitive markets where customer retention is critical, such features enhance the overall experience, encouraging repeat business (Bilgihan, 2016). For African SMEs, where resources are often limited, chatbots provide a scalable and cost-effective solution to customer service challenges. Businesses can deploy chatbots on widely used platforms like WhatsApp or Facebook Messenger to maintain engagement without hiring large customer support teams. This not only saves costs but also allows SMEs to operate more efficiently, particularly in high-demand periods (Chaffey & Smith, 2022).

14.2.2 AI-Based Marketing

Artificial intelligence is revolutionising marketing by enabling businesses to harness data for strategic decision-making (Stone et al., 2020). AI-based marketing employs algorithms to analyse large volumes of customer data, uncovering patterns and insights that would be impossible to identify manually (Bag et al., 2021; Hossain et al., 2022). By leveraging tools like predictive analytics, businesses can anticipate consumer behaviour, optimise marketing campaigns, and target their audiences more precisely (Perifanis & Kitsios, 2023; Mikalef et al., 2023). Kim (2020) and Abrokwah-Larbi and Awuku-Larbi (2024) note that AI-driven marketing is instrumental in reducing inefficiencies and ensuring maximum return on investment. For example, AI tools can analyse engagement metrics from social media campaigns to determine what content resonates most with different demographics. This allows businesses to refine their strategies continuously, ensuring relevance and effectiveness (Islam et al., 2024; Bag et al., 2022). In the context of African SMEs, AI, among other emerging technologies, offers a competitive edge by enabling small businesses to act on data-driven insights typically reserved for larger corporations (Rahman et al., 2023; Amoako et al., 2023). By adopting recommendation engines, for instance, SMEs can provide tailored product suggestions, mirroring the personalised experiences offered by global giants like Amazon (Silvester & Kurian, 2023). This not only enhances customer satisfaction but also drives sales, enabling SMEs to expand their reach and scale operations (Abrokwah-Larbi & Awuku-Larbi, 2024).

14.3 Chatbots and AI-Based Marketing and Customer Engagement

Customer engagement is at the heart of business success, and in Africa, platforms like WhatsApp and Facebook Messenger dominate as primary communication channels (Badran, 2021; Messner, 2022). By integrating chatbots into these platforms, SMEs can engage with their customers seamlessly (Panigrahi et al., 2023). Chatbots are particularly effective in providing instant responses to inquiries, such as product availability or delivery timelines (Selamat & Windasari, 2021). This immediacy enhances customer trust and fosters stronger relationships. Chaffey and Ellis-Chadwick (2019) and Haugeland et al. (2022) emphasise that chatbots are not merely tools for answering questions—they can also engage customers on a deeper level. For example, a clothing retailer might use a chatbot to recommend outfits based on the customer's preferences or previous purchases. These personalised interactions make customers feel valued, increasing their likelihood of returning. Moreover, AI-driven chatbots enable businesses to handle high volumes of inquiries without compromising service quality (Kgakatsi et al., 2024; Omrani et al., 2022; Rawindaran et al., 2021; Chatzoglou & Chatzoudes, 2016). For African SMEs, this is crucial, especially during peak seasons or promotional periods when customer demand spikes. By automating repetitive tasks, businesses can allocate their human resources to more complex customer needs, ensuring a balance between efficiency and personal touch (Rana et al., 2025). For instance, AI-driven marketing tools such as chatbots are increasingly being adopted by small and medium-sized enterprises (SMEs) in Africa, particularly in Ghana and Nigeria (Thottoli et al., 2024), such that in Ghana, a study by Owusu-Afriyie and Salia (2023) on Jumia Online Ghana established that artificial intelligence (AI) improves integrated marketing communication. This is achieved by generating leads, supporting content creation, and improving customer engagement via automation of processes involved in the service delivery (Hinson et al., 2019). This paper therefore proposes that:

P1: The implementation of chatbots and AI-based marketing as a digital marketing communication strategy by SMEs positively and significantly affects customer engagement.

14.3.1 Chatbots and AI-Based Marketing and Cost Efficiency

Running a business, particularly in resource-constrained environments, often involves finding ways to do more with less (Korsgaard et al., 2021). AI-based tools are invaluable in this regard, helping SMEs reduce operational costs while maintaining high levels of service (von Garrel & Jahn, 2023). Chatbots, for instance, can replace human customer service agents for routine tasks like responding to FAQs or confirming orders (Adam et al., 2021). This automation allows SMEs to minimise staffing costs without sacrificing customer satisfaction (Adam et al., 2021; Chong et al., 2021). Saura and Palos-Sanchez (2020) highlight that AI tools go beyond customer service by optimising marketing processes. For example, businesses can use AI to manage ad placements across platforms like Google or Facebook. These tools analyse campaign performance in real time, identifying which ads perform best and reallocating budgets accordingly (Campbell et al., 2020). This ensures that marketing spend is focused on high-impact areas, maximising return on investment. Additionally, AI-driven systems can streamline inventory management by predicting demand trends (Huh et al., 2023). For example, an SME in the retail sector might use AI to forecast which products will be in high demand during a particular season. This reduces the risk of overstocking or understocking, saving costs and improving operational efficiency (Herman et al., 2025). This leads to the proposition that:

P2: The implementation of chatbots and AI-based marketing as a digital marketing communication strategy by SMEs positively and significantly affects cost efficiency.

14.3.2 Chatbots and AI-Based Marketing and Market Reach Expansion

Expanding into new markets has traditionally been a resource-intensive endeavour, often requiring extensive research and significant financial investment (Carneiro et al., 2018; Fleury et al., 2024; Adomako, 2024). However, AI-powered tools have made this process more accessible for SMEs (Kanellopoulou et al., 2025). By analysing customer data and market trends, AI can identify emerging opportunities and guide businesses in tailoring their offerings to meet diverse consumer needs (Adomako et al., 2024; Amoako et al., 2023). In Africa, where cultural and demographic diversity is vast, such insights are invaluable (Kastner et al., 2019;

Gabrah et al., 2024). Tools like Google Analytics and Facebook Ads Manager provide SMEs with detailed reports on consumer behaviour, including preferences, purchasing habits, and geographical trends (Theodorakopoulos et al., 2024). This information enables businesses to customise their marketing strategies, ensuring they resonate with target audiences. Kaur and Kumar (2020) note that AI-driven marketing also facilitates regional and international expansion. For example, an SME selling handmade crafts might use AI to identify markets in Europe or North America where demand for ethically sourced products is growing. By targeting these markets with customised campaigns, the business can extend its reach beyond local customers, tapping into lucrative global opportunities. Furthermore, chatbots play a pivotal role in supporting market expansion (Wang et al., 2022). Multilingual chatbots, for instance, can engage customers in their preferred language, breaking down communication barriers. This feature is particularly beneficial for African SMEs looking to enter neighbouring countries with different languages (Zindi et al., 2024). For instance, Owusu-Afriyie and Salia (2023) observed the essence of optimising AI-generated content for mobile usage to reach wider audiences in developing contexts. Chatbot Africa, a Ghana-based startup, is further assisting small businesses in automating customer interactions and sales channels. This startup uses AI-enabled conversational bots on platforms like WhatsApp. This initiative enables clients to hold real-time conversations with customers. This helps to propose that:

P3: The implementation of chatbots and AI-based marketing as a digital marketing communication strategy by SMEs positively and significantly affects market reach expansion.

14.4 Challenges Faced in Implementing Chatbots and AI-Based Marketing

The adoption of chatbots and AI-based marketing by small and medium enterprises (SMEs) in Africa has the potential to transform their operations. These technologies can improve efficiency, customer engagement, and market competitiveness. However, the integration of these tools is not without its challenges. This section examines the key barriers SMEs face and offers practical recommendations to address them, enabling businesses to leverage these tools effectively.

14.4.1 Infrastructure Deficits

One of the primary obstacles to adopting AI and chatbot technologies in Africa is the lack of reliable digital infrastructure (Peretz-Andersson et al., 2024; Dey et al., 2024). Stable Internet connectivity, which is a prerequisite for implementing these tools, remains a challenge in many regions (Kastner et al., 2019; Gabrah, 2015). High data costs further exacerbate the issue, making it difficult for SMEs to access or sustain the use of these technologies (Chaffey & Ellis-Chadwick, 2019; Gabrah, 2015). Rural areas, in particular, suffer from limited Internet penetration, which restricts their ability to compete in the increasingly digital economy (Millard, 2022). For example, an SME in a rural area looking to deploy a chatbot may face frequent interruptions due to poor connectivity. This not only disrupts customer service but also diminishes the perceived reliability of the business (Liu et al., 2024). Without significant improvements in infrastructure, the digital divide will continue to hinder the potential of SMEs in these regions. Thus,

P4: Infrastructural deficits negatively and significantly affect the implementation of chatbots and AI-based marketing as a digital marketing communication strategy by SMEs.

14.4.2 Skill Gaps

Another major challenge is the lack of technical expertise among SME owners and their employees (Indrawati, 2020). Implementing AI tools requires a fundamental understanding of how these technologies work, from installation to ongoing management (Gill et al., 2022). However, many SMEs lack access to the necessary training and resources to build these skills (Kaur & Kumar, 2020). For instance, an SME owner might acquire an AI-powered marketing tool but struggle to use it effectively due to a lack of understanding of its analytics or campaign management features (Kumar et al., 2024). As a result, the tool fails to deliver the anticipated benefits, leading to wasted investment. The skill gap not only limits the effective use of these technologies but also discourages SMEs from adopting them in the first place (Indrawati, 2020). Therefore, this study proposes that:

P5: Skills gap negatively and significantly affects the implementation of chatbots and AI-based marketing as a digital marketing communication strategy by SMEs.

14.4.3 Data Privacy Concerns

The use of AI-driven tools often involves collecting, analysing, and storing customer data (Kumar et al., 2024). While this enables businesses to personalise their offerings and improve the customer experience, it also raises significant privacy concerns (Asif et al., 2025). SMEs may not have robust data protection measures in place, leaving them vulnerable to data breaches (Saura & Palos-Sanchez, 2020). Such incidents can erode customer trust and damage the reputation of the business. In addition, non-compliance with local and international data protection regulations can result in legal and financial repercussions (Chua et al., 2017). For example, an SME that fails to comply with General Data Protection Regulation (GDPR) requirements while serving European customers may face penalties (Fig. 14.1). Therefore, this study proposes that:

P4: Data privacy concerns negatively and significantly affect the implementation of chatbots and AI-based marketing as a digital marketing communication strategy by SMEs.

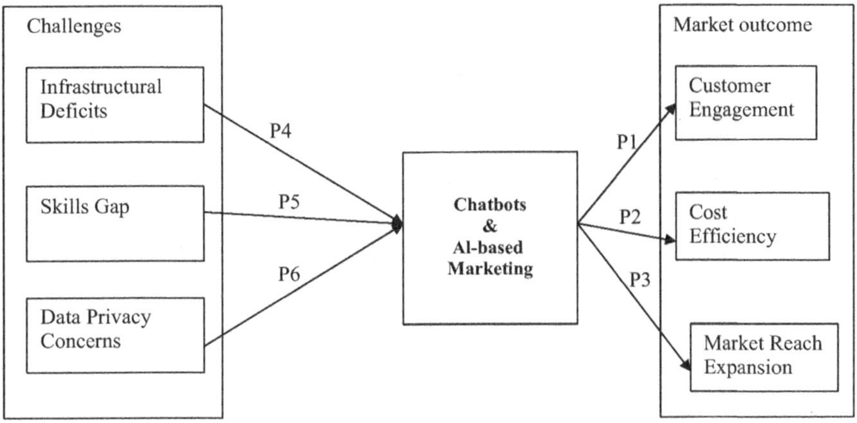

Fig. 14.1 Conceptual framework of the study. (Source: Author's Construct (2025))

14.5 Methodology

The study used a traditional review of literature using articles published in English from 2015 to 2025. In this study, a desk-based research style was used. Prior research is summarised, compiled, and synthesised as part of secondary research. We used a range of datasets to comprehend better how to make more informed business selections. In addition, we studied periodicals, new publications, books, and digital resources from various sectors. During our search, we eliminated any research that did not meet our expansive criteria. Using this method, we gathered the necessary data: First, we conducted an electronic search of relevant databases (Emerald Online Journals; JSTOR Online Journals; Elsevier Online Journals). Keywords used for searching literature include challenges in using chatbots and AI-based marketing such as infrastructural deficits, skills gap, and data privacy concerns and market outcome—customer engagement, cost efficiency, and market reach expansion. These keywords should be covered in the abstract as well as the main document. Articles as well as reports from other organisations were also reviewed. In all, 70 papers were sourced and after screening and scanning, 50 were valid for the review.

14.6 Discussion of the Proposed Conceptual Framework

The study observed that in the implementation of chatbots and AI-based marketing as a digital marketing communication strategy, infrastructural deficits, skills gap and data privacy concerns are the main challenges faced by SMEs. For example, Ghana's National Artificial Intelligence Strategy (2023–2033) outlines how digital infrastructure, education, and policy will enable sustainable AI integration. However, it also highlights persistent barriers such as low digital literacy and Internet access, which limit the scalability of AI for SMEs in rural and peri-urban areas (Ghana Ministry of Communications and Digitalisation, 2023). Similar studies in Nigeria show that SMEs are using AI in the e-commerce space to personalise customer experiences and optimise operations. According to Farmonaut (2024), businesses are employing AI for inventory management, chat-based customer service, and marketing automation. This has significantly improved sales performance and competitiveness. However, the country still faces a gap in AI talent and data infrastructure. A report by Ad-CNG (2023) emphasised the need for educational reform and training programs to build AI expertise among the youth to support the future of digital entrepreneurship. Finally, regional innovations such as the *Dukawalla* project, which is a voice-based AI assistant, have been deployed to support informal sector businesses by enabling verbal interaction with business data (Sankoh et al., 2024). This proves that non-literate users improve business decisions in local languages. Although, the implementation of chatbots and AI-based marketing as a digital marketing communication strategy could positively lead to increased customer engagement, cost efficiency, and help the firm to gain market reach expansion.

14.6.1 Managerial Implications

To address these challenges, a multifaceted approach involving government, private organisations, and SMEs themselves is essential. Governments and private organisations must prioritise investments in digital infrastructure to address connectivity issues (Kastner et al., 2019;

Gabrah, 2015). Expanding broadband networks to underserved regions and reducing data costs can significantly improve accessibility for SMEs (Sidek et al., 2020). Collaborations between public and private sectors can accelerate the deployment of affordable Internet solutions, particularly in rural areas. For example, public-private partnerships can establish community Internet hubs, enabling SMEs in remote areas to access high-speed connectivity. Such initiatives can bridge the digital divide and empower businesses to leverage AI and chatbot technologies effectively (Gabrah et al., 2024).

Training programs tailored to the needs of SMEs are critical to bridging the skill gap. These programs should focus on equipping business owners and employees with practical, hands-on knowledge about AI tools and their applications. Workshops, online courses, and mentorship opportunities can help SMEs gain the confidence to adopt and manage these technologies (Chaffey & Ellis-Chadwick, 2019). Additionally, partnerships with educational institutions and technology companies can provide SMEs with access to training resources and certifications. For instance, a digital marketing workshop hosted by a tech firm could guide SMEs on how to use AI for targeted advertising and customer analytics.

SMEs must adopt stringent data security protocols to safeguard customer information. This includes encrypting sensitive data, regularly updating software, and implementing multi-factor authentication systems. By ensuring compliance with data protection regulations, businesses can build customer trust and avoid legal complications (Saura & Palos-Sanchez, 2020). Furthermore, SMEs should be transparent about their data handling practices, informing customers about how their information is collected, stored, and used. Providing clear privacy policies and obtaining explicit consent for data collection can enhance customer confidence.

Industry associations and technology hubs can play a pivotal role in supporting SMEs. These organisations can facilitate knowledge sharing, provide access to funding opportunities, and advocate for policies that promote digital transformation. For example, a local SME association could host networking events where business owners exchange best practices for AI adoption. Collaboration between SMEs can also foster innovation. By pooling resources, smaller businesses can experiment with AI technologies in a cost-effective manner, sharing both risks and rewards.

14.6.2 Societal Implications

Chatbot and AI-based marketing in Africa present a paradox of high economic potential constrained by systemic challenges. While these technologies enhance customer engagement, operational efficiency, and business growth (The Ghana Report, 2023), their benefits remain unevenly distributed due to infrastructural deficits, limited digital literacy, and weak regulatory frameworks (Ghana Ministry of Communications and Digitalisation, 2023). These structural barriers risk deepening the divide between digitally connected and excluded populations. Addressing these disparities requires targeted policy measures that support infrastructure development, AI-focused education, and robust data governance. In emerging markets like Ghana, the transformative potential of AI for SMEs is clear. However, realising inclusive benefits depends on cross-sector collaboration to ensure that technological advancements contribute to equitable and ethical development rather than reinforce existing inequalities.

14.7 Conclusion, Limitations, and Suggestion for Further Studies

Chatbots and AI-based marketing represent a new frontier for African SMEs, offering transformative benefits that include automating routine tasks, improving customer engagement, and unlocking new market opportunities (Cheng & Jiang, 2022). These tools can significantly enhance the competitiveness of businesses operating in resource-constrained environments, enabling them to thrive in a digital economy (Khan, 2023). For instance, The Ghana Report (2023) reported that

Jumia Nigeria employed chatbots and this helped to track orders. In Ghana, Jumia Ghana deployed AI-based marketing and it promoted personalised marketing and cost efficiency. This led to 40% increase in sales between 2017 and 2021. In the same vein, ExpressPay also used AI-based marketing to ensure an increase in transaction volume by 50% from 2018 to 2022 (The Ghana Report, 2023). To add, restaurants such as Burger King and Relish in Accra, Ghana use WhatsApp as a chatbot interface to manage over 6000 customer interactions (Certaspace, 2024). MTN Ghana and Nigeria implemented Ayoba which supports 35 million users in 22 languages and partners with platforms such as Jumia to ensure market integration (MTN Group, 2023). Finally, MTN like other financial service providers has developed AI chatbot called Zigi which offers support to customers particularly on billing and data inquiries.

However, realising these benefits requires addressing key challenges such as inadequate infrastructure, skill gaps, and data privacy concerns. As Chaffey and Ellis-Chadwick (2019) point out, collaboration between stakeholders is essential to overcoming these barriers. Governments must invest in digital infrastructure, while private organisations should focus on upskilling SME owners and employees. At the same time, SMEs must prioritise robust data protection measures to ensure compliance and build customer trust. Saura and Palos-Sanchez (2020) emphasise that digital tools are not just a convenience but a necessity for sustainable business growth. By addressing these challenges holistically, stakeholders can create an environment where African SMEs are empowered to leverage chatbots and AI-based marketing to their full potential. This collective effort will not only transform individual businesses but also drive economic growth across the continent. The study is non-empirical; hence, the claims should be empirically tested. Thus, the propositions made could be tested in further studies using empirical data. The suggested conceptual framework is put to the test in both developed and developing nations through more research. Further propositions could be made based on a theory.

References

Abrokwah-Larbi, K., & Awuku-Larbi, Y. (2024). The impact of artificial intelligence in marketing on the performance of business organizations: Evidence from SMEs in an emerging economy. *Journal of Entrepreneurship in Emerging Economies, 16*(4), 1090–1117.

Adam, M., Wessel, M., & Benlian, A. (2021). AI-based chatbots in customer service and their effects on user compliance. *Electronic Markets, 31*(2), 427–445.

Adomako, S. (2024). The effect of foreign knowledge acquisition on international performance: The mediating roles of international orientation and business model innovation. *Thunderbird International Business Review, 66*(1), 19–31.

Adomako, S., Shenkar, O., Liu, X., Amankwah-Amoah, J., & Ahsan, M. (2024). Editorial on Doing business in Africa: Navigating opportunities and challenges in Africa's emerging markets. *Journal of International Management, 30*, 101189.

Amoako, G. K., Bonsu, G. A., Gabrah, A. Y. B., & Ampong, G. O. A. (2023). Digital marketing and sustainability competitive advantage: A conceptual framework. In *Handbook of research on achieving sustainable development goals with sustainable marketing* (pp. 170–188). IGI Global.

Asif, M., Fazel, H., & Alghamdi, F. S. (2025). The ethical landscape of immersive marketing: Virtual and augmented reality in advertising. *Marketing Intelligence & Planning*. https://doi.org/10.1108/MIP-07-2024-0519

Badran, M. F. (2021). Digital platforms in Africa: A case-study of Jumia Egypt's digital platform. *Telecommunications Policy, 45*(3), 102077.

Bag, S., Gupta, S., Kumar, A., & Sivarajah, U. (2021). An integrated artificial intelligence framework for knowledge creation and B2B marketing rational decision making for improving firm performance. *Industrial Marketing Management, 92*, 178–189.

Bag, S., Srivastava, G., Bashir, M. M. A., Kumari, S., Giannakis, M., & Chowdhury, A. H. (2022). Journey of customers in this digital era: Understanding the role of artificial intelligence technologies in user engagement and conversion. *Benchmarking: An International Journal, 29*(7), 2074–2098.

Behera, R. K., Bala, P. K., Rana, N. P., & Irani, Z. (2024). Empowering co-creation of services with artificial intelligence: an empirical analysis to examine adoption intention. *Marketing Intelligence & Planning, 42*(6), 941–975.

Bilgihan, A. (2016). Gen Y customer loyalty in online shopping: An integrated model of trust, user experience and branding. *Computers in Human Behavior, 61*, 103–113.

Campbell, C., Sands, S., Ferraro, C., Tsao, H. Y. J., & Mavrommatis, A. (2020). From data to action: How marketers can leverage AI. *Business horizons, 63*(2), 227–243.

Carneiro, J., Bamiatzi, V., & Cavusgil, S. T. (2018). Organizational slack as an enabler of internationalization: The case of large Brazilian firms. *International Business Review, 27*(5), 1057–1064.

Carrasco-Carvajal, O., García-Pérez-de-Lema, D., & Castillo-Vergara, M. (2023). Impact of innovation strategy, absorptive capacity, and open innovation on SME performance: A Chilean case study. *Journal of Open Innovation: Technology, Market, and Complexity, 9*(2), 100065.

Certaspace. (2024). *How WhatsApp is changing the game for small businesses in Africa*. Certaspace. https://certaspace.com/blog/blog_view/42/login

Chaffey, D., & Ellis-Chadwick, F. (2019). *Digital marketing* (7th ed.). Pearson.

Chaffey, D., & Smith, P. R. (2022). *Digital marketing excellence: Planning, optimizing and integrating online marketing*. Routledge.

Chatzoglou, P., & Chatzoudes, D. (2016). Factors affecting e-business adoption in SMEs: An empirical research. *Journal of Enterprise Information Management, 29*(3), 327–358.

Cheng, Y., & Jiang, H. (2022). Customer–brand relationship in the era of artificial intelligence: Understanding the role of chatbot marketing efforts. *Journal of Product & Brand Management, 31*(2), 252–264.

Chong, T., Yu, T., Keeling, D. I., & de Ruyter, K. (2021). AI-chatbots on the services frontline addressing the challenges and opportunities of agency. *Journal of Retailing and Consumer Services, 63*, 102735.

Chua, H. N., Herbland, A., Wong, S. F., & Chang, Y. (2017). Compliance to personal data protection principles: A study of how organizations frame privacy policy notices. *Telematics and Informatics, 34*(4), 157–170.

Dey, P. K., Chowdhury, S., Abadie, A., Vann Yaroson, E., & Sarkar, S. (2024). Artificial intelligence-driven supply chain resilience in Vietnamese manufacturing small-and medium-sized enterprises. *International Journal of Production Research, 62*(15), 5417–5456.

Farmonaut. (2024). *Unleash the AI revolution: How Nigerian small businesses are conquering e-commerce*. https://farmonaut.com/news/unleash-the-ai-revolution-how-nigerian-small-businesses-are-conquering-e-commerce-and-thriving-in-the-digital-age/

Fleury, A., Fleury, M. T. L., Oliveira, L., & Leao, P. (2024). Going digital EMNEs: The role of digital maturity capability. *International Business Review, 33*(4), 102271.

Gabrah, A. Y. B. (2015). *Franchising in emerging markets: Motivations and challenges from a Ghanaian perspective* (MPHIL dissertation, University Of Ghana).

Gabrah (2024). The Impact of Artificial Intelligence on Customer Satisfaction and Customer Loyalty: The Equity Theory Perspectives (Doctoral dissertation, University Of Professional Studies, Accra, Ghana).

Gabrah, A. Y. B., Amoako, G. K., & Ampong, G. O. A. (2023). Africa's Response to SDGs: Barriers and Challenges. In *Corporate sustainability in Africa: Responsible leadership, opportunities, and challenges* (pp. 47–63). Springer International Publishing.

Gabrah, A. Y. B., Amoako, G. K., & Anwana, E. (2024). Stakeholder Integration and Corporate Entrepreneurship. In *Stakeholder management and entrepreneurship in Africa* (pp. 9–22). Routledge.

Ghana Ministry of Communications and Digitalisation. (2023). *National Artificial Intelligence Strategy 2023–2033*. African Data Protection. https://africadataprotection.org/Ghana-AI-Strat.pdf

Gill, S. S., Xu, M., Ottaviani, C., Patros, P., Bahsoon, R., Shaghaghi, A., et al. (2022). AI for next generation computing: Emerging trends and future directions. *Internet of Things, 19*, 100514.

Gołąb-Andrzejak, E. (2023). Measuring the effectiveness of digital communication–social media performance: An example of the role played by AI-assisted tools at a university. *Procedia Computer Science*, 225, 3332–3341.

Haleem, A., Javaid, M., Qadri, M. A., Singh, R. P., & Suman, R. (2022). Artificial intelligence (AI) applications for marketing: A literature-based study. *International Journal of Intelligent Networks, 3*, 119–132.

Haugeland, I. K. F., Følstad, A., Taylor, C., & Bjørkli, C. A. (2022). Understanding the user experience of customer service chatbots: An experimental study of chatbot interaction design. *International Journal of Human-Computer Studies, 161*, 102788.

Hermann, E., Puntoni, S., & Schweidel, D. A. (2025). Conversational AI: The Next Frontier of Digital Platform Monetization. Available at SSRN 5634270.

Hernita, H., Surya, B., Perwira, I., Abubakar, H., & Idris, M. (2021). Economic business sustainability and strengthening human resource capacity based on increasing the productivity of small and medium enterprises (SMEs) in Makassar city. *Indonesia. Sustainability, 13*(6), 3177.

Hinson, R. E., Adeola, O., Nkrumah, K. O., Agyinasare, C., Adom, K., & Amartey, A. F. O. (2019). *Customer service essentials: Lessons for Africa and beyond*. IAP.

Hossain, M. A., Agnihotri, R., Rushan, M. R. I., Rahman, M. S., & Sumi, S. F. (2022). Marketing analytics capability, artificial intelligence adoption, and firms' competitive advantage: Evidence from the manufacturing industry. *Industrial Marketing Management, 106*, 240–255.

Huh, J., Nelson, M. R., & Russell, C. A. (2023). ChatGPT, AI advertising, and advertising research and education. *Journal of Advertising, 52*(4), 477–482.

Indrawati, H. (2020). Barriers to technological innovations of SMEs: How to solve them? *International Journal of Innovation Science, 12*(5), 545–564.

Islam, M. A., Fakir, S. I., Masud, S. B., Hossen, M. D., Islam, M. T., & Siddiky, M. R. (2024). Artificial intelligence in digital marketing automation: Enhancing personalization, predictive analytics, and ethical integration. *Edelweiss Applied Science and Technology, 8*(6), 6498–6516.

Kanellopoulou, D., Giannakopoulos, G., & Karkaletsis, V. (2025). Accelerating AI-powered digital innovation through "APSS": A novel methodology for sustainable business AI transformation. *Journal of Open Innovation: Technology, Market, and Complexity, 11*, 100495.

Kastner, A. N., Mahmoud, M. A., Buame, S. C., & Gabrah, A. Y. (2019). Franchising in African markets: Motivations and challenges from a Sub-Saharan African country perspective. *Thunderbird International Business Review, 61*(2), 169–181.

Kaur, K., & Kumar, P. (2020). Social media usage in Indian beauty and wellness industry: A qualitative study. *TQM Journal, 33*(1), 17–32. https://doi.org/10.1108/TQM-04-2020-0081

Kgakatsi, M., Galeboe, O. P., Molelekwa, K. K., & Thango, B. A. (2024). The impact of big data on SME performance: A systematic review. *Businesses, 4*(4), 632–695.

Khan, S. A. (2023). E-marketing, e-commerce, e-business, and internet of things: An overview of terms in the context of small and medium enterprises (SMEs). In *Global applications of the internet of things in digital marketing* (pp. 332–348). IGI Global.

Kim, H. (2020). Artificial intelligence in marketing: Application, challenges, and implications. *Journal of. Digital Marketing, 12*(3), 45–58. [Insert actual journal if available].

Korsgaard, S., Müller, S., & Welter, F. (2021). It's right nearby: How entrepreneurs use spatial bricolage to overcome resource constraints. *Entrepreneurship & Regional Development, 33*(1–2), 147–173.

Krishnan, C., Gupta, A., Gupta, A., & Singh, G. (2022). Impact of artificial intelligence-based chatbots on customer engagement and business growth. In *Deep learning for social media data analytics* (pp. 195–210). Springer International Publishing.

Kshetri, N., Dwivedi, Y. K., Davenport, T. H., & Panteli, N. (2024). Generative artificial intelligence in marketing: Applications, opportunities, challenges, and research agenda. *International Journal of Information Management, 75*, 102716.

Kumar, V., Ashraf, A. R., & Nadeem, W. (2024). AI-powered marketing: What, where, and how?. *International Journal of Information Management, 77*, 102783.

Liu, L. X., Sun, Z., Xu, K., & Chen, C. (2024). AI-driven financial analysis: Exploring ChatGPT's capabilities and challenges. *International Journal of Financial Studies, 12*(3), 60.

Liu, Z., Han, S., Li, C., Gupta, S., & Sivarajah, U. (2022). Leveraging customer engagement to improve the operational efficiency of social commerce start-ups. *Journal of Business Research, 140*, 572–582.

Magableh, I. K., Mahrouq, M. H., Ta'Amnha, M. A., & Riyadh, H. A. (2024). The role of marketing artificial intelligence in enhancing sustainable financial performance of medium-sized enterprises through customer engagement and data-driven decision-making. *Sustainability, 16*(24), 11279.

Majumder, S., & Mondal, A. (2021). Are chatbots really useful for human resource management?. *International Journal of Speech Technology, 24*(4), 969–977.

Messner, W. (2022). Understanding the influence of culture on customer engagement and recommendation intentions. *Journal of Strategic Marketing, 30*(8), 782–806.

Mikalef, P., Islam, N., Parida, V., Singh, H., & Altwaijry, N. (2023). Artificial intelligence (AI) competencies for organizational performance: A B2B marketing capabilities perspective. *Journal of Business Research, 164*, 113998.

Millard, J. (2022). Rural areas in the digital economy. In *Winning and losing* (pp. 90–123). Routledge.

MTN Group. (2023). *Ayoba – MTN's African super app*. Wikipedia. https://en.wikipedia.org/wiki/Ayoba

Naradda Gamage, S. K., Ekanayake, E. M. S., Abeyrathne, G. A. K. N. J., Prasanna, R. P. I. R., Jayasundara, J. M. S. B., & Rajapakshe, P. S. K. (2020).

A review of global challenges and survival strategies of small and medium enterprises (SMEs). *Economies, 8*(4), 79.

Omrani, N., Rejeb, N., Maalaoui, A., Dabić, M., & Kraus, S. (2022). Drivers of digital transformation in SMEs. *IEEE Transactions on Engineering Management, 71*, 5030–5043.

Owusu-Afriyie, B., & Salia, H. (2023). The role of artificial intelligence in integrated marketing communications: A case study of Jumia Online Ghana. *ResearchGate*. https://doi.org/10.13140/RG.2.2.31725.10725

Panigrahi, R. R., Shrivastava, A. K., Qureshi, K. M., Mewada, B. G., Alghamdi, S. Y., Almakayeel, N., et al. (2023). AI Chatbot adoption in SMEs for sustainable manufacturing supply chain performance: A mediational research in an emerging country. *Sustainability, 15*(18), 13743.

Peretz-Andersson, E., Tabares, S., Mikalef, P., & Parida, V. (2024). Artificial intelligence implementation in manufacturing SMEs: A resource orchestration approach. *International Journal of Information Management, 77*, 102781.

Perez-Vega, R., Kaartemo, V., Lages, C. R., Razavi, N. B., & Männistö, J. (2021). Reshaping the contexts of online customer engagement behavior via artificial intelligence: A conceptual framework. *Journal of Business Research, 129*, 902–910.

Perifanis, N. A., & Kitsios, F. (2023). Investigating the influence of artificial intelligence on business value in the digital era of strategy: A literature review. *Information, 14*(2), 85.

Rahman, M. S., Bag, S., Gupta, S., & Sivarajah, U. (2023). Technology readiness of B2B firms and AI-based customer relationship management capability for enhancing social sustainability performance. *Journal of Business Research, 156*, 113525.

Rana, S., Singh, S. K., & Chandel, A. (2025). AI in customer service automation: Balancing efficiency with human touch. In *AI, corporate social responsibility, and marketing in modern organizations* (pp. 173–194). IGI Global Scientific Publishing.

Rasool, A., Shah, F. A., & Islam, J. U. (2020). Customer engagement in the digital age: A review and research agenda. *Current Opinion in Psychology, 36*, 96–100.

Rawindaran, N., Jayal, A., & Prakash, E. (2021). Machine learning cybersecurity adoption in small and medium enterprises in developed countries. *Computers, 10*(11), 150.

Rawindaran, N., Jayal, A., Prakash, E., & Hewage, C. (2023). Perspective of small and medium enterprise (SME's) and their relationship with government in overcoming cybersecurity challenges and barriers in

Wales. *International Journal of Information Management Data Insights, 3*(2), 100191.

Sankoh, O., Sevalie, S., Mayei, A., Smart, F., N'jai, A. U., & Kenneh, S. (2024). Navigating challenges in health systems strengthening: a closer look at Sierra Leone's journey toward healthcare resilience. *Sierra Leone Journal of Biomedical Research, 15*(1).

Saura, J. R., & Palos-Sanchez, P. (2020). Digital marketing for sustainable growth: Business models and online campaigns using sustainable strategies. *Sustainability, 12*(1003). https://doi.org/10.3390/su12031003

Schwaeke, J., Peters, A., Kanbach, D. K., Kraus, S., & Jones, P. (2025). The new normal: The status quo of AI adoption in SMEs. *Journal of Small Business Management, 63*(3), 1297–1331.

Selamat, M. A., & Windasari, N. A. (2021). Chatbot for SMEs: Integrating customer and business owner perspectives. *Technology in Society, 66*, 101685.

Shafi, P. M., Jawalkar, G. S., Kadam, M. A., Ambawale, R. R., & Bankar, S. V. (2020). *AI—assisted chatbot for e-commerce to address selection of products from multiple products* (pp. 57–80). *A Roadmap Ahead.*

Shahadat, M. H., Nekmahmud, M., Ebrahimi, P., & Fekete-Farkas, M. (2023). Digital technology adoption in SMEs: What technological, environmental and organizational factors influence in emerging countries?. *Global Business Review*. https://doi.org/10.1177/09721509221137199.

Shumanov, M., & Johnson, L. (2021). Making conversations with chatbots more personalized. *Computers in human behavior*, 117, 106627.

Sidek, S., Rosli, M. M., & Khadri, N. A. M. (2020). Fortifying small business performance sustainability in the era of IR 4.0: E-marketing as a catalyst of competitive advantages and business performance. *Journal of Critical Reviews, 7*(12), 2143–2155.

Silvester, S., & Kurian, S. (2023, December). Recommendation systems: Enhancing personalization and customer experience. In *2023 3rd International Conference on Smart Generation Computing, Communication and Networking (SMART GENCON)* (pp. 1–6). IEEE.

Stone, M., Aravopoulou, E., Ekinci, Y., Evans, G., Hobbs, M., Labib, A., et al. (2020). Artificial intelligence (AI) in strategic marketing decision-making: A research agenda. *The Bottom Line, 33*(2), 183–200.

Sun, Y., Chen, J., & Sundar, S. S. (2024). Chatbot ads with a human touch: A test of anthropomorphism, interactivity, and narrativity. *Journal of Business Research, 172*, 114403.

The Ghana Report. (2023, June 10). *AI-powered transformation: Unlocking growth potential for SMEs*. The Ghana Report. https://www.theghanareport.com/ai-powered-transformation-unlocking-growth-potential-for-smes/

Theodorakopoulos, L., Theodoropoulou, A., Kalliampakou, I., Velissaris, P., & Halkiopoulos, C. (2024, September). Revolutionizing Tourism Marketing: Big Data Analytics and Machine Learning for Predictive Accuracy. In *International Conference of the International Association of Cultural and Digital Tourism* (pp. 321–349). Cham: Springer Nature Switzerland.

Thottoli, M. M., Islam, M. A., Ahsan, A., Yusof, M. F., Hassan, M. S., & Chowdhury, R. S. (2024). Exploring mediating and moderating factors of FinTech adoption for innovations in SMEs. *Cogent Economics & Finance, 12*(1), 2387443.

Vashishth, T. K., Sharma, V., Sharma, K. K., Kumar, B., Kumar, A., & Panwar, R. (2024). Artificial intelligence (AI)–powered chatbots: Providing instant support and personalized recommendations to guests 24/7. In *Technology and luxury hospitality* (pp. 211–236). Routledge.

von Garrel, J., & Jahn, C. (2023). Design framework for the implementation of AI-based (service) business models for small and medium-sized manufacturing enterprises. *Journal of the Knowledge Economy, 14*(3), 3551–3569.

Wang, X., Lin, X., & Shao, B. (2022). How does artificial intelligence create business agility? Evidence from chatbots. *International Journal of Information Management, 66*, 102535.

World Economic Forum. The future of learning: How AI is revolutionizing education 4.0 Retrieved from The future of learning: AI is revolutionizing education 4.0 | World Economic Forum. Accessed 13/01/25.

Zindi, B., Ndhlovu, E., & Mhlanga, D. (2024). The Digital Evolution of Global Tourism and the Practical Lessons for African Small Businesses. In Sustainable Finance and Business in Sub-Saharan Africa (pp. 447-471). Cham: Springer Nature Switzerland

Zuhroh, S., & Rini, G. P. (2024). Product innovation capability and distinctive value positioning drivers for marketing performance: A service-dominant logic perspective. *International Journal of Innovation Science*. https://doi.org/10.1108/IJIS-04-2024-0100

15

Dynamics of Small and Medium Enterprises' Borrower Characteristics and Credit Risk in Ghana

George Kwabena Asamoah

15.1 Introduction

Much of the literature on businesses development agrees with the assertion that funding is critical for medium and small businesses' development and sustainability (UNCTAD, 2001). Funding is known to be the lifeblood of any business, big or small (Biswas, 2015). However, high risk and information opacity make it difficult to finance small and medium-sized businesses in Ghana (Abor & Biekpe, 2007). Abor (2017) indicates lending money is a risky endeavour, and as a result, unmistakable comprehension of customers is essential to detect and appraise the dangers associated in any lending situation. To provide acceptable returns to stockholders, lending companies must employ the appropriate risk mitigation technique. They must be cautious while assessing the default risk of their borrowers using solid lending

G. K. Asamoah (✉)
Faculty of Commerce, Rosebank International University College,
Accra, Ghana
e-mail: gkwabena@riuc.edu.gh

E. Amoako Asiedu et al. (eds.), *Entrepreneurship and Small and Medium-Sized Enterprises (SMEs) in Africa*, https://doi.org/10.1007/978-3-032-14174-3_15

standards. Risk homeostasis theory (Wilde, 1982) holds that organizations tend to take more risks when they feel more secure by adjusting their level of risk-taking behaviour in response to the perceived level of risk awareness.

The theory is that financial service providers often offset the risk associated with SME loans by requiring or enforcing higher collateral requirements and charging higher interest rates (Bawumia et al., 2005; International Financial Corporation, 2009). To estimate the probability of default, a credit institution assesses a borrower's creditworthiness by collecting, processing, and analysing accurate, up-to-date information about the borrower. As a result, Tagoe et al. (2005) argue that the amount of money a borrower has in the firm, the degree of profitability and the extent to which profits stay in the business, and the value of security supplied, all play a role in the lending decision. Credit assessors estimate the expected chance of default by emphasizing traditional elements in establishing creditworthiness and ability to pay, according to several research. The 3C's, 4C's, or 5C's of credit, which are character or reputation, capital or leverage, collateral, capacity, and condition, are among these factors (Soares et al., 2011). However, little study has been done on firm and owner-manager characteristics such as firm age, firm size, and owner gender, as well as macroeconomic variables in evaluating trustworthiness and financial capability.

Statistics from the Financial Stability Report of the Bank of Ghana (2016) and the IMF (2013) show that the NPL ratio of SMEs is increasing. The lack of market credibility in the SME sector makes it difficult for lenders to assess risk premiums, creating disparities between the perceived and actual risk profiles of banks (Danquah, & Osei Adu, 2025). In this respect, the extent to which financial institutions lend to SMEs depends on a range of factors. Some of the key factors affecting bank financing for SMEs include the macroeconomic environment, regulatory and regulatory environment, the state of financial sector infrastructure, banks' intrinsic limitations on lending capacity and technology, and little attention to factors specific to SMEs and owner-manager characteristics. These include the track record of SMEs in terms of size, age, industry, gender, and education as agents to determine creditworthiness and solvency (Beck et al., 2008; de la Torre et al., 2010).

As a result, the study addresses these shortcomings by defining two research goals in an effort to fill the vacuum in the literature. The major focus of this research is to look at how the characteristics of borrowers from businesses of all sizes affect credit risk in Sunyani, Ghana. The study's goal was to see if there was a link between a borrower's qualities and counterparty risk, as well as look at the effects of some economic determinants on credit risk.

15.2 Literature Review

15.2.1 Definition and Characteristics of Small and Medium-Sized Enterprises

Various authorities have presented a variety of meanings in the literature. In this study, a small-scale enterprise in Ghana is defined as a corporate entity with less than ten employees, while a medium-scale enterprise is defined as a company with ten to one hundred employees (Abor & Adjasi, 2007; Ghana Statistical Service, 2014). According to McGrath (2005), SME managers with more education and training are more likely to succeed. SMEs' managers, according to Muller and Posel (2004), develop their own management style through trial and error. As a result, rather than being analytical, their management style is visceral, with a focus on day-to-day operations rather than long-term difficulties (Beck & Demirguc-Kunt, 2006). Many SMEs, especially those in developing countries, require operational knowledge and experience. Most SMEs are unregulated and independently controlled, with inadequate human ability, financial resources, and logistics to develop governance policies with clear visions, missions, and goals (Muteti, 2005).

Due to a lack of formal education, SME owners are ill-equipped to carry out managerial tasks for their businesses. From the perspective of Abor and Quartey (2010), the majority of SMEs are one-person operations. Working proprietors are the most prevalent sort of work. In most developing nations, this segment accounts for more than half of the SME workforce. In contrast to those owned by men, Abor and Quartey (2010) discovered that the majority of SMEs are owned by women, with the majority of them being home-based. SMEs are usually involved in retailing, trading, or manufacturing, according to Fisher and Reuber (2000) as well as Hoq et al. (2009). It is often anticipated that the overwhelming of SMEs will be in the retail sector (Abor & Quartey, 2010). The share of SME activity in the retail sector varies significantly across nations, as well as between rural and urban regions within countries.

15.2.2 Firm Characteristics and Credit Risk

According to Lehmann and Neuberger (2001), the age of the company is a sign of credit risk. The longevity of a company can be a measure of its ability to survive and grow, as well as the accumulation of reputational capital, hence its age is often used as a barometer of its quality (Drakos & Giannakopoulos, 2011). Enterprises that have been in operation for a lengthy span of time, according to Jiménez and Saurina (2004), have a reduced credit risk. Older borrowers are less risk averse and thus less prone to default (Boyle et al., 1992; Audia & Greve, 2006). As a result, lenders are more hesitant to lend to young borrowers who are more eager to take risks. In view of the aforementioned, Sapienza et al. (2006) hypothesized that financial service providers could regard younger businesses as riskier than older businesses due to the liabilities associated with newness. Similarly, to Sapienza et al. (2006), Berger and Udell (2006) claim that older firms are safer because financial service providers trust older firms with secured loans and hence have fewer incentives to do adequate screening and credit evaluation.

Brehanu and Fufa (2008) opined that education enhances the borrower's ability to repay. Previous studies have reported that better-educated borrowers are deemed to have more stable and higher incomes, secured employment, and thus a lower default rate (Stiglitz & Uy, 1996). The borrowers' education level can be distinguished from postgraduate to non-high school graduates. Borrowers with a high level of education are more likely to repay their loans since they occupy higher positions with high-income levels. Stiglitz and Uy (1996)'s study on the inverse relationship between borrower status and credit risk is complemented by Cassar's (2004) study on the financing of business start-ups. The relationship between education and loan repayment has been widely investigated, and this view is supported by Bassem (2008), who writes that there is a positive relationship between the level of formal education and the sense of responsibility and reputation, which reduces the probability of default and is very vital to the lender in making lending decisions. Bruns and Fletcher (2008) found that educational status could influence firms' credit risk considerably.

The impact of collateral on credit risk has also received a lot of attention in the literature. The type of collateral used correlates positively with the risk of default. Collateral reduces the financial service providers' risk when loans are made to SME borrowers (Mensah, 2004). According to Gup and Kolari (2005), borrowers' collateral can be a sign of default risk. Thus, the probability of default is very low for loans where a house, for example, serves as a guarantee in support of a loan. This is because of the fear of the borrower losing the house. The higher the collateral value, the higher the incentive for the borrowers to repay the loan, since they do not want to lose their collateral (Menkhoff et al., 2012). There are also theoretical arguments by Manove et al. (2001) supporting the possibility that more collateral implies more non-performing loans or a greater probability of default. Thus, collateral acts as a signal, enabling the financial service provider to mitigate or eliminate the adverse selection problem caused by the existence of information asymmetries between the lender and the borrower at the time of the loan decision (OECD, 2013).

The relationship between gender and credit risk has been analysed in a number of studies. A number of studies found that women consistently outperform men in terms of repayment. The assertion that women are good credit risks is repeatedly put forward by financial advocacy networks and sponsors. A study by Ssendi and Anderson (2009) indicates that women are consistently better in promptness and reliability in payment (Marrez & Schmit, 2009). D'espallier et al. (2011) report that the repayments of loans are higher among female borrowers, mostly due to more conservative investments and lower moral hazard risk. Identically, Kevane and Wydick (2001) state that female groups perform better than male groups in Guatemala in terms of loan repayment. A report on the Grameen Bank, according to Gross et al. (2009), indicates that men are more likely to default than women. Relatedly, Schmit and Marrez (2010) as well as Kevane and Wydick (2001) report that women have better repayment records than men. In a similar vein, Marrez and Schmit (2009) revealed lower default rates for women segments compared to male segments, and as such, the loss rate is lower for women than for men.

15.2.3 Empirical Review on Credit Risk and SME Financing

Wabo (2014), in an effort to identify a mathematical model that can be used in the risk quantification of small and medium-sized enterprises (SMEs), conducted a study in Cameroon. A quantitative approach was employed, and a sample of 110 SMEs out of the population was used for the study. The study found that SMEs in the sample were very risky and this view is supported by Bruns and Fletcher (2008), who write that SMEs are risky and that financial service providers place emphasis on the factors that shift risk, such as requests for collateral, proper financial statements, and knowledge on financial management. In contrast to Wabo (2014), Beck et al. (2008) argue that the SME sector is a profitable venture and very competitive. The finding also revealed that up to 47% of loans granted to small and medium-sized enterprises (SMEs) were defaulted. The finding of Beck et al. (2008) that SMEs sector is profitable and very competitive cannot be generalized in developing economies as there are opposing views. However, the findings from the literature have pointed out clearly that SMEs in developing economies are highly risky.

15.2.4 Risk Compensation Theory

In reaction to a technological approach to safety, Lave and Weber (1970) and Peltzman (1975) proposed the concept of risk compensation (Levym & Miller, 2000). Risk compensation theory states that when a person, a group of individuals, or an institution feels more secure, they will take more risks. As a result, institutions modify their risk-taking behaviour in reaction to the perceived degree of risk, based on the safety measures in place, becoming more cautious when perceiving bigger hazards and less cautious when detecting greater protection (Dolan & Lindsey, 1994; Slovic, 2016; Wilde, 1982). According to the hypothesis, financial institutions usually mitigate the risks of extending loans by demanding or imposing higher debt covenants and charging higher interest rates. Risk compensation theory states that people maximize their utility by comparing the expected costs and benefits of safer and riskier behaviour. Wilde (1982) proposed four elements for personal risk calculation. These include the expected benefits of dangerous behaviour, the expected costs of dangerous behaviour, the expected benefits of safe behaviour, and the expected costs of safe behaviour. The risk compensation theory has been tested in the transport and sports sectors and can be applied to the financial sector (Levym & Miller, 2000).

15.3 Methodology

The study adopted a cross-sectional design to explore associations between SMEs characteristics and credit risk. Levin (2006) asserted that cross-sectional design is employed when the purpose of the study is descriptive. The aim is to describe a population or a subgroup within the population, with respect to an outcome and a set of risk factors. The use of the cross-sectional design also supported the quantitative approach employed in measuring the variables and the statistical techniques employed for the primary data analysis (Pasanen & Luoma, 2021). The distinctive features of this design are that it is executed within a limited period; it studies the relationship between different variables at a single point in time and shows how variables affect each other. The cross-sectional design faces the challenge of the inability to capture social processes or change, subject to recall bias and observer-expectancy effects (Mohammed, 2020).

The population of the study was credit officers of the formal and informal financial institutions and operators of SMEs in the Sunyani municipality. SMEs comprised retailing, wood processing, animal farming, metal works, dressmaking, sawmilling, catering, and hairdressing businesses. For this study, the target population comprised 510 SMEs. SME operators and managers served as proxies for the provision of the primary data for their respective SMEs.

A multi-stage sampling technique was used for the study. First, the sampling frame was categorized into two different sets of population, namely, credit officers and operators of SMEs. Second, SME managers and operators from the various groups of SMEs were categorized into operators of retailing, wood processing, metal works, dressmaking, catering, hairdressing, poultry farming, printing and publishing works, brewing, and agro-processing. To ensure the representativeness of the sample to the population, 217 SME operators were sampled for the study. This was based on the sample size determination table of Krejcie and Morgan (1970), which states that a population of 510 requires a sample size of 217 at a 95% confidence interval, while 64 credit officers of formal and informal financial institutions were sampled for the study.

15.3.1 Data Collection Instruments

Interview schedule was used for the operators of SMEs because they were perceived as largely lacking formal education and thus would need assistance to administer the instruments. This approach guarded against any possible misunderstanding or misinterpretation of the items in the instrument, which might have led to erroneous conclusions.

15.3.2 Theoretical Econometric Model

The probability of default is modelled as:

$$Y_i = X_i \beta + ui \tag{15.1}$$

Where *Xi* is a vector of exogenous explanatory variables; μi is a stochastic error term and β is a vector of parameters. However, in a binary outcome model, the dependent variable yi takes one of these two values:

$$Y = \begin{cases} 1 \; if \; firm \, i \, default \\ 0 \qquad otherwise \end{cases} \tag{15.2}$$

The logit model is systematically specified below: Beginning from a Linear Probability Model (LPM):

$$Pi\left(y = 1/X\right) = P\left(y = 1/X1 + X2 + \ldots + XK\right) \tag{15.3}$$

Pi is the probability that a firm will default;
X1, X2 … Xk denote explanatory variables.
y = *1* means the event does occur (the firm defaulted);
y = *0* means the event does not occur (the firm has not defaulted).

Then, the logistic model specifies that the probability of a firm to default is given by

$$\boldsymbol{P}_i\left(\boldsymbol{Y} = \frac{\mathbf{1}}{\boldsymbol{X}_i}\right) = \frac{\exp\left(\boldsymbol{x\beta}\right)}{\mathbf{1} + \exp^{(x\beta)}} \tag{15.4}$$

The equation implies that the probability of a firm to default ($1-P_i$) can be written as

$$1 - P_i = \frac{\mathbf{1}}{\mathbf{1} + \exp^{x\beta}} \tag{15.5}$$

We can, therefore, write

$$\frac{P_i}{1 - P_i} = \frac{\exp^{(x\beta)}}{1 + \exp^{(x\beta)}}\left(\frac{1 + \exp^{x\beta}}{1}\right) = \exp^{x\beta} \tag{15.6}$$

$\dfrac{\boldsymbol{P}_i}{\mathbf{1} - \boldsymbol{P}_i}$ is simply the odd ratio (OR) in favour of defaulting firms the ratio of the probability that a firm will default to the probability that a firm will not default. The odds ratio is equal to $exp^{(x\beta)}$.

Taking the natural log of Eqn (15.6) gives the logit model as specified below.

$$L_1 = 1n\left(\frac{P_i}{1-P_i}\right) = Z_i \ = \beta_1 + \beta_2 X_i + U_i \tag{15.7}$$

The full regression equations are represented below:

In our model, we postulate that the probability of default is influenced by the following factors: Inflation rate (INFR), Government interference (GOVI), Time of disbursement of loan (TDL), Diversion of funds (DIVF), Staff extortion (STE), while owner-manager and firm characteristics such as Gender of Owner (GENO), Educational Status (EDUSTA), Age of firm (AGE), Size of firm (SIZE), and Collateral value (COLVA) were also modelled.

From Eqn (15.7), the empirical estimation model is given by

$$\begin{aligned}\text{CRPsme} = \beta 0 + \beta 1\text{GOVI} + \beta 2\text{INFR} + \beta 3\text{INTR} + \beta 4 STE \\ + \beta 5 TDL + \beta 6 BRV + \beta 7\text{DIVF} + \mu\end{aligned} \tag{15.8}$$

$$\begin{aligned}\text{CRPsme} = \beta 0 + \beta 1\text{GENO} + \beta 2\text{EDUSTA} + \beta 3\text{AGE} \\ + \beta 4\text{SIZE} + \beta 5\text{COLVA} + \mu\end{aligned} \tag{15.9}$$

15.4 Analysis and Results

This paper foremost examined the characteristics of the SME operators, afterwards correlation analysis and chi-square tests were employed to determine the relationship between SME characteristics and credit risk, while logistic regression was used to model macroeconomic variables and owner-manager characteristics such as gender of owner, educational status of owner, as well as firm characteristics such as age, size of firm, and collateral value. The variables include sex, educational level, and type of enterprise. The study used a total of 217 SME owners and managers that were drawn from the Sunyani Municipality, consisting of 65% of SME owners and 35% of SME managers.

The study collected data from different types of enterprises that had businesses in the Sunyani Municipality. As seen in Table 15.1, more (46.5%) of the SMEs are in retailing, with the least (2.3%) in the hardware business. This finding is consistent with Fisher and Reuber's (2000)

Table 15.1 Types of enterprise

Types of enterprise	Frequency	Percent
Retailing	101	46.5
Hairdressing	50	23.0
Animal farming	25	11.5
Sawmilling and wood processing	15	6.9
Dressmaking	9	4.1
Metal works	6	2.8
Catering	6	2.8
Hardware	5	2.3
Total	217	100.0

Source: Field data (2023)

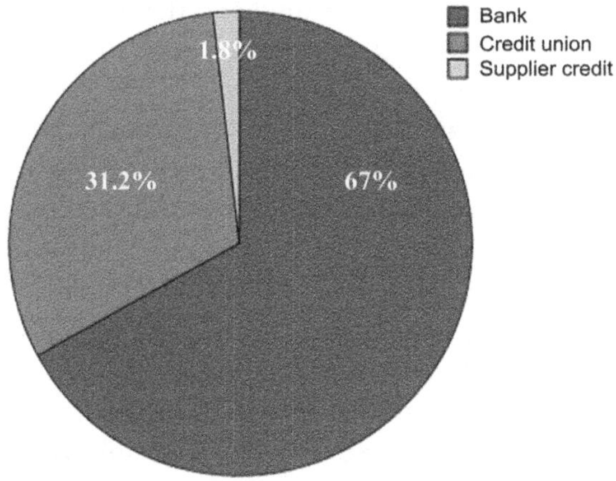

Fig. 15.1 Sources of bank finance. (Source: Field data (2023))

that SMEs are mostly engaged in retailing, trading, or manufacturing. The finding is also consistent with Abor and Quartey's (2010) that the majority of SMEs in Ghana fall into the retailing category.

Figure 15.1 shows the sources from which SME operators borrowed to finance their business activities, and it can be seen that 67% of the respondents borrowed from the bank, while 31.2% borrowed from credit unions. The results show that formal financial institutions play a critical role in financing the SME activities. In accordance with the present results, a previous study by Abor and Quartey (2010) has demonstrated that formal finance plays a key role in SME activities.

The paper further examined the number of times that respondents had applied for a loan, as well as the number of times they had been successful in securing the loan. The aim was to assess the ability of SME operators to meet the credit conditions of financial service providers due to high-risk perception (De la Torre et al., 2010). The study found that the number of times respondents had applied for loans varied from one to four, with a mean of 1.4 (SD = 0.626). The results show that some SME operators had been successful in their attempts to secure loans to finance their businesses. The results also indicate that more loan applications from SME operators were not approved (Awuitor, 2016). The responses on how regular SME borrowers repay loans on time were sought. From the findings, 64.6% of the respondents disclosed that they service their loans on time, while the remaining 35.4% accepted that they occasionally default on repayment.

Beneficiaries of the loans were asked to indicate whether they were able to pay back their loans on time, and how they generated money to repay the loans. These were essential to examine the ability of the entrepreneurs to utilize funds in their businesses to generate additional resources to repay their loans on time (Mensah, 2004). The finding shows that the majority (64.6%) of the beneficiaries of the loan were not able to repay on time. These findings further support the idea of Bawumia et al. (2005) that most SME borrowers were unable to meet the financial obligation. However, a few of the beneficiaries (35.4%) were able to meet loan repayment schedule (Table 15.2).

Table 15.2 Variables in the equation credit risk (SMEs)

	B	S.E.	Wald	Sig.	Exp(B)
Government interference	0.100	0.411	0.060	0.807	1.106
Inflation rate	-1.996	0.465	18.406	0.000	0.136
Interest rate	-1.035	1.454	0.507	0.477	0.355
Time of disbursement	2.923	0.482	36.786	0.000	18.589
Bank regular visits	-3.252	0.728	19.960	0.000	0.039
Staff extortion	-0.354	0.427	0.687	0.407	0.702
Diversion of funds	0.244	0.718	0.116	0.734	1.277
Constant	7.240	5.941	1.485	0.223	1394.90

Source: Field data (2023)

The results of a direct logistic regression analysis performed on credit risk as a dependent variable and seven independent variables: government interference, inflation rate, interest rate, time of loan disbursement, bank regular visits, staff extortion, and diversion of funds. From the output, it is observed that the model can correctly predict 93.8% of default and 90.8% of non-default. Overall, the model predicts 91.7% of the credit risks correctly an improvement over the 68.9% in Block 0. From the model, the chi-square value for the Hosmer Lemeshow Test is 101.208 with a significance level of 0.000. Rousson and Goşoniu (2007) declared the R^2 values of between 0.2 and 0.4 represent a good fit for the model. The model specification is therefore good, given by the significant chi-square for prediction squared. The Cox & Snell *R*-Square and the Nagelkerke *R*-Square values are 0.511 and 0.718, suggesting that between 51.1% and 71.8% of the variability is explained by this set of variables. The chi-square value is 147.530 with 7 degrees of freedom.

The variables that contribute significantly to the predictive ability of the model include inflation rate (z = 18.406; p = 0.000), time of disbursement of loans (z = 36.786; p = 0.000), and banks regular visits (z = 19.960; p = 0.000). Inflation rate is a significant predictor, according to the significant value. The odds ratio for inflation rate, however, is 0.136, a value less than 1. The negative sign of this variable indicates that high inflation rate is associated with lower credit risk. The estimated coefficient of the rate of inflation indicates that a unit increase in the inflation leads to a decrease in the odds that a borrower will default.

Time of disbursing the loan (p = 0.000) is a significant predictor of credit risk. The positive sign of the coefficient for this variable indicates that the longer the time of disbursing the loan, the higher the credit default risk. More specifically, a unit increase in the time of disbursing the loan results in an increase of 18.589 in the odds that a borrower will default. The model indicated a significant (p = 0.000) inverse relationship (b = -3.252) between banks regular visits and credit risk. An increase in monitoring and regular visits by banks would decrease the probability of default by SME operators, all other factors being held constant. A unit increase in the bank regular visits leads to a decrease in the odds that a borrower will default.

Continuous variables such as the size of the firm and age of firm were analysed with Pearson product-moment correlation coefficient. Chi-square test with lambda as statistic was used to measure the association between educational status and credit risk because educational status is an ordinal variable, while credit risk is a nominal variable. Correspondingly, chi-square test with Phi coefficient was used to analyse the association between collateral value and credit risk as well as gender and credit risk because both variables were nominal. The relationship between firms' age as measured by the number of years in operation and credit risk as measured as the potential of a borrower to default or non-default in terms of loan agreement, was first investigated using Pearson product-moment correlation coefficient. Preliminary analyses were performed to ensure no violation of the assumptions of normality, linearity, and homoscedasticity.

As noted from Table 15.3, there is a strong but negative significant relationship between firms age and credit risk ($r = -0.680$, $p < 0.01$). Thus, older firms are associated with lower credit risk. The explanation for this is that SME operators who have been in operation for a longer period are viewed as an indicator of a firm's quality, since the longevity of the firm may provide a signal for survival ability and quality of management as well as the accumulation of reputational capital (Diamond, 1991). This finding corroborates the ideas of Boyle et al. (1992) as well as Sachs and Cohen (1982) that older borrowers are more risk-averse, and therefore, less likely to default.

The study found a large but negative correlation between a firm's size and credit risk ($r = -0.092$, $p > 0.01$). Thus, as the size of the firm increases,

Table 15.3 Correlation between firms age and credit risk

		Credit risk	Firms age
Credit risk	Pearson Correlation	1	-0.680**
	Sig. (2-tailed)		0.000
	N	217	215
Firms age	Pearson Correlation	-0.680**	1
	Sig. (2-tailed)	0.000	
	N	217	217

**Correlation is significant at the 0.01 level (2-tailed)
Source: Field data (2023)

credit risk decreases. The explanation for this is that larger firms have lower credit risk. The relationship is consistent with studies by Schiffer and Weder (2001) in the USA, World Bank (2005), as well as Gabriel (2015) that smaller firms have higher risk and, as such, have a higher rate of failure compared to large firms.

The association between gender of the owner and credit risk was investigated using the chi-square test of independence. From the chi-square test (χ^2 (1) = 0.024, p = 0.878: $p > 0.05$), there is no statistically significant association between gender and credit risk. This means that the proportion of males that default is not significantly different from the proportion of females that default. This relation contradicts the finding of Marrez and Schmit (2009) as well as Schmit (2004) in Belgium that the default rates for women segments are lower compared to male segments, and as such, the loss rate is lower for women than for men.

The association between collateral and credit risk was investigated using the chi-square test with Phi coefficient. From the Chi- square test, a p-value of 0.00 (X^2 = 62.783, df = 1) with Phi coefficient = 0.615, and a $p < 0.000$, indicated a strong significant positive association between collateral value and credit risk. An increase in collateral value is associated with higher credit risk. The relation observed corroborates the findings of Manove, Padilla, and Pagano (2001) that collateralized loans have a high possibility of default because financial service providers tend to trust the borrowers with secured loans and hence, have fewer incentives to undertake adequate screening and credit assessment.

The association between educational status and credit risk was investigated using the chi-square test with lambda as a statistic. The findings indicated a moderate significant, but positive association between the educational status of SME operator and credit risk. From the Chi-square independence test, a p-value of 0.00 (χ^2 (4) = 61.261, p = 0.000) shows that there is a statistically positive but moderate significant association between the levels of education of SME operators and credit risk. This is because the p-value of 0.00 is lesser than the acceptable error margin of 0.05. The lambda value = 0.285, $p < 0.05$. The implication is that differences in the level of education determine borrowers' potential to default. Thus, SME operators with different levels of education were equally capable of defaulting on loans.

15.5 Logistic Regression Results

Table 15.4 presents the results of a direct logistic regression analysis performed on credit risk only as the dependent variable and five independent variables: Firm's size, Gender of owner, Age of firm, educational status of owner, and collateral value.

The Cox & Snell *R*-Square and the Nagelkerke *R*-Square values are 0.386 and 0.555, suggesting that between 38.6% and 55.5% of the variability is explained by this set of variables. The chi-square value is 79.979 with 5 degrees of freedom. The variables that contribute significantly to the predictive ability of the model include firm's size ($z = 5.532$; $p = 0.019$), firm's age ($z = 5.449$; $p = 0.020$), educational status ($z = 8.593$; $p = 0.003$), and collateral value ($z = 22.606$; $p = 0.000$). Gender of owner did not contribute significantly to credit risk.

Firm's age varies inversely with credit risk. The negative sign of this variable indicates that younger firms are more likely to default compared to older firms. The firm's age is statistically significant at 5%. The estimated coefficient of the age of firm indicates that a unit increase in the years of a firm leads to a decrease of 0.877 in the odds that a firm will default. The possible explanation for this is that, as a firm ages, the greater the capital structure and financial strength. This view is supported in an earlier study by Jiménez and Saurina (2004) that firms that have been in operation for a longer period have lower credit risk.

Firm's size is a significant predictor, according to the Sig. value. The odds ratio for firm's size, however, is 0.261, a value less than 1.00. The negative sign of this variable indicates that small firms are more likely to default compared to older firms. The estimated coefficient indicates that

Table 15.4 Variables in the equation (owner-manager/firm characteristics)

	B	S.E.	Wald	Sig.	Exp(B)
Firm size	-1.342	0.571	5.532	0.019	0.261
Gender of owner	-0.103	0.301	0.116	0.733	0.902
Firm age	-0.131	0.056	5.449	0.020	0.877
Educational status	0.168	0.057	8.593	0.003	1.183
Collateral value	2.709	0.570	22.606	0.000	15.018
Constant	-2.180	1.659	1.727	0.189	0.113

Source: Field data (2023)

a unit increase in the firm's size leads to a decrease in the odds that a borrower will default. Thus, as the size of the firm increases, credit risk decreases.

Collateral value is expected to increase the propensity to default, all other things being equal. While the results in the logit model confirm this claim, the positive sign of the coefficient for this variable indicates that the higher the collateral value, the higher the credit risk. This variable is significant at 5%. Thus, an increase in collateral value is associated with higher credit risk. More specifically, a unit increase in the collateral value results in an increase of 15.018 in the odds that a firm will default.

Educational status is also a significant predictor ($p = 0.003$). The positive coefficient of this variable indicates that SMEs entrepreneurs with higher levels of education tend to default more than those with lower levels of education. This variable is significant at 5%. Thus, a 1% increase in the educational status has 1.183 odds in favour of credit risk. Thus, SME operators with different levels of education were equally capable of defaulting on loans. This relation supports the findings of Reta (2000) that educational level is positively related to credit risk.

15.6 Conclusion and Policy Implications

Majority of the loans are diverted for the purpose unintended, as a result of, poor monitoring and irregular banks' visits undertaken by the credit officials to monitor customers. Credit policies, inflation rates and interest rates influence credit risk. For instance, a decline in default rate is associated with improved credit policies. High interest rates charged compensate the financial service providers for the high risk of default. The predominant reasons why most financial service providers charge higher risk premiums on SME loans are linked with SMEs' susceptibility to failure and changes in the external environment. The firms' characteristics such as age, size, and collateral value influence credit risk. In view of the findings, the study recommends that as a policy measure, SME entrepreneurs should take steps to seek clarification on the conditions attached to loans to reduce the number of unsuccessful applications. Further, SME entrepreneurs should state the ideal time they wish to receive loans from financial service providers for their businesses. This will help financial service providers to disburse the loan on time in order to generate maximum impact on the businesses of SMEs and also help to reduce the moral hazard problem.

References

Abor, J., & Adjasi, C. K. (2007). Corporate governance and the small and medium enterprises sector: Theory and implications. *The International Journal of Business in Society, 7*(2), 111–122.

Abor, J., & Biekpe, N. (2007). Small business reliance on bank financing in Ghana. *Emerging Markets Finance and Trade, 43*(4), 93–102.

Abor, J., & Quartey, P. (2010). Issues in SME development in Ghana and South Africa. *International Research Journal of Finance and Economics, 39*(6), 215–228.

Abor, J. Y. (2017). *The financial environment and small businesses. Entrepreneurial finance for MSMEs*. University of Ghana Business School, Accra: Palgrave Macmillan.

Audia, P. G., & Greve, H. R. (2006). Less likely to fail: Low performance, firm size, and factory expansion in the shipbuilding industry. *Management Science, 52*(1), 83–94.

Awuitor, J. A. (2016). *Optimizing banks' loan portfolio in Ghana. A case study of Nkoranman Rural Bank, Sunyani* (Doctoral Thesis, KNUST, Ghana). http://hdl.handle.net/123456789/8361.

Bank of Ghana. (2016). *Annual Reports*. Buck Press.

Bassem, B. S. (2008). Determinants of successful group loan repayment: An application to Tunisia. *Journal of Sustainable Development in Africa, 10*(2), 766–800.

Bawumia, M., Belnye, F., & Ofori, M. E. (2005). The determination of bank interest spreads in Ghana: An empirical analysis of panel data. *African Development Review, 20*(3), 378–399.

Beck, T., & Demirguc-Kunt, A. (2006). Small and medium-size enterprises: Access to finance as a growth constraint. *Journal of Banking & Finance, 30*(11), 2931–2943.

Beck, T., Demirguc-Kunt, A., & Martinez Peria, M. S. (2008). *Bank financing for SMEs around the world: Drivers, obstacles, business models, and lending practices*. (Policy Research Working Paper, 4785). Bell, Canada: The World Bank.

Berger, A. N., & Udell, G. F. (2006). A more complete conceptual framework for SME finance. *Journal of Banking & Finance, 30*(11), 2945–2966.

Biswas, A. (2015). The widening financing gap and micro, small and medium enterprises in India. *International Journal of Research, 2*(4), 528–541.

Boyle, M., Crook, J. N., Hamilton, R., & Thomas, L. C. (1992). Methods for credit scoring applied to slow payers. In L. C. Thomas, J. N. Crook, & D. B. Edelman (Eds.), *Credit scoring and credit control* (pp. 75–90). Oxford University Press.

Brehanu, A., & Fufa, B. (2008). Repayment rate of loans from semi-formal financial institutions among small-scale farmers in Ethiopia: Two-limit Tobit analysis. *The Journal of Socio-Economics, 37*(6), 2221–2230.

Bruns, V., & Fletcher, M. (2008). Banks' risk assessment of Swedish SMEs. *Venture Capital, 10*(2), 171–194.

Cassar, G. (2004). The financing of business start-ups. *Journal of Business Venturing, 19*(2), 261–283.

Danquah, D. A., & Osei Adu, K. (2025). Effects of lending rates and financial development on loan portfolio in sub-Saharan Africa. *Future Business Journal, 11*(1), 227.

De la Torre, A., Pería, M. S. M., & Schmukler, S. L. (2010). Bank involvement with SMEs: Beyond relationship lending. *Journal of Banking & Finance, 34*(9), 2280–2293.

Despallier, B., Gurin, I., & Mersland, R. (2011). Women and repayment in microfinance: A global analysis. *World Development, 39*(5), 758–772.

Diamond, D. W. (1991). Monitoring and reputation: The choice between bank loans and directly placed debt. *Journal of political Economy, 99*(4), 689–721.

Dolan, E. G., & Lindsey, D. E. (1994). *Economics*. Dryden Press.

Drakos, K., & Giannakopoulos, N. (2011). On the determinants of credit rationing: Firm-level evidence from transition countries. *Journal of International Money and Finance, 30*(8), 1773–1790.

Fisher, E., & Reuber, R. (2000). *Industrial clusters and SME promotion in developing countries*, (Commonwealth Trade and Enterprise Paper No. 3). London, United Kingdom: Commonwealth Secretariat.

Gabriel, K. U. K. (2015). *Factors influencing small and medium enterprises' access to funding in Kenya: A case study of westlands division*. Mount Kenya University.

Ghana Statistical Service (2014). *2010 Population and housing census report*. Accra, Ghana statistical service. www.statsghana.gov.gh/pop_stats.html.

Gross, J. P., Cekic, O., Hossler, D., & Hillman, N. (2009). What matters in student loan default: A review of the research literature. *Journal of Student Financial Aid, 39*(1), 19–29.

Gup, B. E., & Kolari, J. W. (2005). *Commercial banking: The management of risk*. John Wiley & Sons Incorporated.

Hoq, M. Z., Ha, N. C., & Said, S. M. (2009). SMEs in the Malaysian economy. *International Business Journal, 1*(2), 3–17.

IFC. (2009). *The SME banking knowledge guide*. The World Bank Group.

International Monetary Fund. (2013). *Ghana Country Report* No. 13/187. IMF, Washington, DC.

Jiménez, G., & Saurina, J. (2004). Collateral, type of lender and relationship banking as determinants of credit risk. *Journal of Banking & Finance, 28*(9), 2191–2212.

Kevane, M., & Wydick, B. (2001). Microenterprise lending to female entrepreneurs: Sacrificing economic growth for poverty alleviation? *World Development, 29*(7), 1225–1236.

Krejcie, R. V., & Morgan, D. W. (1970). Determining sample size for research activities. *Educational and Psychological Measurement, 30*(3), 607–610.

Lave, L. B., & Weber, W. E. (1970). A benefit-cost analysis of auto safety features. *Applied Economics, 2*(4), 265–275.

Lehmann, E., & Neuberger, D. (2001). Do lending relationships matter? Evidence from bank survey data in Germany. *Journal of Economic Behavior & Organization, 45*(4), 339–359.

Levin, K. A. (2006). Study design III: Cross-sectional studies. *Evidence-Based Dentistry, 7*(1), 24–25.

Levym, D. T., & Miller, T. (2000). Risk compensation literature- the theory and evidence. *Journal of Crush Prevention and Injury Control, 2*(1), 75–86.

Manove, M., Padilla, A. J., & Pagano, M. (2001). Collateral versus project screening: A model of lazy banks. *Rand Journal of Economics, 32*(4), 726–744.

Marrez, H. (2010). Credit risk in microcredit: how does gender matter?. *Savings and Development*, 369–388.

Marrez, H., & Schmit, M. (2009). *Credit risk analysis in microcredit: How does gender matter?* (CEB Working Paper No. 09/053). Brussels Belgium: Solvay Brussels School of Economics and Management.

McGrath, S. (2005). Skills for productive citizenship for all: The place of skills development for micro and small enterprises in South Africa. *Journal of Education and Work, 18*(1), 111–125.

Menkhoff, L., Neuberger, D. K., & Rungruxsirivorn, O. (2012). Collateral and its substitutes in emerging markets' lending. *Journal of Banking & Finance, 36*(3), 817–834.

Mensah, S. (2004). *A review of SME financing schemes in Ghana. In UNIDO regional workshop of financing small and medium scale enterprises*. United Nations Industrial Development Organisation.

Mohammed, A. A. (2020). *The Effects of Disability Labeling on Teachers' Referrals of Twice-exceptional Children to Gifted Programs in Saudi Arabia*. University of Northern Colorado.

Muller, C., & Posel, D. (2004). Concerns with measuring informal sector employment: An analysis of national household surveys in South Africa, 1993–2001. *Journal for Studies in Economics and Econometrics, 28*(1), 1–19.

Muteti, J. (2005). *SME lecture notes*. Catholic University of Eastern Africa.

OECD. (2013). *Financing SMEs and entrepreneurs: An OECD scoreboard*. OECD Publishing.

Pasanen, J., & Luoma, A. (2021). How can social insurers promote return to work in occupational rehabilitation? A quantitative, cross-sectional study. *BMC Public Health, 21*, 1–11.

Peltzman, S. (1975). The effects of automobile safety regulation. *Journal of Political Economy, 83*(4), 677–725.

Reta, G. (2000). *Women and micro finance: The case of women fuel wood carriers in Addis Ababa*. Unpublished Master's Thesis (MA), Department of Economics, University of Addis Ababa.

Rousson, V., & Goşoniu, N. F. (2007). An R-square coefficient based on final prediction error. *Statistical Methodology, 4*(3), 331–340.

Sachs, J. D., & Cohen, D. (1982). *LDC borrowing with default risk* (Working Paper No. 925). Massachusetts Ave: National Bureau of Economic Research.

Sapienza, H. J., Autio, E., George, G., & Zahra, S. A. (2006). A capabilities perspective on the effects of early internationalization on firm survival and growth. *Academy of Management Review, 31*(4), 914–933.

Schmit, M. (2004). Credit risk in the leasing industry. *Journal of banking & finance, 28*(4), 811–833.

Schmit, M., & Marrez, H. (2010). Credit risk in microcredit: how does gender matter?. *Savings and Development*, 369–388

Schiffer, M., & Weder, B. (2001). *Firm size and the business environment: Worldwide survey results*. World Bank Publications.

Slovic, P. (2016). *The perception of risk*. Routledge.

Soares, J. O., Pina, J. P., Ribeiro, M. S., & Catalão-Lopes, M. (2011). Quantitative vs. qualitative criteria for credit risk assessment. *Frontiers in Finance and Economics, 8*(1), 242–289.

Ssendi, L., & Anderson, A. R. (2009). Tanzanian micro enterprises and micro finance the role and impact for poor rural women. *Journal of Entrepreneurship, 18*(1), *1–19*.

Stiglitz, J. E., & Uy, M. (1996). Financial markets, public policy, and the East Asian miracle. *The World Bank Research Observer, 11*(2), 249–276.

Tagoe, N., Nyarko, E., & Anuwa-Amarh, E. (2005). Financial challenges facing urban SMEs under financial sector liberalization in Ghana. *Journal of Small Business Management, 43*(3), 33–43.

United Nations Conference on Trade and Development [UNCTAD]. (2001). *Improving the competitiveness of SMEs in developing countries. The role of finance to enhance enterprise development*. UNCTAD.

Wabo, L. B. (2014). Evaluation of SME and bank financing: Development of a rating model for banks from a sample of 179 SMEs in Cameroon. *Journal of Small Business & Entrepreneurship, 27*(1), 43–66.

Wilde, G. J. (1982). The theory of risk homeostasis: Implications for safety and health. *Risk Analysis, 2*(4), 209–225.

World Bank. (2005). *World development indicators*. World Bank.

16

Conclusion and Reflections

Emelia Amoako Asiedu, Richard Kofi Asravor, Robert Ebo Hinson, and George Oppong Ampong

16.1 Introduction

This concluding chapter synthesises the essential findings, insights, and thematic lessons from the preceding chapters, offering an all-inclusive reflection on the dynamics of entrepreneurship and SME development in Africa, particularly within the post-COVID-19 context. It revisits the overarching objectives of the book by highlighting major contributions to theory and practice, and exploring the broader implications for

E. Amoako Asiedu
Department of Marketing, Ghana Communication Technology University, Accra, Ghana
e-mail: easiedu@gctu.edu.gh

R. K. Asravor (✉) • G. Oppong Ampong
Ghana Communication Technology University, Accra, Ghana
e-mail: rasravor@gctu.edu.gh; gampong@gctu.edu.gh

R. E. Hinson
University of Ghana Business School, Accra, Ghana

E. Amoako Asiedu et al. (eds.), *Entrepreneurship and Small and Medium-Sized Enterprises (SMEs) in Africa*, https://doi.org/10.1007/978-3-032-14174-3_16

entrepreneurs, policymakers, and researchers. While acknowledging certain limitations, this chapter also provides recommendations for future inquiry and engagement. Ultimately, it underscores the critical role of entrepreneurship in fostering inclusive economic recovery and sustainable development across the continent.

16.2 Recapitulating the Central Themes

The discussion opens by exploring the major realities that African SMEs encountered in the wake of the COVID-19 pandemic. These enterprises were deeply affected by disruptions in supply chains, restricted access to finance, and regulatory hurdles. Yet, in the midst of these pressures, new avenues also emerged, particularly in the form of digital innovations and stronger engagement with stakeholders. From a conceptual standpoint, the conversation draws attention to the increasing importance of ethical and sustainable business conduct not just as a compliance requirement, but as a strategy rooted in values. Business leaders and policymakers alike are encouraged to build resilience by developing supportive ecosystems that provide access to finance, infrastructure, and training.

Building on these foundations, the narrative turns to the critical role of innovation, with Ghanaian SMEs serving as a focal point. Digital tools like mobile payments and online commerce proved vital in helping firms navigate pandemic-related challenges. Innovation, in this context, is not just a buzzword but a bridge between resources and business performance. Especially in the informal sector, there is a strong case for fostering affordable, practical innovation. To make this possible, governments must ensure that digital skills training and access to technology are widely available and affordable.

Attention then shifts to how SMEs can develop and maintain a competitive edge in a rapidly evolving business environment. Strategic thinking, particularly around brand development and customer loyalty, is highlighted as essential for long-term growth. While tangible resources are important, intangible assets such as reputation and client relationships often determine market staying power. As a result, small business owners are encouraged to invest in tools like customer relationship management

(CRM) software and digital marketing strategies, while policy support is needed to build SMEs' capacity for strategic planning and execution.

Technology adoption is another recurring theme. Although many SMEs are quick to adopt basic technologies such as mobile money, uptake of more advanced solutions has been slow often due to cost and limited expertise. The message is clear: for technology to be transformative, it must be both scalable and accessible. Governments can play a role by addressing infrastructure gaps and offering incentives for digital integration. At the same time, further research is needed to understand how these technologies translate into financial performance over the long term.

Sustainability and ethical business practices are also brought into focus. Many SMEs now see environmental and social responsibility not as obligations, but as ways to differentiate themselves and create value. However, despite this positive shift in mindset, practical constraints like limited resources and capacity often get in the way. The recommendation here is for tailored support measures that align sustainability goals with the realities of smaller enterprises. There is also a call for more research into how informal businesses across Africa interpret and implement sustainability in everyday operations.

The importance of customer service, especially in the digital age, is another critical insight. In sectors like delivery services, managing complaints effectively has become central to building customer trust. Digital tools that combine automation with a human touch have proven especially effective. But success in this area depends on cultural understanding and responsiveness. For SMEs, developing basic digital literacy and adopting thoughtful service recovery strategies can make a significant difference. There is also scope for further study on how cultural norms shape customer expectations and complaint resolution in African markets.

The volume turns its lens to marketing strategies in the context of the Fourth Industrial Revolution. Traditional approaches are no longer enough. Today's SMEs must build relationships, not just transactions, and learn to engage with customers in dynamic, data-driven ways. Businesses that embrace experimentation, feedback, and ongoing learning are more likely to thrive. On the policy side, there is a need to create access to digital marketing infrastructure and to provide training that helps SMEs navigate emerging tools and platforms. As technologies like artificial intelligence continue to evolve, their impact on marketing in Africa warrants deeper exploration.

One of the key insights explored in this volume centres on a fresh way to understand how marketing works in African SMEs. A context-specific framework known as TAPE (Transformation, Assimilation, Prediction, Exceptionality) offers a structured approach to how businesses can blend innovation with deep local market knowledge. SMEs that stand out in performance often combine digital solutions with grassroots understanding of customer needs. The key lesson for business leaders is to strike a balance: use data to inform decisions but never lose sight of the human and cultural context in which customers operate. On the policy front, there is a clear need to build marketing capabilities across SMEs, particularly in areas like data analytics and digital brand building. Additionally, more research is needed to explore how informal marketing tactics interact with modern digital strategies.

The significance of strategic marketing planning in ensuring business competitiveness also features strongly. When SMEs develop clear and flexible marketing strategies—grounded in understanding their target segments, value proposition, and data-informed choices, they are better equipped to thrive in fast-changing environments. These structured planning efforts become intangible assets that support long-term growth. Entrepreneurs are encouraged to align marketing goals with their broader business objectives and leverage user-friendly analytics tools to guide decision-making. At the policy level, tailored support in the form of planning templates, mentoring, and digital platforms is crucial. There's also an open field for research into how small businesses, especially in informal settings, adapt structured planning to fit their unique cultural and operational realities.

Another emerging theme is the growing role of AI and digital advertising in strengthening SME brand visibility. As businesses embrace tools like chatbots and automated content creation, new possibilities for customer interaction are unfolding. However, the use of artificial intelligence in branding must be handled with care. Over-reliance on automation can erode emotional connection and cultural sensitivity qualities that matter deeply to consumers. The takeaway for managers is to be strategic with AI, blending measurable performance with authentic storytelling.

Policymakers, on the other hand, are called to close digital skills gaps through targeted training and to develop ethical standards for the responsible use of AI in marketing. Important questions remain around fairness, bias in algorithms, and how micro-enterprises can remain competitive in an increasingly digital landscape.

Financial management among Ghanaian SMEs also comes into sharp focus. Findings suggest that discipline in financial practices like budgeting, cost control, and seeking financial advice—often matters more than simply gaining access to credit. The study reveals how internal financing choices, shaped by gender and firm size, influence sustainability. Policies that encourage sound financial habits and offer affordable access to accounting tools can go a long way in boosting SME resilience. Long-term studies are needed to track how digital tools and financial practices evolve, especially across different segments of the SME sector.

The interplay between entrepreneurial mindset and digital marketing effectiveness also stands out. SMEs that show strong entrepreneurial traits like being proactive and innovative tend to use social media more effectively than those that just maintain an online presence. The most successful firms tend to focus their energy on select platforms, particularly Instagram and WhatsApp, where engagement is highest. For policymakers, the establishment of digital marketing support centres across regions could provide much-needed infrastructure and training. Further research should explore how algorithmic visibility and informal sector actors interact in the social media space.

Turning to the broader challenge of building an online presence, successful SMEs are found to follow a phased and customer-focused digital strategy. Discoverability, engagement, and conversion serve as the three pillars of an effective digital ecosystem. These businesses do not just adopt technology for its own sake; instead, they tailor digital tools to local user habits and preferences. Practical support in the form of mobile-optimised website templates and cybersecurity awareness can strengthen digital confidence among small businesses. There's a need for more research into voice-enabled platforms and local-language tools, which could expand digital access to underserved communities.

In examining the adoption of AI-powered tools like chatbots, the evidence shows gradual but promising uptake among urban-based and tech-oriented SMEs. These tools can enhance operational efficiency, but their success depends on how well they're adapted to local language and customer expectations. The study cautions against full automation and emphasises the importance of preserving human interaction, especially in service delivery. For governments and developers, this means investing in low-cost, culturally adapted digital tools while setting clear ethical standards. Future research should examine how consumers perceive AI, especially in multilingual markets, and how these tools fit into the broader growth of e-commerce across

16.3 Africa

Finally, the analysis of credit access among SMEs sheds light on how informal business realities influence borrowing behaviour. Rather than defaulting due to dishonesty, many entrepreneurs struggle to repay loans because of unpredictable business demands. This insight suggests the need for flexible and context-aware credit solutions. A hybrid approach that blends traditional scoring with alternative data like mobile money history can improve loan decisions. Financial literacy on responsible borrowing remains essential. There is also an urgent need for more studies into how digital lending platforms (fintechs) are reshaping credit relationships and access across Africa.

16.4 Integrative Insights from the Chapters

This volume brings together a wide range of perspectives that, when viewed collectively, paint a vivid picture of how African SMEs, especially those in Ghana, have responded to the post-COVID landscape. Three main themes stand out: building resilience through innovation, integrating digital tools strategically, and crafting context-aware policies and management approaches. These threads run through all the studies, highlighting how SMEs are not just reacting to disruption but are also actively reshaping how they operate and compete in a rapidly digitising world.

16.4.1 Innovation as a Core Driver of Resilience

A recurring insight is the vital role of innovation in helping small businesses weather uncertainty. Whether it's low-cost technology, grassroots marketing, or flexible business planning, the more adaptive SMEs have leaned into change rather than resisted it. This innovation extends beyond product development to how services are delivered, how relationships with customers are maintained, and how day-to-day operations are managed. Traits like creativity, calculated risk-taking, and forward-thinking, hallmarks of entrepreneurial spirit, proved especially useful when embedded into digital platforms and communication tools.

16.4.2 Digital Transformation as a Strategic Necessity

Far from being an optional enhancement, digitalisation has emerged as a lifeline for many SMEs. Tools like e-commerce platforms, mobile money, AI-powered customer service, and chatbots have opened new opportunities, making businesses more visible, efficient, and responsive. But successful adoption isn't just about the technology itself; it depends on how well digital solutions align with the local business context. Many SMEs are taking a phased approach to digital transformation, building capacity step by step, and choosing tools that fit their size, capabilities, and customer preferences.

16.4.3 The Need for Context-Specific Support Structures

Another key message is that traditional policy models often fall short in addressing the realities faced by African SMEs, particularly those in informal or resource-constrained environments. What works in highly structured markets may not translate well in African contexts marked by fragmented supply chains and informal business practices. Instead, policies must focus on ecosystem development, such as improving digital infrastructure, offering practical training, enabling financial access, and promoting regulatory flexibility. Cross-sector collaboration, especially between public and private actors, emerges as crucial for making such support effective and inclusive.

16.4.4 Adapting and Extending Existing Theories

On a theoretical level, the studies in this volume adapt established frameworks—such as Stakeholder Theory, the Resource-Based View, the Technology Acceptance Model, and Pecking Order Theory—to the specific conditions of African SMEs. Rather than applying these models rigidly, the research shows the value of contextualising them. This not only improves their relevance but also contributes to a broader academic understanding of how small businesses operate in emerging markets.

16.4.5 Strategic Thinking in Resource-Limited Settings

From a managerial standpoint, a clear takeaway is the importance of embedding strategy into all aspects of the business. Financial planning, marketing, and customer service all benefit when guided by a clear, adaptable strategy. The studies illustrate that scarcity does not necessarily hinder innovation; on the contrary, it can drive creative and efficient solutions. Business owners are encouraged to prioritise continuous learning, invest in technology that adds real value, and blend traditional methods with modern tools to stay competitive.

16.4.6 Operating in the Space Between Formal and Informal

A deeper insight reveals how many SMEs operate at the intersection of formality and informality. This duality allows for flexibility and grassroots connection but also creates barriers in terms of regulation, data visibility, and access to capital. Many SMEs, for instance, use platforms like WhatsApp and mobile money for transactions and marketing, yet remain largely outside formal financial or regulatory systems. This reality calls for support structures that respect and leverage informality, rather than trying to replace it with rigid formal systems.

16.4.7 Shifting Definitions of Customer Value

In today's markets, delivering value goes beyond offering a good product at a fair price. Customers increasingly respond to convenience, personalisation, and meaningful engagement. Digital tools such as social media, AI-driven PR, and chatbots allow SMEs to craft brand identities that resonate on both local and global levels. This ability to blend digital tools with cultural authenticity offers African SMEs a distinct advantage in a connected world.

Innovation Born from Constraints One of the more powerful insights is that limitations can be fertile ground for innovation. Several examples across the volume highlight how SMEs have turned constraints into opportunities using lean budgets to drive creativity, building informal credit systems, or improvising marketing approaches. This challenges the common assumption that more resources automatically lead to better outcomes and suggests a need to rethink how success and competitiveness are measured in SME contexts.

16.4.8 Understanding Gender Dynamics in SME Development

The chapters also bring to light gendered differences in how SMEs are managed and supported. Women-led enterprises often approach financial management and customer engagement differently and tend to rely more on community-based strategies. Yet, they also face additional barriers to digital tools, credit access, and formal training. Addressing these gaps calls for policies and programmes that not only acknowledge but directly address the intersection of gender with other systemic challenges.

16.4.9 Strengthening the Broader Ecosystem

Finally, the studies argue for a collaborative, multi-level approach to SME support. Universities, development agencies, the private sector, and governments all have roles to play. Whether it produces relevant research, provides funding, designing technologies, or enacting enabling policies, coordinated action is essential. SMEs themselves must be seen not as passive beneficiaries of support, but as active partners in building a resilient and inclusive business ecosystem.

16.4.10 Contributions to Theory, Policy, and Practice

This book offers a comprehensive contribution to the evolving discourse on entrepreneurship and SME development in Africa, particularly in the aftermath of the COVID-19 pandemic. The insights gathered extend beyond case-specific observations, offering deeper reflections that inform theoretical development, policymaking, and managerial decision-making in resource-constrained environments.

On a theoretical level, the volume enriches key frameworks such as the Resource-Based View (RBV), Stakeholder Theory, the Technology Acceptance Model, and entrepreneurial marketing theory. The analysis underscores the strategic importance of intangible assets such as brand equity, customer loyalty, digital capabilities, and entrepreneurial orientation as core drivers of resilience and competitiveness in African SMEs. Additionally, the work introduces novel perspectives, including frameworks that adapt existing theories to local contexts, such as customer-centric models for digital transformation and marketing in platform-based economies.

The stakeholder-oriented approach that emerges throughout the text contributes to a broader understanding of how SMEs in Africa view sustainability and social responsibility not merely as compliance mandates, but as integral to long-term strategy. By aligning business goals with community and environmental needs, these enterprises are shown to be forging innovative pathways towards inclusive development. In terms of policy, the book advocates for adaptive and inclusive frameworks that reflect the lived realities of African entrepreneurs. It calls for the creation of enabling environments that foster innovation, bridge the digital divide, and promote financial inclusion. Specific areas for intervention include expanding access to affordable Internet and digital infrastructure, supporting mobile-first technology solutions, and offering simplified regulatory procedures for small and informal enterprises. The findings also reinforce the need for public investment in skills development particularly digital literacy, AI readiness, and customer analytics to prepare SMEs for a fast-evolving business landscape.

From a practical standpoint, the book presents a roadmap for SME managers to rethink operational strategies in the face of volatility. It stresses the role of strategic marketing planning, disciplined financial management, and agile customer engagement. Entrepreneurs are encouraged to adopt cost-effective technologies, invest in digital branding, and embrace innovation as a continuous, learning-driven process. Furthermore, there is a strong emphasis on balancing digital automation with human connections, ensuring that tools like chatbots and AI are implemented thoughtfully and in line with local cultural expectations.

Financial decision-making is also explored through the lens of behavioural and relational finance, emphasising the importance of trust, transparency, and accountability in SME-lender relationships. Practical suggestions are made for alternative credit assessment models that go beyond traditional collateral requirements, especially for women- and youth-led businesses operating in the informal sector.

Generally, this book affirms that African SMEs are not simply surviving through improvisation but are strategically adapting, blending traditional practices with emerging technologies to meet the demands of a rapidly changing world. The volume thus contributes meaningfully to scholarship, offers clear and timely policy direction, and equips practitioners with grounded, actionable strategies for growth and sustainability.

16.5 Implications for Entrepreneurs, Policymakers, and Stakeholders

As we look back over the fifteen chapters of this book, one message becomes clear: the future of African SMEs is full of promise, but only if the right lessons are applied and the right support systems are in place. Whether it's a small shop in Kumasi embracing mobile payments, or a growing enterprise in Accra tapping into digital advertising, the road ahead will be shaped by how well entrepreneurs, governments, and support institutions work together.

For entrepreneurs and SME managers, the biggest takeaway is that adaptability is key. The SMEs that have weathered the post-COVID storm are not necessarily the biggest or most well-funded; they are the most flexible, innovative, and digitally savvy. Whether using WhatsApp for customer service, social media for brand promotion, or basic AI tools to automate responses, those who embraced technology have reached more customers and operated more efficiently. But technology alone isn't enough. Chapters on marketing and strategy have shown that having a clear plan, knowing your market, and telling your brand's story well are just as important. Additionally, good financial habits like tracking expenses, budgeting, and planning ahead give a formula for long-term survival.

Entrepreneurs are also being asked to think differently about sustainability. Ethical business practices, environmental awareness, and social responsibility are no longer the concern of big corporations alone. African consumers are becoming more conscious, and SMEs that show they care about people, the planet, and fair practices are increasingly winning customer loyalty. For policymakers and government institutions, the findings in this book are a call to action. The business environment needs to be made simpler, fairer, and more inclusive. One of the major barriers for SMEs, especially those in informal or rural areas, is access whether it's access to the Internet, electricity, finance, or markets. Governments have a role to play in fixing this. Investments in rural broadband, reliable power, and fintech infrastructure can open new doors for entrepreneurs who were previously left behind.

At the same time, the rules of doing business need to be easier to understand and follow. Many small businesses are held back by complex registration processes, unclear tax obligations, or burdensome compliance requirements. A streamlined, digital-first approach can change that. And when it comes to financing, traditional bank models that rely on heavy collateral just don't work for most small businesses. It's time for credit models to consider alternative data like mobile money usage or utility payments to assess risk more fairly.

Education is another big piece of the puzzle. Governments should invest in training programmes that teach digital skills, financial literacy, and entrepreneurial thinking, especially for youth and women. Chapters on AI, marketing, and innovation have shown that small businesses are willing to learn; they just need the opportunity and the right tools.

For SME support networks such as business associations, NGOs, universities, and development agencies, there is a huge opportunity to build stronger, more connected ecosystems. Entrepreneurs need mentors, access to affordable services, and a community that understands their challenges. Whether it's creating digital hubs for start-ups, forming regional SME clusters, or running peer learning programmes, support organisations can help SMEs grow faster and smarter.

There is also room for partnerships. When public and private actors come together to co-design policies, offer shared platforms, or provide bundled services, everyone benefits. And as African markets continue to evolve, global business models and technologies must be adapted to fit local realities, taking into account language, infrastructure, and cultural preferences.

Finally, what this book makes clear is that SME growth is not something that happens in isolation. Entrepreneurs must take the lead, but they cannot do it alone. Policymakers must create environments that reward innovation and reduce red tape. Financial institutions must think beyond collateral and find ways to support small businesses based on their potential, not just their past. And support organisations must be proactive in helping entrepreneurs navigate challenges and seize opportunities. In a continent where small businesses drive most of the economic activity, building strong, digital, and inclusive SMEs is more than just good policy; it is essential for sustainable development. With the right mix of innovation, cooperation, and commitment, Africa's SMEs can lead the way into a more resilient, prosperous future.

Index

E. Amoako Asiedu et al. (eds.), *Entrepreneurship and Small and Medium-Sized Enterprises (SMEs) in Africa*, https://doi.org/10.1007/978-3-032-14174-3

The manufacturer's authorised representative in the EU is Springer
Nature Customer Service Centre GmbH, Europaplatz 3, 69115 Heidelberg,
Germany. If you have any concerns regarding our products, please
contact ProductSafety@springernature.com

Printed and bound by CPI Group (UK) Ltd, Croydon, CR0 4YY
22/09/2026
02220984-0008